Ethical Dilemmas in the Creative, Cultural and Service Industries

Ethical Dilemmas in the Creative, Cultural and Service Industries enhances professional ethical awareness and supports students' development of skills for ethical decision-making in these growing sectors.

It focusses on the shaping of personal and professional values, and dealing with the moral and ethical issues that (future) professionals may encounter in practice. Including a multitude of varied and interdisciplinary case studies, this textbook adopts an applied ethical approach which enables the student to combine basic ethical theory with relevant and 'real-life' cases. Major ethical issues such as CSR, ethical leadership, human rights, fraud, employee rights and duties, new technology and (social) entrepreneurship are addressed.

This will be invaluable reading for students studying tourism, hospitality, leisure, events, marketing, healthcare, logistics, retail and game development. It will also be a suitable resource for in-company training of practitioners already working in this wide range of domains.

Johan Bouwer is Professor of Ethics in Business and Profession at Breda University of Applied Sciences, The Netherlands. Formerly he held the positions of Senior Researcher in Meaning and Leisure at the Academy for Leisure, Director of Research, and acting Rector Magnificus at the same university. He received his PhD from the Free University in Amsterdam in 1992. From 1997 to 2008, he was Professor of Spiritual Care in Health Care Institutions at Groningen University and the PThU in Kampen, The Netherlands.

Any book on ethics within the creative, cultural, and service industries (aka hospitality, tourism, recreation and leisure) is to be applauded, but this one is particularly useful as it is designed to help the industry leaders of tomorrow to think in an ethical manner. It covers such a huge range of important debates that it should arguably become required reading for everyone, from students to industry practitioners, in the field. The book's importance is underlined by its clear alignment to the Sustainable Development Goals of the United Nations.
Dr Neil Carr, Professor and Head of the Department of Tourism at the University of Otago, New Zealand, and Managing Editor of *Annals of Leisure Research*.

The authors demonstrate a deep commitment to ethical business practice. This masterfully edited collection is concerned with ethics in the cultural, creative and service industries, right now, but better than that, it shows what it is to be an ethical practitioner at any time. It is absolutely contemporary, but it is set to be an enduring classic.
Dr Tony Blackshaw, Professor of Leisure Studies and Sociology at Sheffield Hallam University, United Kingdom and Editor of Routledge's Critical Leisure Studies book series, amongst other things.

Hardly a week goes by without adverse headlines about the creative, cultural or service industries whether related to over-tourism and the related danger to sustainability; state-sponsored doping in sport: poor corporate governance of public and third sector organisations; the fallacy of legacy of major events or the arrogance of unchallenged leadership in the commercial sector. So often these relate to poor personal values among those in leadership roles which translate into questionable organisational principles and performance. This important textbook and its experienced authors will make a valuable and vital contribution to the field, providing analysis of a wide range of ethical dilemmas which in turn will inform and promote best practice in these ever-growing industries.
Dr Derek Casey, Chair Emeritus of the World Leisure Organization, which advises the United Nations in areas such as sport, leisure and tourism, has been Chief Executive of the Sports Council in the UK and Chair of the Council of Europe's Committee on Sport. He has received several honorary doctorates, is a guest professor to universities in different parts of the world and is a senior fellow of the American Leisure Academy.

Designed to develop ethical awareness, Ethical Dilemmas in the Creative, Cultural and Service Industries, *provides a comprehensive and sensitive range of material to inculcate ethical values among students. Reflecting on leadership, governance, culture, integrity, social responsibility, privacy and human rights across all streams of the supply chain, the authors support the ideals of ethical business practices with numerous case studies. The result is a toolkit that has the potential to positively influence the ethical behavior of graduates locally and internationally.*
Dr Barry O'Mahony, Professor and Chief Academic Officer at Ecole hôtelière de Lausanne (EHL), Switzerland. He occupied several leadership positions at a number of universities across the world, including the Universities of Wollongong, Swinburne, Melbourne and Victoria.

Ethical Dilemmas in the Creative, Cultural and Service Industries

Edited by Johan Bouwer

LONDON AND NEW YORK

First published 2019
by Routledge
2 Park Square, Milton Park, Abingdon, Oxon OX14 4RN

and by Routledge
52 Vanderbilt Avenue, New York, NY 10017

Routledge is an imprint of the Taylor & Francis Group, an informa business

© 2019 selection and editorial matter, Johan Bouwer; individual chapters, the contributors

The right of Johan Bouwer to be identified as the author of the editorial material, and of the authors for their individual chapters, has been asserted in accordance with sections 77 and 78 of the Copyright, Designs and Patents Act 1988.

All rights reserved. No part of this book may be reprinted or reproduced or utilised in any form or by any electronic, mechanical, or other means, now known or hereafter invented, including photocopying and recording, or in any information storage or retrieval system, without permission in writing from the publishers.

Trademark notice: Product or corporate names may be trademarks or registered trademarks, and are used only for identification and explanation without intent to infringe.

British Library Cataloguing-in-Publication Data
A catalogue record for this book is available from the British Library

Library of Congress Cataloging-in-Publication Data
A catalog record has been requested for this book

ISBN: 978-0-367-21011-3 (hbk)
ISBN: 978-0-367-21015-1 (pbk)
ISBN: 978-0-429-26483-2 (ebk)

Typeset in Frutiger
by codeMantra

Printed and bound in Great Britain by
TJ International Ltd, Padstow, Cornwall

Contents

List of contributors	xi
Preface	xiii

1 Introduction — 1
Johan Bouwer

1.1	Introduction	1
1.2	The creative, cultural and service industries	3
1.3	Using cases: Pedagogical support	5
1.4	The structure of the book	6
1.5	The content of the book	7
1.6	Conclusion	14
1.7	Questions for discussion	15
1.8	Concluding thoughts	15

Part I Ethics, culture, moral development and decision-making in business contexts — 19

2 Ethics and business — 21
Johan Bouwer

2.1	Introduction	21
2.2	What is ethics?	21
2.3	What is business?	28
2.4	Ethics and business	33
2.5	Conclusion	42
2.6	Questions for discussion	43
2.7	Concluding thoughts	43

3 Culture, business and ethics in a globalising world — 48
Esther Peperkamp

3.1	Introduction	48
3.2	Globalisation and culture	49

Contents

	3.3	Culture and business	51
	3.4	Organisational culture and ethical decision-making	54
	3.5	Conclusion	57
	3.6	Questions for discussion	58
	3.7	Concluding thoughts	58

4 Moral development, moral positioning and decision-making   **63**
Marco van Leeuwen

4.1	Introduction	63
4.2	Foundations of moral reasoning	64
4.3	Moral development I: Evolution and psychology	66
4.4	Moral development II: Hierarchy and normativity	69
4.5	Conclusion: Moral positioning and ethical decision-making	73
4.6	Questions for discussion	74
4.7	Concluding thoughts	74

5 Ethical dilemmas and decision-making (models)   **77**
Johan Bouwer

5.1	Introduction	77
5.2	What is an ethical dilemma?	78
5.3	What is ethical decision-making?	80
5.4	Frameworks and models for making ethical decisions	84
5.5	Conclusion	93
5.6	Questions for discussion	93
5.7	Concluding thoughts	94

Part II Ethical dilemmas in the creative, cultural and service industries   **97**

6 Professional ethics   **99**
Roy Wood, Lieke Sauer, Raymond Boland and Jan-Willem Proper

6.1	Introduction to professional ethics *Roy Wood*	99
6.2	Professional ethics in hospitality – the case of managers and employee reward *Lieke Sauer and Roy Wood*	103
	Case 6.2.2: Professional behaviour, fairness and ethical standards	*106*

6.3	The art of whistle-blowing *Raymond Boland*	107
	Case 6.3.2: Loyalty and spilling the beans	*110*
6.4	Managers' roles in ethical conduct *Jan-Willem Proper*	112
	Case 6.4.2: Being ethical in the market of home medical products	*116*
6.5	Concluding thoughts	118

7 Organisational ethics — 122
Celiane Camargo-Borges, Liliya Terzieva, Jalal Atai, Johan Bouwer and Mata Haggis

7.1	Introduction to organisational ethics *Celiane Camargo-Borges*	122
7.2	Effective leadership in the context of libraries *Liliya Terzieva*	127
	Case 7.2.2: Effective leadership in the library	*132*
7.3	Good corporate governance and fraud *Jalal Atai and Johan Bouwer*	133
	Case 7.3.2: Deterring fraud in the hotel industry	*136*
7.4	Responsible business in the video-game industry *Mata Haggis*	139
	Case 7.4.2: Employee crunch versus making profits	*143*
7.5	Concluding thoughts	144

8 Corporate social responsibility — 149
Marisa de Brito, Jan-Willem Proper, Han Verheijden and Françoise van den Broek-Serlé

8.1	Introduction to corporate social responsibility *Marisa de Brito*	149
8.2	Supply-chain integrity *Jan-Willem Proper*	155
	Case 8.2.2: Selling solar TVs in Benin City	*159*
8.3	Productivity: Effective and efficient operations *Han Verheijden*	160
	Case 8.3.2: Profits, productivity and corporate social responsibility	*163*
8.4	Ethical sourcing and (electronic) waste management *Françoise van den Broek-Serlé*	165
	Case 8.4.2: The mobile phone as a change agent?	*171*
8.5	Concluding thoughts	173

Contents

9	**Sustainability and business**	**179**
	Frans Melissen, Ko Koens, Paul Peeters and Jeroen Nawijn	
	9.1 Introduction to sustainability and business	179
	Frans Melissen	
	9.2 Sustainable business models	183
	Frans Melissen	
	Case 9.2.2: Hospitality 2.0	*186*
	9.3 Balancing interests in urban tourism governance	189
	Ko Koens	
	Case 9.3.2: Balancing sustainable tourism and liveability in an urban context	*191*
	9.4 Carbon footprint and human well-being	194
	Paul Peeters and Jeroen Nawijn	
	Case 9.4.2: Climatic sustainability, tourism and the eradication of poverty	*198*
	9.5 Concluding thoughts	200
10	**Human rights and business**	**205**
	Rami Isaac, Mata Haggis and Esther Peperkamp	
	10.1 Introduction to human rights and business	205
	Rami Isaac	
	10.2 Human dignity and the presentation of minorities and women in video games	210
	Mata Haggis	
	Case 10.2.2: New York Dawn's race, gender and social dialogues	*212*
	10.3 Tourism, human rights and ethics	216
	Rami Isaac	
	Case 10.3.2: Palestine, tourism and human rights	*217*
	10.4 The working poor	220
	Esther Peperkamp	
	Case 10.4.2: Amusement parks, wages and poverty	*223*
	10.5 Concluding thoughts	226
11	**Responsible entrepreneurship and innovation**	**231**
	Marco van Leeuwen, Diana van Dijk and Greg Richards	
	11.1 Introduction to responsible entrepreneurship and innovation	231
	Marco van Leeuwen	

	11.2 Healthcare, entrepreneurship and managing costs *Diana van Dijk*	237
	Case 11.2.2: Fairness in administering scarce and expensive medicine	*241*
	11.3 Cities, entrepreneurship and events *Greg Richards*	243
	Case 11.3.2: The FIFA World Cup and Olympic Games	*245*
	11.4 Social entrepreneurship and social innovation *Marco van Leeuwen*	248
	Case 11.4.2: Social entrepreneurship using voluntourism	*253*
	11.5 Concluding thoughts	254
12	**Information technology and business** *Hayleigh Bosher, Marnix van Gisbergen, Adriaan van Liempt and Pieter de Rooij*	**258**
	12.1 Introduction to information technology and business *Hayleigh Bosher*	258
	12.2 Intellectual property (IP) and privacy in the entertainment industry *Marnix van Gisbergen and Hayleigh Bosher*	263
	Case 12.2.2: Photographs and videos taken inside a football stadium	*266*
	12.3 Downloading films and the ethical customer *Adriaan van Liempt*	268
	Case 12.3.2: Killing Popcorn Time	*272*
	12.4 Big data and marketing *Pieter de Rooij*	273
	Case 12.4.2: Using customer data at Carnegie Hall	*278*
	12.5 Concluding thoughts	280
Index		**285**

Contributors

Jalal Atai is a lecturer in accounting, finance and research at Breda University of Applied Sciences in the Netherlands.

Raymond Boland is a lecturer in English language at Breda University of Applied Sciences in the Netherlands.

Hayleigh Bosher is a lecturer in intellectual property (IP) law at Brunel University London (UK), IP Consultant specialising in IP, Media and Entertainment (HBLegal.org), and Director of the Intellectual Property Awareness Network (IPAN). She was formerly a lecturer in IP, Media and Entertainment Law at Breda University of Applied Sciences in the Netherlands.

Johan Bouwer is Professor of Ethics in Business and Profession at Breda University of Applied Sciences in the Netherlands.

Marisa de Brito is a senior lecturer and researcher in place-making and events at Breda University of Applied Sciences in the Netherlands, and an Active Member of the International Association for Tourism and Leisure Education (ATLAS) and of the Dutch Centre for Expertise on Leisure, Tourism and Hospitality.

Françoise van den Broek-Serlé is Professor of Logistics and Sustainability at Breda University of Applied Sciences in the Netherlands (part-time) and owner of Duionlog (Logistics, Innovation and Sustainable Entrepreneurship).

Celiane Camargo-Borges is a senior lecturer and researcher in design approaches such as imagineering, experience design and process design, as well as in tourism destination management, at Breda University of Applied Sciences in the Netherlands. She is also an Associate and Board Member of the TAOS Institute (USA).

Diana van Dijk is a senior lecturer and researcher in communication skills and in healthcare logistics at Breda University of Applied Sciences in the Netherlands.

Marnix van Gisbergen is Professor of Digital Media Concepts at Breda University of Applied Sciences in the Netherlands.

Mata Haggis is Professor of Creative and Entertainment Games at Breda University of Applied Sciences in the Netherlands.

Rami Isaac is a senior lecturer and researcher in tourism at Breda University of Applied Sciences in the Netherlands, and Assistant Professor of Tourism and Hospitality Management at Bethlehem University, Palestine.

Contributors

Ko Koens is a senior lecturer and researcher in sustainable tourism and hospitality at Breda University of Applied Sciences in the Netherlands and Research Associate at the University of Johannesburg in South Africa.

Marco van Leeuwen is a senior lecturer and researcher in philosophy, leisure and imagineering at Breda University of Applied Sciences in the Netherlands.

Adriaan van Liempt is a senior lecturer and researcher in leisure and sociology at Breda University of Applied Sciences in the Netherlands.

Frans Melissen is Professor of Sustainable Business Models at Breda University of Applied Sciences in the Netherlands.

Jeroen Nawijn is a senior lecturer in tourism at Breda University of Applied Sciences in the Netherlands.

Paul Peeters is Professor of Sustainable Transport and Tourism at Breda University of Applied Sciences in the Netherlands, Member of the ICAI CAEP International Aviation Environmental Standards Working Group 3, and a contributing author of the IPCC AR5 Working Group 3 Report on Transport.

Esther Peperkamp is a senior lecturer and researcher in leisure, sociocultural anthropology, and qualitative research methods at Breda University of Applied Sciences in the Netherlands.

Jan-Willem Proper is Professor of Transport and Logistics at Breda University of Applied Sciences in the Netherlands.

Greg Richards is Professor of Place-Making and Events at Breda University of Applied Sciences, and Professor of Leisure Studies at Tilburg University in the Netherlands.

Pieter de Rooij is a senior lecturer and researcher in experience marketing and customer relationship management at Breda University of Applied Sciences in the Netherlands.

Lieke Sauer is a lecturer in sustainable business models and researcher in sustainable food at Breda University of Applied Sciences in the Netherlands.

Liliya Terzieva is a senior lecturer and researcher in creative entrepreneurship, leadership, complex adaptive systems and multifunctional leisure locations at Breda University of Applied Sciences in the Netherlands.

Han Verheijden is Professor of Productivity at Breda University of Applied Sciences in the Netherlands (part-time) and founder and owner of Verheijden Concepts BV (leisure sector).

Roy Wood is a senior lecturer in the Faculty of Business and Law, University of Northampton, and a visiting professor at the University of Hertfordshire Business School. He was formerly Professor of Hospitality Management at Breda University of Applied Sciences in the Netherlands.

Preface

This textbook is designed to increase professional ethical awareness and the ability to make sound ethical decisions in the domains of the creative, cultural and services industries, and to support the teaching and study of (business) ethics in the context of undergraduate professional education. Since it takes a multidisciplinary, multi-contextual and applied ethical approach, which enables both tutor and student to combine (basic) ethical theory with relevant and 'real-life' cases that (future) professionals might encounter in practice, it is also suitable for in-company training of practitioners already working in these domains.

The idea for this book was born a few years ago when Breda University of Applied Sciences in the Netherlands started a project leading to the inclusion of (facets of business) ethics in all of its educational programmes, thereby acknowledging the industry's need to attract professionals who are also able to address ethical dilemmas in their work. These programmes cover the domains of tourism, leisure and events, hospitality, facility, media, games, logistics and the built environment. They represent industries which employ skills and talent in order to generate economic value – also through the provision of intangible products and services such as transport, retail, marketing and even healthcare – but additionally, they cover industries which focus on creating social, cultural and environmental value.

The main challenge was to find a way of combining these fields, which have no watershed divisions between them, in such a way that students, trainees and lecturers from different educational programmes and disciplines could profit from it. The answer was found in a format which, on the one hand, includes themes and issues that are formally discussed within the broad field of business ethics (including theory), but on the other hand includes cases which are, materially speaking, specifically relevant to the three mentioned domains. Twenty-one cases have been included in the book; these cover a wide range of ethical dilemmas, allowing users to relate to and learn from professional fields other than their own. The ethical issues addressed transcend national borders and aim to shape personal and professional values and decision-making. The textbook will serve a variety of courses within the domains of the creative, cultural and service industries. For more background information and a description of the structure and content of this collection, see Chapter 1.

I would like to thank for their (moral) support all 24 of the authors, who contributed to this textbook with great enthusiasm. I am grateful to Hayleigh Bosher, Marisa de Brito, Celiane Camargo-Borges, Rami Isaac, Marco van Leeuwen, Frans Melissen and Roy Wood for the coordination work they have done on the chapters they wrote introductions to. Last, but not least, a special word of thanks to the

Preface

editors' team at Routledge, Emma Travis, Lydia Kessell and Frances Tye, for their professional assistance in putting this collection together.

I sincerely hope that this book will inspire many who study, teach and work in the domains of the creative, cultural and service industries to be more aware of the (adverse) impacts business behaviour could have, and contribute to adequately addressing the ethical dilemmas which might emerge in their professional practices.

Johan Bouwer

Chapter 1

Introduction

Johan Bouwer

1.1 Introduction

Educational institutions all around the globe are, against the background of the many scandals witnessed in the world of business in the last decades, still in search of adequate ways to educate responsible professionals who, on the one hand, will be able to serve their companies with integrity and display responsible behaviour in that context, whilst also living up to the needs and moral expectations of society and behaving like responsible global citizens, on the other. Those scandals and (financial) crises have prompted the educators of future business men and women to seriously study business ethics. This discipline fundamentally evaluates and judges economic practices on the basis of their 'acceptability', rightness or wrongness and on their ability to prevent harm to people, communities, society and the environment; but also, and especially, on their ability to foster benefit and value (well-being, quality of life) for all. In addition, the many challenges the world faces today – such as dealing with the impacts of climate change; pursuing sustainability; eradicating poverty and inequality; addressing the exclusion of groups of people (cultures and minorities), and the negative impacts of technological development; ensuring the availability and safety of food for all; addressing the unavailability of good healthcare globally; turning around the high rates of child mortality in the world, and ensuring good education for all – add to the necessity that educational institutes address these urgent issues in their curricula in order to contribute to ensuring a sustainable planet for both current and future generations. The world has become a global village and decisions taken in one part of the world (could) have an impact on the others. This applies to business as well: it has become globalised, and is faced by the challenged of (re-)evaluating the very foundations of its existence, (re-)defining its relationship with society and nature and becoming more and more involved in the contexts in which it operates, and (re-)considering the impacts of its operations, products and services on human beings and on the planet itself. Businesses are invited to join hands with those trying to find solutions to these challenges and to take care not to be a part of the problems that have given rise to them. This not only applies to large international companies, but also to smaller and medium-sized ones. More precisely, it applies to every leader, manager and employee. One cannot speak of (responsible and ethical) business without speaking of (responsible and ethical) people.

Johan Bouwer

Therefore, in order to deliver well-equipped future professionals who will be able to resort to morally sound practices in business and management, scholars and practitioners have pursued their quest to find adequate and effective ways of teaching/training ethics in business and management education with quite some fervour. The debate and discussions amongst scholars on how ethics could/should be taught might be called lively and intense. An astonishing amount of work has been done in studying, amongst other things: (the content of) business ethics courses; teaching methods; the pedagogical presuppositions behind those methods; the perceptions of both lecturers and students with regard to the importance and purpose of ethics education; models for and principles of ethical decision-making; the effects of (business) ethics education on moral behaviour; moral development, and the determinants and moderators of moral behaviour. A Google search on 'business ethics education' delivered 338,000,000 hits, which testifies to the magnitude of this scholarly activity (the search was carried out on 6 March 2019). Apart from the many books that have been written on business ethics, and the stream of publications on 'teaching (business) ethics' that have been accepted in 'regular' journals for business ethics (such as the *Business Ethics Quarterly*, *Business & Professional Ethics Journal*, *Journal of Business Ethics*, *International Journal of Business Governance and Ethics*, and *Business Ethics: A European Review*), the field also comprises several scholarly journals which specialise in (business and management) ethics education. To mention a few: the *Journal of Business Ethics Education*, the *Academy of Management Learning and Education*, the *Journal of Management Education*, and, the latest addition, the *International Journal for Ethics Education*, which was launched at the end of 2016. Even so, the search for ways in which educational institutes could teach ethics effectively, or rather, educate responsible professionals for the world of business and management has not come to an end, yet.

This textbook contributes to this endeavour in a very specific way. It follows an approach to business ethics that sees it as 'ethical decision-making' and tries to pre-empt the critique made of many textbooks by Murphy, Sharma and Moon (2012). Quoting Adams, Murphy et al. observed that these textbooks, in representing ethical decision-making, fail to reflect on decision-making at the individual level (instead of at the corporate level); they convey material that mainly focusses on theory rather than practice, they rarely embed ethical dilemmas 'in the context of other aspects of the workplace' (2012: 324) by resorting to the integration of themes and practices in education and, most of all: they fail to devote attention to the shaping of personal and professional values. Therefore, the book is composed in such a way as to introduce basic knowledge of ethical theory and the factors that influence ethical decision-making, but concentrates especially on case studies. The discussion questions related to these cases arguably facilitate the enhancement of ethical awareness, critical personal and professional reflexivity, and the skills needed in order to make sound ethical judgements and decisions. The cases cover a vast range of broad ethical issues in the field of business ethics, but especially focus on experiences (or possible exposure to ethical problems and dilemmas) employees might encounter in professional practice within the domains of the creative, cultural and service industries. These focal points are related to the three broad domains that make up the educational scope of Breda University of Applied Sciences in the Netherlands, an institution for higher, professional/vocational and academic education. This university offers educational programmes which cover the fields of tourism, leisure, hospitality, facilities, logistics, mobility, urban development, game development and media and entertainment – fields which are not widely addressed in books on business ethics, at least not cohesively. For example, publications like *Issues in Recreation and Leisure: Ethical Decision-Making* (McLean and Yoder, 2005); *Ethics in the Hospitality and Tourism Industry* (Liebermann and Nissen, 2008); *Values in Tourism: An Itinerary to Tourism Ethics* (Gras-Dijkstra, 2009); and *The Ethics of Tourism: Critical and Applied Perspectives* (Lovelock and Lovelock, 2013) certainly contribute to the theme, but they mainly aim to cover issues – to some extent exhaustively – that are at stake within a *specific* sector. This textbook provides for ethical reflection on different, (inter)related fields in one publication.

The authors are predominantly senior scholars who are affiliated with Breda University of Applied Sciences and use different perspectives to explicate their themes. They represent quite a range of cultural backgrounds, such as Dutch, British, Irish, Portuguese, Brazilian, Palestinian, Afghan, Albanese and South African. Three of the contributors have appointments at other universities as well.

In conclusion: this textbook does not claim to be comprehensive, nor does it aim at educating business ethicists, or even building character; rather, as indicated earlier, it wants to be of service to lecturers and undergraduate students in higher and vocational education in the three domains mentioned. Based on an integrated and a multidisciplinary approach, it aims at raising moral sensitivity and ethical awareness, and supporting the development of the skills required for ethical decision-making. There is no overkill of (theoretical) information and the book could therefore also be of service to professionals who currently work in these industries, encounter similar dilemmas in their professional practice and are in need of training that could support moral development and ethical decision-making within their organisations.

In the following sections, the focus, pedagogical presuppositions, structure and content of the book, including an overview of the cases and ethical dilemmas explicated within it, will be discussed more broadly.

1.2 The creative, cultural and service industries

As indicated above, the focus of this book will be on recognising and addressing the ethical dilemmas that (future) professionals within the domains of the creative, cultural and service sectors might encounter in their work. Within Breda University of Applied Sciences, these domains include industries like tourism, leisure and hospitality, which focus not only on economic, but also on cultural and social value; industries that employ creative skills and talent in order to generate economic value, and also those industries that create such value through the provision of intangible products and services such as transport, retail, marketing and healthcare. There are no watershed divisions between those domains. On the contrary, leisure sectors such as tourism, sports, culture, events and media are becoming increasingly interlinked and require an integrated and multidisciplinary approach. Moreover, some sectors, such as leisure and tourism for example, have become interlinked with other (public) sectors in society, such as healthcare (as seen in the influence of leisure on health and the phenomenon of medical tourism), which adds to the relevance of bringing those fields together in one book. To illustrate the overlap between these industries, the scope of their domains will be briefly addressed next.

The *creative industries* are generally conceived as an increasingly important economic sector that rests on knowledge and information (intellectual property) that has been generated through creative action and innovation. This field is also referred to as the creative economy or the cultural sector, which apparently makes 'creative industries' a fuzzy term. It comprises forms such as video games, art, advertising, fashion, TV and radio, (online) publishing, film, music, crafts, design, museums and galleries (see Creative Industries, n.d.). Some scholars go to such lengths as to consider the educational industries, and the (public and private) services they provide, to be part of the creative industries (Hesmondhalgh, 2002: 12).

The *cultural industries* is generally understood to cover the production of, for example music, television, film, publishing, crafts, design, architecture, the visual and performing arts and advertising; but also, tourism, sports, events, entertainment, food, pastimes and festivals. Cultural activities are conceived as embracing those activities people, groups and communities value and enjoy. There is clearly an overlap with the themes mentioned under the umbrella of the creative industries. In fact, the cultural industries are considered by UNESCO, for example, to be identical with the creative industries and to comprise the creation, production and distribution of cultural goods, which are usually subjected to intellectual property rights (see Cultural industry, n.d.).

The *service industries*, also called the tertiary sector, comprises 'intangible products' such as services delivered to customers. Usually activities such as marketing and offering guidance and advice are central to these services. Here again, some overlap with themes from the other two domains mentioned is visible. Services could be delivered in fields such as accounting, banking, insurance and computer services, but also in those of hospitality, tourism, transport, entertainment, distribution and food services (see Service industries, n.d.).

Without going into it too deeply, it should be noted that a critique of strict distinctions between these three domains has, apart from any alleged conceptual confusion due to overlap in the fields they cover, also been made on a more fundamental level. Miller argues that the term 'cultural' has to a large extent been overtaken by 'creative', which has been adopted by economists to indicate activities which produce profit. *Creativity* is seen as input and not output. Since all economic sectors have cultural elements and since culture relates to 'all the questions of managing populations and coping with a life after manufacturing', the cultural industries deserve a 'new' conceptualisation and therefore should take their rightful place amongst these three (2009: 95–97). This endeavour will not be explored here, but the conceptual distinction between the three domains will be maintained (at least in the title of this book).

It would be impractical and unsatisfactory to attempt to address all the possible ethical dilemmas that could emerge within all these fields in one book. Therefore, a selection of cases has been made that covers fields from all three of those domains, which enables students to, by making cross-references, get an overview of (possible) dilemmas and problems that could be at stake in their own (future) professional practice.

1.3 Using cases: Pedagogical support

Education should arguably ideally contribute to students' attainment of critical personal and professional reflexivity, moral maturity and the status of responsible global citizens. Taking responsibility for one's own personal and professional actions presupposes, in the words of Michael Mann, winner of the German Sustainability Award 2016, a mindset which is oriented towards 'looking and understanding', which he regards as the first and most important step that needs to be taken to become an ethical citizen, but one which, at the same time is the most challenging to take (freely cited). In order for 'looking and understanding' to lead to ethical behaviour, education should be directed towards strengthening and increasing practical wisdom (Wittmer, 2013: 173).

Practical wisdom ('phronesis') is a kind of knowledge that especially focusses on making good decisions or judgements, often within a specific (professional) role an individual has to play. It is distinct from theoretical or scientific knowledge ('episteme'), which primarily grapples with general principles in understanding the nature of things, and 'craft' knowledge ('techne'), which is used to produce something (usually a product, although it could also be used to develop and/or implement a business plan, for example). Practical wisdom is usually gained from practice and experience, and is arguably a foundational asset or skill that (future) professionals in the field of business and management need. Attaining practical wisdom should therefore be the primary goal in educating responsible professionals, but of course, it should be complemented with some (basic) theoretical and 'craft' knowledge. In the words of Betta: professionals should have an 'ethicmentality', a term which refers to the merging of ethical understanding with 'social life', such as business or economic practices (2016: 179).

This approach to teaching (business) ethics is not new. On the contrary, there are currently many voices in the field of education and training advocating pedagogies with the following qualities: they (i) facilitate knowledge that is 'created through the transformation of experience' (Murphy et al., 2012: 322); (ii) help students to 'think critically about their values and realize them in practice' (Hartman, 2013: 190); (iii) are about 'educating more than just a technically well-equipped manager', but someone who will 'pursue what is best for the common good in ways that are ethical, responsible and sustainable' (Smit, 2013: 51); (iv) lead to the development of sound ethical decision-making 'which includes the ability to reconcile personal and professional values' (Ametrano, 2014: 160); (v) impact 'significantly on students' capacities to act on and express their values when faced with ethical dilemmas' (Chappell, Edwards and Webb, 2013: 214); and (vi) help to acquire virtues which are based on a consciousness of 'personal innate values' and 'habitual practice' (Culham, 2015: 82). Scholars are concerned that these outcomes cannot be reached by continuing to implement the 'traditional ethical courses' which primarily focus on content (theoretical knowledge), use a 'high degree of practice using logical analysis' and are often 'too abstract to have any practical value for students', rather than assessing the 'rightness or wrongness of students' conclusions or decisions regarding an ethical issue' (Ohreen, 2013: 241–242). Dialogue or debate should be pursued: students should be given the opportunity to raise questions and hold discussions about the ethicality of their own (anticipated) behaviour in real or realistic cases within the fields in which they will work one day. Hence, this textbook is constructed in a way designed to optimise the attainment of practical wisdom (see Section 1.4). And hence the choice to concentrate on case studies.

Of the many effective teaching methods that scholars experiment with, such as problem-based learning (PBL), stories, biographies, role-play, literature, vignettes, games, videos and film, it seems that the 'analysis and discussion of cases is generally considered the most effective method for teaching business ethics' (Cavanagh, 1998: 624). Falkenberg and Woiceshyn hold this consensus on the use of cases in education to be related to its ability to enhance ethical awareness, improve 'reasoning and judgement abilities', stimulate the 'moral imagination', and help students to become aware of their own values and the ways in which they could apply them when confronted with ethical dilemmas (2008: 213).

However, the proof of the pudding lies in the eating: whether or not the use of case studies in education is effective can only be determined by the way a person has reacted to an ethical dilemma. And as is known, ethical behaviour is determined by both social and individual factors, such as culture, socialisation (family, peers, education), the law, personal values, world view/religion, and (stage of) moral development. These determinants, amongst others, are studied in psychology, sociology and anthropology. Drumwright, Prentice and Biasucci have put forward that, in getting closer to understanding the outcomes of ethical behaviour, behavioural ethics – a relatively new field of study which draws upon disciplines including psychology and sociology, and which studies how people make (un)ethical decisions – could give a new impulse to teaching (business) ethics effectively (2015). Behavioural ethics focusses on 'understanding cognitive errors, social and organisational pressures, and situational factors that can prompt people who do not intend to do anything wrong to engage in unethical behaviour' (Drumwright et al., 2015: 451). Although this needs further study, the compelling analysis made by Drumwright and colleagues supports, for example, Rest's model for ethical decision-making: moral awareness, moral decision-making, moral intent and moral action, which will feature further on in Chapter 5. And, last but not least, their recommendation to pursue critical thinking, multiple framing, practical reasoning and reflection in education fully resonates with those skills that working with cases is thought to develop.

In conclusion, there is ample pedagogical and scholarly support for working with cases in education. Students need moral sensitivity and awareness, but they also need some theory and tools with which to act in solving ethical dilemmas. This textbook represents an attempt to provide these. It can be used as a standalone course book, but should ideally function as an integrative, 'embedded' companion to 'regular' lectures on the themes included in it (for example, supply-chain management), such that students' ethical sensitivity can be addressed and will become 'second nature'.

1.4 The structure of the book

The book consists of two main parts. Part I is theoretical in nature and is titled 'Ethics, culture, moral development and decision-making in business contexts'. It has four chapters (2–5), conveying foundational information which lays the groundwork for reflection on ethical theory, the influence of culture and diversity, individual moral development and ethical decision-making. Although Part I is predominantly theoretical in nature, the fifth chapter also contains several models which could be used for assessing and solving ethical dilemmas.

Part II is an 'applied' section and titled 'Ethical dilemmas in the creative, cultural and service industries'. It contains seven chapters (6–12), each of which is structured as follows. First, a general introduction is given on the main theme of the chapter (for example, professional ethics), which has been written by a senior scholar who also acted as coordinator of the chapter. This introduction is followed by three cases which, in turn, are each preceded by an introductory section which paves the way to the (usually mainly fictitious) case. The cases offer insights into different kinds of ethical dilemmas and problems which professionals working in the creative, cultural and service industries could encounter, and conclude with five questions for discussion. These questions are formulated in such a way as to stimulate moral awareness and reflection on sound ethical behaviour. In fact, all the chapters of this book contain questions for discussion – including the theoretical chapters. The chapters end with a brief section containing 'concluding thoughts', written by the editor of this book, and a few suggestions for further reading.

The contents of the 12 chapters will be described very briefly in the next section.

1.5 The content of the book

This section gives, first, an outline and brief summary of the chapters of the book and, secondly, an overview of the cases and the ethical dilemmas that are linked to them.

1.5.1 Outline and summary of the chapters

Chapter 1, written by Bouwer, gives an introduction to the backgrounds, focus, pedagogical presuppositions, structure and content of the book. As indicated above, the book especially aims at enhancing ethical awareness and the ability to make sound ethical decisions in the domains of the cultural, creative and service industries, and to support the study/integration of (business) ethics in the higher, professional education of undergraduate students.

Chapter 2, the first of the four theoretical chapters in Part I of the book, written by Bouwer, discusses the nature of 'ethics' and 'business' and their interrelatedness. He concludes that ethics (how to live a good life) and business (economic activity) can never be separated. Their foci – well-being and welfare respectively – are two sides of the same coin and are underpinned by the moral virtues of responsibility and integrity. In Chapter 3, Peperkamp addresses the influence of culture on business decisions in a globalising context. However complex, culture can never be ignored by organisations since it shapes individuals' attitudes, values, expectations and habits and therefore has an impact on ethical decision-making. Peperkamp suggests that companies, in order to find corporate agreement on shared values that could lead to corporate ethical behaviour, should resort to constructive dialogue. Van Leeuwen reflects on moral development and the impact it has on ethical decision-making in Chapter 4. Critically drawing on the developmental psychology of Kohlberg and Gilligan, he argues that the moral position a person eventually takes when making decisions is not necessarily related to a specific moral stage, but, apart from being a mix of rational, affective and emotional influences, could also be determined by the nature of the ethical dilemma itself. Chapter 5 concludes Part I and is titled 'Ethical dilemmas and decision-making (models)'. Bouwer conveys the theoretical constituents of ethical decision-making, such as the factors that influence it and the process of decision-making itself, as well as a 'toolkit' consisting of different frameworks and models that could be used for either ethical screening or ethical decision-making.

Chapter 6 is the first of the seven 'applied' chapters in Part II of the book. Wood writes an introduction to the theme of the chapter – 'professional ethics'– and discusses the nature of a profession and the need for professional ethics. It is followed by three cases. The introduction to the first case is written by Sauer and Wood. It discusses professional ethics in the hospitality industry, more specifically the attitudes of managers towards, and the management of, employee reward. The case itself regards the apparent unfairness of extreme ethical standards in human resource practice as seen in a situation in which someone was fired due to an unfortunate coincidence of events. The second case introduction, written by Boland, offers insights into the phenomenon of whistle-blowing and its associated ethical dilemmas. His case describes how a person could feel crushed by loyalty when a good employer does something in business that is seemingly not kosher. In the introduction to the third case, Proper ruminates on some of the facets of the individual-organisational interface of ethics, with a special focus on the roles of the manager. The case itself revolves around the dilemmas three members of a management team encounter when discovering that their company is buying in uncertified products which could lead to clients being harmed.

Chapter 7 addresses organisational ethics, and Camargo-Borges, drawing on social constructionist thinking, argues that classical theories of organisational ethics are in danger of becoming obsolete if they do not align better with current forms of interaction. Instead, a relational approach should be followed, which takes locally crafted moral orders into account. Terzieva writes the first case study. The introduction to the case deals with the role of a library director who urgently needs to initiate change in the organisation despite resistance from the employees to changes in what they feel their roles to be. The case itself introduces the concept of dynamic leadership, proposing an innovative way to lead in complex and continuously changing times. The second case is introduced by Atai and Bouwer, who discuss the relationship between good corporate governance and fraud and argue for the emplacement of effective internal control mechanisms. The case itself demonstrates how the Fraud Triangle could help to deter fraud in the front office of a Bangalore hotel. The introduction to the third case, dealing with the theme of responsible business in the video-game industry, is written by Haggis. His case elaborates on the ethics of employer responsibilities in this industry.

Introduction

The central theme of Chapter 8 is 'corporate social responsibility' (CSR). It focusses on ethical dilemmas in supply-chain networks – as all three cases demonstrate. De Brito writes the general introduction to the chapter and indicates that CSR, which generally refers to self-regulation of companies in balancing profits with social and environmental issues, is more than acting lawfully: it is also about acting on ethical issues like transparency, responsibility and ensuring the well-being of future generations. The first case study is introduced by Proper, and focusses on supply-chain integrity depicting the goal of minimising the risk of unethical corporate behaviour. His case reflects on the ethical dilemmas that could emerge from doing business in a foreign country when there seems to be a discrepancy between the positive and negative impacts on different stakeholders in the supply chain. Verheijden writes the second case study and points out in the introduction that, especially in the leisure and hospitality sectors, capital productivity is exposed to higher risk than labour-productivity, and illustrates in his case how the interactions between profit, productivity and CSR could lead to dramatic challenges to young entrepreneurs. In the third case, van den Broek-Serlé indicates in the introduction how organisations can make their CSR visible in the way they deal with extended responsibility regarding ethical sourcing and waste management, and her case deals with the intriguing question of how 'fair' the manufacturing of a 'fair' mobile phone fundamentally is when we consider the consequences and impacts of retracting business from the developing countries where e-waste had initially been dumped.

Chapter 9 reflects on sustainability in business. Melissen writes both the general introduction and the first case study. In the introduction he elaborates on what specifically needs to change in the way business operates in order for it to contribute to sustainable development: business models should be based on and supported by sustainability thinking instead of being founded on the principles of capitalism. His case study is preceded by an explication of the thesis that 'traditional' business models have lost their relevance, and should be replaced by 'new' models based on sustainable thinking. The case itself reflects the main principles for a 'new' business model in the context of hospitality. This is followed by the second case, written by Koens. Koens introduces his case with a description of the interrelationships between sustainability, tourism and governance. In the case itself, he demonstrates which ethical dilemmas are in play for different stakeholders with different interests and opinions with regard to which plans should be implemented to ensure the practice of sustainable tourism in a big metropolis. In the chapter's third case study, Peeters and Nawijn provide up-to-date information about the impact of tourism's carbon footprint on climate change and human well-being, and also on the ethical dilemmas surrounding them. The case itself identifies the factors which should be dealt with when working towards climatic sustainability and the eradication of poverty.

Ethical dilemmas that could emerge within the realm of human rights are discussed in Chapter 10. In the general introduction to this chapter Isaac puts forward that human rights in business cannot be guaranteed by governments alone. He argues that the international community should adopt a human rights regime that provides more effective protection for individuals and communities against corporate-related human rights harm than is the case right now. Haggis introduces the first case by pointing out that people of colour, for example, are often negatively portrayed in games. This necessitates continuous debate. He demonstrates the negative portrayal of people of colour in video games through a vast array of reflections – negative and positive, and from different target groups – on a fictitious case in which a black woman is the protagonist. Isaac writes the second case study, revolving around the interactions between tourism, human rights and ethics as reflected in the case of Palestine within the setting of an illegal Israeli occupation. The case illustrates that continuing up to the present day, Palestine is never been able to fully explore its tourism potential. This problem requires broad international reflection and action on individual as well as societal and political levels. Chapter 10 closes with a case study on the 'working poor', written by Peperkamp. She offers insight into people's values with regard to paid work and the importance thereof to human identity, and illustrates this with a case in which people are exploited within the attraction park sector in Germany despite the existence of a national minimum wage regulation there.

Chapter 11, with an introduction by van Leeuwen, offers insights into the dilemmas that could emerge within the interplay between entrepreneurship, innovation and responsibility. Van Leeuwen reflects on the different transitions entrepreneurial thinking has gone through, the kind(s) of moral value that entrepreneurship creates and the entrepreneur as responsible agent. The introduction to the first case, written by van Dijk, touches upon the interactions between entrepreneurship, healthcare and the management of costs. Van Dijk identifies the moral dilemmas that could emerge when healthcare institutes, like hospitals, are forced to start behaving like companies, need to deal with the dynamics of the market, including economic efficiency, and are pressurised to specialise and compete with other hospitals. She demonstrates, in her case, that, at grass-roots level, 'entrepreneurial pressure' could lead to unfair allocation of scarce medicine, making it less accessible to the people who desperately need it. Richards proposes in the introduction to the second case that cities can act as entrepreneurs if they wish to market themselves as relevant locations for investors and tourists. One of the tools at their disposal is the attempt to organise a large-scale event (e.g. the FIFA World Cup, the Olympic Games) as an attention-grabbing strategy. His case shows that bribes, mismanagement, self-enrichment and fraud are part and parcel of the process of organising a major event. The third case, written by van Leeuwen, deals with social entrepreneurship and social innovation and the ethical dilemmas that are attached to that. The introduction to van Leeuwen's case discusses how some forms of business transform in such a way that they become focussed on increasing social value. This includes the efforts entrepreneurs make to redesign or improve specific systems in accordance with a specific ideology. His case compellingly explicates the potential (adverse) impacts of an activity (voluntourism) within the framework of social entrepreneurship. Genuine intentions to do good do not necessarily lead to good outcomes in terms of behaviour.

Part II of this collection concludes with Chapter 12. This chapter considers the legal and ethical impact of new technologies on businesses, which, on the one hand, provide new opportunities and challenges for them, such as increasing their profit margins by improving and innovating their services and products; but on the other, as is often the case with the good things in life, also harbour a negative side. The introduction to Chapter 12 was written by Bosher. She also, together with van Gisbergen, provides the first case, which discusses intellectual property (IP) and privacy in the entertainment industry. The authors show that copyright is a regulatory tool for remunerating creators which provides restrictions on the use of works such as books, films, music and pictures. The case itself demonstrates the moral and legal implications of football fans filming in stadiums without the consent of the organisers of the game or owners of the stadium. The second case is introduced by van Liempt, who reflects on the theme of downloading films and the ethical customer. His case shows that the uploading and downloading of copyright-protected material on the Internet without permission or a licence is considered illegal under European law, but that many studies have demonstrated that this behaviour does not resonate, particularly with younger people, as an ethical wrong. De Rooij closes the chapter with its third case, which deals with the issue of big data and marketing. His case ponders the question of whether a good cause legitimises the use of big data, and if so, to what extent. The answer seems to align with the statement that whilst the use of data can be extremely valuable to marketers, the collection and use of such data must also be balanced with people's privacy rights.

1.5.2 Overview of cases and ethical dilemmas

The cases included in this study are portrayed below. An indication is given of the (main) ethical dilemmas they represent. Obviously the discussion questions included at the end of the cases also call forth other dilemmas than those that have been registered in the book. But those displayed below can be considered the 'leading' dilemmas' expressed in a specific case. For an overview depicting the dilemmas in relation to a specific industry, see the case matrix box included at the end of this section.

Chapter 6: Main theme: Professional and managerial ethics.
Case 6.2.2 Professional behaviour, fairness and ethical standards.
Dilemma: How to be fair in judging the apparent 'criminal' behaviour of a hotel employee.
Case 6.3.2 Loyalty and spilling the beans.
Dilemma: How to discern when professional loyalty to a tourism company requires an employee to blow the whistle.
Case 6.4.2 Being ethical in the market of home medical products.
Dilemma: How to judge and fulfil managerial roles in an ethical way.
Chapter 7: Main theme: Organisational ethics.
Case 7.2.2 Effective leadership in the library.
Dilemma: How to be an ethical leader in transforming an organisation.
Case 7.3.2 Deterring fraud in the hotel industry.
Dilemma: How to address the culture of fraud in the front office of a hotel.
Case 7.4.2 Employee crunch versus making profits.
Dilemma: How a games-development company can be responsible and fair towards *all* employees.
Chapter 8: Main theme: Corporate social responsibility.
Case 8.2.2 Selling solar TVs in Benin City.

Dilemma: How to – as a company pursuing fair business – balance the interests of all stakeholders.

Case 8.3.2 Products, productivity and corporate social responsibility.

Dilemma: How to balance the close relationship between low capital productivity and the shift of capital-risk in the leisure sector for the benefit of all stakeholders.

Case 8.4.2 The mobile phone as a change agent?

Dilemma: How to manage supply chains in a sound way with regard to the disposal of electronic waste.

Chapter 9: Main theme: Sustainability and business.

Case 9.2.2 Hospitality 2.0.

Dilemma: How to evaluate, construct and implement sustainable business models in the hospitality sector.

Case 9.3.2 Balancing sustainable tourism and liveability in an urban context.

Dilemma: How to make a case for sustainable tourism in cities.

Case 9.4.2 Climatic sustainability, tourism and the eradication of poverty.

Dilemma: How to balance the welfare and well-being of local communities and the environment at tourism destinations.

Chapter 10: Main theme: Human rights and business.

Case 10.2.2 *New York Dawn*'s race, gender and social dialogues.

Dilemma: How to judge and avoid racial stereotyping in video games.

Case 10.3.2 Palestine, tourism and human rights.

Dilemma: How to judge and do business with regard to tourism in countries where human rights are violated.

Case 10.4.2 Amusement parks, wages and poverty.

Dilemma: How to formulate the responsibility of business to society with regard to paying fair wages and eradicate poverty in the leisure industry (amusement parks).

Chapter 11: Main theme: Responsible entrepreneurship and innovation.

Case 11.2.2 Fairness in administering scarce and expensive medicine.

Dilemma: How to deliver optimum care to all those who deserve it in the face of the 'entrepreneurial road' hospitals are expected to travel.

Case 11.3.2 The FIFA World Cup and the Olympic Games.

Dilemma: How to judge the behaviour of 'entrepreneurial' cities competing for the right to organise major sport events.

Case 11.4.2 Social entrepreneurship using voluntourism.

Dilemma: How to assess the ethicality of social entrepreneurship and innovation.

Chapter 12: Main theme: Information technology and business.

Case 12.2.2 Photographs and videos taken inside a football stadium.

Dilemma: How to consider the protection and regulation of intellectual property with regard to taking photos at football games.

Case 12.3.2 Killing Popcorn Time.

Dilemma: How to create 'ethical customers' with regard to the illegal download of music from the Internet.

Case 12.4.2 Using customer data at Carnegie Hall.

Dilemma: How to use customer data ethically in marketing in the leisure industry (privacy in the performing arts).

Case Matrix

Industry	Type of dilemma	Chapter	Page
Tourism	Whistle-blowing, loyalty and professional ethics	6.3.2	110
	Balancing sustainable tourism and liveability in cities	9.3.2	191
	Carbon footprint, tourism and human well-being	9.4.2	198
	Business, human rights and ethics	10.3.2	217
Leisure	Profits, productivity and corporate social responsibility (CSR)	8.3.2	163
	Responsible business, fair wages and the eradication of poverty	10.4.2	223
	The ethicality of social entrepreneurship and innovation	11.4.2	253
	Marketing and the ethical use of customer data	12.4.2	278
Hospitality	Fair judgement of suspected 'criminal' behaviour by an employee	6.2.2	106
	Good corporate governance and addressing a culture of fraud	7.3.2	136
	Constructing and implementing sustainable business models	9.2.2	186
Gaming/creative	Corporate ethics and the well-being of all employees	7.4.2	143
	Avoiding racial and gender stereotypes in video games	10.2.2	212
Cultural	Ethical leadership in an organisation in transition	7.2.2	132
	Entrepreneurial cities, competition and organising sports events	11.3.2	245
	Intellectual property (IP) and privacy in taking photos inside a football stadium	12.2.2	266
	Downloading films and the ethical customer	12.3.2	272

(continued)

Case Matrix (continued)

Industry	Type of dilemma	Chapter	Page
Logistics/ service	Management ethics and selling substandard products	6.4.2	116
	Balancing fair business and interests of all stakeholders in the supply chain	8.2.2	159
	CSR, electronic waste management and sustainability thinking	8.4.2	171
	Healthcare, entrepreneurship and managing costs	11.2.2	241

Comments: There are no watershed divisions between the creative, cultural and service industries. This also applies to the cases linked to the industries mentioned in the first column of the matrix. For example, the ethical dilemmas represented by cases connected to the tourism sector (indicated in the second column of the matrix) could also emerge in the leisure, hospitality and 'cultural' sectors. Moreover, issues like human rights, ethical leadership, sustainability, CSR, responsible business, new technology, ethical marketing, fraud, employee rights and duties, (social) entrepreneurship, innovation and stakeholders (also in the supply chain) – to mention but a few – are relevant to all the industries mentioned above. Instructors and students alike are therefore advised to be creative when studying the cases and also consider the applicability and relevance of the ethical dilemmas expressed in industries other than their own.

1.6 Conclusion

This textbook is designed to enhance ethical awareness and the ability to make sound ethical decisions in the domains of the creative, cultural and service industries. Its focus is on the shaping of personal and professional values and the moral and ethical issues that (future) professionals might encounter in practice. The book is usable at both basic and professional educational levels and could therefore also serve as a source for in-company training of professionals/practitioners in the relevant work field. In addition, by taking a multidisciplinary, multi-contextual, applied ethical and case study approach, the book takes into account pedagogical concerns regarding teaching (business) ethics.

This introduction provides: (i) an explication of the book's backgrounds (educational concerns in the face of scandals in the world of business and management), (ii) its focus (the creative, cultural and service industries), (iii) its pedagogical underpinnings (raising ethical awareness and improving decision-making skills through studying cases), and (iv) the structure of the book (two parts, of which one deals with theory and the other with practice); as well as (v) a brief description of the chapters of the book (including an outline, and matrix, of the themes of the cases and the ethical dilemmas they represent).

1.7 Questions for discussion

- Can 'character' be taught? Give reasons for your answer.
- Is having a 'virtuous character' a prerequisite for displaying ethical behaviour in following up on business decisions/strategy? Why?
- There are two perspectives with regard to the question whether ethics should be included in business and management education: one regards it a waste of time, and the other a necessary activity. Could you think of arguments supporting these two positions? Which position do you favour? Why?
- If there is a good argument in favour of teaching (business) ethics at universities, what would, to your mind, the best net outcome/effect be? Which didactics could effectuate that?
- In what way can teaching itself be considered a moral activity? Use the notions of 'agency', 'educational practice' and 'educational intent' to build a case for or against it.

1.8 Concluding thoughts

Teaching itself can be considered a moral activity, since the lecturer inevitably functions as a role model for students through the integrity, honesty, fairness, respect, care and compassion he/she displays in contacts with them, but also in the choices he/she makes with regard to the selection, prescription and examination of literature, and the envisaged goals, intentions and outcomes he/she has in mind regarding the educational activities. There is more to teaching at the end of the day than merely steering students towards control and mastery of a specified bulk of knowledge, investing a specified amount of time and complying with specified (professional) competencies. Education is 'more than the learning of facts; it is the training of the mind to think' (Einstein; 'Einstein on Education', 2015); it is the 'most powerful weapon you can use to change the world' (Mandela, 2003) and it is 'not preparation for life – it is life itself' (Dewey; 'John Dewey Quotes', n.d.). The education of young people is always infused with values, norms and beliefs: those of the student, but also of the lecturer. These are constantly in dialogue with one another, and in the choices that both have to make. Therefore teaching is about carefully enabling and equipping students to follow a path that could lead them to flourish as responsible and ethical human beings in their personal and professional lives. In teaching (business and management) ethics then, 'explicit' knowledge and insights should ideally be paired with 'tacit' experiential knowledge and insights in a process of dialogue which leads to the student's gaining moral sensitivity, awareness and know-how in dealing with ethical dilemmas, and becoming a global citizen. Ethics could be taught in many ways, but arguably an integrated and embedded approach is more 'natural' and has the greatest chance of enabling students to 'see' the ethical questions that always hover above every (business and management) decision that one has to take.

Further reading

Bryson, J.R. and Daniels, P.W. (2007). *The Handbook of Service Industries*. Cheltenham/Northampton, UK: Edward Elgar.

Fenwick, T. and Nerland, M. (2014). *Reconceptualising Professional Learning: Sociomaterial Knowledges, Practices and Responsibilities*. London/New York: Routledge.

Hesmondhalgh, D. (2013). *The Cultural Industries* (3rd ed.). London/Thousand Oaks, CA: Sage Publications.

Jones, C., Lorenzen, M. and Sapsed, J. (Eds.) (2015). *The Oxford Handbook of Creative Industries*. Oxford: Oxford University Press.

Mahoney, J. (2013). *Teaching Business Ethics in the UK, Europe and the USA: A Comparative Study*. London/New York: Bloomsbury Publishing.

Ogonyemi. K. (Ed.) (2015). *Teaching Ethics Across the Management Curriculum: A Handbook for International Faculty*. New York: Business Expert Press.

References

Ametrano, I.M. (2014). Teaching Ethical Decision Making: Helping Students Reconcile Personal and Professional Values. *Journal of Counseling and Development*, 92: 154–161.

Betta, M. (2016). *Ethicmentality – Ethics in Capitalist Economy, Business, and Society*. Dordrecht: Springer Science + Business Media B.V.

Cavanagh, G.F. (1998). Teaching Business Ethics. In Werhane, P.H. and Freeman, R.E. (Eds.), *Blackwell Encyclopedic Dictionary of Business Ethics* (pp. 622–625). Oxford/Malden: Blackwell Publishers.

Chappell, S., Edwards, M.G. and Webb, D. (2013). Sustaining Voices: Applying Giving Voice to Values to Sustainability Issues. *Journal of Business Ethics Education*, 10: 211–230.

Creative Industry. (n.d.). In *Wikipedia*. Retrieved 14 September 2017 from https://en.wikipedia.org/wiki/Creative_industries.

Culham, T. (2015). Virtue Ethics as a Framework for Teaching and Evaluating Business Ethics. *Journal of Business Ethics Education*, 12: 77–100.

Cultural Industry. (n.d.). In *Wikipedia*. Retrieved 14 September 2017 from https://en.wikipedia.org/wiki/Cultural_industry.

Dewey, J. (n.d.). John Dewey Quotes. In *Brainy Quote*. Retrieved 13 March 2019 from https://www.brainyquote.com/quotes/john_dewey_154060.

Drumwright, M., Prentice, R. and Biasucci, C. (2015). Behavioural Ethics and Teaching Ethical Decision Making. *Decision Sciences Journal of Innovative Education*, 13(3): 431–458.

Einstein on Education. (2015, 7 July). In *The Unity Process*. Retrieved 13 March 2019 from https://theunityprocess.com/einstein-on-education-vs-programming/.

Falkenberg, L. and Woiceshyn, J. (2008). Enhancing Business Ethics: Using Cases to Teach Moral Reasoning. *Journal of Business Ethics*, 79: 213–217.

Gras-Dijkstra, S. (2009). *Values in Tourism: An Itinerary to Tourism Ethics*. Meppel: Edu'Actief b.v.

Hartman, E.M. (2013). *Virtues in Business: Conversations with Aristotle*. Cambridge/New York: Cambridge University Press.

Hesmondhalgh, D. (2002). *The Cultural Industries*. London/Thousand Oaks, CA: Sage Publications.

Liebermann, K. and Nissen, B. (2008). *Ethics in the Hospitality and Tourism Industry* (2nd ed.). Orlando, FL: American Hotel & Motel Association.

Lovelock, B. and Lovelock, K.M. (2013). *The Ethics of Tourism: Critical and Applied Perspectives*. London/New York: Routledge.

Mandela, N.R. (2003). Lighting Your Way to a Better Future. Address by Nelson Mandela at launch of Mindset Network, Johannesburg. Retrieved 13 March 2019 from http://www.mandela.gov.za/mandela_speeches/2003/030716_mindset.htm

McLean, D.J. and Yoder, D.G. (2005). *Issues in Recreation and Leisure: Ethical Decision-Making*. Champaign, IL: Human Kinetics.

Miller, T. (2009). From Creative to Cultural Industries: Not All Industries Are Cultural, and No Industries Are Creative. *Cultural Studies*, 23(1): 88–99.

Murphy, R., Sharma, N. and Moon, J. (2012). Empowering Students to Engage with Responsible Business Thinking and Practices. *Business and Professional Ethics Journal*, 31(2): 324.

Ohreen, D. (2013). Rationalism and a Vygotskian Alternative to Business ethics Education. *Journal of Business Ethics Education*, 10: 231–260.

Service Industries. (n.d.) In *Wikipedia*. Retrieved 14 September 2017 from https://en.wikipedia.org/wiki/Category:Service_industries.

Smit, A. (2013). Responsible Leadership Development through Management Education: A Business Ethics Perspective. *Africa Journal of Business Ethics*, 7(2): 45–51.

Wittmer, D. (2013). Developing Practical Wisdom in Ethical Decision Making: A Flight Simulator Program for 21st Century Business Students. *Journal of Business Education*, 10: 169–184.

PART I

Ethics, culture, moral development and decision-making in business contexts

Chapter 2

Ethics and business

Johan Bouwer

2.1 Introduction

Business ethics is often regarded an oxymoron, as it seems impossible to combine two concepts representing two totally different fields of meaning and purpose into one construct (Crane and Matten, 2010: 4). They just do not seem to fit together, because ethics is about good and bad behaviour while the core business of business – making profits – apparently does not fit that distinction. Some people maintain that business is not about right or wrong. It is an amoral endeavour whose purpose cannot be evaluated or judged by categories of good or bad. Business is a 'neutral' activity. But reality is quite stubborn and recalcitrant, as will become clear below.

Today, the connection between ethics and business is manifested in the realm of 'business ethics', which has found its place in both academia and business practice. It seems to be more relevant than ever before. The future of business ethics appears bright, since the many ethical dilemmas faced by the world, and therefore also by business, at different levels of society challenge both scholars and practitioners alike to reflect on the implications these dilemmas have for both education and business practice and also on the conditions for solving them. There is a sense of an urgent need to find answers and solutions to many (global) ethical dilemmas and problems, and business is more and more frequently invited to join hands with governments and societies to ensure a liveable and fair planet for future generations.

This chapter offers theoretical background information about the very nature of the concepts 'ethics', 'business' and the construct 'business ethics'. First, the nature, history and purpose of, and approaches to ethics are introduced, followed, secondly, by an explication of the nature, history, characteristics and purpose of business. Thirdly, business ethics is discussed with regard to its history, nature, scope and domain, as are approaches to theory.

2.2 What is ethics?

Ethics, also conceived as moral philosophy, relates to what is morally good or bad, right or wrong conduct. It studies moral values, beliefs, principles and theory. In practice, ethical behaviour is basically directed towards not harming others, but ideally it is, more positively, directed towards doing well unto others. Fundamentally, ethics addresses only one question: 'How should we live our lives?' (DesJardins, 2014: 13).

Two key concepts are used for situating and clarifying the nature of ethics. These are 'ethics' and 'morality'. They demarcate the study of human behaviour in the context of moral philosophy. And yet, there is no consensus about their exact meanings.

2.2.1 'Ethics' and 'morality'

The term 'ethics' is derived from the Greek *ethikos*, which in turn, comes from the word 'ethos'. 'Ethos' means 'habit, custom, conventional' (DesJardins, 2014: 14) or 'character, manners' (Skorupski, 2003: 203). This has led ethics to be associated with, on the one hand, the rules and conventions of a society or community that steer the conduct of its members, but also, on the other, people's feelings and their reasons for acting in a specific way (Skorupski, 2003: 204). The term 'morality' is derived from the Latin word *mos* (plural *mores*) and also means 'custom'.

So, in popular usage 'ethics' and 'morality' are most often seen as synonyms, because morality is conceived to be a way of life in which the norms and values of a society or community are reflected (see also Chapter 4). However, as said before, there is – also in academia – a lack of conceptual consensus. Some scholars use the term interchangeably (e.g. Cohen, 2004: 12), while others make a distinction between them – sometimes in quite different ways. Singer (2015) attributes this situation to the way 'ethics' is understood: it is associated with a discipline that has morality as its subject of study, but it is also equated with morality itself. Apart from reflection on right and wrong behaviour, ethics is also associated with 'personal preferences, emotional responses, religious beliefs, social expectations and genetic determinism' (Lynn, 2007: 790). This expands the domain of ethics even further. As far as 'morality' is concerned, the philosopher Rachels deems it impossible to come up with 'a simple uncontroversial definition' of what it actually is. There are just too many conceptions of what it means to live a moral life (1999: 1). Yet, when one reflects on the connections between the nature of knowledge and 'beliefs and justification' it is, for the sake of epistemological clarity, quite important to make a distinction between 'ethics' and 'morality'.

Ten Have, ter Meulen and van Leeuwen point out that the word 'morality' can be used in two ways: it can either have a more general (or broader) meaning analogous to 'ethics', in the sense of conduct that is seen as according with the conventions of a certain society or community; or a specific (or narrow) meaning that is synonymous with positive qualifications like 'good, desirable, right or permissible' (1998: 10). The opposites of 'morality' in the general sense of the word are 'a-moral, or non-moral or non-ethical', and its opposite in its specific meaning is 'immoral' (Bouwer and van Leeuwen, 2017: 98). When it comes to making sound moral or ethical decisions, Rachels holds, one needs to underpin one's arguments with sound reasoning and also consider the interests of everyone involved. This he calls 'the minimum conception of morality' (1999: 19), which should be taken as a starting point irrespective of the theory used.

So, for the purpose of this section it is sufficient to conclude that 'ethics' as a discipline, as moral philosophy, refers to the study of the language of morality, the

Ethics and business

justification of ethical norms and the development of congruent ethical theories (Knoepffler, 2009: 18). In other words, it concerns the 'study of morality and the application of reason to elucidate specific rules and principles that determine right and wrong for a given situation' (Crane and Matten, 2007: 8). 'Morality', in turn, is concerned with 'the norms, values, and beliefs embedded in social processes which define right and wrong for an individual or a community' (Crane and Matten, 2007: 8). Ethics is therefore rationalised and codified morality and has been subjected to reflection, study and debate for more than 2000 years. Philosophical renditions of the foundations of morality have shifted over time (Burns, 2008:13) and it would therefore go too far to provide a complete sketch of the historical development of moral thinking over the past centuries. For the purpose of this chapter, only a few lines will be drawn which reflect the main ethical positions in history.

2.2.2 A brief historical sketch of the development of ethics

Ethics originated when people started to reflect on the best way to live their lives. This is 'paradigmatically' reflected in roughly three epochs in (Western) history. The accounts of the epochs presented are complemented with information from the online source, the *New World Encyclopedia* ('History of Ethics', n.d.).

In the *premodern era*, philosophers looked for the foundations of morality in 'the nature of man, his place in the cosmos, and his constitutive relationship with the divine' (Burns, 2008: 9). To act morally was to realise one's very nature. Metaphysics and teleology (metaphysics is about studying 'being', all that is, and telos literally means 'purpose') steered moral thinking in this period. The leading question was how to be happy and lead a good life by finding one's own role in the cosmos. Both Ancient Greek ethics, represented by philosophers like Socrates, Plato and Aristotle, and later Greek ethics, represented by Epicurean and Stoic thinking, emerged in this period. In addition, the medieval ethics represented by the church fathers and the Scholastic period of Aquinas, Scotus and Ockham can also be placed within this specific historical 'paradigm'.

In the *modern era*, the limelight turned towards the human mind. Knowledge 'begins not with metaphysics or teleology but with epistemology' (Burns, 2008: 11) (epistemology studies human knowledge). Human beings cannot know things themselves, but can only realise understanding when they deem the object of knowing to be 'sensible' and empirical. Thought itself becomes the new foundation of moral thinking and reality consists of mechanical processes. The central ideas in this period – which is represented by the philosophers Hobbes, Hume and Kant respectively – are the following: there is no such thing as an ultimate good, but only human desires; reason is eventually determined by human passion; and established good is the result of the human will to fulfil his/her duty. Kant's notion that morality yields 'categorical imperatives', meaning that human behaviour can be steered by universally valid principles, is a matter that is still discussed by modern ethicists.

In the *'post'-modern period*, moral thinking is (largely, but not solely) expressed in language and action. This enhances the accessibility of the moral domain. Pre-existing entities are rejected as unsuitable and invalid for laying foundations for the building of a moral system. Moral questions should be analysed on the basis of the consequences of human behaviour. At the same time, the need for theories that provide ontological foundations (basic structures of being and existence) for morality became stronger in the moral discourse towards the end of the previous century. The golden thread running through moral thought during this period is that one has an inescapable ethical responsibility towards others. Two leading scholars representing this historical 'paradigm' are Levinas and Bauman. Levinas' philosophy calls selfishness and egoism into question and poses the notion of the inalienability of the 'Other', whose 'face' tells me that 'I am the same', while Bauman pursues morality without an ethical code. In Bauman's view, traditional ethical thinking (principles and rules, for example) has gone bankrupt and humanity needs to acknowledge that personal morality is the main 'driver' in reaching moral consensus between people and parties.

This very brief (and incomplete) sketch can be seen as the historical bedrock of a variety of ethical theories that the modern ethicist has inherited. The sketch is incomplete, amongst other reasons, because it only takes into account the development of ethics in Western contexts. Other ethical traditions such as Eastern ethics (for example, Indian/Asian (mainly drawing on Hinduism and Buddhism) and Chinese ethics (mainly drawing on Confucianism and Taoism)) and Arabic ethics (mainly drawing on Islamic religion) have not been attended to. Decision-making based on these philosophies might lead to the same ethical conclusions as Western philosophies have come to, but the journeys they might take to reach that point are different. It is said that Western ethicists often hold truth finding in high regard, while Eastern ethicists cherish protocol and respect. But broadly speaking, there is no theoretical consensus about moral issues, their fundamental nature and the principles that could be implemented in solving ethical dilemmas (Baggini and Fosl, 2013: xv). Yet, in order to get a general view of the broad domain ethics is concerned with, it might be helpful to distinguish between the major areas of study and the ethical approaches they embrace.

2.2.3 Approaches to mapping the domain of ethics

Different approaches to organising ethics can be traced in the literature. One way of mapping the terrain of ethics is to distinguish between theoretical ethics and applied ethics (Gras-Dijkstra, 2009: 97) – despite the fact that applied ethics fully incorporates theoretical ethics as well. As will be indicated further on, there is a discussion going on about whether applied ethics could be equated with 'practical' ethics. However, the terrain of theoretical ethics will be outlined first.

2.2.3.1 Theoretical ethics

Theoretical ethics – as one of the pillars holding up the roof of ethics – is oriented towards those criteria which explain the essence of morality. It is usually divided into three branches:

- Meta-ethics, which is concerned with the nature of moral judgement and the foundations or principles of ethical theory;
- Descriptive ethics, which studies people's beliefs about morality;
- Normative ethics, which examines the standards and principles applied to assess the rightness or wrongness of actions themselves, and is therefore sometimes called 'prescriptive'.

Ethics and business

In turn, normative ethics – in reflecting on the moral or ethical quality of behaviour or an action – applies different ethical approaches that can be characterised either as 'traditional' or 'contemporary' (Gras-Dijkstra, 2009: 100).

2.2.3.1.1 TRADITIONAL NORMATIVE ETHICAL APPROACHES

Usually three traditional theoretical ethical approaches are distinguished. They are the following:

- Deontology, which focuses on the duties to be followed and the principles that lead to right and good actions;
- Teleology – also called 'consequentialism' – which focusses on the goal of an action and the consequences that behaviour has for the self or others. Consequentialism is probably the most widely used approach to moral decision-making in ethics and is based on the philosophical assumption that all action is aimed at a specific goal, and that all that is has an inherent purpose (telos). The main theories that resort to consequentialist approaches are the following:

    - utilitarianism (which looks for the greatest good or happiness for the greatest number of people)
    - hedonism (which pursues pleasure or happiness as a goal in life) and
    - egoism (which is about acting for one's own benefit) (Thompson, 2010: 71–79)

- Virtue ethics, which focuses on the character qualities one should acquire in order to be able to act well or rightly.

2.2.3.1.2 CONTEMPORARY NORMATIVE ETHICAL APPROACHES

As far as contemporary normative ethical approaches are concerned, scholars also differentiate between three categories. They are:

- The ethics of (human) rights, fairness and justice. This approach can be seen as a representation of the deontological approach in ethics;
- The ethics of care, empathy and compassion. An important feature of this approach is its emphasis on relationality between people and parties. In a certain sense it represents consequentiality, because the impact of care and good relations might lead to the good;
- Virtue ethics, which is a refinement and further clarification of the traditional virtue ethics. Modern theories of virtue ethics also reflect on the character traits of the actor, but broaden their scope to include eudaemonism (the idea that the final goal of action is human flourishing, well-being or happiness – see section 2.2.4) and phronesis (meaning that someone has the (practical) wisdom to decide which virtue is applicable in a specific situation; Gras-Dijkstra, 2009: 131).

Section 2.4.4 will shed more light on these theories.

2.2.3.2 Applied and/or practical ethics

The other pillar that holds up the roof of ethics is applied ethics. Some scholars distinguish applied ethics from practical ethics. This might look like a contradiction in terms, since ethics is fundamentally concerned with practice and therefore per definition 'applied' or 'practical'. Yet the concept 'applied' was coined and 'institutionalised' due to moral discourses about, for example, the legitimacy of war, freedom and sexuality, civil rights and developments in the field of medicine, subjects that began to dominate the public domain in the United States in the 1960s (Haldane, 2003: 492). Since then, professionals in different fields have experienced the need to reflect on their responsibilities and the moral edges to which their actions could take them. Different fields of application have seen the light. Take for example business ethics, medical or bioethics, ethics of law, media ethics, environmental ethics, animal ethics, consumer ethics and also leisure and tourism ethics. So, applied ethics studies the way in which moral awareness has been put into practice (by professionals), and the way in which theory could be or has been implemented (by professionals), with the purpose of solving ethical dilemmas within a specific realm of reality.

What, then, could the arguments of those scholars be who make a distinction between 'applied' and 'practical' ethics? Lynn, for example, regards 'applied' ethics as the application of 'the answers from theoretical ethics to concrete cases in a top-down, linear and deductive manner', while 'practical' ethics 'seeks out the best answer by integrating what we learn from a concrete case about a moral problem and the conceptual insights that help us best understand and resolve that moral problem' (2007: 791). Practical ethics, in his mind, is concerned with hermeneutics: it is 'an ethics that is simultaneously conceptually rich and situated in real life' and which seeks moral understanding by 'accounting for a person's intentions, concepts, meanings, interpretations and communications' (Lynn, 2000: 6). Another scholar, Knoepffler, puts forward that applied ethics could be used in two ways. On the one hand, it could apply a top-down approach (in concordance with Lynn's assessment of applied ethics), but on the other, it could use a bottom-up one. To his mind, the bottom-up approach proceeds from the belief that a specific case itself, the concrete situation, conveys the norms and values needed to solve an ethical dilemma (Knoepffler, 2009: 52). He rejects both these applications of ethics. Instead, Knoepffler advocates a holistic approach, which resembles Lynn's definition of *practical* ethics. He holds that, apart from working with the criteria, rules and principles which are present in the concrete situation itself, one should also have a dialogue with the current 'tradition' or 'reality' in which the case has emerged. This 'tradition' or 'reality' contains transcending principles that could be used to amend or correct those related to the case itself (Knoepffler, 2009: 55–57). This line of reasoning shows that 'practical' ethics depicts a more comprehensive approach towards solving ethical dilemmas, which reckons with more than one set of ethical principles. Both case and context provide the information that is used in reaching a decision.

However, whatever the mode in which the study of ethics is structured or organised, the foundational aim – as indicated above – remains the same; namely, to reflect on the preconditions for leading a good life and/or on the different ways of becoming (human).

2.2.4 Ethics and the purpose of the good life

The answer to the question of how to live a good life is determined by another question, namely 'what is the end or purpose of a/the good life?' Sylvester considers an 'end' to be something that is good in itself; it has intrinsic goodness and is therefore 'is chosen for its own sake' (1987: 174). The end, purpose or ultimate value of the good life, then, can be seen as the encompassing ethical goal towards which human behaviour and actions are directed. The Greek philosopher, Aristotle, considers this ethical goal of the good life, or the highest aim in human life, to be eudaemonia. The concept of eudaemonia, or the highest human good, consists of two Greek terms, namely, 'eu' (good) and 'daimon' (god, spirit, demon). Eudaemonia literally means 'good spirit' or 'blessed with good godliness' (Holowchak, 2004: xi) or 'being true to one's inner self' (Begum, Jabeen and Awan, 2014: 314). It is usually translated into English as 'happiness'.

In modern times, scholars from a wide range of disciplines have filled happiness with conceptual meaning: it is defined by some as 'the greatest good, pleasure, highest level of satisfaction, the power to overcome fears, obeying God or having a good conscience' (Begum, Jabeen and Awan, 2014: 314); by others, as a condition of enjoyment and feeling good (Layard, 2005: 12); and by yet others as feeling excited (in the case of young people) or peaceful (in that of elderly people) (Mogilner, Kamvar and Aaker, 2011: 401). Yet, apart from 'pleasure', philosophers also conceive of happiness as a virtue, the 'fulfilment of human nature', 'our natural end' and 'something impossible for us to obtain' (Pawelski, 2013: 247). There is no universal consensus about the exact meaning of happiness, since it is quite subjective and individually bound. However, the attitude, world view or moral stance that takes happiness to be the ultimate goal or end of life is called hedonism.

Hedonism, broadly speaking, is concerned with 'maximizing pleasure and minimizing pain' (Peterson, 2006: 78). This applies to both sensory or bodily and intellectual pleasures (Thompson, 2010: 74). Hedonism is about human well-being (Stebbins, 2014: 28); it influences moral choice and drives human behaviour. Ayn Rand warns that happiness should not be taken as a standard, an abstract principle that steers human choice and behaviour in the 'achievement of a concrete specific purpose', but rather as the 'purpose of ethics'. She argues that happiness can be best achieved by accepting one's *life* as one's primary concern and pursuing the 'rational values it requires', but not by posing happiness itself as an undefined primary concern that steers one's life (Moen, 2012: 115). Although Rand's position on morality and ethics evokes resistance in a wide circle of philosophers due to its egoist foundation, her warning to be critical of the 'standard' that leads human action should be taken seriously.

However, 'eudaemonia' harbours other meanings than 'happiness' or 'well-being' alone. Huta, for example, argues that it is better to translate eudaemonia as 'flourishing or excellence', since Aristotle's explication of the term transcends and encompasses the happiness denotation. Aristotle describes eudaemonia as 'active behaviour that exhibits excellence or virtue in accordance with reason and contemplation' (Huta, 2013: 202). Eudaemonia is the end or purpose of a life that expresses both intellectual virtues (practical and pure theoretical thinking) and character (or moral) virtues. Although all three kinds of virtue are deemed important for the good life, Aristotle favours the pure theoretical virtues that can be reached through contemplation (Brown,

2003: 611–612). Whereas 'happiness' refers to moral goodness only when activities have led to it (Brown, 2003: 612), eudaemonia is about self-fulfilment (Yacobi, 2015: 85), and, conceived as flourishing or excellence, it fundamentally embraces 'moral goodness as an *integral* part of the good life' (Brown, 2003: 612).

In sum, living a life that is good is a 'way of being' (van Zyl, 2015: 184) and leads to eudaemonia (happiness/well-being, flourishing/excellence). Hedonic approaches mostly focus on those actions that lead to happiness and evaluate them either on deontological or consequentialist bases, while eudaemonic approaches are more concerned with the worth and value humans allocate to issues in life, and the way these values are reflected in 'feelings, reactions, attitudes and desires'. Such approaches ponder upon the question of what kind of human being one wants to be (van Zyl, 2015: 184) and therefore often consult virtue ethics.

The purpose of ethics, therefore, is to reflect on human behaviour and the principles underpinning that behaviour from the perspective of the good life. This is true for all the levels of society at which individuals operate, meaning that it can be studied on the micro, (individual), meso (group/organisational/institutional) and macro (societal/state) levels. Individual ethics investigates the obligations an individual has towards him/herself, fellow human beings and also to nature, while organisational ethics reflects systematically on good and just institutions. Social or public ethics studies the behaviour of governments in all social realms that have an impact on the well-being of the general public (Göbel, 2013: 43–46).

To prepare us for a reflection on how this relates to human conduct within a business setting, the meaning and nature of 'business' will be explored first.

2.3 What is business?

This section provides a brief introduction to the meaning and nature, history, characteristics, and aims and purpose of business.

2.3.1 The meaning and nature of 'business'

Several online dictionaries indicate that the concept 'business' has a long history. The word stems from the old English word 'bisignis', which carries meanings such as 'anxiety, 'care', 'attentiveness' and 'occupation' ('Business', n.d., *Merriam-Webster.com*; 'Business', n.d., *Dictionary.com*). In Middle English it came to be spelt 'busyness', and from the 14th until about the end of the 18th and beginning of the 19th centuries, this word was mainly used to indicate a 'state of being busy' or 'state of being much occupied or engaged' (Cresswell, 2010: 65). The need emerged to make a distinction between simply being busy and having a business to attend to. 'Busyness' gradually acquired the connotation of having 'an appointed task' ('Business', n.d., *Oxford Dictionaries*). The sense of having a 'trade' or 'commercial engagements' grew from that. The *Online Etymological Dictionary* even records that in order to accentuate the exact meaning of 'busyness', the word 'busiless' was coined ('Business', n.d., *Online Etymological Dictionary*). 'Busiless' indicated that a person was at leisure, unemployed, and 'without business'. This concords with the distinctions that are made in Latin, for example. The word used for 'business' is *'negotium'* and indicates the opposite of *'otium'*, which means 'leisure'.

Today, it is not easy to provide one general and universally applicable definition of 'business'. There are just too many kinds of businesses, and they come in different sizes and shapes. Think of banks, newspaper kiosks, florists, supermarkets, cafés, estate agents, tourist operators, hotels, accountancy firms, game developers, caterers, one-man (or -woman) businesses (such as coaches); and there are many more. Yet they all share certain commonalities, which are clarified by the following definitions of 'business':

- 'A business is an organization or enterprising entity engaged in commercial, industrial or professional activities. A company transacts business activities through the production of a good, offering of a service or retailing of already manufactured products. A business can be a for-profit entity or a non-profit organization that operates to fulfil a charitable mission' ('Business', n.d., *Investopedia.com*);
- 'The organized effort of individuals to produce and sell, for a profit, the goods and services that satisfy society's needs' (Pride, Hughes and Kapoor, 2014: 29);
- 'The activity of making, buying, or selling goods or providing services in exchange for money' ('Business', n.d., *Merriam-Webster.com*);
- 'An organizational entity involved in the provision of goods and services to consumers' ('Business', n.d., *Wikipedia*);
- 'A form of activity conducted with an objective of earning profits for the benefit of those on whose behalf the activity is conducted' (Akrani, 2011);
- 'Human activity directed towards producing or acquiring wealth through buying or selling of goods' (Akrani, 2011);
- 'Any profit-seeking organization that provides goods or services designed to satisfy customers' needs' (Dewhurst, 2014: 15).

These definitions indicate that business is fundamentally an economic or commercial phenomenon which, in satisfying societal needs, entails the trading of goods and/or services to customers in exchange of money. Yet behind this rough explication of what business stands for, there are more characteristic features that have to be taken into account in order for a person or an organisation to 'qualify' as, or as the driver of, a business. These characteristics will be discussed further on (see section 2.3.3).

2.3.2 A brief history of business

Although the concept 'business' as it is used today is relatively young, this should not lead one to think that the subject matter covered by the word is also recent. On the contrary: 'doing business' has quite a long history. Business history forms part of the history of economic thinking, and goes hand in hand with the history of trade. Economic history dates back to ancient times. Aristotle, for example, reflected on *oeconomicus* (management of the household) and put forward that one could distinguish between the natural way of acquiring goods, like farming, fishing and hunting – which are related to producing goods for the necessities of living – and the unnatural way, which entails acquiring goods beyond one's needs (Brue and Grant, 2013: 1). Yet as far as physical trade between people is concerned, there is evidence that it existed much earlier than the times of the ancient Greeks. People exchanged goods and services as far back as the prehistoric era ('Trade History', n.d.).

Johan Bouwer

It is not easy to convey a consistent systematic and chronological explication of economic history, because economic thinking evolved 'in jumps, through a succession of epochs of revolution consolidation; of language confusion and "classical" periods' (Screpanti and Zamagni, 2005: 1). Yet several scholars have tried to create order in economic history by identifying broad epochs each of which function as an umbrella for a wide range of people, ideas, models, theories, contexts and the like to be found within it. It would be beyond the scope of this book to describe this history in depth. For the purpose of this chapter it will suffice merely to sketch a brief outline, which describes (in giant leaps) the 'way' business has travelled from its inception until today. The *Wikipedia* entry on the history of economic thought, for example, identifies 14 broad 'historical clusters', which give some indications of themes. These 'clusters' are as follows:

- Ancient economic thought (before AD 500)
- Economic thought in the Middle Ages (AD 500–1500)
- Mercantilism and international trade (16th to 18th centuries)
- Pre-classical period (17th and 18th centuries)
- Classical period (18th and 19th centuries)
- Neo-classical period (19th and 20th centuries)
- Alternative schools (19th century)
- World wars, revolution and the Great Depression (early to mid-20th century)
- Alternative schools (20th century)
- Keynesianism (20th century)
- Chicago School (20th century)
- Games, evolution and growth (20th century)
- Post-World War II and globalisation (mid to late 20th century)
- Post-2008 economic crisis (21st century)

('History of Economic Thought', n.d.)

When, more specifically, it comes to the history of *trade*, *Wikipedia* offers a timeline of international trade made up of five historical periods:

- The ancient period
- The Middle Ages
- The early modern period
- The later modern period
- Post-World War II

('Timeline of International Trade', n.d.)

However, Priddat has proposed a reduction of the historical epochs portraying the development of economic thinking to three. In addition, he adds three 'broad' economic lines of thinking to each of these epochs, thereby conveying their main focus. These are:

- The transition from the ancient *oeconomica* to the economic view of the accumulation of capital that was vibrant in the 18th century, also called the era of the creation of wealth.

- The transformation of the old theories of production (and labour) to the theories of the attribution of value up to the marginal utility theory in modern times. (indicating the 'extra' satisfaction a customer will achieve when buying more than one product or making use of the same service more than once).
- The modernisation of the theory of values that forms the foundation for modern economy in the debates at the end of the 20th, beginning of the 21st century.

(Priddat, 2002: 9–10)

From these historical outlines one can deduce that the prevailing economic, or business philosophy could historically be situated as originating in the period after World War II, and more specifically, after the 2008 economic crisis period. Priddat indicates in his categorisation that the leading question in this epoch concerns the value(s) of economic activity. What value do the economy and business pursue in the context of the current global, highly competitive and technologically challenging environment, and what value do they in reality generate, and to whom (Pride et al., 2014: 26)? This touches upon the question of the aims and purpose of business (see section 2.3.4). Yet in order to set the scene for a reflection on these, the features of business will be introduced next.

2.3.3 Characteristics of business

From a 'pure' business perspective, as Pride, Hughes and Kapoor's definition has shown above, a business displays three basic features. These are 'the organised effort of individuals' to make 'business profit' by 'satisfying the needs' of customers (2014: 8–9). Material, human, financial and informational resources of a company are applied and managed in a concerted and integrated way, so that (potential) buyers are 'seduced' into acquiring the products offered, thereby heightening the company's profitability through the increase of sales and/or reduction of costs. To help a business be successful in this endeavour, there are several other characteristic features it may adopt. So, to sum up, apart from:

- the economic/commercial activities entailing the production and distribution of goods and services,
- satisfying the needs of customers through the buying and selling (trading) of high-quality goods and services at a reasonable price, and
- ensuring that a profit is made, which is driven by the return on investment, and is the major indicator of the success of a company,

it could also follow these guidelines:

- bearing in mind that business or entrepreneurship harbours risks and uncertainty of different kinds. These include foreseeable risks, such as taxes that have to be paid, costs of supplies or equipment, overheads, salaries and the costs of the goods and services that are offered; but also the unforeseeable ones, such as changes in customer tastes and in the reigning trends in society, the impact on the economy of (potential) customers and the actions taken by competitors;

- staying fresh and creative in order to improve one's existing goods and services or invent new products and services through innovation;
- keeping the laws, rules and regulations of a country in mind and having an effective system of governance and control in place;
- using both the material and non-material resources of the company optimally; and
- realising that business continuously needs the support of different social groups like investors, employees, customers and creditors, which makes it a socio-economic activity.

The notion that business is fundamentally a socio-economic activity (last bullet point) points to its interdependence with society. This implies that it has a certain undeniable (social) responsibility (see Chand, n.d.) – an aspect which forms an important cornerstone in the discussion of the moral and ethical responsibilities of a company. This will be dealt with next.

2.3.4 The aims and purpose of business

Questions about the relationship between business and society, business and the environment, and about the moral and ethical responsibilities of business towards those domains, align well with the aims and purpose of business.

Since the Industrial Revolution, the idea of 'shareholder primacy', has prevailed, especially after Milton Friedman's work on this area in the mid-20th century. It entails that the only responsibility of business is to create profit (Fleming and Jones, 2013: 50), and therefore its aim is to maximise the wealth of a company's owners; or, as Vallance has put it, it is all about the 'maximisation of shareholder *value*' (2001: 33). This position can be seen as business-purpose number one. Although it is commonly accepted that business has a moral obligation to make a profit, and that the creation of welfare is the prime responsibility of a business, there are scholars who think otherwise. Over the last decades of the 20th century and the early years of the 21st, trust in business has plunged to all-time low, fed by the many scandals in, for example, the food, real estate, accounting and banking sectors. But the world has changed as well. The concerns it faces, for example, climate change, poverty and inequality in the world, wars and violence, and the problem of the liveability of the planet for future generations, as mentioned in the introduction, are quite grave. This has arguably led to a stretching of the shareholder-value position to encompass a *long-term* shareholder value (Preston, 2010: 55).

The second theory, which posits that the aim of business is to prioritise its long-term shareholder value, holds that a business should treat its employees and suppliers in a just and fair manner, and adopt ethical policies to secure more trust from the public and (potential) customers, thus ensuring the company's profitability. However, this position does not fully satisfy the critics of shareholder value, because all the adaptations made to the theory still serve the purpose of maximising shareholder wealth. In times of crisis, the primacy of shareholder value will still prevail (Preston, 2010: 55–56).

A third business theory identified by Preston is the multi-stakeholder approach (2010: 56). See also the work of Freeman on this topic (1984). This approach presupposes that businesses fundamentally have responsibilities to more than just one stakeholder (the shareholders). Customers, employees, suppliers, local communities and the environment should be considered stakeholders as well. In addition, businesses should realise that they enjoy certain privileges, such as tax relief and government subsidies, and that they make use of societal resources. Business can never deny its connection to and even dependence on society. To be more specific, while society depends on business for wealth creation, business needs society as an environment in which it can create that wealth.

Then there is a fourth position, which goes beyond the multi-stakeholder approach. This argument puts forward that business should be proactively involved in shaping society for the better. Based on its influential position in society, business should always be aware of both the negative and positive impacts its activities could have on people, communities and the environment, and take (proactive) action to minimise or eradicate the negative impacts and enhance positive ones (Preston: 2010: 56).

What these four positions have shown – and this concords with Priddat's assessment of the nature of current economic thinking, above – is that the world has reached a point at which economic value can no longer be defined or represented by price and money only (2002: 214). It can no longer be determined by pure financial calculation, because economic theories are not 'neutral instruments of pure knowledge' (Screpanti and Zamagni, 2005: 514). The majority of scholars in business and economics, and (potential) businesspeople, agree that the value of business should be considered to include socio-contextual values and *meanings* as well. Research has shown that 88 per cent of Master of Business Administration (MBA) graduates in the Unites States are willing to accept a lower wage if they have the choice to work for a company with ethical business practices (Clark and Babson, 2012: 821). This means that, in satisfying the needs of society, or customers, businesses do indeed have a moral responsibility to make a profit (generate welfare), but at the same time they should not forget that the way in which they generate that welfare has an impact on the people and environment (the context) it operates in. Economic and financial value go hand in hand with moral value. In the same vein, Heertje suggests that welfare and well-being should not be considered antonyms, but should be embraced as one and the same aim of economic activity (2007: 13). Therefore, economics, and thus also business, cannot be detached from the virtues underlying a sound society and it can no longer treat social problems as simple 'technical issues'; rather, it should see them as 'an aspect of the general quest for the Good Life' (Screpanti and Zamagni, 2005: 515). These statements show that the discussion has quite emphatically and specifically moved towards the question of the relationship between ethics and business.

2.4 Ethics and business

As indicated at the beginning of this chapter, there is still no universal consensus that business has any other responsibility than making profits, let alone linking it to the issue of 'ethics'. The question of whether ethics and business could ever 'meet' to some extent, is still occupying the minds of even the most hard-headed business leaders and thinkers. Apparently, these two concepts are seen as so contradictory that it would be untenable to put them together into one construct of meaning, namely 'business ethics'. But, as has been assessed, at this stage business ethics seems to be alive and well. Motives for considering the ethical side of business might, as one example, relate to the above-mentioned scandals in the field of business. These events imply that businesses have behaved unethically and that the decisions they have made did not live up to the moral standards and expectations of the public, or of the law. If business has nothing to do with ethics, could these scandals then be attributed to the very nature of business, implying that it is inherently 'bad', or does it mean that business belongs to another 'moral' domain than the rest of society? Doesn't it suffice if business obeys the laws and regulations of the country it is residing in? Why a need for ethics then? Or is the uneasiness to deal with ethics attributable to mere reluctance?

In any case, there seem to be good reasons to accept that 'business ethics' as a phenomenon has a right to exist. Not only does the explication of the characteristics, aims and purpose of business given above, the current state of economic thinking; the mutual interdependence between business and society, and the increasing public awareness of the role and function business plays, and is expected to play in the world, suggest that business has a responsibility to fulfil regarding all of its stakeholders; there is also the challenge of understanding why business has made 'bad' decisions and what could have been done to avoid them in future, or, even better, how business could make 'good' decisions from the outset. The general public expects business to behave responsibly. And 'responsibility' is a concept from the domain of ethics. Surveys have shown that 49 per cent of US consumers reported having boycotted companies that had displayed behaviour not considered to be in the best interest of society; 87 per cent of customers indicated that they were prepared to switch to other brands if they were manufactured in a more socially responsible way than their usual choice; and 69 per cent of employees indicated that they weighed and evaluated the social and environmental track record of a company before they decided to accept a job offer (Clark and Babson, 2012: 820–821).

Whether the relationship between ethics and business is a smooth and easy one or not, the reality is that they have formed a partnership for quite some time now. In the following sections a brief history of business ethics will be provided, along with an explication of its nature and definition, its scope and domains, and approaches to its study.

2.4.1 A brief history of business ethics

Moral sensitivity with regard to the impact of economic and business activities is not new. Close reading of sections 2.2.3 and 2.2.4 will reveal that ethical issues in business were at stake even at the very beginnings of economic or commercial history. Consider the reference to Aristotle's notion of the natural and unnatural acquisition of goods. Schwartz describes the early moral awareness of business in his entry on 'Business Ethics' in *The Encyclopaedia of Business Ethics and Society* as follows:

> (…) the Code of Hammurabi, created nearly 4,000 years ago, records that Mesopotamian rulers attempted to create honest prices. In the fourth century BCE, Aristotle discussed the vices and virtues of tradesmen and merchants. The Old Testament and the Jewish Talmud discuss the proper way to conduct business,

Ethics and business

including topics such as fraud, theft, proper weights and measures, competition and free entry, misleading advertising, just prices, and environmental issues. The New Testament and the Koran also discuss business ethics as it relates to poverty and wealth. Throughout the history of commerce, these codes have had an impact on business dealings. (Schwartz, 2008: 216)

McMahon adds to that:

> The Egyptians were not to take money for passage across the river until after the passenger was safely there. In the Old Testament interest was not to be taken on loans. (...) Cicero asked about price justice for goods in a starving city. Dionesian Roman Law prescribed that justice requires to grant to each person what is his/her due. (McMahon, 1998: 317)

An awareness of the impacts of business activity was also present in the early and late Middle Ages. Issues to be mentioned here, which were often discussed within the fields of philosophy and theology, include the influence of the market on (i) the price of a product, (ii) slavery and the creation of monopolies, (iii) power and rights, (iv) the relationship between labour and capital, (v) conflicts between employer and employee, (vi) fair wages, capitalism and morality and (vii) poverty and fair prices (McMahon, 1998: 317; Ferrell, Fraedrich and Ferrell, 2015: 11).

It was only in the 1960s that the star of ethics in business started to rise due to public discussions about civil rights, 'the environment, safety in the workplace and consumer issues' (Schwartz, 2008: 2017). Ferrell, Fraedrich and Ferrell give a handy overview of the issues that were at stake in the United States from the 1960s until the 2000s.

- 1960s: environment, civil rights, employer–employee tensions, changing work ethic and drug use.
- 1970s: Employee militancy, human rights, covering up issues instead of correcting them, disadvantaged consumers and transparency.
- 1980s: Bribes and illegal contracting, influence peddling, deceptive advertising, financial fraud (savings and loans).
- 1990s: sweatshops and unsafe working conditions in third-world countries, rising corporate liability for personal damages, financial mismanagement and fraud, organisational ethical misconduct.
- 2000s: cybercrime, financial misconduct, global issues such as Chinese product safety, sustainability, intellectual property theft.

(Ferrell, Fraedrich and Ferrell, 2015: 10)

For the sake of completion, another bullet point is added representing the issues that are currently at issue (and have been since 2010):

- 2010s: in the last few years attention has been directed towards the foundations of the free market (capitalism), corporate governance, business leadership, compliance, climate change and energy, responsible business conduct, metrics regarding business and well-being, humanistic management, the next generation of corporate social responsibility and sustainability, information technology, big data and privacy, fake news and the media, human rights (again) and poverty and inequality.

As an academic discipline, business ethics started to emerge in the 1970s and was acknowledged as a field of study in the 1980s. Companies 'became more concerned with their public image, and as social demands grew, many businesses realised they needed to address ethical issues more directly', which lead to their institutionalisation; as a result, organisations started to implement ethical compliance programmes in the 1990s (Ferrell, Fraedrich and Ferrell, 2015: 11). From 2000 onwards, discussions about organisational ethical behaviour have focussed mainly on ethical or responsible leadership, accountancy and sound financial reporting.

Business ethics seems to have found its place in academia as a mature discipline. Scholars (and practitioners alike) study questions such as 'can business ethics be taught? What factors actually influence ethical behaviour? What should a firm's ethical obligations (i.e., beyond the law) consist of? (…) How can business ethics be best integrated into a firm's corporate culture?' (Schwartz, 2008: 219). The list of associated issues, problems and questions is much longer. Globalisation and internationalisation have added to the complexity of the issues business ethics has to deal with. It is forced to look over the fences of its own (national) borders and resort to thorough inquiry in order to come up with innovative solutions that are good for business and society.

2.4.2 What is business ethics?

Business ethics is generally characterised as a form of applied ethics. Applied ethics, in turn, 'covers a vast range of subjects' in 'a range of key areas of human life' (Thompson, 2010: 189–190) – some of which have been mentioned in section 2.2.3.2. As has been indicated above, applied ethics utilises insights from general ethical theory pertaining to what is good or bad, and also from meta-ethics, in reflecting on and offering solutions to the urgent practical dilemmas and problems that have emerged within a specific practice. However, it should be noted that in order to be credible to and relevant for a specific domain, applied ethics can no longer be regarded as a mere application of principles and standards from the existing general theory on solving ethical problems. On the contrary, the starting point for theorising and finding acceptable 'answers' to ethical problems should be practice (and its context) itself. That is why Lynn speaks rather of practical ethics, and Knoepffler wants to 'cross-check' between the principles linked to a specific case and those present in the context in which it is embedded. Practical ethics searches for moral understanding – fed by honest and thorough analysis of the practice itself – as the basis for finding ways to solve ethical dilemmas or formulate principles and standards for good behaviour. This also goes for business ethics.

2.4.2.1 Defining business ethics

Finding a generally accepted definition of business ethics is not easy, despite the many attempts that have been made to capture its essence in one clear all-explaining sentence. The following definitions give an impression of how different scholars conceive of business ethics. Note that some definitions are formulated in a formal way while others are presented in a more substantial, material way.

- 'Business ethics is the application of moral standards to business situations' (Pride et al., 2014: 35).
- 'Business ethics comprises a subdivision of applied ethics which has the task to deduce practical recommendations with regard to the (concrete) application of norms in the economic subsystem' (Holzmann, 2015: 19).
- 'Business ethics, then, can be described as the study of how we ought to conduct business; the study of what makes certain actions within the business context the right, rather than the wrong thing to do, from a value-based perspective. It often involves making choices between conflicting values. It is about more than obeying the law. And it is the concern of all types of organisations, not just profit-seeking, private companies' (Preston, 2010: 52).
- 'Business ethics comprises organizational principles, values, and norms that may originate from individuals, organizational statements, or from the legal system that primarily guide individual and group behaviour in business' (Ferrell, Fraedrich and Ferrell, 2015: 5).
- 'Business ethics refers to the values and standards that determine the interaction between business and its stakeholders' (Rossouw and van Vuuren, 2017: 5).
- 'Business Ethics is the study of business situations, activities and decisions where issues of right and wrong are addressed' (Crane and Matten, 2010: 5).
- 'Business ethics is the study of business action – individual or corporate – with special attention to its moral adequacy' (Goodpaster, 1997: 51).
- 'Business ethics studies the social responsibility of corporations from the perspective of the moral concept "responsibility" itself' (Jeurissen, 2009: 110).
- 'Business ethics is the study of moral principles and conduct within a business environment' (van Syckle and Tietje, 2010: 184).
- 'Business ethics is too often conceived as a set of impositions and constraints, obstacles to business behaviour rather than the motivating force behind that behaviour' (Solomon, 1999: 67). 'The ethics of business is not simply confined to "business" but begin [sic] by examining the very nature of the good life and living well in a business society' (Solomon, 1998: 531). '(…) the three most basic business virtues: honesty, fairness and trustworthiness' (Solomon, 1999: 69).

Arguably, when two issues like ethics and business are joined together into one construct, and the characteristic features of both are 'known', then it seems plausible that those characteristics could be blended together into another set of attributes describing that construct. This means that there should be some congruence between those attributes that have been described above as those of 'business' and those of 'ethics'. Although the vast majority of the definitions of 'business ethics' portrayed in this section revolve around the formal aspects of business – like the kind of ethics it resorts to (applied ethics); the task of ethics (studying the morality of business conduct and providing principles, values and norms for decision-making); the setting (business/economic activity); the actors (person or an organisation); and the nature and context of its agency (situations, activities and decisions – towards all stakeholders), they also refer to substantial, material notions such as right and wrong, living well, the good life, and virtues like responsibility, honesty, fairness and trust.

It has been pointed out earlier that the concept 'responsibility' is increasingly regarded as a leading value or virtue in business behaviour. Solomon defines another foundational virtue for business behaviour that encompasses the three virtues of honesty, fairness and trust, and which can be regarded as complementary to responsibility. It is the virtue of integrity (Solomon, 1999). Therefore, these two notions can arguably be seen as the leading principles for good business behaviour which hold up the roof of business ethics. This idea is supported by the work of scholars such as Hartman, DesJardins and MacDonald (2014) who approach business ethics from the perspectives of social responsibility and personal integrity, Jeurissen (2009), who does so from those of moral responsibility and integrity, and Rossouw and van Vuuren (2017), from moral responsibility and moral integrity. It will be demonstrated by an overview of the scope and domain of business ethics in the next section.

2.4.3 The scope and domain of business ethics

Section 2.2.4 concludes with the statement that ethics can be studied at different levels of aggregation such as the micro, meso and macro levels. This is also applicable to the study of business ethics. Fryer conveys several indicative insights with regard to these three levels, which are portrayed in the schema below (2015: 6–7). The views of other scholars have been added to his as well. However, the explanation does not fully cover all the (specific) ethical issues that business ethics has to deal with, but it does offer an indication of which (kinds of) issues or possible dilemmas are related to which level:

- As far as the *micro level* is concerned, business ethics studies issues related to the ethical behaviour of and decisions taken by individual managers or employees of a certain company on a day-to-day basis. Is it, for example, in cases where contracts have to be made, ethically acceptable for an employee to withhold vital information from his or her manager, to accept gifts from suppliers in exchange for information, or to give preference to companies (or a personal friend) with whom he or she has a long-standing relation? In other words, business ethics studies the ethical implications of economic activity 'within the organisation itself' (Rossouw, 2004: 2). More specifically, the main theme on the individual level concerns the professional and moral roles that individuals play, the functions they have within the organisation and the personal and professional ethical dilemmas they encounter within it. Think about the roles of receptionist, buyer or seller, employee, manager, leader and the like. How do these individuals behave personally towards 'other people, their colleagues, customers, partners or the general public?' (Preston, 2010: 55). What rights and obligations do they have, which activities are permissible in the organisation and what moral virtues could be expected from them? The important moral virtues at stake here are *moral integrity and moral responsibility* and relate to questions such as whether individual behaviour is fair, honest and trustworthy.

- On the *meso level*, business ethics has to deal with questions related to the right or wrong behaviour of companies or industry sectors, for example, in cases where they try to avoid paying taxes (in certain countries), or choose the cheapest way to get rid of waste (e.g., by dumping it in an African country) or take irresponsible risks in an attempt to increase profits. In other words, on this level, business ethics studies the implications of economic activity 'between organisations and those with whom they interact' (Rossouw, 2004: 2) – more specifically its impacts on other people, communities and the natural environment (Preston 2010: 54). This level has two branches, namely the intra-organisational and extra-organisational ones:

    - The intra-organisational branch concerns good corporate governance and employees' rights and obligations (as one stakeholders of the company). Business ethics deals here with issues like job security, job safety, non-discrimination, sexual harassment, privacy issues, misuse of company resources, participation and loyalty. How does the company legitimise the rights, obligations and responsibility of its employees? What is the culture of the organisation? Does it, for example, have an implemented ethical code of conduct or does it follow other international treaties and/or codes? The moral value or virtue at stake here is *responsibility* (with regard to governance).
    - The extra-organisational branch concerns corporate responsibility, and sales and marketing. Business ethics deals here with issues like (sound) advertising, lying and deception, manipulation, conflicts of interest, corruption, bribery, fraud, financial misconduct, and pricing. The moral value or virtue at stake here is social *responsibility* (towards all other stakeholders than the employees of a company, for example, the customers, suppliers, stockholders, communities, competitors, trade unions, government and environment).

- The *macro level* (also called the systemic level) considers the actual or desirable role a company plays within the broader context, society. Think of questions, as mentioned before, pertaining to whether business has a responsibility towards society and the environment as well, or only towards making as much money as possible, or whether governments should give the market a free hand in 'going its way'. Or should they do some steering in order to secure (or improve) the well-being of society, communities and the environment? Which principles, standards and/or procedures should be followed in order to be certain that good ethical behaviour is properly regulated at this level? In other words, business ethics at the systemic level concerns the 'broad policy framework within which economic exchange occurs' which 'is being decided upon at the national level by the political power of the state' (Rossouw, 2004: 2). It therefore covers all issues related to and influenced by globalisation and/or internationalisation, and deals with issues like the economy, market, inequality, poverty, human rights, environment, instability, fraud and corruption, economy and sustainability. The moral value or virtue at stake here is (social) *responsibility*.

In closing this section, it seems important to state that the two foundational virtues indicated here – *responsibility* and *integrity* – are arguably two sides of the same coin. Both virtues guide the good (moral) business behaviour of both individuals and companies. Professional moral behaviour, for example, is not steered or judged by integrity, as a character trait, alone. One should also consider the moral responsibility of a person, which can be regarded as the action-related guideline for professional behaviour. This is also true for companies. A company is not only steered or judged by the virtue of responsibility, but also by the virtue of integrity. In practice, when a person or company has to relate to and/or deal with an ethical dilemma, these two virtues will most probably be used in a differentiated way. Yet it is good to keep in mind that whether one refers to individual professional behaviour or to corporate behaviour, it is always a *person* that is acting within the confinements of the role or functions he/she fulfils, or the mandate he or she has within the company. People act, not firms or companies (notwithstanding the fact that a firm can be regarded a legal person). Integrity, as indicated earlier, incorporates other virtues such as honesty, transparency, truthfulness and openness, while responsibility incorporates values such as care, respect, compassion and wisdom in handling power and status. Both integrity and responsibility are needed in order to make good ethical decisions. This aspect will be treated more extensively in Chapter 5.

2.4.4 Approaches to business ethics and theory

As a mature academic discipline within the realm of applied or practical ethics, business ethics is a (multi-disciplinary) field which is studied by different branches of learning and also from different ethical perspectives. At a disciplinary level, it can, for instance, be studied within economics, management studies, history, anthropology, sociology, psychology and philosophy. Yet there are also other ways of addressing and communicating about business ethics. Scholars use different approaches to do this. Schwartz identifies five 'formal' modes that are generally used to approach business ethics in the literature (2008: 218). They are the following:

- The normative and descriptive approach: the normative stance conveys how business practice and behaviour *should* be, while the descriptive stance tells us what the state of business behaviour currently *is*.
- A functional approach: business activities are categorised based on the different functions a company carries out, such as marketing, finance and accounting.
- An issues approach: business activities are categorised based on themes that are representative of important 'issues' companies have to deal with. Think of issues such as responsible business conduct, the relationship between employer and employee, the company's relationship with its customers and sustainable business models.
- A stakeholder approach: this approach concerns reflection on those stakeholders of a company who will be most directly influenced (for good or ill) by its business activities.
- A mixed approach: the mixed approach is more comprehensive in nature and draws on more than one perspective to approach business ethics as a discipline. For example, it uses a combination of the other approaches we have mentioned (stakeholder + issues + functionality or normative/descriptive + stakeholder, etc.).

Other scholars look at business ethics through the lens of ethical theory. Kaplan Financial Limited, for example, makes a distinction between two strands of theory: the absolutism/relativism dichotomy and the deontological/teleological dichotomy (2009: 318–324).

- The first distinction is made between a dogmatic position (absolutism), which holds that there is one truth that has to be imposed on all ethical dilemmas, whatever the context might be, and a more pragmatic approach, which pursues a solution of an ethical dilemma that is based on the moral system of individuals and not on one universal truth (relativism).
- The second distinction entails two of the main classical ethical traditions: on one hand, the presupposition that an ethical dilemma within the domain of business can only be solved by assessing whether the activities themselves are good or bad (deontology), or that it can only be solved by considering the outcomes or impact of business activities on the other (teleology).

The deontological position is characterised by the principles of universality (is the action condoned by others?), human dignity (are the human beings affected regarded as means or ends?) and consistency (would everyone be prepared to do the same under the circumstances?); while the teleological position represents two ethical positions, namely egoism (choosing for reasons of self-interest might benefit society as well) and utilitarianism (do the impacts and outcomes of business activity lead to the greatest amount of good to the greatest number of people?).

DesJardins embraces the three classical traditional ethical theories, consequentialism, deontology and virtue ethics – the idea that a good character and personal moral virtue are most likely to be instrumental in solving ethical dilemmas in a sound manner and in leading a good and happy life) – to guide him through the field of business ethics (2014: 44–45).

Rossouw and van Vuuren work with the three classical ethical positions as well, but supplement them with three modern theories of the modern corporation. These ethical positions take public moral sentiment into account and fundamentally encompass the two foundational virtues identified in section 2.4.3: moral integrity and moral responsibility.

- The first posits the question whether a company has moral responsibilities (theory of corporate social responsibility).
- The second inquires whether a company could be regarded as a moral agent (theory of corporate moral agency).
- The third reflects on the question about whose interests a company should serve (stakeholder theory).

(2017: 86–99)

The list of scholarly positions regarding perspectives and approaches to business ethics is endless, but to conclude this section, a brief summary will be given of current approaches to business and business ethics. Business ethics is becoming more and more integrated within business philosophy, and also into the fibre of companies. It draws inspiration from the significant challenges the world is facing and is – to some extent – advocated through terms like corporate social responsibility and sustainability.

Think about documents like the ISO 26000 guidelines for social responsibility, and the United Nations (UN) Global Compact on corporate sustainability; the UN's Sustainable Development Goals (SDGs) leading its 'Agenda 2030', goals for both people and planet (such as creating a world in which poverty is eradicated, injustice and inequality are fought and the planet is protected on behalf of future generations); and the OECD Guidelines for Multinational Enterprises, which make recommendations for responsible business conduct. In order to pursue responsible business practices, companies are challenged to use their innovative power to implement new business models which embrace integrity and other values, to ensure that their business activities cause no harm to stakeholders. Companies are also urged to collaborate with other parties in order to address the many urgent issues the world is facing today.

This sense of urgency about working towards a better future for all is also expressed in global initiatives such as the OECD Better Life Initiative, which measures well-being and progress in the world; the Humanistic Management Network, which, amongst other activities, studies the relationship between economy and freedom, and advocates for human dignity, well-being and the flourishing of people and communities; and the Social Enterprise Initiatives (SEIs) which are found all around the globe and which pursue positive social impacts in business – impacts that go beyond the goal of making profits for the owners or stakeholders. Arguably, social enterprise and sustainability thinking gave birth to, for example, Benefit Corporations (B Corps), which have redefined 'success' in business. Their primary goal is to have a positive impact on society, employees, communities and the environment, while still making a profit.

These are examples of 'other' or 'new' approaches to business ethics. They demonstrate that, in facilitating a 'good life' for business, people, communities and the environment, business ethics can (and should) walk hand in hand with economical aims.

2.5 Conclusion

This chapter offers a theoretical foundation for reflection on the notions of 'ethics' and 'business' and the way they come together in the concept of 'business ethics'. The nature, history, purpose of and different approaches to ethics were introduced first, followed, secondly, by an explication of the nature, history, characteristics and purpose of business. *Ethics* reflects on how to lead a good life and 'answers' are traditionally found in deontological, teleological and virtue ethical approaches. Yet 'modern' versions of these three positions – such as justice and fairness, care and new forms of virtue ethics – are also used by scholars. *Business* is fundamentally a socio-economic activity, which, in making a profit through the buying and selling of goods and services to customers, thereby satisfying their needs, also has a responsibility to try to prevent its activities from having any negative impacts on people and the environment. Rather, business should, ideally, actively pursue the well-being of society and the environment in policy and behaviour. Thirdly, *business ethics*, as the field in which ethics and business are joined together, was discussed in terms of its history, nature, scope and domain, and approaches to theory. Business ethics studies the moral principles and conduct of people and organisations within a business setting. It takes place on the individual, organisational and systemic levels and evaluates business behaviour alongside the measuring bar of responsibility and integrity – two virtues that are foundational in realising sound business practices. Business ethics covers moral reflection on issues related to finance and accountancy, marketing, management, human rights, leadership, sustainability, and many others. It is implemented from a number of different kinds of perspectives and is based on diverging ethical theories as well. There is ample evidence that business ethics, apart from being an academic discipline, has also found its way in quite a range of global initiatives and guidelines which inspire and urge business to join forces in ensuring a better future for all.

2.6 Questions for discussion

- Make a list of the top five most important personal and top five most important professional values you cherish. Which of those values are moral values? How can you tell when a value is moral and when it is not?
- Crane and Matten posit that morality is concerned with 'the norms, values, and beliefs embedded in social processes which define right and wrong for an individual or a community'. Can you define norms, values and beliefs and also tell the difference between morality and ethics?
- Can you tell the difference between business ethics, corporate social responsibility and sustainability? Which values are foundational to each of these three issues?
- Imagine you have the job of your dreams within the field you are working in right now or want to work in one day (for example, in hospitality, tourism, leisure, etc.). Your manager asks you to come up with a plan which steers the company towards realising a greater positive impact on people, communities and the environment, while still making a profit. What would your advice entail?
- Can you think of ways in which the impact of business activities could be assessed or measured?

2.7 Concluding thoughts

Business, fundamentally a commercial, economic activity, has a very long history. And from its inception up to the present day, moral issues have been ascribed to business and also addressed. This means that there is an inescapable interdependent connection between business and society: the one cannot flourish without the other. Welfare cannot go without well-being. Given the fact that business activity could have either a negative or positive impact on society, and also on the environment, there is a need to assess the nature of the impact of such activities, and to evaluate the morality of the persons and companies that engage in them, but also the ethical principles and norms that govern their behaviour. This is the task of business ethics.

Business ethics studies the impact of business conduct on three levels: the individual, organisational and the systemic. The questions leading ethical inquiry on these levels are: (i) 'How can professionals behave in an ethically sound way to their colleagues, customers, partners and the general public?'; (ii) 'How does a company legitimise its policy and behaviour towards both its internal (employees) and external stakeholders (customers, suppliers, owners, society, environment, etc.) given the great challenges the world currently faces?'; and (iii) 'How can the economic activity of business and the market be regulated nationally and globally so that a sustainable and just world is ensured for future generations?' In other words: 'How do the foundational virtues of responsibility and integrity figure on these three levels?'

Business is a value-laden practice and should be approached and evaluated through a value-sensitive lens. Therefore, it should walk hand in hand with ethics. The ultimate purpose of business is/should be to create value, which guarantees a 'good life' for business, people, communities and the environment.

Further reading

Brenkert, G.G. and Beauchamp, T.L. (Eds.) (2010). *The Oxford Handbook of Business Ethics*. Oxford/New York: Oxford University Press.

Frederick, R.E. (Ed.) (2002). *A Companion to Business Ethics*. Oxford/Malden: Blackwell Publishing.

Fryer, M. (2015). *Ethics Theory and Business Practice*. London/Thousand Oaks, CA: Sage Publications.

Kolb, R.W. (Ed.) (2008). *The Encyclopaedia of Business Ethics and Society*. London/Thousand Oaks, CA: Sage Publications.

Luetge, C. (Ed.) (2013). *Handbook of the Philosophical Foundations of Business Ethics*. New York/London: Springer (Vol. I and II).

Matsui, N. and Ikemoto, Y. (2015). *Solidarity Economy and Social Business: New Models for a New Society*. London/New York: Springer.

Peil, J. and Staveren, I.M. van (Eds.) (2009). *Handbook of Economics and Ethics*. Cheltenham/Northampton, UK: Edward Elgar Publishing.

Pride, W.M., Hughes, R.J. and Kapoor, J.R. (2014). *Business* (12th ed.). Mason, OH: Cengage Learning.

References

Akrani, G. (2011). What Is Business? Meaning, Definitions Features of Business. In *Kalyan City Life*. Retrieved 13 July 2017 from http://kalyan-city.blogspot.nl/2011/03/what-is-business-meaning-definitions.html.

Baggini, J. and Fosl, P.S. (2013). *The Ethics Toolkit: A Compendium of Ethical Concepts and Methods*. Oxford/Malden: Blackwell Publishing.

Begum, S., Jabeen, S. and Awan, A.B. (2014). Happiness: A Psycho-Philosophical Appraisal. *The Dialogue*, IX(3): 313–325.

Bouwer, J. and Leeuwen, M. van (2017). *Philosophy of Leisure: Foundations of the Good Life*. Abingdon/New York: Routledge.

Brown, L. (2003). Plato and Aristotle. In Bunnin, N. and Tsui-James, E.P. (Eds.) *The Blackwell Companion to Philosophy*. (2nd ed.). Malden/Oxford: Blackwell Publishers, 601–619.

Brue, S.L. and Grant, R.R. (2013). *The Evolution of Economic Thought* (8th ed.). Mason, OH: Cengage Learning.
Burns, R.P. (2008). On the Foundations and Nature of Morality. *Harvard Journal for Law and Public Policy*, 31(1): 7–21.
Business. (n.d.). In *Dictionary.com*. Retrieved 12 July 2017 from http://www.dictionary.com/browse/business?s=t.
Business. (n.d.). In *Investopedia*. Retrieved 12 July 2017 from http://www.investopedia.com/terms/b/business.asp#ixzz4meIzq47Z.
Business. (n.d.). In *Merriam-Webster*. Retrieved 12 July 2017 from https://www.merriam-webster.com/dictionary/business.
Business. (n.d.). *Online Etymological Dictionary*. Retrieved 12 July 2017 from https://www.etymonline.com/search?q=Business.
Business. (n.d.). *Oxford Dictionaries*. https://en.oxforddictionaries.com/definition/business. Accessed 12 July 2017.
Chand. S. (n.d.). Top 10 Important Characteristics of Business. In *Your Article Library*. Retrieved 14 July, 2017, from http://www.yourarticlelibrary.com/business/top-10-important-naturecharacteristics-of-business/7494/.
Clark, W.H. and Babson, E.K. (2012). How Benefit Corporations are Redefining the Purpose of Business Corporations. *William Mitchell Law Review*, 38(2): 817–851.
Cohen, S. (2004). *The Nature of Moral Reasoning: The Framework and Activities of Ethical Deliberation, Argument and Decision-Making*. Oxford: Oxford University Press.
Crane, A. and Matten, D. (2007). *Business Ethics* (2nd ed.). Oxford/New York: Oxford University Press.
Crane, A. and Matten, D. (2010). *Business Ethics* (3rd ed.). Oxford/New York: Oxford University Press.
Cresswell, J. (2010). *Oxford Dictionary of Word Origins*. Oxford: Oxford University Press.
DesJardins, J. (2014). *An Introduction to Business Ethics* (5th ed.). New York: McGraw-Hill.
Dewhurst, J.A. (2014). *An Introduction to Business and Business Planning*. Bookboon.com.
Ferrell, O.C., Fraedrich, J. and Ferrell, L. (2015). *Business Ethics: Ethical Decision Making and Cases* (10th ed.). Stamford, CT: Cengage Learning.
Fleming, P. and Jones, M.T. (2013). *The End of Corporate Social Responsibility: Crisis and Critique*. London/Thousand Oaks, CA: Sage Publications.
Freeman, R.E. (1984). *Strategic Management: A Stakeholder Approach*. Boston, MA: Pitman.
Fryer, M. (2015). *Ethics Theory and Business Practice*. London/Thousand Oaks, CA: Sage Publications.
Göbel, E. (2013). *Unterhehemensethik. Grundlagen und Praktische Umsetzung* (3rd ed.). Konstanz/München: UVK Verlagsgesellschaft.
Goodpaster, K.E. (1997). Business Ethics. In Werhane, P.H. and Freeman, R.E. (Eds.). *Blackwell Encyclopaedic Dictionary of Business Ethics* (pp. 51–57). Oxford/Malden: Blackwell Publishers.
Gras-Dijkstra, S. (2009). *Values in Tourism. An Itinerary to Tourism Ethics*. Meppel: Edu' Actief.
Haldane, J. (2003). Applied Ethics. In Bunnin, N. and Tsui-James, E.P. (Eds.), *The Blackwell Companion to Philosophy* (2nd ed.) (pp. 490–499). Malden/Oxford: Blackwell Publishers.
Hartman, L., DesJardins, J. and MacDonald, C. (2014). *Business Ethics: Decision Making for Personal Integrity and Social Responsibility* (3rd ed.). New York: McGraw-Hill.
Have, H.A.M.J. ten, Meulen R.H.J. ter, and Leeuwen, E. van (1998). *Medische Ethiek*. Houten/Diegem: Bohn Stafleu Van Loghum.
Heertje, A. (2007). *Economie in een Notendop*. Amsterdam: Prometheus.

History of Economic Thought. (n.d.). In *Wikipedia*. Retrieved 17 July 2017 from https://en.wikipedia.org/wiki/History_of_economic_thought.

History of Ethics. (n.d.). In *New World Encyclopedia*. Retrieved 23 July 2017 from http://www.newworldencyclopedia.org/entry/History_of_Ethics.

Holowchak, M.A. (2004). *Happiness and Greek Ethical Thought*. London/New York: Continuum.

Holzmann, R. (2015). *Wirtschafsethik*. Wiesbaden: Springer/Gabler.

Huta, V. (2013). Eudaimonia. In David, S.A., Boniwell, I. and Ayers, A.C. (Eds.), *The Oxford Handbook of Happiness* (pp. 201–203). Oxford: Oxford University Press.

Jeurissen, R.J.M. (Ed.) (2009). *Bedrijfsethiek een Goede Zaak*. Assen: Van Gorcum.

Knoepffler, N. (2009). *Angewandte Ethik*. Cologne/Vienna: Böhlau Verlag.

Kaplan Financial Limited (2009). *Understanding Professional Ethics*. Wokingham, UK: Kaplan Publishing.

Layard, R. (2005). *Happiness: Lessons from a New Science*. New York: Penguin.

Lynn, W. (2000). Situating Ethics. In *Geoethics: Ethics, Geography and Moral Understanding*. Doctoral Dissertation. Department of Geography, University of Minnesota, Minneapolis, 1–17.

Lynn, W. (2007). Practical Ethics and Human–Animal Relations. In Bekoff, M. (Ed.), *Encyclopaedia of Human–Animal Relationships* (pp. 790–797). Westport, CT: Greenwood Press.

McMahon, T.F. (1998). History of Business Ethics. In Werhane, P.H. and Freeman, R.E. (Eds.), *Blackwell Encyclopaedic Dictionary of Business Ethics* (pp. 317–320). Malden/Oxford: Blackwell Publishers.

Moen, O.M. (2012). Is Life the Ultimate Value? A Reassessment of Ayn Rand's Ethics. *Reason Papers* 34(2): 84–116. Retrieved 21 March 2016 from http://reasonpapers.com/pdf/342/rp_342_9.pdf.

Mogilner, C., Kamvar, S.D. and Aaker, J. (2011). The Shifting Meaning of Happiness. *Social Psychological and Personality Science*, 2(4): 395–402.

Pawelski, J.O. (2013). Introduction to Philosophical Approaches to Happiness. In David, S.A., Boniwell, I. and Ayers, A.C. (Eds.), *The Oxford Handbook of Happiness* (pp. 247–251). Oxford: Oxford University Press.

Peterson, C. (2006). *A Primer in Positive Psychology*. Oxford/New York: Oxford University Press.

Preston, D. (2010). *What is a Business?* (3rd ed.). Milton Keynes, UK: The Open University.

Priddat, B.P. (2002). *Theoriegeschichte der Witschaft*. Munich: Wilhelm Fink Verlag.

Pride, W.M., Hughes, R.J. and Kapoor, J.R. (2014). *Business* (12th ed.). Mason, OH: Cengage Learning.

Rachels, J. (1999). *The Elements of Moral Philosophy* (3rd ed.). New York/London: McGraw-Hill.

Rossouw, D. (2004). *Developing Business Ethics as an Academic Field*. Johannesburg: BEN-Africa.

Rossouw, D. and Vuuren, L. van (2017). *Business Ethics* (5th ed.). Cape Town: Oxford University Press.

Schwartz, M.S. (2008). Business Ethics. In Kolb, R.W. (Ed.), *The Encyclopaedia of Business Ethics and Society* (pp. 216–219). London/Thousand Oaks, CA: Sage Publications.

Screpanti, E. and Zamagni, S. (2005). *An Outline of the History of Economic Thought*. New York/Oxford: Oxford University Press.

Singer, P. (2015). Ethics. In *Encyclopaedia Britannica*. Retrieved 18 November 2015 from http://www.britannica.com/topic/ethics-philosophy.

Skorupski, J. (2003). Ethics. In Bunnin, N. and Tsui-James, E.P. (Eds.), *The Blackwell Companion to Philosophy* (2nd ed.) (pp. 202–230). Malden/Oxford: Blackwell Publishers.

Solomon, R.C. (1998). The Moral Psychology of Business: Care and Compassion in the Corporation. *Business Ethics Quarterly*, 8(3): 515–533.

Solomon, R.C. (1999). *A Better Way to Think About Business: How Personal Integrity Leads to Corporate Success*. Oxford/New York: Oxford University Press.

Stebbins, R.A. (2014). Leisure, Happiness and Positive Lifestyle. In Elkington, S. and Gammon, S.J. (Eds.), *Contemporary Perspectives in Leisure: Meanings, Motives and Lifelong Learning* (pp. 28–38). London/New York: Routledge.

Syckle, B. van and Tietje, B. (2010). *Anybody's Business*. Upper Saddle River, NJ: Pearson Education.

Thompson, M. (2010). *Understand Ethics*. London: McGraw-Hill.

Timeline of International Trade. (n.d.). In *Wikipedia*. Retrieved 17 July 2017 from https://en.wikipedia.org/wiki/Timeline_of_international_trade.

Trade. (n.d.). In *Wikipedia*. Retrieved 17 July 2017 from https://en.wikipedia.org/wiki/Trade#History.

Vallance, E.M. (2001). *Business Ethics at Work*. Cambridge/New York: Cambridge University Press.

Yacobi, B.G. (2015). Life and the Pursuit of Happiness. *Journal of Philosophy of Life*, 5(2): 82–90.

Zyl, L. van (2015). Eudaimonistic Virtue Ethics. In Besser-Jones, L. and Slote, M. (Eds.), *The Routledge Companion to Virtue Ethics* (pp. 183–196). New York/London: Routledge.

Note

Parts of section 2.2 were published previously in J. Bouwer and M. van Leeuwen (2017), *Philosophy of Leisure: Foundations of the Good Life* (Abingdon/New York: Routledge), 97–102. The permission granted by Routledge/Taylor & Francis for the use of this material is greatly appreciated.

Chapter 3

Culture, business and ethics in a globalising world

Esther Peperkamp

3.1 Introduction

Over the past decades, there has been growing interest in the influence of culture on conducting (international) business. This also impacted on the field of business ethics. Extensive surveys on dimensions of culture have been carried out and reported on (Hofstede, 1980, 2001; House et al., 2004). Some textbooks focus on ethics in international management (e.g., Carroll and Gannon, 1997) and on international business ethics (e.g. Fisher and Lovell, 2009). Other publications aim to 'provide a practical toolkit for managers and leaders by helping them to develop a new mindset for working with and across cultures' (Trompenaars and Woolliams, 2004: 3). Whereas early research and cross-cultural comparisons focussed on Europe and North America, more recently a number of studies have also been published about African (Oumlil and Balloun, 2009; D. Rossouw, 2002; G. J. Rossouw, 2005) and Asian countries, in particular those societies relevant to international business, such as Korea and China (Christie et al., 2003; Feldman, 2013; Gupta and Sulaiman, 1996). Cross-cultural comparisons have also been made for specific aspects of business ethics, such as the willingness to justify ethically suspect behaviour (Cullen et al., 2004), whistle-blowing (Park et al., 2008), codes of ethics (Wood, 2000), and corporate social responsibility (Visser, 2008; Waldman et al., 2006) – to name just a few areas of interest.

Culture is a complex concept. The *Merriam-Webster* online dictionary provides four definitions of the term. In a very general sense, culture is defined as 'the integrated pattern of human knowledge, belief and behaviour that depends upon the capacity for learning and transmitting knowledge to succeeding generations'. More specifically, it is defined as 'the customary beliefs, social forms, and material traits of a racial, religious, or social group', as well as a 'set of shared attitudes, values, goals, and practices that characterizes an institution or organization' and a 'set of values, conventions, or social practices associated with a particular field, activity, or societal characteristic' (see Culture, n.d.). In other words, 'culture' does not only refer to national culture, but one can also speak of the culture of an organisation or a phenomenon (such as the culture of book reading). These different levels of culture are also important when studying culture in relation to business ethics.

Culture, business and ethics

Companies are increasingly confronted with cultural differences in a context of international business relations, expatriate employees, cultural diversity amongst employees, and ensuing cross-cultural communication. The culture of a company (corporate culture) is also influenced by the larger culture in which a company operates. There is a need for knowledge about how to deal with these cultural differences in business; these have been the object of study in many different academic disciplines.

Many studies of this area have sprung out of the disciplines of psychology and management, and quantitative research still dominates the field, although there is an increasing amount of qualitative, ethnographic work available, as Crane (1999) and Brand (2009) observed some time ago. Some might take the view that qualitative, especially ethnographic, research efforts should not be recognised as valid examples of studies about business ethics and ethical dilemmas in cross-cultural management, because such studies are predicated on a different ontology and epistemology. They utilise different idioms to describe ethics-related issues, and tend to focus on understanding local perspectives and specific situations instead of generalising national contexts. Nevertheless, there exists quite a large interest in the field of anthropology in issues of morality in economic behaviour, as the following examples will show: Browne and Milgram (2009), especially the later chapters; also Dunn (2004), Ferraro and Briody (2017), Hamada (1991), Mandel and Humphrey (2002) and Yang (1994).

The growing interest in these matters relates to the phenomenon of globalisation – a process that has rendered the question of the role of culture in today's world more urgent. This chapter will therefore address the question of how culture relates to business ethics, i.e. ethical decision-making in the context of globalisation. In exploring this, firstly, the nature of and connection between globalisation and culture will be explicated, followed, secondly, by reflection on the relationship between culture and business. Reference will be made to research done in this area and critiques of that research. Thirdly, the implications of the interconnections between organisational culture and ethical decision-making will be examined, since culture could affect ethical decision-making in different ways and in different situations. The question of which position to adopt in order to accept and overcome cultural and ethical differences will be addressed as well.

3.2 Globalisation and culture

The ongoing process of globalisation has sparked off interest in the role of culture in business, and therefore also in business ethics (Cragg, 2005; Crane and Matten, 2016). To pave the way for a discussion of the interconnectedness between culture and business ethics, and the implications of this for organisational behaviour, the nature of globalisation itself will be described first.

3.2.1 Globalisation

Broadly speaking, globalisation is understood as an increasing interconnectedness between different parts of the world. It is important to realise that interconnectedness in itself is not a new phenomenon. Large trade networks extended from China to Europe (the famous Silk Road was established in 130 BC ('Silk Road', 2017)), and from the African east coast to South East Asia, for example, even earlier (Wood, 2011: 24). Via the Indian Ocean, crops, pottery, and fabrics found their way to Africa in return for gold and ivory amongst other commodities. Trading inevitably involves intercultural contacts, and those influences can be seen up to this day (see for example Middleton, 1994). Such trading networks must also have involved ethical and moral dimensions, although little is known about this, as we have seen in Chapter 2.

Against the background of the historical existence of extensive trading networks, globalisation is regarded as a modern, contemporary phenomenon. The magnitude of the scale and pace at which interconnectedness between societies is developing, and of the number of people affected by these connections, has not been seen in history before. Globalisation is, amongst other qualities, characterised by disembedding, speed, standardisation, interconnectedness and interdependence (Eriksen, 2014). Disembedding refers to the decrease in significance of place and locality, which is enhanced by the increased speed of information and transportation. In practice, this makes it possible for companies to be located in different places than their clients or suppliers. Moreover, technology makes it possible for (many) white-collar employees to work wherever they want. Standardisation supports this process: exchange between different parts of the world has become much easier through the acceptance of universal standards such as a limited range of international currencies, industry standards, and even the clock. Exchange take place in the form of ideas and goods, but also people. Take for instance mass tourism, migration, and business travel, all of which have steadily increased over the past decades. These developments have led to an increasing interconnectedness between people and parties around the world, supporting the notion that we currently live in a network society (Castells, 2011). However, interconnectedness also implies increased interdependence, which, in turn, introduces new vulnerabilities (Eriksen, 2014). To mention a few: economic developments in one part of the world affect economies in other parts, and information technology (IT) is not only used to sustain friendships or build business relationships, but also to support organised crime and terrorism.

A key question in globalisation debates is whether cultures will become more alike because of standardisation and interconnectedness. A frequently coined term in this respect is 'McDonaldization' (Ritzer, 1993), an idea that predicts that the rational principle upon which McDonalds is based will be adopted by other companies and in other societies around the world. Indeed: incorporation in a global market economy necessarily implies the adoption of certain principles and values. Where transactions between individuals are monetised, the social relationships in societies whose economic system was based on reciprocity become unsettled and local moral systems are affected (Hutchinson, 1996).

This phenomenon has led to some thinkers predicting 'the end of history', because it is expected that liberal capitalist democracy will be adopted all over the world (Fukuyama, 1992). Others have countered these expectations, and have argued that cultural and religious identities will become major sources of conflict in the post-Cold-War world (Huntington, 1996). Communities that feel threatened by globalisation emphasise their uniqueness and also their right to be unique – paradoxically by invoking universal standards such as human rights and using modern technology such as Internet. Social movements resist disembedding and emphasise, for example, slow living, as well as resorting to local consumption. The trend of globalisation goes hand in hand with the trend of localisation, which gives it a 'double face'. Scholars have thus adopted the term *glocalisation* to denote this (Robertson, 1995).

3.2.2 The continuing importance of culture

The discussion about whether cultures are becoming alike because of globalisation, also has implications for business and management. After all, if people do indeed become alike, cultural differences will no longer play a role in international organisations and business. On the other hand, research suggests that culture does have an impact on organisations. For example, companies from different countries emphasise the importance of ethics to different degrees, either through the implementation of ethical codes (Langlois and Schlegelmilch, 1990; Palazzo, 2002; Vogel, 1992) or through emphasising different aspects of ethical codes (Singh et al., 2005). Scholars find explanations for these variations in the cultural impact of differences between legal systems: in countries where legal regulations are more strict, there is less need for a separate ethical code of conduct. This shows that culture could influence both the legal system and the need for ethical guidelines. Pallazzo (2002), for example, argues that the reluctance of German companies to create formal business ethics programmes (as US companies do) can be explained by their different cultural background, or the so-called habits of the heart (Palazzo, 2002). His argument resonates with the thesis posited by Max Weber that particular branches of Protestantism have instilled certain values that lay at the foundation of the development of capitalism (Weber, 1930).

To conclude, culture is a significant factor when it comes to values and practices in the areas of business and business ethics; even more so, given the globalising forces that work towards increasing standardisation. However, the exact role of culture can be – and has been – conceptualised in a number of different ways, which will be explored in the next section.

3.3 Culture and business

The last few decades have seen an increasing amount of research on the subject of culture and business. Researchers generally agree that culture influences the way business is conducted in different countries. The organisational cultures of companies are influenced by the cultures in which they operate. However, scholars also point out that different conceptualisations of culture are in use. For example, culture can be seen as a variable, or as a metaphor which stands for the core values that guide a company's goals and performance (Smircich, 1983). As a variable, correlations are calculated with other variables, usually cognitive aspects such as ethical beliefs and attitudes. The approach to culture as a variable will be explored below, after which alternative views on the relationship between culture, business and ethics will be presented.

3.3.1 Dimensions of culture and ethics

An example of research on the relationship between culture and business is a well-known study, popular with business and management researchers, carried out by Hofstede (1980). Based on a sample of IBM employees from different countries, Hofstede drew up country profiles. He argued that countries can be hierarchically ordered according to a limited number of dimensions of so-called *national culture*. One of those dimensions is the degree to which different societies are oriented towards individualism versus collectivism, indicating the extent to which a society puts the interest of the individual first, or that of the community or group. Other dimensions pertain to power distance (how societies deal with inequalities), masculinity (how societies value competition), uncertainty avoidance (how societies deal with uncertainty and the unknown), long-term orientation (how societies think about the future) and indulgence (how societies value pleasure and enjoyment). Hofstede found, for example, that with regard to organisations, both US and German employees tend to be individualistic, but that Germany scores higher on *long-term orientation*, which implies that Germans value tradition more and view societal change with suspicion.

Hofstede's cultural dimensions are also related to particular values and ethical guidelines. For example, one could expect that societies with high scores on *long-term orientation* value social responsibility and sustainability more – as is currently the case in Germany. Dimensions of national culture are also thought to influence the organisational culture of companies from a particular country, including the way in which companies deal with business ethics. It seems that individualism and uncertainty avoidance are positively correlated with a firm's ethical policy (at least on paper), whereas a negative correlation exists between the latter and masculinity and power distance. In other words, in societies that emphasise the importance of individuals over the group, and in which people tend to feel threatened by uncertain situations, firms are more likely to have adopted policies about human rights, ethics systems, ethics communication and implementation, and corruption (Scholtens and Dam, 2007).

3.3.2 Cultural complexity

Studies of the above-mentioned dimensions of culture have often been the target of critique for portraying a simplified image of culture (for an extensive critique of Hofstede, see McSweeney, 2002). Such criticism relates to philosophical underpinnings, which question whether culture can be measured by reducing it to a few variables. In this way, cultures could easily become a pastiche of themselves: 'Western societies are individualistic' versus 'Asian societies are collectivistic'. In the African context for example, the concept of *ubuntu* is often cited to claim the existence of a special, communal approach to life and business. The concept, meaning 'I am, because we are' is appealing, and seems to epitomise African culture. However, evidence that *ubuntu* is in reality practised as the most central value in African culture is lacking, as is evidence to the contrary, one should add (West, 2014). It is always easy to explain social phenomena in hindsight by referring to culture.

Consider the following example: a participatory management project in an African context (Mbigi, 1992) can conveniently be interpreted as a case of *ubuntu*.

However, similar management projects are implemented in non-African societies, as West reports (2014). In a non-African context, similar cases of participatory management can without difficulty be interpreted as a manifestation of local values as well, such as egalitarianism, which raises the question of what the distinctive quality of *ubuntu* then is. Explaining particular behaviour through referring to culture feels like reading a horoscope: no matter what the horoscope says, it will always come true, precisely because the horoscope is broad and vague enough to make it applicable to everybody. This problem is also noticed by West, who argues that the idea that *ubuntu* is a distinctive ethic can be questioned, and that greater clarity is certainly on the actual meaning of the term is needed, in order to judge its distinctiveness (West, 2014). Yet, the baby should not be thrown out with the bathwater. Native concepts such as *ubuntu* may provide local people with tools to attribute meaning to the world and their role in it. They may refer to *ubuntu* in constructing their identity. In addition, it cannot be denied that cultural differences between African and Western societies exist. However, it can be questioned whether the origins of these differences could be attributed to a single concept like *ubuntu*. Apart from cultural complexity, one also needs to take into account that cultures change, especially in a world in which there are a lot of interactions between different societies.

3.3.3 Cultural change

It is quite difficult and perhaps even inappropriate to reduce cultures to a kind of essence, because cultures also change. Contact with other cultures and external environmental circumstances force people to reorganise their lives. And political decisions have an impact on people's beliefs and behaviour too.

The Chinese practice of *guanxi*, for example, may be seen by both insiders and outsiders as a set of cultural practices, but should also be interpreted in the historical context of the Cultural Revolution, as Yang (1994) argues. *Guanxi*, meaning personal connections, is a form of gift-exchange in interpersonal relationships through the granting of favours. International companies operating in China believe they have to take this practice into account when doing business, although gift giving in Western society is often seen as an indicator of corruption and bribery.

Although the concept resonates with cultural values (derived from Confucianism), the practice is not set in stone, and originally had different meanings and implications for people depending on their ethnicity, class, and gender. According to Yang, this initially positive practice acquired negative dimensions with the development of Chinese capitalism, when *guanxi* started to predominantly benefit the elite (Yang, 1994, 2002). Not surprisingly therefore, though also somewhat an ethnocentrically, the concept has been invoked by others to describe petty corruption (Dunfee and Warren, 2001; Lovett et al., 1999). In any case, in 2012 the Chinese government under General Secretary Xi Jinping started a campaign against corruption. Where gift giving was earlier considered to be good business etiquette, culturally appropriate and part of Chinese culture, it was now legally considered bribery. Such legal rules cannot be seen as detached from culture: they are often the expression of cultural change, or they are an impetus for such change (when people internalise the new law). The role of culture should therefore always be considered in a *historical* and *holistic* context.

When studying organisational culture, the same caveats that apply to national culture should be kept in mind, as will be argued in the following paragraph.

3.3.4 Organisational culture

As shown above, national culture impacts the way business is conducted. But as was shown in the introduction, culture is not only about national culture. The term also refers to 'shared attitudes, values, goals, and practices that characterizes an institution or organization' (See Culture, n.d.). It has been pointed out that a company's culture is influenced by the cultural context in which it operates, but also that cultures in general are complex and subject to change. This also applies to organisational culture. This topic has also received increasing attention over the past decades as well, not least because of the assumption that a strong organisational culture positively contributes to profitability. Yet one could question whether there ever exists one, homogeneous culture in an organisation. Within organisations, values, beliefs and practices might vary between departments, or between managers and employees, for example. Therefore, studying organisational culture is not an easy task and there are a variety of different possible approaches. Martin, for example, advocates that the complexity of organisational culture should be taken into account, and that the study of it should focus in particular on how it includes some employees and excludes others, and look at the prevalent inconsistencies, paradoxes, and conflicts in organisational behaviour (2001). This leads to the question of the interactions between organisational culture and ethical decision-making.

3.4 Organisational culture and ethical decision-making

In order to gain a better understanding of the influence of culture on organisational behaviour and ethical decision-making, it is important to address not only the question of the role individuals play in this, but also how their values and behaviour should be judged, given the different cultural backgrounds and positions that they might have. After all, it is individuals, more specifically the employees, who are confronted with cultural differences in their organisations, and who need to make decisions on how to act in situations that raise ethical dilemmas. As stated above, culture inevitably influences individual actions and, given the reality that culture itself can change, this raises the question of to what extent people who seem to share the same cultural background might exhibit different values and behaviour. It is therefore also important to reflect on the question of how cultural values and behaviour should be judged.

3.4.1 Culture and the individual

The explication above especially addressed the concept of culture at group level, and warns against generalisation, simplification and determinism. Yet another way of looking at culture relates to a more individual level. It might just be the case that individuals from different societies have more in common than individuals with the same cultural background. Take for example Indian ICT specialists who have finished their studies in the United States, and work for an international company. They might have more in common with their fellow workers than with people from their home country who have manual jobs. Especially in times of globalisation, it can be questioned to what extent clear boundaries can be drawn between cultures, and to what extent national cultures actually influence individuals. Culture is never homogeneous. Especially in large and complex societies, one expects a fair amount of variation.

People are not just unwitting products of their culture. The structure–agency debate as manifested in the social sciences posits that individual behaviour is not necessarily the result of the structural arrangements of that person's society (such as culture), but that people are also capable of acting independently as free agents. Culture may provide a set of moral values and ethical guidelines, but individual members of a culture may endorse and enact those values and principles to different degrees and in different ways. It is therefore useful to adopt a *situational* and *relational* perspective, which entails that how people act and identify themselves, depends on the (situational) context. Cultural elements may become more or less salient when that context changes. The concept of *ubuntu,* for example, becomes especially relevant and salient in relation and opposition to what is perceived as Western individualism. The global world is always interpreted locally, with reference to local cultural and historical repertoires. Dunn (2004) has shown that when an American company took over a Polish company and introduced American-style management, Polish workers attributed meaning to those changes and negotiated them by drawing on their experiences of socialism, Catholicism, kinship and gender ideologies. Kaneff (2002) shows in another ethnographic study that appreciation of specific economic activities differs according to which aspect of a person's identity is emphasised. One woman could experience participation in market trading as a shameful activity, because of her previous employment as an official, on the basis of a work ethic grounded in socialism, whereas another women might experience it as an honourable activity, since it enables her to provide for her family. To the second woman, the household is more central to her identity (Kaneff, 2002). The example shows that which aspect of cultural values (family versus work ethic) is emphasised in a given situation might depend on generation and occupation. Factors like class, gender, religion, and the like may also influence which values are emphasised in which way. These findings point to the complexity surrounding the discussion of the role 'culture' plays in organisations and business ethics. How, then, can one find an adequate and valid way to evaluate this role?

3.4.2 Evaluating cultural positions

To start with a brief résumé: cultural complexity also complicates the discussion about culture and ethical decision-making. Different cultural groups hold different moral beliefs and ethical standards. Even if there are values that are universally acknowledged, such as honesty or respect, the way these values are conceived and applied might be different between societies. In cultures in which kinship relations are valued, it may be perfectly acceptable to grant favours to kinsmen, which in other societies would be seen as an instance of nepotism and corruption. And while gifts between local businessmen are accepted as an appropriate practice, this might not be the case in international business relations. Moreover, the way individuals within the same society conceive and apply such values in particular situations might be different as well. How then, can we judge cultural values and behaviour?

Understanding these cultural differences would seem to call for *cultural relativism* as opposed to *ethnocentrism*. Whereas ethnocentrism involves judging another culture by the values and standards of one's own, cultural relativism holds that cultures are equal and should be treated and fully respected in their own right. By this reasoning, all cultures have the same worth and value. This means that behaviour can only be judged by the standards of the cultural context in which it takes place. The cultural relativist position seems therefore to be quite reasonable, and easy to uphold in a world with distinct cultural groups who live separate lives. However, in a globalised world where economic systems overlap, it is much more difficult to pursue cultural relativism. Questions arise such as: should internationally operating companies adopt the principles of the country of origin, or of the country in which they operate? Should they accept local ethical values, principles and legal frameworks, even when these are in conflict with their own ethical principles of the company and the country in which they originated? Medical companies, for example, test medicines in countries like India and Kenya, where people are often not even informed that they are taking part in such testing. Regulations for testing medicines are less strict or easier to circumvent in those countries. And when hiring international employees, to what extent are employees free to live and work according to their own culturally specific ethical principles? A cultural relativist position may also fail to acknowledge to a sufficient extent the existence of heterogeneity. Pinning people down to a supposed specific culture may not do justice to those individuals who do not identify with a generalised characterisation of that culture. In addition, since cultures can change, a cultural relativist position may also fail to do justice to those individuals who wish for a change in their culture.

So what could the solution to this apparent dilemma be? Ethnocentrism is, due to its exclusionary character clearly not a valid option for judging values and behaviour in organisations, and cultural relativism apparently also has its shortcomings. Yet, if one agrees that one can neither claim that there are universal values, nor accept all cultural values as equally valid, one might want to look for a middle position. Such a middle position could be an agreement that some values are universal, while others are relative. This position demands constructive dialogue with other, and between, cultural positions; respecting and upholding the fundamental equality of all cultures – without denouncing one's own. This has been referred to as *cultural pluralism* (Wernaart, 2015: 294).

Now, what do the reflection on the individual as a cultural change agent within organisations, and the different positions from which cultural values and behaviour could be evaluated and judged, actually mean for addressing ethical dilemmas within an organisation?

3.4.3 Implications for ethical decision-making

The way attitudes, expectations and habits of a company are cultivated is greatly shaped by organisational culture and determines ethical decision-making to a large extent (see also Chapter 5). A strong ethical culture could prevent damage being done to both internal and external stakeholders of a company, and improve good ethical behaviour in the long run. Therefore, if a company adopts a so-called cultural pluralist position and adopts constructive dialogue within its organisation, this might lead to the conclusion of internal agreements on 'universal company values' and on the generally accepted ways in which the corporation and individuals should act. It could also turn towards existing examples of constructive dialogue such as, for example, the Declaration of Human Rights. Scholars like Bowie (2001) and Smeltzer and Jennings (1998) have argued that there is a need for international codes of business ethics. This might to some extent relieve the complexity of working in a situation whereby different cultural positions exist between countries and in organisations themselves. Many important treaties and guidelines have seen the light since the start of the 21st century. Take for instance the OECD Guidelines for Multinational Enterprises, the ISO 26000 Guidelines for Social Responsibility and the Millennium Development Goals (MDGs), which were replaced by the Sustainable Development Goals (SDGs) in 2016 – as we saw in Chapter 2.

Such codes will not solve all dilemmas on how to act; it is rather the constructive dialogue giving rise to such codes that will help companies progress towards building value-based corporate cultures, as well as enabling them to enhance their corporate reputation and providing them with concrete guidance for internal decision-making. Doing business with a mission statement that explicitly honours culture and ethical behaviour might inspire employees to do the right thing, identify with shared corporate values like trust, transparency and respect, and take responsibility for business behaviour that treats all the organisation's stakeholders in a responsible and honourable manner.

However, the discussion about the interconnections between culture, business and ethics has not, and will not, come to an end. There will always be a need for further reflection on culture, because of its dynamic nature: such reflection will focus not only on the nature of the role it actually plays in international business and business ethics, but also on the role that business, society and the international community want it to play, currently and in future.

3.5 Conclusion

The relationships between culture, business and ethics in the context of a globalised world have been explored in this chapter. Globalisation has made questions about culture and the role of culture in doing business and business ethics more pressing in the context of the modern world. Although many scholars interested in this relationship would adopt a definition of culture as a set of shared values, beliefs, and practices, when it comes to exploring the relationship between culture, business, and ethics, the concept of culture is much more complex, as the examples in this chapter have shown. First, attention needs to be paid to the possibility of change due to internal as well as external factors: politics, history, and intercultural contacts all play a role. Especially under conditions of globalisation, culture is affected by intercultural contacts. Secondly, it can also be questioned to what extent a culture is actually shared between its members. Modern society is becoming increasingly complex, with its members drawing their beliefs and convictions from many different sources. Thirdly, culture is not only about the values we say we uphold, but also how we enact them, which is influenced by the context and the meaning we attribute to other people's actions. These comments apply not only to national, but also to organisational culture: businesses are becoming increasingly international and complex. Organisational culture is never homogeneous, not only because employees may originate from different countries, but also because it cannot be presupposed that people born in the same culture automatically share the same value and belief system. This seems to ask us to approach organisational culture from a pluralist perspective, which cherishes dialogue between different cultural positions. Although it will never be a perfect and an adequate solution for creating a 'common moral discourse' within an organisation, adopting ethical codes and referring to international guidelines could unite different positions.

3.6 Questions for discussion

- One set of the cultural dimensions Hofstede has described is the dichotomy between *individualism* and *collectivism*. Give yourself a score on a scale from 1 to 10 for each of the following statements:

    - (a) *Individualism*: 'I do not have any responsibility for the well-being of my colleagues at work, because my only moral obligation is to take care of myself and my family.'
    - (b) *Collectivism*: 'I expect the company I work for (my boss and colleagues) to take care of me in times of trouble. This will greatly enhance my loyalty to the company.'

    Which position have you given the highest score, and what does this say about your cultural identity and personal ethics?

- Section 3.4.1 describes a situation in which two women evaluate doing the same job in quite different ways. Can you think of a role in your current or probable future career area to which a colleague of yours might aspire, but that you would never take? Think of reasons for this.
- Consider the three approaches which people could apply in dealing with the different cultures described in paragraph 3.4.2. Which of those positions appeal to you most? Why? Could you identity the values that are foundational to each of these positions?
- Imagine you were asked to develop a mission statement for a local hotel chain operating in a culturally diverse country overseas. What would the core values and main themes of the mission statement be?
- Debate the following statement: 'Ethical and behavioural codes of conduct within organisations guarantee ethical behaviour.'

3.7 Concluding thoughts

Culture is often seen as the sum of attitudes, beliefs, practices, customs, norms and values that is shared by a specific group of people, and that distinguishes them from other groups within a specific society. Instrumental in a culture's transmission from one generation to another are language, material objects, ritual, institutions and art. Culture is fundamentally a dynamic phenomenon, since it can change under the influence of social, political and economic forces in societies and countries. Due to globalisation, many cultures have developed 'hybrid' characteristics: individuals adopt values from other countries they are exposed to, while still adhering to (some) values they were raised with. This means that many business organisations cannot be regarded as culturally homogeneous – even when situated in the 'home country'. The implication of this is that business, in making ethical decisions, should always be aware of the close relationship between ethical values and cultural values, and work in accordance with that. In cultivating corporate culture, an organisation could either create cultural 'unity' through sharing common values related to predefined ethical or behavioural codes of conduct, or give room to a more dynamic scenario which honours the co-existence of diverse cultural positions within the organisation and gives them a voice through respectful dialogue in order to formulate desired ethical behaviour and take responsible business decisions. The second scenario, although quite intensive and time-consuming, ensures that the richness of all cultural positions within an organisation are exploited in favour of a dynamic ethical corporate culture, which is able to adapt to demanding times and developments relatively fast.

Further reading

Gannon, M.J. and Newman, K.L. (Eds.) (2001). *The Blackwell Handbook of Cross-Cultural Management*. Oxford: John Wiley & Sons.
Gesteland, R.R. (2002). *Cross-Cultural Business Behaviour: Marketing, Negotiating, Sourcing and Managing Across Cultures* (3rd ed.). Copenhagen: Copenhagen Business School Press.
Homan, K., Koslowski, P. and Luetge, C. (Eds.) (2007). *Globalisation and Business Ethics*. Hampshire/Burlington, VT: Ashgate.
Lavoie, D. and Chamlee-Wright, E. (2000). *Culture and Enterprise: The Development, Representation and Morality of Business*. London/New York: Routledge.
Trompenaars, F. and Woolliams, P. (2003). *Business Across Cultures*. Chichester, UK: Capstone Publishing.

References

Bowie, N.E. (2001). Business Ethics and Cultural Relativism. In Malachowski, A. (Ed.), *Business Ethics: Critical Perspectives on Business and Management* (pp. 135–146). London: Taylor & Francis.
Brand, V. (2009). Empirical Business Ethics Research and Paradigm Analysis. *Journal of Business Ethics*, 86(4): 429–449.
Browne, K.E. and Milgram, B.L. (Eds.). (2009). *Economics and Morality: Anthropological Approaches*. Lanham, MD/New York/Toronto/Plymouth: Altamira Press.
Carroll, S.J. and Gannon, M.J. (1997). *Ethical Dimensions of International Management*. London/Thousand Oaks, CA: SAGE publications.
Castells, M. (2011). *The Rise of the Network Society: The Information Age: Economy, Society, and Culture*. Malden/Oxford: Wiley-Blackwell.

Christie, P.M.J., Kwon, I.W.G., Stoeberl, P. A. and Baumhart, R. (2003). A Cross-Cultural Comparison of Ethical Attitudes of Business Managers: India, Korea and the United States. *Journal of Business Ethics*, 46(3): 263–287.

Cragg, W. (Ed.). (2005). *Ethics Codes, Corporations, and the Challenge of Globalization.* Cheltenham, UK: Edward Elgar Publishing.

Crane, A. (1999). Are You Ethical? Please Tick Yes☐ or No☐: On Researching Ethics in Business Organizations. *Journal of Business Ethics*, 20(3): 237–248.

Crane, A. and Matten, D. (2016). *Business Ethics: Managing Corporate Citizenship and Sustainability in the Age of Globalization.* Oxford: Oxford University Press.

Cullen, J.B., Parboteeah, K.P. and Hoegl, M. (2004). Cross-National Differences in Managers' Willingness to Justify Ethically Suspect Behaviours. *Academy of Management Journal*, 47(3): 411–421.

Culture. (n.d.). In *Merriam-Webster.* Retrieved 4 October 2017 from https://www.merriam-webster.com/dictionary/culture.

Dunfee, T.W. and Warren, D.E. (2001). Is Guanxi Ethical? A Normative Analysis of Doing Business in China. *Journal of Business Ethics*, 32(3): 191–204.

Dunn, E.C. (2004). *Privatizing Poland: Baby Food, Big Business, and the Remaking of Labor.* Ithaca, NY: Cornell University Press.

Eriksen, T.H. (2014). *Globalization: The Key Concepts.* London: Bloomsbury Academic.

Feldman, S.P. (2013). *Trouble in the Middle: American–Chinese Business Relations, Culture, Conflict, and Ethics.* London/New York: Routledge.

Ferraro, G.P., and Briody, E.K. (2017). *The Cultural Dimension of Global Business.* Oxford/New York: Routledge.

Fisher, C. and Lovell, A. (2009). *Business Ethics and Values: Individual, Corporate and International Perspectives.* Harlow, UK: Prentice Hall.

Fukuyama, F. (1992). *The End of History and the Last Man.* New York: Free Press.

Gupta, J.L. and Sulaiman, M. (1996). Ethical Orientations of Managers in Malaysia. *Journal of Business Ethics*, 15(7): 735–748.

Hamada, T. (1991). *American Enterprise in Japan: Other Ways of Loving and Knowing.* Albany, NY: SUNY Press.

Hofstede, G. (1980). *Culture's Consequences: International Differences in Work-Related Values.* Beverly Hills, CA: Sage.

Hofstede, G. (2001). *Culture's Consequences: Comparing Values, Behaviors, Institutions and Organizations Across Nations.* Thousand Oaks, CA: Sage.

House, R.J., Hanges, P.J., Javidan, M., Dorfman, P.W. and Gupta, V. (Eds.) (2004). *Culture, Leadership, and Organizations: The GLOBE Study of 62 Societies.* Thousand Oaks, CA: Sage Publications.

Huntington, S.P. (1996). *The Clash of Civilizations and the Remaking of World Order.* New York: Simon & Schuster.

Hutchinson, S.E. (1996). *Nuer Dilemmas: Coping with Money, War, and the State.* London/Los Angeles: University of California Press.

Kaneff, D. (2002). The Shame and Pride of Market Activity: Morality, Identity and Trading in Post Socialist Rural Bulgaria. In Mandel, R. and Humphrey, C. (Eds.) *Markets and Moralities: Ethnographies of Post Socialism* (pp. 33–52). London: Berg.

Langlois, C.C. and Schlegelmilch, B.B. (1990). Do Corporate Codes of Ethics Reflect National Character? Evidence from Europe and the United States. *Journal of International Business Studies*, 21(4): 519–539.

Lovett, S., Simmons, L. and Kali, R. (1999). Guanxi versus the Market: Ethics and Efficiency. *Journal of International Business Studies*, 30(2): 231–247.

MacSweeney, B. (2002). Hofstede's Model of National Cultural Differences and Their Consequences: a Triumph of Faith; a Failure of Analysis. *Human Relations*, 55(1): 89–118.

Mandel, R. and Humphrey, C. (2002). *Markets and Moralities: Ethnographies of Post Socialism*. London: Berg.

Martin, J. (2001). *Organizational Culture: Mapping the Terrain*. Thousand Oaks, CA/London: Sage Publications.

Mbigi, L. (1992). Unhu or Ubuntu: The Basis for Effective HR Management. *People's Dynamics* (11): 20–26.

Middleton, J. (1994). *The World of the Swahili: An African Mercantile Civilization*. New Haven, CT: Yale University Press.

Oumlil, A.B. and Balloun, J.L. (2009). Ethical Decision-Making Differences between American and Moroccan Managers. *Journal of Business Ethics*, 84(4): 457–478.

Palazzo, B. (2002). US-American and German Business Ethics: An Intercultural Comparison. *Journal of Business Ethics*, 41(3): 195–216.

Park, H., Blenkinsopp, J., Oktem, M.K. and Omurgonulsen, U. (2008). Cultural Orientation and Attitudes Toward Different Forms of Whistle Blowing: A Comparison of South Korea, Turkey, and the UK. *Journal of Business Ethics*, 82(4): 929–939.

Ritzer, G. (1993). *The McDonaldization of Society: An Investigation into the Changing Character of Contemporary Social Life*. Newbury Park, UK: Pine Forge Press.

Robertson, R. (1995). Glocalization: Time-Space and Homogeneity-Heterogeneity. *Global Modernities*, (2): 25–45.

Rossouw, D. (2002). *Business Ethics in Africa*. Cape Town: Oxford University Press.

Rossouw, G.J. (2005). Business Ethics and Corporate Governance in Africa. *Business & Society*, 44(1): 94–106.

Scholtens, B. and Dam, L. (2007). Cultural Values and International Differences in Business Ethics. *Journal of Business Ethics*, 75(3): 273–284.

Silk Road. (2017, 3 November). In *History*. Retrieved 14 March 2019 from https://www.history.com/topics/ancient-middle-east/silk-road.

Singh, J., Carasco, E., Svensson, G., Wood, G. and Callaghan, M. (2005). A Comparative Study of the Contents of Corporate Codes of Ethics in Australia, Canada and Sweden. *Journal of World Business*, 40(1): 91–109.

Smeltzer, L.R. and Jennings, M.M. (1998). Why an International Code of Business Ethics Would Be Good for Business. *Journal of Business Ethics*, 17(1): 57–66.

Smircich, L. (1983). Concepts of Culture and Organizational Analysis. *Administrative Science Quarterly*, 28(3): 339–358.

Trompenaars, F. and Woolliams, P. (2004). *Business across Cultures*. Chichester, UK: Capstone.

Visser, W. (2008). Corporate Social Responsibility in Developing Countries. In Crane, A. McWilliams, A, Matten, D., Moon, J. and Siegel, D.S. (Eds.). *The Oxford Handbook of Corporate Social Responsibility* (pp. 473–499). London: Oxford University Press.

Vogel, D. (1992). The Globalization of Business Ethics: Why America Remains Distinctive. *California Management Review*, 35(1): 30–49.

Waldman, D.A., De Luque, M.S., Washburn, N., House, R.J., Adetun, B., Barassa, A. (...) Wilderom, C.P.M. (2006). Cultural and Leadership Predictors of Corporate Social Responsibility Values of Top Management: A GLOBE Study of 15 Countries. *Journal of International Business Studies*, 37(6): 823–837.

Weber, M. (1930). *The Protestant's Ethic and the Spirit of Capitalism*. New York: Scribner's.

Wernaart, B. (2015). *Ethiek en Economie: Een Grensoverschrijdende Inleiding*. Groningen/Houten: Noordhoff Uitgevers.

West, A. (2014). Ubuntu and Business Ethics: Problems, Perspectives and Prospects. *Journal of Business Ethics*, 121(1): 47–61.

Wood, G. (2000). A Cross Cultural Comparison of the Contents of Codes of Ethics: USA, Canada and Australia. *Journal of Business Ethics*, 25(4): 287–298.

Wood, M. (2011). *Interconnections: Glass Beads and Trade in Southern and Eastern Africa and the Indian Ocean – 7th to 16th centuries AD*. Studies in Global Archeology 17. Uppsala: Department of Archaeology and Ancient History, Uppsala University. Retrieved 8 March 2017 from: http://uu.diva-portal.org/smash/get/diva2:463276/FULLTEXT01.pdf

Yang, M. (1994). *Gifts, Favours and Banquets: The Art of Social Relationships in China*. Ithaca, NY: Cornell University Press.

Yang, M. (2002). The Resilience of Guanxi and its New Deployments: A Critique of Some New Guanxi Scholarship. *China Quarterly*, 170: 459–476.

Chapter 4

Moral development, moral positioning and decision-making

Marco van Leeuwen

4.1 Introduction

Ethics and *morality* deal with the fundamental question that confronts humans time and time again: 'what is the right thing to do'? *Ethics* is a branch of philosophy that refers to rules and regulations that are defined in a social group, and are intended to be applied in that context, while *morals* or *morality* refers to the corresponding internal, private rules, habits or principles that characterise and guide what is judged to be acceptable behaviour. *Moral* principles in individuals' private lives determine how they act individually and interact with others, and how they make decisions and weigh all the relevant options about what to do (see also Chapter 2). However, it is common knowledge that people often make different decisions on how to act when confronted with the same ethical dilemma. This is arguably because their behaviour is steered by different sets of moral principles. This gives rise to the following intriguing questions. First of all, 'How come?' And, given the fact that such principles in business define acceptable conduct in professional contexts, and should, ideally, determine how everybody, from the company's management to the trainee on the factory floor, makes decisions: 'What implications do the different moral positions of employees, for example, have for ethical decision-making within organisations'? These two questions are the main pivotal points around which the reflection in this chapter revolves.

Therefore, this chapter will, more specifically, contain an exploration of the concept of *moral development*. This concept can be unpacked in several different ways. For instance: where, in a biological and cultural evolutionary sense, does the human capacity for moral behaviour come from? And: once humans are dealing with an organism that is, in principle, capable of exhibiting moral behaviour, which factors come into play in determining the kinds of morality that emerge? These two questions refer to what the capacity of making moral judgements is rooted in, i.e. to moral psychology, and ask how that capacity could have developed. A second approach is to regard moral development in a normative sense: is something like 'moral growth' possible? Is it possible to develop 'better' morals? Is it possible to conceive of a coherent hierarchy of moral judgement types? These questions refer to the possibility of a classification scheme for the actions and ideas of an organism who has the capacity to make moral judgements (e.g. a human being), in order to determine how 'highly developed' that organism's judgements are.

The following route will be taken: section 4.2 will start with some words about the kinds of judgements that moral judgements are. Then, in sections 4.3 and 4.4, each of the two approaches to the concept 'moral development' will be discussed in turn. Section 4.3 is about moral psychology, and section 4.4 about moral hierarchies. In conclusion, section 4.5 will briefly reflect on the implications of these discussions for ethical decision-making within organisations.

4.2 Foundations of moral reasoning

For something that is so important to what we do and how we do it, establishing what actually counts as appropriate moral behaviour is surprisingly (and perhaps frustratingly) difficult. Part of the reason for this has to do with the fact that in many theories, the process in question is considered to be a type of judgement, i.e. a (largely) rational deliberation that terminates in a decision ('this is right', 'that is wrong', 'this is what I should do') (see also Chapter 5). The problem becomes visible once we realise that making moral judgements is often not a straightforward decision-making process based on uncontested facts, but rather a deliberation that has a decidedly hybrid character. That is, how a moral decision-making process unfolds can be very context-dependent (in that specific parameters being different, with all else being equal, can lead to different outcomes); the character of such a process might be not just rational and analytical but also emotional or intuitive, and therefore moral decision-making can be a very personal and dynamic process (circumstances and people evolve, develop different attitudes and change opinions). The context-dependence notion will be discussed first. Based on this discussion it will become apparent that the point about the emotional basis of morality needs to be discussed as well. This will be done in section 4.3, which in turn, will lead to an account of the third point in section 4.4, which discusses the ways in which people can develop their moral skills.

To illustrate the first point (that moral decision-making is context-dependent): it helps to distinguish between judgements in aesthetics, judgements pertaining to facts, and moral judgements. In *aesthetics* (the study of beauty), value judgements are, by and large, subjective. Judgements of whether a painting, a landscape or a person is considered to be beautiful usually come down to personal preference. They are *opinions*. *Factual statements* are different: they are (at least in principle) objective. The number of people in a room, the distance between two cities, the number of cells in someone's body – the truth or falsity of a statement about these things has to do with a matter of fact: what is claimed either is or is not accurate, and it is not a matter of opinion (even if one cannot be certain what the actual fact is: one cannot accurately count the cells in one's body). But *ethical/moral statements* and judgements fall in neither of the two categories above: they tend to deal with neither purely subjective opinion, nor with wholly objective facts, but with something that shares traits with both. These are statements such as 'murderers deserve the death penalty', 'abortion should be legal', or 'when a country possesses weapons of mass destruction, it is okay for another country to attack it'.

Moral development and decision-making

When it comes to these ethical issues, many people feel decisions in those cases should not rely solely on personal preference (so they are not subjective in the same way that aesthetic judgements are), and neither do they involve observing/measuring whether or not something is factually true (so they are not objective the same way factual judgements are). However, these cases tend to be of the kind in which something important is at stake: in each case, many people feel strongly that it is supposed to be a certain way.

As far as the emotional, or intuitive argument mentioned above is concerned: it counters the idea that there might be ethical facts (i.e. objective ethical truths), and also opposes subjectivism about moral rules – i.e. basing judgements on personal approval or disapproval without systematic reference to extrinsic standards. Subjectivism about ethics is a possible position, but by its nature sabotages those activities that make ethics possible: constructive criticism (because a staunch reliance on personal reference kills the discussion) and systematic analysis (because personal preference can be quite unpredictable). Still, there is a story to be told about where the intuitions come from, and how subjective (dis)approval emerges. The next section below will look at the possibility of a *shared* biological foundation of moral reasoning, i.e. the idea that embodied emotions help explain such moral intuitions, and that there are regularities across the human race in moral behaviour. While to accept that account is not the same as to claim that there are ethical facts, it does help to strengthen the notion that morals are not wholly contingent or subjective.

The idea that moral rules are not-quite-subjective but still contingent (namely, contingent upon the sociocultural context), is espoused in relativism about ethics. One important inspiration of ethical relativism was formed by the decolonisation processes following the European colonisation campaigns of the 17th–19th centuries: emerging voices from non-Western societies (gradually) undermined the idea of a universal ethical system (i.e., one in the Western European mould). The proliferation of localised or context-dependent ethical systems makes determining what 'morally acceptable' means rather more complicated. How, then, do people determine what 'morally acceptable' or 'good' means? Common sources of moral judgements are argumentation, personal intuition and majority opinion.

The first source of a moral judgement, *argumentation*, implies that figuring out what it means for an action or decision to be 'good', is to *justify* the moral standards people use. That is, people evaluate the moral character of an action by assessing to what extent it is possible to provide a *rational justification* of that action. This evaluation consists of establishing whether someone truly believes that an action is morally correct, and whether this belief is consistent with the person's other beliefs, the totality of which should reflect a coherent evaluation of actions over time being morally correct. We should add some nuance now, because it makes a difference which aspect of a morally ambiguous situation is evaluated. Do we evaluate someone's *actions*, or is it the *person* as such (regardless of the actual effects of her actions) that is evaluated? Do a person's 'good' motivations and beliefs make the action good even if the result of this action is bad? Or, vice versa: is someone to be blamed for having 'bad' motives if the result of his actions is good? Different answers to these questions correlate with different attributions of responsibility for someone's actions. Can the wind/a dog/a child/an adult be blamed for knocking over an expensive vase in the same ways?

There are certain rules and regularities associated with the procedure of actually making moral judgements. Cornman, Lehrer and Pappas (1992: 284) suggest two main rules with which to critically evaluate ethical issues:

- 'If a person feels certain that a specific action is morally incorrect, and this belief is not inconsistent with any of his other beliefs, and an ethical standard dictates that this action is morally correct, then the person has some reason to reject the ethical standard'.
- 'If a person feels certain that a large number of actions are morally correct, and none of these beliefs is inconsistent with any of his other beliefs, and he has not been biased in choosing these actions for consideration, and he finds that an ethical standard agrees in all these cases with his beliefs, then the person has some reason to accept the ethical standard'.

The insights or claims underlying these rules are as follows:

Ethics involves rational deliberation about whether beliefs (about the appropriateness of an ethical rule) are consistent with a person's other beliefs. These beliefs are beliefs in the philosophical sense, so not 'whatever you happen to believe', but 'what you are certain of'. Based on such a rational deliberation, a person can then generate *some* reason to accept or reject an ethical rule, which suggests that this weighing of reasons (and therefore ethics as such) is not an exact science, but a decision-making process dependent on the context within which said reasons are thought to be valid. This decision can be made when someone *feels certain* that something is the case.

This means that even when the evaluation criterion of an ethical rule or dilemma is rational, still in the end there is some reference to a 'feeling' (of being certain) that has a non-trivial influence on the outcome of the evaluation. The question to be answered is therefore as follows: where do such feelings come from? Discussing this means to address the *second* source of a moral judgement, namely *personal intuition*. Both *personal intuition* and *majority opinion* will, due to their thematic and foundational prominence in this chapter, be discussed in separate (main) sections under the heading of 'moral development'.

4.3 Moral development I: Evolution and psychology

In following up on *personal intuition* as a source of moral judgement, the origins of the human capacity for moral behaviour will be investigated next. That is the first of the two approaches to the concept 'moral development', as defined earlier.

In determining where the human capacity to make moral judgements comes from, it might be useful to start with a common-sense approach. That is, if asked point blank, many people will state that they try to live their lives by following a rule that has become known as the 'Golden Rule'. In its general formulation, this rule says that you should treat others as you would want them to treat you. It is sometimes thought that this rule is from the Bible; it is indeed to be found there, in various forms, e.g. in Leviticus (19:18), Matthew (7:12) and Luke (6:31), but the core

Moral development and decision-making

idea is older and much more widespread. The idea could/can be found in Ancient Egypt, Ancient Greece, the great Eastern religions, Christianity, Islam and also humanism. However, a major problem with accepting this rule as the guiding principle of one's ethics is that differences in subjective preference are not accounted for. Suppose that a *masochist* (someone who enjoys particular kinds of pain) decided to use this rule – many people would be very unhappy with the (emotional or physical) pain that this person would cause to others.

A more careful version of the Golden Rule's core idea was developed by Immanuel Kant (1724–1804). Kant's *categorical imperative* is as follows: 'Act only according to that maxim whereby you can at the same time will that it should become a universal law' (Kant, 1993/1785: 30). If human behaviour is understood as following specific rules, would it work if all people followed those rules? If someone steals things because he likes to get expensive items for free, one could say that that person lives according to the rule 'stealing from others is okay'. However, if everyone decided to follow that rule, would that result in a stable society? Can this personal rule be a generally applicable *law*? The answer in this case, of course, should be *no*. Kant's categorical imperative has a problem: it speaks of a person's rule becoming a *universal* law. The question then is: with so many different kinds of people in the world, can there be such a thing as a *universal* moral law?

R.M. Hare (1963) claims that *universalisability* is a logical feature of a moral judgement, but the idea that any rule is universally applicable or true is inherently problematic. Even the strong and widespread moral conviction that it is not permissible to kill a person can and will be contested in a variety of circumstances, especially in countries or cultures that still have the death penalty. In these countries, it is considered to be possible for someone to commit such a heinous crime that that person's right to live is forfeited, and he or she can legally and morally be sentenced to death.

So, different cultures or social groups tend to have different ideas about even the most strongly held moral beliefs. Cultural differences will cause a *divergence* in the set of possible moral laws, with people from different cultures or groups tending to select different subsets of that broad set as 'acceptable moral laws'. This indicates a *cultural relativism* about morals. (For a broader discussion on this, see Chapter 3).

There is also an anti-relativistic 'force' in play: the simple fact that human beings share an evolutionary history means that their biological similarities, specifically the similarities in emotional responses, result in a *convergent* force, constraining the possible variation in ethical beliefs. This would indicate a kind of *biological universalism* about morals. The proof for this view comes from the fact that not all, but a vast majority of people across cultures will be inclined to feel repelled by excessive violence and cruelty, for instance. There is a reason for this, and that reason can be found in the biological 'programming' (the apostrophes are added to indicate explicitly that this is a non-literal use of the word) that constrains our moral intuitions. That is, our *emotions* are largely embodied, automatic and intuitive, and our conscious decisions often have an emotional basis (see e.g. Gallagher, 2005; Damasio, 1999). This means that most people across cultures (except sociopaths) are 'biologically programmed' to react to the emotional expressions of others in a particular way, and hence make similar kinds of choices when responding to or dealing with others. This, in turn, means that there are few, if any, truly 'universal' moral laws, but the laws that do find use tend to gravitate towards a fairly compact region of similarity.

A prominent version of the position that morality is shaped by biology is *ethical naturalism*. Prinz (2007), for instance, makes a case for the claim that morality is a by-product of particular biological predispositions. The idea is, in other words, that moral norms are sentimental norms. Important proof for this claim comes from psychology, psychiatry and neuroscience. Wheatley and Haidt (2005), for instance, found that moral judgements can be altered by eliciting specific emotions. They report that when test subjects were hypnotised to feel disgust upon hearing the word 'often', stories containing many instances of this word caused the subjects to give more negative moral appraisals. Another important indication that ethical naturalism, broadly conceived, is likely to be correct, is that emotional deficits (e.g. the inability of a psychopath to feel certain emotions) correlate strongly with moral blindness: if someone cannot feel a particular emotion, or is incapable of recognising that emotion in others, the capacity to make the correlated moral judgement is similarly impaired.

What seems more counter-intuitive, perhaps, is that Prinz (2007) makes his case in favour of ethical naturalism while simultaneously *denying* that morality is innate. He argues that humans are not born with moral rules, but rather that their moral capacities almost inevitably flow from the presence and functioning of other capacities, most prominently *emotions*, which can token intuitive sensations of disgust, approval, desire, etc. in relation to people, objects and their actions; *meta-emotions* (emotions about emotions) such as feelings of guilt about being angry with a child, or about being happy about someone else's misfortune; and *theory of mind*, the capacity to take on someone else's perspective, and care about that person and what happens to her based on this understanding of her position.

All this suggests that moral judgements are, to an important extent, based on emotions, but there is also sufficient room for the possibility that they are not exclusively determined by them. The other component, as has already been discussed in section 4.2, is rational deliberation. Haidt and Bjorklund (2008) refer exactly to this combination of emotion and rationality in the defence of their position, social intuitionism, which similarly affords the emotions a major role in the making of moral judgements. In interviews about the moral judgement process, they asked where moral beliefs came from, and they found that many of these involve intuitive, emotion-based snap judgements, followed by ad hoc rational-justification attempts. In these justification attempts, many people allow themselves to be influenced by the ethical standards prevalent in their environment. This shows the importance of the sociocultural context, within which people make moral judgements, and in which they learn to do so: the acquisition of moral insight is a balancing act between 'nature' (emotion-based moral tendencies) and 'nurture' (the idea that certain kinds of moral judgements and responses are rewarded by one's sociocultural niche). In their account, the foundation of these intuitions underlying moral behaviour is formed by five core intuition clusters, which they metaphorically describe as 'moral taste buds' (just as humans have receptors for flavours that are sweet, bitter and salty, etc.). These core virtue categories are harm/care; fairness/reciprocity; authority/respect; purity/sanctity; in-group/out-group (Haidt and Bjorklund, 2008: 203).

Moral development, then, is the process in which the intuitive tendencies in these categories are honed in interaction with the virtues that are applicable in whatever social context that person generally operates in. In other words, children learn how to interpret (which is at least in part a cognitive process) what to say and how to act, based on their own emotions in relation to the rules that apply in their sociocultural environment. This social influence is an important manifestation of *majority opinion*, the third source of a moral judgement, as mentioned before, and which will be addressed in the next section.

4.4 Moral development II: Hierarchy and normativity

In the balance between emotion-based intuition, rational deliberation and social influence, there are different types of moral judgements that one can make. There have been attempts to classify those types, and some of those attempts include a ranking of sorts – suggesting that some kinds of moral judgement are better, or more evolved, than others. One of the most (in)famous of these is the classification of the stages of moral development by psychologist Lawrence Kohlberg. In this section, a brief overview will be given of his cognition-based six-stage schema, as well as a more emotion-based adaptation of his schema by Carol Gilligan, one of his students.

Kohlberg cast his schema in the mould defined by the Swiss psychologist Jean Piaget. Piaget claimed that the cognitive development of children occurs in stages, and in each of these stages a child is typically in possession of particular emotional, cognitive and behavioural capacities. The transitions from stage to stage tend to occur at roughly around the same ages, and these transitions are characterised by qualitative shifts in the aforementioned capacities. Several of these shifts are relevant to the development of moral capacities. In the preoperational stage (generally from age 2 to 7), children are egocentrically focussed; as they enter the concrete operations stage (age 7 to 11), they learn how to take on other perspectives, but generally still lack the capacity for sustained abstract reasoning; this cognitive capacity starts to rise to prominence around age 11 (Piaget and Inhelder, 1967/1948).

In line with these transitions, Crain (1985) describes the main differences in moral reasoning between children under 10, and children over 12, i.e. before and after the acquisition of abstract reasoning skills in addition to the capacity to take on other perspectives, as follows: for children under 10, moral rules are usually fixed and absolute, and moral judgements are based on consequences (generally to the extent that these consequences are relevant to the child herself). Children over 12 are capable of more relativistic reasoning, for instance, acknowledging that rules can be changed if many people agree. These older children are also capable of making moral judgements based on the intentions of a person rather than her actions. Rodriguez provides the following example to explain this idea: 'When, for example, the young child hears about one boy who broke 15 cups trying to help his mother and another boy who broke only one cup trying to steal cookies, the young child thinks that the first boy did worse' (2009: 123).

Marco van Leeuwen

Kohlberg designed a 'Piagetian' developmental sequence for moral reasoning, e.g. as outlined in his 1981 book. This sequence is divided in three levels of two stages each, so six stages in all, which outline progressively 'advanced' moral understanding, justification and rationalisation skills, loosely correlated with a person's cognitive development from birth to adulthood. It could be portrayed as follows:

- Level 1: Pre-conventional (ages 0–9).

    - Stage 1: Dominant moral orientation: obedience and punishment.
    - Stage 2: Dominant moral orientation: self-interest.

- Level 2: Conventional (age 9–20).

    - Stage 3: Dominant moral orientation: interpersonal accord and conformity.
    - Stage 4: Dominant moral orientation: authority and social-order maintaining.

- Level 3: Post-conventional (age 20+).

    - Stage 5: Dominant moral orientation: social contract.
    - Stage 6: Dominant moral orientation: universal ethical principles.

Kohlberg's moral development stages were based on interviews of adults and children, which investigated their reasons for moral decisions. He used a variation of the Heinz Dilemma, a widely used story containing a moral conundrum, as the basis for his analysis. Paraphrasing the story from Kohlberg (1981), the Heinz dilemma goes like this:

> Heinz's wife was dying from cancer. A newly developed drug, made from radium, would be able to cure her. The chemist who invented the drug was willing to sell Heinz the drug, but wanted to charge ten times his personal material costs, to pay for development costs and to cover his profit margin. Heinz borrowed money from friends and family to purchase the drug, but was only able to raise half the money needed to buy a dose. Heinz begged the chemist to sell him the drug for less, or to allow him to pay later, or else his wife would die of the untreated disease. The chemist refused, claiming he owned the drug, and that it was his right to make money off of it. Desperate, Heinz broke into the chemist's store to steal the drug.

The dilemma is whether Heinz was right or wrong in doing so. Kohlberg's findings show, in answering this dilemma, that in his moral judgement hierarchy, there can be *twelve* possible positions (arguments pro and contra in each of the six stages). The schema below explicates the pro and contra arguments for Heinz stealing or not stealing the medicine.

- Level 1: Pre-conventional (age 0–9)

    - Stage 1: Dominant moral orientation: obedience and punishment.
      PRO: The medicine is not worth what the chemist wants for it.
      CONTRA: Heinz should not do it in order to avoid punishment.

- Stage 2: Dominant moral orientation: self-interest.
    PRO: Heinz will be much happier if he can save his wife.
    CONTRA: Suffering in prison will be much more painful than witnessing his wife suffering.

- Level 2: Conventional (age 9–20)

  - Stage 3: Dominant moral orientation: interpersonal accord and conformity.
    PRO: Heinz's wife expects him to come up with the medicine.
    CONTRA: Heinz cannot be blamed for following the rules.
  - Stage 4: Dominant moral orientation: authority and social-order maintaining.
    PRO: Stealing the drug will mean breaking the law; Heinz will need to accept the consequences.
    CONTRA: The law is clear: stealing is illegal.

- Level 3: Post-conventional (age 20+)

  - Stage 5: Dominant moral orientation: social contract.
    PRO: Choosing what is right for Heinz's wife is more important than what the law says.
    CONTRA: The law protects the chemist's right to his product, and it is not right to violate that right.
  - Stage 6: Dominant moral orientation: universal ethical principles.
    PRO: Saving a human life is of more fundamental value than property rights.
    CONTRA: Heinz's wife's life is not more important than the lives of those who would be able to afford the medicine.

As explained, Kohlberg designed his stages of moral development in the mould cast by psychologist Jean Piaget. However, more modern theories in developmental psychology no longer support such a rigid structure of separate stages that correspond with age brackets. Instead, the consensus is that there are many parallel and interacting developmental trajectories of properties and capacities. Still, even in Piaget's sequence of stages, an important component of cognitive development in the later years of childhood is the acquisition of the ability to see things from someone else's perspective. Interestingly, this capacity of perspective-taking, which in Piaget's frame is defined in a cognitive sense, is also a key component of moral insight. However, in ethical naturalism, as discussed in section 4.3, being able to assume and understand someone else's position in a rational sense is very much informed by non-cognitive emotional dispositions.

One of Kohlberg's students, Carol Gilligan, took issue with some of Kohlberg's findings, which found that women scored lower than men. On a hierarchical understanding of Kohlberg's schema, i.e. defining behaviour in accordance with the higher stages as morally superior, this would imply that women are morally inferior to men. Gilligan (1982) hypothesised that Kohlberg arrived at his results in part because he only interviewed *male* respondents about their moral decision-making. As was mentioned, Kohlberg's moral development stages were based on interviews of adults and children, which investigated the reasons for moral decisions. This focus on reasons can explain why the hierarchy of stages is still defined in terms of cognitive capacities. As Haidt and Bjorklund (2008) mention, Kohlberg paid little attention to the *emotions* as an explanatory capacity in moral judgement. Gilligan, instead, purposefully interviewed *women* about their moral decision-making, finding that they tended to be less focussed on a rational analysis of moral dilemmas, or whatever rules would apply in a given situation, than Kohlberg's male interviewees, and instead attached greater significance to actions that would express *care*. Consequently, Gilligan came to claim that women are not morally inferior, but merely tend to prefer a *different* ethical style, which focusses on social relationships rather than the more abstract ideals of justice that infuse Kohlberg's schema. This 'ethics of care' implies a change in moral perspective, relinquishing a focus on justice and rules in favour of a preference for social interaction and trying to find out the right way to acknowledge the needs of the other.

Gilligan suggests that moral development, which can be described as climbing through the stages in this schema, does not primarily involve the development of cognitive or analytical skills, but rather growth in the capacity to *reflect on oneself*. If Kohlberg's theory is male-centred, Gilligan's account can then be seen as a feminist alternative. Working within that conceptual frame, Gilligan suggested a different developmental sequence within the ethics of care. In the earliest years of a child's development (the pre-conventional stage), the child's goal is self-preservation. As the child grows older (into the conventional stage), she becomes less selfish and develops the capacity for self-sacrifice, the ability to care for others, and take responsibility for their wellbeing. The post-conventional stage, ultimately, is characterised by a capacity for self-reflection, which would support non-violence (hurting neither oneself nor the other) as a moral principle.

As stated, Gilligan hoped to provide an alternative to Kohlberg's male-biased, cognition-favouring schema. However, perhaps there is a way to find a constructive and generative interpretation within which both can be valuable. One step towards that end is to accept the core idea of *ethical naturalism*, which is that the moral decision-making of human beings in general, i.e. not just women, is rooted in emotions, including the desire to care for others. This idea has been borne out in other studies, which show that both men and women can and do make both care-based and rule-based moral judgements, but that perhaps on average men and women tend to have different preferences on which needs to be more prominent. Men do not make purely rational moral judgements, nor do women always prefer the caring solution; all people are capable of both, but in different mixtures. A second step has to do with the point highlighted earlier: the 'Piagetian', highly compartmentalised developmental sequences that both Kohlberg and Gilligan's systems are based on are no longer considered to be accurate.

A more caritative or useful application of Kohlberg and Gilligan's sequences could be to understand them not as hierarchical road maps for developmental psychology (or, in this case, developmental ethics), but as classifications of moral reasoning styles. These classifications then need to allow for variations in moral style choices in the same person, depending on what moral dilemma needs to be solved, and under which sociocultural conditions this solution needs to be found. The stages as defined might still be used to map out a person's moral development, perhaps in the form of (1) a moral career, as a person trains her cognitive capacities, finds herself in different sociocultural contexts and/or learns how to process the emotions underlying her moral intuitions in different ways; or (2) on a smaller scale, the contemplation process pertaining to a single dilemma, which might cycle through different stages and their associated moral considerations before landing on a (more or less) definitive judgement. But perhaps, due to the coarseness of the classification that is inherent to these Piagetian sequences, one should resist the temptation to execute strong normative judgements (as in: claiming that a judgement at stage 5 is intrinsically superior to a judgement at stage 3). It is perfectly possible that individuals adopt different strategies for moral behaviour, the arguments of which are related to the nature of the ethical dilemma. For example, in one case a person's behaviour could be led by level 2, stage 4 arguments, while the same person could adopt level 3, stage 6 arguments to act in another case. Moral deliberations are always context-bound, as stated before, and therefore never 'fixed'.

Which lessons can now be drawn from the discussion of all the theories and ideas in this chapter for the moral positions individuals or people in business contexts could take when confronted with an ethical dilemma at work?

4.5 Conclusion: Moral positioning and ethical decision-making

An important lesson to be learned is that moral decision-making depends on many different sources of input. Moral judgements are neither exclusively based on rational rules, nor fully democratic and context-determined, nor wholly intuitive and emotion-based. They are often a little bit of each of these things. That is what makes it so difficult to pin down the exact status of a moral judgement: 'is this truly the right or wrong thing to do or think?' It often truly is the case that the outcomes of a decision taken are different for everyone. However, this does not mean that everybody can do and say and believe whatever they want, and expect that to be the end of it. In a business setting, for example, embracing a relativistic position like this would result in chaos when, as an organisation, trying to reach some kind of mutual consensus with regard to ethical policy or resolving ethical dilemmas. No, one should be aware that there are always reasons for moral convictions, whether or not these reasons were an intrinsic part of the moral decision-making process, whether or not they would need to be constructed after the fact, or whether they are cognitive, affective or emotional in nature. This concords with the notion that apparently the majority of people in society resorts to what Kohlberg calls the conventional level of moral reasoning and most often are susceptible to external influences, meaning that in the context of organisations they would most probably look for external guidance when confronted with an ethical dilemma at work (May, n.d.). The reasons are thus most often constructed after the fact. However, when there are reasons, there are grounds for *debate* about how and why specific moral decisions were reached. That – an *open exchange between morally mature human beings* – is the foundation of ethics as a discipline, as well as the beginning of politics, of responsible and sustainable business and of a healthy society. This challenges business organisations to embrace the enhancement of corporate moral awareness and exert their wisdom in listening to the polyphony of reasons their employees might have for resolving ethical dilemmas, and to give voice to those reasons when opting for a corporate moral consensus with regard to the decisions that have to be taken, despite the diversity in moral dispositions within the organisation.

4.6 Questions for discussion

- Imagine or recall a situation in which you have organised a surprise event in honour of a dear friend of yours, but because of unforeseen circumstances, it turned out to be disastrous. Your friend was not amused at all and has decided to cut all ties of friendship between you and him/her. Does this mean that this disastrous event, given the fact that it was organised from the goodness of your heart and with good intentions, is fundamentally bad? Give reasons for your position.
- Consider Immanuel Kant's notion of the categorical imperative described in section 4.3. Could you think of an ethical principle that could serve as a universal law for all mankind?
- Read the 'Heinz Dilemma' in section 4.4 again and put yourself in Heinz's shoes. What would you have done? Give a moral argument for your decision. To which developmental stage does your argument belong? Does this stage say something about the values that are central to your world view? Would you have done the same for a refugee in a nearby asylum centre and used the same argument in support of your decision?
- Is the moral argument you have given for your proposed behaviour in the second part of the previous question (with regard to the refugee) based on rational considerations or emotions? Does you answer say anything about the way you *usually* make decisions?
- Putting forward that any team of employees working together in an organisation represents a vast range of different moral positions: what would you consider the best way for a manager to align and mould those positions in such a way that, in solving an ethical dilemma, a sound ethical decision could be taken, which has the support of the whole team?

4.7 Concluding thoughts

Most mature individuals, both inside and outside the realms of business and management, do most of the time have an idea or a feeling about what is the right thing to do in a specific situation. Yet it still happens that good people, under certain conditions, often involuntarily make decisions that could be typified as irresponsible or unethical. In order to better understand why people take the (unethical) decisions they often do, scholars started a few years ago to study ethical decision-making from, amongst other perspectives, a (moral) psychological one. This implies that the centuries-old (moral) philosophical approach to discerning what a good person is, what a good decision is and *which* decision could lead to desired behaviour in a specific situation, is complemented by questions about *how* individuals take decisions, how they think about moral issues and how those insights have developed or evolved over time. This approach, which is relatively young, is called behavioural ethics, or empirical ethics, and studies the interplay of cognitive, social and contextual factors that could lead an individual to take an 'unfortunate' or downright unethical decision. In order to make a good decision, it is presupposed that a person should be morally 'aware' (a cognitive category) that an issue at stake is, indeed, an ethical issue. However, behavioural ethics has discovered that people sometimes fail to recognise or label an issue as 'moral' or 'ethical', due to 'bounded ethicality' or 'moral disengagement'. The first entails that an action is deemed to be 'fair' because the outcomes are in favour of the agent him/herself. The second rests upon a feeling that an action is justified because its outcomes are less harmful towards other people than they actually are, which, in turn, lessens feelings of guilt. The intriguing conclusion is: moral awareness, and therefore also moral reasoning (and thus (im)moral behaviour), is less cognitively and more affectively and intuitively determined than has until now been generally accepted.

Further reading

Joyce, R. (2006). *The Evolution of Morality*. Cambridge, MA/London: The MIT Press.
Killen, M. and Smetana, J. (Eds.) (2006). *Handbook of Moral Development*. Mahwah, NJ/London: Lawrence Erlbaum Associates Publishers.
Kvalnes, Ø. (2015). *Moral Reasoning at Work: Rethinking Ethics in Organizations*. Basingstoke, UK/New York: Palgrave Macmillan.
Lapsley, D.K. and Narvaez, D. (Eds.) (2004). *Moral Development, Self, and Identity*. Mahwah NJ/London: Lawrence Erlbaum Associates Publishers.
Schumaker, D.M. and Heckel, R.V. (2007). *Kids of Character: A Guide to Promoting Moral Development*. Westport, CT/London: Praeger Publications.
Tiberius, V. (2015). *Moral Psychology: A Contemporary Introduction*. London/New York: Routledge.

References

Cornman, J.W., Lehrer, K. and Pappas, G. (1992). *Philosophical Problems and Arguments: An Introduction* (4th ed.). Indianapolis, IN: Hackett Publishing Company.
Crain, W.C. (1985). *Theories of Development*. Upper Saddle River, NJ: Prentice-Hall.
Damasio, A.R. (1999). *The Feeling of What Happens: Body and Emotion in the Making of Consciousness*, New York: Harcourt Brace.
Gallagher, S. (2005). *How the Body Shapes the Mind*. Oxford: Clarendon Press.
Gilligan, C. (1982). *In a Different Voice: Psychological Theory and Women's Development*. Cambridge, MA: Harvard University Press.
Haidt, J. and Bjorklund, F. (2008). Social Intuitionists Answer Six Questions about Moral Psychology. In Sinnott-Armstrong, W. (Ed.), *Moral Psychology, Vol. 2: The Cognitive Science of Morality: Intuition and Diversity*. Cambridge, MA/London: The MIT Press.

Hare, R.M. (1963). *Freedom and Reason.* Oxford: Oxford University Press.
Kant, I. (1993/1785). *Grounding for the Metaphysics of Morals.* Translation by J. W. Ellington (3rd ed.). Indianapolis, IN: Hackett Publishing Company.
Kohlberg, L. (1981). *Essays on Moral Development, Vol. I: The Philosophy of Moral Development.* San Francisco, CA: Harper & Row.
May, D.R. (n.d.). Ethical Decision-Making Process – Organizational and Psychological Influences. EESE Faculty Development Workshop. Retrieved 9 October 2017 from https://research.ku.edu/sites/research.ku.edu/files/docs/EESE_ethical_decision_making_process_psychological_organizational_influences.pdf.
Piaget, J. and Inhelder, B. (1967/1948). *A Child's Conception of Space* (Translated by F. J. Langdon and J. L. Lunzer). New York: Norton.
Prinz, J. (2007). Is Morality Innate? In Sinnott-Armstrong, W. (Ed.), *Moral Psychology, vol. 1: Evolution of Morals.* Cambridge, MA: MIT Press.
Rodriguez, T.J. (2009). *Understanding Human Behavior – A Psychology Work Text.* Manila, Philippines: Rex Book Store, Inc.
Wheatley, T. and Haidt, J. (2005). Hypnotically Induced Disgust Makes Moral Judgements More Severe. *Psychological Science* (16): 780–784.

Chapter 5

Ethical dilemmas and decision-making (models)

Johan Bouwer

5.1 Introduction

As has been shown in Chapter 2, business ethics entails assessing and evaluating the ethical principles and norms which govern the behaviour of individuals and organisations within a business setting. Business behaviour, in turn, rests upon decisions that have been made with regard to activities that have been, or are to be, undertaken at all three levels of business performance; the individual, the organisational and the systemic. Although business activities are steered by policy (strategy), and sometimes also by codes of conduct, their (negative or positive) impacts on their own profitability, people, communities and the environment are mainly determined by the way business officials deal with the ethical dilemmas they encounter during their interactions with other people, situations and contexts. Business is a dynamic and entrepreneurial enterprise, which involves taking risks. Miscalculation and the pressure to optimise financial performance could lead to adverse outcomes, or worse: to downright disaster. As mentioned in previous chapters, the business scandals and economic crisis of the late 20th/early 21st centuries, and the resulting loss of public trust, testify to that. In reaction to this, some business owners are focussing once more on the very purpose of business: to create both economic and moral value. There can be no welfare without well-being. In order to get back on track, or to keep going on the right track, companies should take care that business activities are carried out in an ethically sound way and cause no harm to any of the company's stakeholders; or even better, they should proactively focus on doing the right thing. This presupposes an orientation towards ethical decision-making.

Therefore, a valid case could be made for approaching business ethics differently. Many options have been mentioned already in Chapter 2, section 2.4.4 – but apart from these, there is also the argument that business should be viewed from a pragmatic perspective, typified as 'ethical decision-making in business contexts'. There is hardly a textbook on business ethics that does not have included a chapter on ethical or moral decision-making. Some scholars even wrote their textbooks specifically from that perspective. To mention a few: Hartman, DesJardins and MacDonald wrote *Business Ethics: Decision-Making for Personal Integrity and Social*

Responsibility (Hartman, DesJardins and MacDonald, 2014); *Business Ethics: Ethical Decision Making and Cases*, by Ferrell, Fraedrich and Ferrell (Ferrell, Fraedrich and Ferrell, 2015) and Schwartz's *Business Ethics: An Ethical Decision-Making Approach* (Schwartz, 2017). Ethical decision-making in business contexts can therefore be seen as the 'spine' of all business activities. Business ethics, from this perspective, is about doing practical or moral reasoning; it is about making choices; and it is about dealing with ethical dilemmas and problems.

This chapter has a twofold purpose: on the one hand it will convey a brief theoretical basis for understanding the constituents of ethical decision-making, and on the other, it will provide a kind of 'toolkit' consisting of frameworks and models that could be used when encountering ethical dilemmas in the workplace in order to solve them in a satisfactory and sound way. First, the nature of an ethical dilemma will be explored. Secondly, the nature and process of ethical decision-making will be described, followed, thirdly, by a description of a range of different existing ethical decision-making models, which could be used either in the classroom or professional practice.

5.2 What is an ethical dilemma?

5.2.1 The nature of an ethical dilemma

The word 'dilemma' stems from Greek and literally means 'double proposition' or 'perplexing situation'. It refers to a position in which someone feels 'trapped' and does not really know how to act in order to get out of it in a satisfying and plausible way ('Dilemma', n.d.). Thus an ethical dilemma concerns making a choice between two or more options or ways of acting, which are of such a nature that the agent is not able to make a clear and reasonable choice for the 'best option'. To be more specific: Kvalnes defines an ethical dilemma as follows:

> Situations where two or more moral values or duties make demands on the decision-maker, who can only honour one of them, and thus will violate at least one moral concern, no matter what he or she decides to do (2015).

McConnell uses the following description to characterise an ethical dilemma:

> The agent is required to do each of two (or more) actions; the agent can do each of the actions; but the agent cannot do both (or all) of the actions. The agent thus seems condemned to moral failure; no matter what she does, she will do something wrong (or fail to do something that she ought to do) (2014).

An ethical dilemma is thus paradoxical in nature, because a person is expected to act on a specific issue, but the outcomes of the choice that has to be made will not be straightforwardly preferable or acceptable. This could be demonstrated by a situation in which a person has to choose between telling the truth and saving a life (for example, deciding whether or not to tell the truth to corrupt policemen about the whereabouts of someone who is known to be innocent, but whose arrest might

Ethical dilemmas and decision-making

lead to their possible torture or death). Both moral options can be characterised as 'virtuous' or 'good' or 'just' behaviour, but not doing one of them will lead to moral failure. It also applies to situations in which one has to choose between two bad options, for example, where someone is not able to complete an important assignment on time and resorts to either paying someone else to do that for him/her, or using (copying) information from other resources. These options are both undesirable and immoral.

However, framing the exact nature of an ethical dilemma could be more complex than that. McConnell (2014), for example, distinguishes between different kinds of ethical dilemmas, which, for example, refer to either epistemology, ontology, obligation or prohibition. Yet, given the purpose of this chapter, all these different (more complex) kinds of dilemma will not be explicated in full. The general description of the nature of an ethical dilemma that was described above will continue to apply. Moreover, it should be noted that even on this quite basic, relatively elementary level, different kinds of ethical dilemma can be identified. Even the most 'basic' choices people have to make between good and bad every day of their lives could also harbour ethical dilemmas (although these were described as false dilemmas by Kvalnes (2015: 9)). This is certainly the case when a virtuous choice could lead to bad outcomes (for others). For example, in dire situations in which food is shared with starving people, but can be allocated only to a specific category of victim; say, only men, or women, or the elderly, or infants. The good act of 'feeding the hungry' then becomes tainted, because only a specific group will gain from the 'good' act.

To conclude this section: the most common kinds of ethical dilemma, which professionals are likely to encounter in their work, are the following:

- Having to choose between a good and a bad act, especially when the bad act could lead to a good outcome as well.
- Having to choose between two good acts, in which the choice of one will result in failing to do good by means of the other.
- Having to choose between two good acts, in which a decision not to choose will result in failing to do good at all.
- Having to choose between two bad acts, in which the choice of one might result in an (uncertain) less bad outcome than when choosing the other.
- Having to choose between two bad acts, in which neither option can or will lead to a good outcome.

To repeat: the choice to be made could also concern more than two possible actions.

5.2.2 Examples of ethical dilemmas within the creative, cultural and service industries

In order to provide more insight, a few examples of dilemmas that professionals within the domains of the creative, cultural and service industries might encounter will be mentioned next. Some of them are discussed as cases in Part II of this book (see also the case matrix in Chapter 1).

Johan Bouwer

- Choosing between increasing profits and 'crunching' employees in the gaming industry.
- Choosing between allowing a hotel to go bankrupt, and doing business with suppliers who use child labour in the hospitality industry.
- Choosing to keep investors in or owners of theme parks satisfied by deliberately underpaying seasonal workers.
- Choosing to establish branches of a company in the service industry (logistics, for example) in countries where human rights are violated.
- Choosing to make use of 'green labels' (sustainability) in order to attract more customers in the hospitality and tourism industry, although the business effectively does not deserve those labels.
- Choosing to remain silent out of fear of the consequences when discovering that the tour operator one works for is paying bribes.
- Choosing to twist the truth about the quality of amenities at holiday destinations in advertising if this will deliver more customers.
- Choosing to clandestinely buy potential customers' private information, in order to attract more people to events in the leisure industry.

How, then, can one handle ethical dilemmas when they emerge in professional practice? More specifically, how can one make sound decisions in order to uphold responsible business conduct and act with integrity?

5.3 What is ethical decision-making?

In order to fully understand ethical decision-making as a phenomenon, we need to take the most important dimensions of this process into consideration. These dimensions will be addressed next.

5.3.1 Moral reasoning

The basis for ethical decision-making is moral reasoning. And moral reasoning, according to Cohen, is 'an attempt to bring moral principles and specific judgements into harmony, consistency, or alignment, or to get a "fit" between the principles and the judgements' (2004: 57). Expressing opinions, or making a moral judgement about a situation, individual or organisational behaviour, policy or ethical dilemma, presupposes the application of moral values and ethical principles. Cohen's statement suggests that there should be an equilibrium or perfect 'match' between the evaluation of a dilemma and the principles used to make that evaluation.

Moral reasoning often takes place intuitively (see Chapter 4), but sometimes it becomes necessary for individuals, teams or organisations to consciously resort to structured forms of moral reasoning when trying to solve an ethical dilemma (see also Chapter 7, section 7.1.4). The ethical principles people use in such cases offer some clarification of the moral nature of planned (business) behaviour, the outcomes of actions already taken, or those that have to be taken. These principles usually rest upon one of the three (main) ethical traditions mentioned in Chapter 2.

These are the deontological, teleological (or consequentialist) and virtue-ethical approaches. In some cases people argue from the Kantian (deontological) perspective of rights and duties, or of what is just and fair, and in other cases their reasoning is based upon utilitarian consequences – favouring those actions that will deliver benefit for the most people or stakeholders. The consequentialist approach is most frequently used in the field of business ethics. The third tradition, virtue ethics, although excluded as a valid basis for moral reasoning by some scholars, because it is concerned with 'noble' character and therefore not based on principles, stimulates companies to ask themselves which character traits their business officials and employees should have in order for them to act in such a way that unethical business conduct is avoided and ethical business conduct is promoted in a 'natural' way.

There are other factors involved in moral reasoning and ethical decision-making than these formal ethical principles alone. Those factors belong, broadly speaking, to the contextual-cultural and personal-psychological categories – as has been shown in Chapters 3 and 4 respectively.

5.3.2 Factors influencing moral reasoning and ethical decision-making

Ethical or unethical behaviour depends on the interplay between the perceived intensity and importance of an ethical dilemma and the opportunity to act properly or improperly. To zoom in on the perceived intensity of an ethical dilemma: the moral reasoning and ethical decision-making applied to solve the dilemma are (also) determined by the personal and professional values and norms of the official or employee, the culture of the organisation and the society (culture) it is doing business in (see Chapters 3 and 4). These two frames of reference (personal and cultural values) interact with each other. They are, in a business setting, for example, fed by individual factors, such as gender, education, work experience, nationality, age and locus of control (how people see themselves in relation to power); but also by organisational factors such as corporate culture (the values employees share within the organisation) and ethical culture (the integrity with which decisions are made within the organisation) (Ferrell et al., 2015: 131–134).

If an organisation does not have a high ethical culture, it is most likely that an employee with less established and less strongly articulated values will follow the adage of 'when in Rome, do what the Romans do'. In addition, the setting (society or country), with its specific form of government, regulation and control, obviously also contributes to the outcomes of ethical decisions. Much research has been done on the influence of socialisation, human development and personal moral identity (for example by Rest et al. (1999) and Kohlberg (1981) and, more recently, in the field of behavioural ethics (Gintis, 2009)) and situational variables on ethical decision-making (for example by Ford and Richardson (1994), and by Trevino (1986)), which suggests that moral awareness is of fundamental importance in perceiving and assessing the moral nature of a business decision. Some people develop moral sensitivity in a 'natural way', through their upbringing and socialisation; others have to develop it later on in their lives and careers.

5.3.3 Ethical decision-making

Whereas moral reasoning concerns the implementation of principles in a moral discourse in supporting or rejecting a moral judgement of business activities that have been or are to be performed (see section 5.3.1 above), ethical decision-making goes a step further in actively trying to find a solution for an ethical dilemma. Although the line between these two processes is quite thin, they are quite certainly different processes. Whereas ethical decision-making is about 'selecting the best solution from among feasible alternatives' (Bloisi, Cook and Hunsaker, 2003: 478), moral reasoning describes the process leading to the point at which a selection can be made. The Wikipedia entry on 'Ethical decision' confirms this description: 'Ethical decision-making requires a review of different options, eliminating those with an unethical standpoint, and then choosing the best ethical alternative' ('Ethical decision', n.d.).

5.3.4 The process of ethical decision-making

'An ethical decision is one that engenders trust, and thus indicates responsibility, fairness and caring' ('Ethical decision', n.d.). It must be added: the path leading to the realisation of trust, responsibility and care is often slippery and crooked. Ethical dilemmas within a business context are often quite complex and cannot be solved without careful consideration of all factors involved and weighing all the pros and cons of the anticipated activities. Therefore, people often make use of frameworks for moral reasoning and/or models for ethical decision-making when trying to reach consensus about the steps that have to be taken. This is the case in many different professions in society, such as medicine and law, but it also goes for business.

Generally speaking, any process in which a decision, assessment or diagnosis has to be made has roughly three stages:

- The gathering, selecting and arranging of data or information.
- Interpreting the data or information.
- Naming or describing the issue, dilemma or problem.

The purpose of any decision-making process is to lay a basis on which to formulate an action plan or to act on reliable data or information which, in attempting to understand or interpret the issue at hand properly, conveys the constitutive aspects of, or patterns in, the identified dilemma or problem. These three stages are the precondition for any follow-up steps that will be taken in the ethical decision-making process. The few examples explicated below shed more light upon this process.

Adair uses a three-step outline, which could be seen as the core of ethical decision-making (2007: 65):

- Define the problem (*definition*: describing the facts, values and principles, and stating the ethical issue or problem).
- Generate feasible options (*analysis*: weighing of values and principles, external factors, duties to other parties and discussion of applicable ethical theories).
- Choose the optimum course/solution (*decision*: including a defence of its moral quality).

Yet Kaplan Financial Limited's position (2009: 389), in adopting Rest's Four Component Model for ethical decision-making (see Klinker and Hackmann, 2004: 439), is a bit more robust. They distinguish between the following stages:

- Recognise the moral issue (awareness/sensitivity).
- Make a moral judgement (judgement).
- Establish moral intent (intention/motivation).
- Engage in moral behaviour (implementation: action/behaviour).

Most scholars use Rest's model to build their own ethical decision-making models (Schwartz, 2017: 277). In literature and on the Internet, one can find models consisting from three to even twelve steps respectively.

The following five-step model is known as the 'classical approach to decision-making' and provides an insightful illustration of the general outline/process of decision-making (Adair, 2007: 25). Each step contains several sensitising and quite specific instructions which are meant to lead a person to realise the aims envisaged with each step.

- Define the objective.
- Collect relevant information.
- Generate feasible options.
- Make the decision.
- Implement and evaluate.

Many of the models for ethical screening and decision-making that are described later on in section 5.4 make use of these steps. Before getting to that, a question which occupies the minds of many (business)people will be addressed first, namely, 'why do business people have to go through the pains of ethical decision-making if there is a law that regulates business behaviour?'

5.3.5 Ethical decision-making and the law

The law can be regarded an instrument which regulates behaviour in society and therefore also in business contexts. In this sense it is related to and even based upon ethical principles. Crane and Matten essentially consider the law to be 'an institutionalization or codification of ethics into specific social rules, regulations, and proscriptions' (2016: 5). This implies that there is an overlap between the law and ethics, but they are nonetheless quite different in nature and have different purposes and fields of 'jurisdiction'.

The law consists of a 'systematic set of universally accepted rules and regulation created by an appropriated authority such as government (...) which is used to govern the action and behaviour of the members and can be enforced, by imposing penalties', while ethics can be seen as the 'principles that guide a person or society, created to decide what is good or bad, right or wrong, in a given situation' (Surbhi, 2015, *Key Differences*). By applying those principles, individuals can live a good life, and organisations can resort to responsible business conduct. Therefore, the law's set of rules and principles are legally binding and judge conduct by judicial standards, while ethics' set of guidelines are not binding, except, maybe, in an individual's conscience, and they judge behaviour by moral standards. The law can be seen as a kind of filter because it 'effectively screens out much unethical behaviour, but it does not deal with all such behaviour' (Major, 2012: 64). It is possible for the law to overlook issues which might be of ethical importance. It is perfectly possible that a person or an organisation acts within the boundaries of the law, although that act is unethical. But the reverse might be true as well. Take for example a situation in which an individual drives through a red light (which is illegal) because he or she is rushing to a hospital with an child on board who has been run over, and does so in order to save that child's life (which is ethical). Or think about countries whose law does not respect human rights (for example, by excluding certain groups of the population from certain jobs or other privileges in a specific sector of society): if a business discriminates there, it is acting according to the laws of that a country. However, its actions would be fundamentally unethical.

To conclude: business ethics reflects on those areas in business in which a clashing of values occur, but which are not covered or regulated by (a) law, or not yet covered or regulated by (a) law. Business ethics encourages companies to distinguish between what they *must* do and what they *should* do. Considering the latter, what a company *should* do entails actively looking at the impacts of its conduct on all stakeholders, and assessing what is the right thing to do under given circumstances. This presupposes that managers and employees alike should consciously seek ways to reach this aim. This is often realised through the application of ethical screening- or decision-making frameworks and models.

5.4 Frameworks and models for making ethical decisions

A distinction can be made between informal and formal approaches to ethical decision-making (van Syckle and Tietje, 2010: 190–191). The informal approaches use 'quick checks' to assess 'whether you're headed down an ethical path' (van Syckle and Tietje, 2010: 190) or not, while the formal approaches use ethical frameworks or models which require careful, systematic and critical reflection on the issue at stake. The informal assessment can also be called ethical 'triage' or ethical 'screening', because it intends to reveal the existence, nature and relevance of ethical risk when one has to act on a decision being taken within a business context.

The next two sections describe several frameworks and models regarding the assessment of, firstly, ethical risk and, secondly, ethical dilemmas or problems. There is some overlap in the phases and steps, but the models offer a range of options that can be used in (lecturing or professional) practice. Which one works 'best' under which conditions and circumstances is left to the judgement, preference and context of the user.

5.4.1 Ethical triage or screening: Assessing ethical risk

Four frameworks for doing ethical screening are displayed below:

Ethical dilemmas and decision-making

5.4.1.1 Framework 1: TI ethics quick test

The Texas Instruments (TI) code of conduct includes an 'Ethics quick test' (Texas Instruments, 2015: 8). This framework consists of seven prompts by means of which the assessor could do a quick scan in order to decide whether the outcomes necessitate further decision-making based on a more robust model. This would be the case when answers to the questions and prompts raised enough doubt about the right way to act.

- Is the action legal?
- Does it comply with our values?
- If you do it, will you feel bad?
- How will it look in a news story?
- If you know it's wrong, don't do it!
- If you're not sure, ask.
- Keep asking until you get an answer.

5.4.1.2 The navigation wheel

Kvalnes' (2015: 42–48) framework for ethical screening is a variation of the TI one. Although it can also be used as a (more robust) model for ethical decision-making, it has been introduced here as a screening framework because of its clear and accessible structure.

- Law: Is it legal?
- Identity: Is it in accordance with our values?
- Morality: Is it right?
- Reputation: Does it affect our goodwill?
- Economy: Is it in accordance with business objectives?
- Ethics: Can it be justified?

5.4.1.3 Framework 2: Venn diagram model

This model (Carroll and Buchholtz, 2008: 250) consists of three circles, representing the ethical, legal and economic domains of business. They partly overlap and therefore intersect with one another. Ethical screening takes place in the model's four intersection areas (the fourth is in the middle).

- Area 1: When a decision accords with all three domains, profit, ethics and the law, then go for it (proceed with implementing the decision).
- Area 2: When a decision accords with only the law and profit (thereby excluding ethics), then proceed cautiously.
- Area 3: When a decision accords with only ethics and profit (thereby excluding the legal aspect), then proceed cautiously, because if it is ethical, then it is possible that it is legal too.
- Area 4: When a decision accords only with ethics and the law (thereby excluding profit), then ignore the decision and find other ways to generate profit.

Johan Bouwer

5.4.1.4 Framework 3: The Rossouw and van Vuuren model

This model (Rossouw and van Vuuren 2013: 161–165) can be used for both ethical screening and ethical decision-making. The authors advise that the questions raised by their model should be internalised by all employees – as a 'mindset which is infused in the normal business decision-making process'. It should become 'second nature' (160).

- Is it legal? (Assessing the ethicality of legal standards and evaluating business decisions and conduct related to them: if the law is unethical, then the decisions or conduct based on that will be also).
- Does it meet company standards? (Assessing the ethicality of the codes and standards of a company and evaluating business decisions and conduct related to them: if the decisions and conduct contradict sound ethical codes and standards, then they should be denounced or abandoned).
- Is it fair to all stakeholders? (Assessing whether business decisions and conduct consider and respect the interests of all stakeholders: if so, then they could be considered fair).
- Can it be disclosed? (Assessing whether one is confident that business decisions and conduct are defendable before a broader forum: if the decision-maker is willing to disclose them to parties such as the general public or the press, or subject them to the scrutiny of their own conscience and those of significant others, then they might be considered sound).

5.4.2 Models for assessing and solving ethical dilemmas

The following ten models arguably have the same core, but they have different underlying philosophies and implement different phases and steps in gathering the needed information and reaching ethical consensus.

5.4.2.1 The ETHIC decision-making model

This model (Dempsey, 2013) has been included in an overview of different approaches to ethical decision-making and is presented here due to its 'ETHIC' acronym', which could be of help in remembering the different steps of the decision-making process.

- **E**xamine personal, professional, client, agency, societal values.
- **T**hink about the applicable ethical standards, laws and legal precedents.
- **H**ypothesise different decisions, their outcomes and the impact on relevant systems.
- **I**dentify who will benefit and who will be harmed by these specific decisions, keeping in mind professional values and mission.
- **C**onsult.

5.4.2.2 The DISORDER model for moral decision-making

Here is another example (Newton, 2013: 12–13) of an approach to ethical decision-making which can easily be remembered thanks to its acronym, which indicates the phases of the moral reasoning procedure.

- Definition of the dilemma.
- Inquiry to obtain all necessary information.
- Sorting out the stakeholders.
- Options and outcomes.
- Rights and rules.
- Determination and decision-making.
- Evaluation of effects.
- Review and reconsideration.

5.4.2.3 A guide to moral decision-making

MacDonald (2010) regards this model as 'an aid', which does not necessarily guarantee good decisions. He suggests that the order of the steps could be changed, depending on the situation in which one has to make an ethical decision.

- Recognising the moral dimension.
- Who are the interested parties? What are their relationships?
- What values or principles are involved?
- Sketch out options – not just actions, but *courses* of action.
- Weigh the benefits and the burdens.
- Look for analogous cases.
- Discuss with relevant others.
- Does this decision accord with legal and organisational rules?
- Am I comfortable with this decision?

5.4.2.4 Potter Box model (PB model)

In this section the outlines of two models using the Potter Box (PB) logic are shown. The first is the 'classic' PB model, which uses four dimensions to make an ethical analysis, and the second is a 'modified' PB model, proposed by Watley (2014: 1–14). This model follows five steps to reach an ethical consensus.

The 'classical' PB model:

- Situation (facts): Gathering all relevant facts without making any judgement.
- Values: Distinguish between the kinds of values that could influence ethical decision-making (for example: aesthetic, professional, sociocultural and moral values).
- Principles: Identify those principles based on relevant ethical theories, which will throw more light on both personal norms and on relevancy with regard to the ethical dilemma at stake (for example: Aristotle's golden mean, Kant's categorical imperative, Mill's principle of utility, Rawls' veil of ignorance, etc. ('Potter Box', n.d.).
- Loyalties: This step concerns the loyalty the decision-maker has towards certain agents (for example, himself or herself, employer, colleagues, the public, etc.).

The 'modified' PB model (Watley):

- Situation: Gather relevant facts and identify all applicable assumptions.
- Stakeholders: Identify those stakeholders on whom the decision could have an impact (now and in the future).

- Obligations: Which obligations does the decision-maker have towards these stakeholders? (These are based on a list of prima facie duties such as non-injury; beneficence; self-improvement; justice; reparation; gratitude; promise-keeping; truth-telling; liberty; and duty of manner, some of which have subcategories in the form of values and virtues.)
- Values: Which duties carry specific weight and significance? Do they imply or refer to a specific action? Which action will satisfy most obligations?
- Universalise: If this means that the decision to be taken rests on a precedent, will it then be good for both the decision-maker and all the other stakeholders?

5.4.2.5 Markkula framework for ethical decision-making

The Markkula framework for ethical decision-making (Markkula Center for Applied Ethics, 2015: see website) intends to increase ethical sensitivity. It has a structure which enables decision-makers to explore the ethical aspects of a decision and weigh the considerations which should impact on the choice that someone makes.

- Recognise an ethical issue.
  - Could this decision or situation be damaging to someone or to a specific group? Does this decision involve a choice between a good and bad alternative, or perhaps between two 'goods' or two 'bads'?
  - Does the issue at hand concern more than only what is legal or what is the most efficient solution? If so, how?
- Get the facts.
  - What are the relevant facts of the case? What facts are not known? Can I learn more about the situation? Do I know enough to make a decision?
  - What individuals and groups have an important stake in the outcome? Are some concerns more important? Why?
  - What are the options for acting? Have all the relevant persons and groups been consulted? Have I identified creative options?
- Evaluate alternative actions.
  - Which option will produce the most good and do the least harm? (The utilitarian approach.)
  - Which option best respects the rights of all who have a stake? (The rights approach.)
  - Which option treats people equally or proportionately? (The justice approach.)
  - Which option best serves the community as a whole, not just some members? (The common good approach.)
  - Which option leads me to act as the sort of person I want to be? (The virtue approach.)
- Make a decision and test it.
  - Considering all these approaches, which option best addresses the situation?
  - If I told someone I respect (or told a television audience) about the option I have chosen, what would they say?

- Act and reflect on the outcome.
  - How can my decision be implemented with the greatest care and attention to the concerns of all stakeholders?
  - How did my decision turn out and what have I learned from this specific situation?

5.4.2.6 Van Es model for ethical decision-making

Van Es' model (2011: 288–293) has three phases which are related to the three Aristotelian (basic) stages of rhetoric. The ethical process takes place on two levels: that of the moral debate and the moral dialogue. Each of those levels has its own set of values, such as equity, propriety, solidarity (debate), and reciprocity, respect and trust (dialogue) (2011: 228).

- Phase 1: Moral assessment.
  - What are the moral intuitions?
  - What are the facts and who are the stakeholders?
  - Which stakeholder values are at stake here?

  (guided by the following values: personal, professional, organisational and public)

- Phase 2: Moral judgement.
  - Based on a perspective that focusses on consequences, including interests and ideals.
  - Based on a perspective focussed on principles, including rights and duties.
  - Based on a perspective focussed on virtues, including integrity and commitment.

  (guided by pro and contra arguments regarding all three perspectives)

- Phase 3: Moral decision.
  - Taking responsibility for the action: both positive and negative consequences.
  - Taking responsibility for rapprochement: keeping the dialogue alive.
  - Taking responsibility for personal development: keeping on learning consciously and taking responsibility for personal aspirations, culture and commitments.

  (guided by the way the actor deals with his/her responsibility)

5.4.2.7 The Wittmer model for ethical decision-making

Wittmer (2015: 54) calls his model a general (cognitive) behavioural model for ethical decision-making. As expressed in the schema below, ethical decision-making entails the sum of the ethical decision processes (characterised by sensitivity, judgement and choice), which are influenced by *individual attributes* (such as personal value systems and a sense of compliance to rules and the law), and *environmental factors* (such as an organisational culture of risk-taking, and settings which are remote from cultural values), and actual ethical conduct.

- Ethical situation.
- Ethical sensitivity (first step of the decision process): includes individual and situational influences.
- Ethical judgement (second step of the decision process): includes individual and situational influences.
- Ethical choice (third step of the decision process): includes individual and situational influences.
- Ethical behaviour: includes individual and situational influences.

5.4.2.8 Cognitive development model for ethical decision-making (CMD-model)

The cognitive moral development model, or CMD (Collins, 2012: 157, and Kaplan Financial Limited, 2009: 390–391), is based on the work of the social psychologist Kohlberg. He studied individual moral development and, famously, distinguished between six stages of this, related to three cognitive moral development levels (see also Chapter 4, section 4.4).

Pre-conventional level: Individual is focussed on self-interest and external rewards or punishment
- Stage 1: Obedience/punishment avoidance.
    Question: Does the action hurt me?
    Ethical principle: Egoism.
    Comment: Right and wrong are defined according to rewards and/or punishment from authority (obedience to rules due to a fear of authority).
- Stage 2: Instrumental purpose/reward seeking.
    Question: Does the action benefit me?
    Ethical principle: Egoism.
    Comment: Right is defined according to what is regarded as 'fair' and delivers benefit for the individual personally (self-interest, fairness to self, reciprocity).

Conventional level: Individual is focussed on what is expected of them by others
- Stage 3: Mutual interpersonal expectations/interpersonal accord and conformity.
    Question: Is the action supported by my peers?
    Ethical principle: Social group relativism.
    Comment: Actions are defined by what individuals feel that their peers and those close to them deem good behaviour (well-being of friends and colleagues).
- Stage 4: Social system/social accord and system maintenance.
    Question: Does the action maintain and respect current laws and customs?
    Ethical principle: Cultural relativism.
    Comment: Social accord determines the rightness of actions (there is a duty towards the customs, laws and traditions in society).

Post-conventional level; Individual has an autonomous, internalised personal view of right and wrong
- Stage 5: Prior individual rights, social contracts, utilities.
    Question 1: Does the action treat every stakeholder with respect?
    Question 2: Does the action guarantee the greatest good for the greatest number?
    Ethical principles: Deontology (question 1) and utilitarianism (question 2).

Ethical dilemmas and decision-making

Comment: Right and wrong are determined by basic rights, values and 'social contracts' (human rights).
- Stage 6: Universal ethical principles.
    Question 1: How would a virtuous person act?
    Question 2: Does the action treat every stakeholder with respect?
    Ethical principles: Virtue ethics (question 1) and deontology (question 2).
    Comment: Individuals make decisions based on self-chosen ethical principles which they believe apply to every human being (important values are justice, equality, fairness to everyone, universal human rights).

It is important to note that individual factors such as age, gender and experience will have an influence on the final decision. In addition, these factors become more important at the higher levels of the model (for example, at stages 5 and 6). Individuals' decisions will rest upon their personal convictions that they are right. Furthermore, situational factors (for example, related to the organisational or societal culture) also have an influence on an individual's decisions, but seem to be more important at the lower levels of the model (for example, levels 1 and 2): they are not fundamentally based on a person's personal values and beliefs, but rather on what a person feels is expected from him/her (external influences).

5.4.2.9 The rational problem-solving process

This model is based on the assumption that individuals could take a clear and valid decision only when it rests upon a rational assessment of the underlying ethical dilemma (as is the case in many other models). This model incorporates a handy set of indicators which steer users through the whole process of decision-making (Bloisi et al., 2003: 479):

- Problem awareness

    - Establish trust
    - Clarify objectives
    - Assess the current situation
    - Identify problems

- Problem definition

    - Analyse problems
    - Agree on problems to be solved

- Decision-making

    - Establish decision-making criteria
    - Develop action alternatives
    - Evaluate alternatives
    - Decide on a plan

- Action-plan implementation

    - Assign tasks and responsibilities
    - Establish an implementation schedule

- Reinforce commitment
- Activate the plan

- Follow-through

  - Establish criteria for success
  - Determine how to measure performance
  - Monitor the results
  - Take corrective action.

5.4.2.10 The integrated EDM model (I-EDM model)

Schwartz (2017: 60–80) describes an integrated model of ethical decision-making (I-EDM) which is based on the work of Rest (1986), Jones (1991), Trevino (1986), Tenbrunsel and Smith-Crowe (2008), Hannah, Avolio and May (2011) and Haidt (2001), and also of himself (Schwartz, 2016). This model caters for both the process of ethical decision-making and the factors that influence the process. The outline below shows that individual and situational variables, or moderating factors, specifically interfere with the *moral judgement stage* in the decision-making process. However, they can influence the other main stages as well.

- Moral awareness, or recognition of the presence of an ethical dilemma (could be absent).

  - Influenced by moral attentiveness, mindfulness, imagination and framing (building blocks for moral awareness).

- Moral judgement (Evaluation of the best course of action amongst alternatives).

  - Individual influences:
    Personal intuition (sense); emotion (feel), reason (reflect) and rationalisation (justify)
    Personal moral character disposition and integrity (including demographics, personality/psychology and ethical experience)
  - Situational influences:
    Importance, intensity and complexity of the ethical issue at hand
    Ethical infrastructure of the organisation (communication, training, sanctioning systems)
    Perceived need for personal gain (financial loss, high debts, time)
  - Influence by moral consultation (code of ethics, other people)

- Moral intention (commitment to act according to moral values of self/company.

  - Determined by moral character (moral identity, willpower and courage to act)

- Ethical behaviour (actions supported by moral standards).

  - Could relate to actions which are directed towards either the avoidance of harm (proscriptive) or the promotion of good (prescriptive).

5.5 Conclusion

Entrepreneurial thinking prompts business organisations to take risks. In order to minimise adverse and negative impacts on stakeholders, or even better, ensure that business activities have a positive impact on all, companies are increasingly resorting to systematic reflection on, and evaluation of the impacts of those risks, and ways to solve ethical dilemmas which might have emerged in business practice. An ethical dilemma emerges when a person, in attempting to find a solution to a problem, has to make a choice between two options, in a situation whereby either: both are desirable, meaning that not doing one of them will result in moral failure; or where none of the options will lead to a satisfactory, morally sound, solution to the problem. The decision-maker will have to resort to moral reasoning and establish an equilibrium between the nature of a dilemma and the principles or standards used to solve it. This becomes clearer when one reflects on the nature and process of ethical decision-making. The process displays a fourfold structure, which is usually integrated in most of the ethical decision-making models used in business contexts. The process starts with moral awareness, passes through a stage of moral judgement – weighing and evaluating options for good conduct, based on principles coming from one (or more) major ethical traditions, the deontological, teleological and virtue-ethical – then a stage of moral intent, and ends with moral behaviour.

Four frameworks for ethical triage, or screening, and ten models for ethical decision-making have been included in this chapter. The triage frameworks entail a less formal 'quick-check' approach which enables the decision-maker to assess whether he/she is on the 'right track' and whether a more in-depth and structured analysis of the ethical dilemma is needed. The decision-making models included have different levels of sophistication. Whereas some are quite straightforward and easy to use due to the acronyms in their names, representing the different phases or steps of the model, others are more complex. These also include the assessment of intervening individual and situational factors, such as moral character and organisational culture. The context and (personal) preferences of the decision-maker will determine which model provides adequate help in ensuring good and responsible business conduct.

5.6 Questions for discussion

- In solving ethical dilemmas: which of the three traditional ethical theories would you most likely use (deontology, consequentialism or virtue-ethical theory)? Why?
- What does the CMD-model for ethical decision-making tell you about your personal values and norms, and approach in solving ethical dilemmas (see section 5.4.2.8)? Does this align with the choice you made in the first question?
- Describe an ethical dilemma you were confronted with recently. Could you recall the phases you went through in solving the dilemma, starting from the nature of the dilemma and ending with a statement as to whether it was solved

to your satisfaction (or not)? How do these phases compare with the steps explicated in the Markkula framework for ethical decision-making (see section 5.4.2.5)? Would the outcome have been different if you have used this model for decision-making in the first place? Which step of the model has helped you most? Why?
- What is the most important question or issue one should consider when trying to solve an ethical dilemma?
- Read section 5.3.5 (Ethical decision-making and the law) once more and then reflect on the question whether a company which resorts to 'greenwashing' should be put on trial in a court of law. Use both legal and ethical considerations (and the way they interact with each other) to make your position clear.

5.7 Concluding thoughts

Business ethics is about assessing and evaluating the ethical principles and norms that govern the behaviour of individuals and organisations within a business setting. Business behaviour, in turn, rests on decisions that have been made with regard to activities that have been, or are to be, undertaken at all three levels of business performance; the individual, the organisational and the systemic. Making a decision means choosing between alternatives which are related either to a problem that has emerged in business practice, or to an opportunity that has emerged which a company believes should be taken advantage of.

Choosing between alternatives often has a moral character. The alternatives are often of such a nature that the decision-maker is confronted with an ethical dilemma, comprised of the difficulty of having to choose between options of which some might be desirable, but none will lead to a satisfactory solution. Under such circumstances it is essential that individuals and organisations critically reflect on the exact nature of the dilemma and problem, make an ethical judgement based on weighing the alternatives and the ethical principles to which they refer, take a decision on the preferred action, implement it and evaluate whether the outcomes and impacts accorded with the anticipated 'good' for all stakeholders. This kind of reflection is ideally 'second nature' to employees, but it can also be supported by the application of structured ethical decision-making models which can lead actors systematically through the whole process of moral reasoning and ethical decision-making.

Further reading

Cohen, S. (2004). *The Nature of Moral Reasoning: The Framework and Activities of Ethical Deliberation, Argument and Decision-making*. Oxford/New York: Oxford University Press.

Hartman, L.P., DesJardins, J. and MacDonald, C. (2014). *Business Ethics: Decision-Making for Personal Integrity and Social Responsibility*. New York: McGraw-Hill.

Newton, L. (2013). *Ethical Decision-Making: Introduction to Cases and Concepts in Ethics*. London/New York: Springer.

Schwartz, M.S. (2017). *Business Ethics: An Ethical Decision-Making Approach*. Oxford/Chichester: John Wiley & Sons.

References

Adair, J. (2007). *Decision Making and Problem Solving Strategies*. London/Philadelphia: Kogan Page.

Bloisi, W., Cook, C.W. and Hunsaker, P.L. (2003). *Management and Organizational Behaviour* (pp. 476–522). Maidenhead: McGraw-Hill Education.

Carroll, A.B. and Buchholtz, A.K. (2008). *Business and Society: Ethics and Stakeholder Management* (7th ed.). Mason, OH: Cengage Learning.

Cohen, S. (2004). *The Nature of Moral Reasoning: The Framework and Activities of Ethical Deliberation, Argument and Decision-Making*. Oxford/New York: Oxford University Press.

Collins, D. (2012). *Business Ethics: How to Design and Manage Ethical Organisations*. Hoboken: John Wiley & Sons.

Crane, A. and Matten, D. (2016). *Business Ethics* (4th ed.). Oxford: Oxford University Press.

Dempsey, A.L. (2013). *Approaches to Ethical Decision Making*. Association of Professional Engineers and Geoscientists of British Columbia (APEGBC). Retrieved 20 January 2017 from https://www.apeg.bc.ca/getmedia/07a7c376-4d6d-4548-a3fc-f6fd620ccf48/Approaches-to-Ethical-Decision-Making-ALD.pdf.aspx.

Dilemma. (n.d.). In *Literary Devices*. Retrieved 27 July 2017 from https://literarydevices.net/dilemma/.

Es, R. van (2011). *Professionele Ethiek: Morele Besluitvorming in Organisaties en Professies*. Deventer: Kluwer.

Ethical Decision. (n.d.). In *Wikipedia*. Retrieved 27 July 2017 from https://en.wikipedia.org/wiki/Ethical_decision.

Ferrell, O.C., Fraedrich, J. and Ferrell, L. (2015). *Business Ethics: Ethical Decision Making and Cases*. Stamford, CT: Cengage Learning.

Ford, C.F. and Richardson, W.D. (1994). Ethical Decision-Making: A Review of the Empirical Literature. *Journal of Business Ethics*, 13(3): 205–221.

Gintis, H. (2009). *Behavioral Ethics*. Santa Fe Institute and Central European University. Retrieved 11 March 2019 from http://www.umass.edu/preferen/gintis/Behavioral Ethics.pdf.

Haidt, J. (2001). The Emotional Dog and its Rational Tail: A Social Intuitionist Approach to Moral Judgment. *Psychological Review*, 4: 814–834.

Hannah, S.T., Avolio, B.J. and May, D.R. (2011). Moral Maturation and Moral Conation: A Capacity Approach to Explaining Moral Thought and Action. *Academy of Management Review*, 36: 663–685.

Hartman, L.P., DesJardins, J. and MacDonald, C. (2014). *Business Ethics: Decision-Making for Personal Integrity and Social Responsibility*. New York: McGraw-Hill.

Jones, T.M. (1991). Ethical Decision Making by Individuals in Organizations: An Issue-Contingent Model. *Academy of Management Review*, 16: 366–395.

Kaplan Financial Limited. (2009). *Understanding Professional Ethics*. Wokingham, Berkshire: Kaplan Publishing.

Klinker, J.F. and Hackmann, D.G. (2004). An Analysis of Principals' Ethical Decision Making using Rest's Four Component Model of Moral Behaviour. *Journal of School Leadership*, 14(4): 434–448.

Kohlberg, L. (1981). *Essays on Moral Development, Vol. I: The Philosophy of Moral Development*. San Francisco, CA: Harper & Row.

Kvalnes, O. (2015). *Moral Reasoning at Work: Rethinking Ethics in Organisations*. Hampshire/New York: Palgrave Macmillan.

MacDonald, C. (2010). *A Guide to Moral Decision Making*. Retrieved 26 July 2017 from http://www.ethicsweb.ca/guide/.

McConnell, T. (2014). Moral Dilemmas. In *Stanford Encyclopaedia of Philosophy*. Retrieved 27 July 2017 from https://plato.stanford.edu/entries/moral-dilemmas/.

Major, A.E. (2012). Law and Ethics in Command Decision Making. *Military Review*, May/June: 61–74. Retrieved 28 July 2017 from https://www.law.upenn.edu/institutes/cerl/conferences/cyberwar/papers/reading/Major.pdf.

Markkula Center for Applied Ethics. (2015). *Markkula Framework for Ethical Decision Making*. Santa Clara, California: Markkula Center for Applied Ethics at Santa Clara University. Retrieved 29 July 2017 from https://www.scu.edu/ethics/ethics-resources/ethical-decision-making/a-framework-for-ethical-decision-making/.

Newton, L. (2013). *Ethical Decision-Making: Introduction to Cases and Concepts in Ethics*. London/New York: Springer.

Potter Box. (n.d.). In *Wikipedia*. Retrieved 14 March 2019 from https://en.wikipedia.org/wiki/Potter_Box.

Rest, J.R. (1986). *Moral Development: Advances in Research and Theory*. New York: Praeger.

Rest, J.R., Narvaez, D., Bebeau, M. and Thoma, S. (1999). *Postconventional Moral Thinking: A Neo-Kohlbergian Approach*. Mahweh, NJ: Lawrence Erlbaum Associates.

Rossouw, D. and Vuuren, L. van (2013). *Business Ethics* (5th ed.). Cape Town: Oxford University Press.

Schwartz, M.S. (2016). Ethical Decision-Making Theory: An Integrated Approach. *Journal of Business Ethics*, 139: 755–776.

Schwartz, M.S. (2017). *Business Ethics: An Ethical Decision-Making Approach*. Oxford/Chichester: John Wiley & Sons.

Surbhi, S. (2015, 24 December). Difference between Law and Ethics. In *Key Differences*. Retrieved 29 July 2017 from http://keydifferences.com/difference-between-law-and-ethics.html.

Syckle, B. van, and Tietje, B. (2010). *Anybody's Business*. Upper Saddle River, NJ: Pearson Education.

Tenbrunsel, A.E. and Smith-Crowe, K. (2008). Ethical Decision Making: Where We've Been and Where We're Going. *Academy of Management Annals*, 2: 545–607.

Texas Instruments (2015). *Code of Conduct: Our Values and Ethics*. Texas Instruments Incorporated. In *Texas Instruments*. Retrieved 29 July 2017 from http://www.ti.com/corp/docs/investor_relations/downloads/TI_Code_of_Conduct_our_values_and_ethics.pdf?keyMatch=TI%20Ethics%20Quick%20Test&tisearch=Search-EN-Everything.

Trevino, L.K. (1986). Ethical Decision Making in Organizations: A Person–Situation Interactionist Model. *Academy of Management Review*, 11: 601–617.

Watley, L.D. (2014). Training in Ethical Judgement with a Modified Potter Box. *Business Ethics: A European View*, 23(1): 1–14.

Wittmer, D. (2015). Developing a Behavioural Model for Ethical Decision-Making in Organisations. In Frederickson, H.G. and Ghere, R.K. (Eds.). *Ethics in Public Management* (pp. 49–69). London/New York: Routledge.

PART II

Ethical dilemmas in the creative, cultural and service industries

Chapter 6

Professional ethics

Roy Wood, Lieke Sauer, Raymond Boland and Jan-Willem Proper

6.1 Introduction to professional ethics

Roy Wood

The flavour of attitudes to business ethics can be quite broad. Let us consider three different positions. The British Conservative politician and former UK Deputy Prime Minister Michael Heseltine once stated that 'The market has no morality'; B.R. Ambedkar, the first law and justice minister of the independent republic of India held that 'History shows that where ethics and economics come in conflict, victory is always with economics'; and Anita Roddick, founder of the Body Shop, said 'Being good is good business'. Heseltine's conviction is perhaps the most depressing, for what are ethics without morals? Ambedkar's sceptical viewpoint is to a degree seemingly justified in the quotation 'People of the same trade seldom meet together, even for merriment and diversion, but the conversation ends in a conspiracy against the public, or in some contrivance to raise prices' from Adam Smith, who is, somewhat ironically in this context, generally regarded as the godfather of right-wing economics (see Ambedkar, n.d.; Heseltine, n.d.; Roddick, n.d.).

Anita Roddick's observation implies what has become a fashionable view since the 1970s – that holding to high standards in the conduct of business brings both material and non-material benefits.

In general there is, in the wider population, as well as amongst theorists of business ethics, at least a mistrust of the ethical behaviour of those engaged in commerce. The late Sumantra Ghoshal, a leading management theorist and educator, remarked that 'Many of the worst excesses of recent management practices have their roots in a set of ideas that have emerged from business school academics over the last 30 years' (2005: 75). Ghoshal argued against what he saw as academic management's 'pretence of knowledge', highlighting the need for management to be understood in its social context. Khurana and Nohria opened their now well-known article advocating a universal managerial code of ethics by stating baldly 'Managers have lost legitimacy over the past decade in the face of a widespread institutional breakdown of trust and self-policing in business' (2008: 70).

6.1.1 The 'professional' part of professional ethics

While they are by no means the only commentators to do so, and Ghoshal focusses on the behaviour of business-school academics while Khurana and Nohria focus on managers, both are essentially concerned with professional ethics, the nature of which is not as easy to define as might first appear. Sociologists and others have expended considerable energy agonising over how a profession should be defined (MacDonald's 1995 text, while dated, gives a good overview of the issues) but are agreed that professions differ from other occupations in a number of ways, as indicated in the following list.

- Professions embody a form of specialist expertise which presupposes an equally specialist form of education and/or training and/or apprenticeship.
- Professions are almost always internally regulated, and often also externally regulated (by, for example, law).
- The internal regulation of a profession often (though not always) relies on restrictions on the numbers allowed to practice that profession – this may be managed by quota and/or access being enabled and restricted by competitive examinations.
- Professions often require their members to comply with a code or codes of ethics and have the right to remove formal membership of that profession from those found guilty of serious breaches of such code(s).

Until relatively recently, the law, medicine and the clergy were seen as the major, and by some, only, professions, although the *Wikipedia* entry for 'profession' suggests that by the end of the nineteenth century, in addition, surveying, actuarial science, dentistry, civil engineering, logistics, architecture, accounting, pharmacy, veterinary medicine, psychology, nursing, teaching, librarianship, optometry and social work had all met one or more criteria to justify being called a profession ('Profession', n.d.). No doubt, which occupations should be classified in this way will remain a controversial and complex matter. It is perhaps significant that 'management' is not routinely regarded as a profession, but it is not surprising. The category is a broad one and lends itself to numerous specialisations, some of which might qualify managers with that specialisation to claim the status of professionals, while others would not confer such entitlement.

6.1.2 The 'ethics' part of professional ethics

Possibly the oldest code of professional ethics is the Hippocratic Oath, 'sworn' by many medical doctors to this day and, of course, now part of much more extensive codes of practice maintained by professional and regulatory medical bodies. Other professional bodies have their own codes of ethics. These normally include specifying both standards of conduct and behaviour of a general kind as well as behaviours particular to the profession. As professionals tend to be highly specialised in one or more relatively scarce skills, profession-specific codes of ethics will often deal with how and in what circumstances those skills should be deployed, as well as specifying how a breach of ethical standards may be punished (by a professional regulatory body and/or prevailing law).

Professional ethics

Khurana and Nohria's (2008) advocacy of the professionalisation of management and the creation of a code of ethics for managers has been noted earlier. The sheer range of people who have the word 'manager' in their job title together with the range of functions they perform would seem to make this a worthy but impractical ambition, though not necessarily one that should be dismissed. Perhaps of more interest here is to consider why professional ethics may be necessary at all. Put another way, why is an individual's own common sense and moral compass apparently deemed unreliable in guiding their actions and ensuring the routine practice of ethical behaviour? First, a code of ethics serves as a warning to those bound by its terms. It says 'you may think of doing this at some point, but you should not do it for fear of a negative outcome'. The underlying assumption is that even exalted members of professions cannot be relied upon all the time to 'do the right thing'. We are, after all, all human and therefore imperfect and there are occasions when our moral compass might fail. Secondly, most professions (and many other occupations) are, or are increasingly, knowledge-based and for those who create, control and otherwise 'steward' knowledge, 'common sense' is *the* enemy. This view is most obviously present in the academic profession, where despite a distinguished analytic heritage, the concept of common sense is viewed by many as little more than a vehicle for articulating reactionary and uncritical value judgements. Thus Frank Lloyd Wright, the American architect, was able to state (a similar sentiment is also attributed to the French thinker, Voltaire) that 'there is nothing more uncommon than common sense' (Wright, n.d.) and Albert Einstein is reputed to have observed that 'common sense is the collection of prejudices acquired by age eighteen' (Einstein, n.d.).

6.1.3 Who are professional ethics for?

Those who would bind us together under the umbrella of an ethical code or codes fear common sense. In Charles Dickens' *Bleak House* (1853[2003]), we are introduced to the legal case of Jarndyce versus Jarndyce which concerns the fate of a large inheritance. At the start of the book the case has already been making its way through the English court of Chancery for several generations such that, when it is resolved as part of the novel's narrative, the whole estate has been consumed in legal costs. One possible perspective on codes of professional ethics is thus that they oppose common sense and bolster what are largely abstract concepts of professional expertise in order to make that expertise scarcer and more expensive. In this view, codes of ethics exist primarily to protect and reassure the 'professionals' rather than their clients.

Near absurdist examples of this can be found in American hospitals, where codes of ethics can be policed vigorously in order to reduce the possibility of dubious litigation by patients against doctors or the institution itself. Medical doctor Harold Shipman, one of the UK's (indeed, world's) most notorious serial killers, was not prevented by professional ethics from killing an estimated 200-plus patients over an extended period. Indeed, in an indirect way, the power conferred on Shipman as a medical professional supposedly operating within both general and specific moral and ethical codes may actually have prolonged his killing spree and deferred the advent of those events that finally led to him being apprehended. One function of codes of ethics is, in essence, to invite the non-specialist, the client, to uncritically trust the professional.

6.1.4 Professional ethics in business

One of the great difficulties in establishing codes of ethics is that professions can differ considerably as to the range and quality of skills they employ. It would be a matter of deep concern if, after opening you up on the operating table, a surgeon could not recognise organs such as the heart, lungs and kidneys. A greater tolerance might be extended to an expert art historian who failed to initially and correctly identify the well-known artist of an unsigned painting. There are many managerial positions which by virtue of the expertise required are fundamentally professions, and whose practitioners are thus bound by codes of ethics (finance, accounting, legal advisors). Others, as we have noted, are not so bound.

In professional ethics, probably the two most important questions to pose are 'what is a manager's primary duty?' and 'to whom does a manager owe their primary duty?' For some, the answer to both questions comes in the form of the Friedman Doctrine, named for neo-liberal economist Milton Friedman, who argued that the only responsibility of managers is to maximise profit for shareholders (1970). For others, this view is, intrinsically, ethically compromised. Business activity is such a fundamental aspect of society that its impacts cannot be ignored or assumed to be morally neutral. This approach has given rise, amongst other things, to the many debates about 'corporate social responsibility' (CSR), although CSR also has equally important applications to small and medium-sized enterprises (see also Chapter 8). Wider debates about sustainability also increasingly bear down on the social roles of business (see also Chapter 9).

The economic crisis which engulfed much of the developed world in 2008 and which, at the time of writing, has not fully abated, led to increased scrutiny of dubious business practices although without much evidence of positive change. At the same time, the main means by which such matters as CSR and sustainability would usually be addressed – political discourse – is evidencing increasing polarisation on a global scale. This increases the difficulties attendant on putting aside one's own base and other prejudices, including political prejudices, to focus as objectively as possible on analysing and solving problems, many of which may well threaten the long-term future of the whole planet.

Whether in business or any other kind of human activity there will always be those who behave in a way deemed by others as 'unethical'. Why might someone behave in such a way? The answer is because they can, and because often they can get away with whatever nefarious action they take – and of course, because they may additionally benefit in some material way from that action. For some commentators, only governments, through legal regulation, can hope to achieve the necessary change to contain the many forms of unethical behaviour that impact on society. The increasingly fissiparous nature of politics noted above would seem to make that particular prospect unlikely. How then are we to deal with unethical behaviour: through more codes of practice, and/or more severe penalties for those who transgress such codes? The answer may well lie in our acceptance of the inevitability of unethical conduct while simultaneously doing everything possible at the individual, human, level to imbue in individuals an understanding of right and wrong – or acceptable and unacceptable – behaviours. This is an old-fashioned idea and it is not untouched by relativistic considerations (what is right? what is wrong?). Yet it addresses ethics and ethical behaviour as a human construct and allows for the possibility of change, it is an approach that can be simultaneously loose and rigorous, and, as with any human construct, it can be easily discarded if its utility is found wanting.

6.1.5 In conclusion

This introduction points out that ethical standards are frequently codified, following general principles, into sets of rules of behaviour appropriate to particular professions. In this first part of the chapter, consideration is given to the nature of professions and the need for professional ethics, together with the problematic nature of classifying management positions in general as 'professional'. At the same time, the text reflects on the need for codified rules of professional ethical behaviour as against trusting general moral judgements as to 'good' behaviour. The remainder of the chapter consists of three discussions. In the first commentary, Sauer and Wood offer an insight into macro-level professional behaviour in the hospitality industry, specifically managers' attitudes to and management of reward. The following case study by Sauer invites readers to reflect and comment upon the apparent unfairness of extreme ethical standards in human resource practice. Next, Boland offers insights into the phenomenon of whistle-blowing and its associated ethical dilemmas. Motivation for blowing the whistle and having a keen eye for the very nature of the ethical dilemma, and overseeing the consequences of one's decision, are key pillars in understanding this phenomenon. He illustrates the complexity of whistle-blowing in a case study which describes how a person could feel crushed by loyalty when a good employer does something in business that is seemingly not kosher. Finally, Proper ruminates on some of the facets of the individual–organisational interface of ethics with a special focus on the roles of the manager. Managers should reactively and proactively act with integrity and responsibility, thereby correcting and preventing unethical behaviour within their own organisations, but also when it comes to the ethical behaviour of their suppliers and other connections. His case study deals with the dilemmas three members of a management team express when discovering that their company is buying in uncertified products which could lead to clients being harmed.

6.2 Professional ethics in hospitality – the case of managers and employee reward

Lieke Sauer and Roy Wood

6.2.1 Introduction to professional ethics in hospitality

Winston Churchill, Britain's Prime Minister in World War II, once commented of his deputy and immediate post-war successor: 'Mr. Attlee is a very modest man. Indeed he has a lot to be modest about' ('Winston Churchill Quotes', n.d.). The modern hospitality industry is not especially modest. Indeed, its leaders are constantly boasting of its importance, together with tourism, to the global economy. However, the sector does arguably have a great deal to be ethical about. Frequently promoting itself as a 'people industry' (which industries are not 'people' industries?) commercial hospitality organisations have an almost global reputation for poor human resource management practices and in those countries where the sector is viewed favourably as a source of employment it is often only because government imposes relatively rigorous legal requirements via labour legislation. Specific concerns about hospitality industry labour practices focus on the (supposedly poor) quality of hospitality jobs; the absence of meaningful training to perform those jobs; long hours of work; the overly demanding nature of some jobs in the sector; the absence of work–life balance; and, of course, poor remuneration (for a review of these issues and the industry more widely, see Wood, 2015).

There is no reason to suppose that professional behaviour in hospitality should differ from such behaviour in general, thus complying with whatever moral and ethical codes societies consider to be generally and specifically appropriate to their circumstances and those of the organisations that operate within their territories. Although not widely studied within the hospitality management field, there are some examples of both empirical research into business ethics (e.g. Ghiselli, 1999; Lee et al., 2014) and industry-specific applications of usually hypothetical ethical cases (e.g. Liebermann and Nissen, 2013). Often, these present an optimistic and formalistic view of ethics in the sector, invoking to varying degrees that trusty moral imperative 'should' as in 'this is what should happen'.

Unfortunately, despite grandiose 'values statements' promulgated by hospitality companies on their websites and elsewhere, what 'should' happen rarely – or at least infrequently – does happen. To develop this point we shall briefly instance three examples of managerial behaviour towards remuneration practices in the sector.

6.2.1.1 Managerial attitudes towards remuneration in hospitality – three examples

First, in the UK during the 1990s, the hospitality industry's representative body the British Hospitality Association (BHA) supported the then Conservative government's efforts to reduce and ultimately eliminate minimum-wage protection in the hospitality sector. When the opposition Labour Party indicated that if elected to government (which it duly was in 1997) it would introduce a global minimum wage for the British economy there was much consternation, with the BHA amongst others predicting that such a measure would lead to a reduction in the capacity of industries to create jobs because of excessive wage bills. In fact, in the early years of the national minimum wage's operation hospitality labour costs rose by about 2 per cent, with no evidence of significant job losses (Williams, Adam-Smith and Norris, 2004).

Secondly, employers often argue that tips are a valuable supplement to hospitality workers' wages but, dependent on what system is employed for distributing gratuities, it is not always the case that all employees receive them – often the only beneficiaries are those working in customer-facing roles, notably food and beverage service. Furthermore, many employers do not distribute tips as a supplement but use them to subsidise basic pay of employees and/or effectively charge employees for distributing gratuities, as in the following example identified by Hickman, Usborne and Grice (2008):

Gondola Holdings, Britain's largest casual dining giant with annual sales of £228m, deducts an 8 per cent administration charge from tips to staff at Pizza Express... [.] The British Hospitality Association, which represents restaurants, denied that its members were mean – and blamed the Inland Revenue for failing to provide a clear lead. Its deputy chief executive, Martin Couchman, said that there were 'legitimate' costs involved in distributing service charges and credit card tips.

Thirdly, in parts of the global hospitality industry there has been a substantial increase in the use of zero-hours contracts and their variants. Zero-hours contracts do not guarantee work to workers, who are paid only for work performed. Workers who sign zero-hours contracts are expected to be available when their employer needs them but are not legally obliged to accept such work. In the UK the biggest user of zero-hours contracts is the hotels and restaurants sector, and in 2013 90 per cent of McDonald's employees were governed by such instruments (Hall, 2013).

6.2.1.2 What is 'ethical'?

Are the above examples characteristic of 'ethical' professional behaviour? From the perspective of neo-liberal economics we might argue a resounding 'yes'. Because labour is normally the hospitality sector's largest and most easily controlled variable cost, managers are under constant pressure to find ever more ingenious ways of reducing it and if they follow, without much qualification, the Friedman Doctrine (that the only social – and by extension, ethical – responsibility of businesses and their managers is to maximise profit for shareholders, see Friedman, 1970) then they are clearly behaving ethically and professionally. From other economic, ethical and social perspectives one might doubt that the singular and uncompromising pursuit of profit, if it leads to the behaviours described, is in any way desirable in terms of the wider, potentially negative, impact it has on large numbers of people.

We can analyse ethical behaviour in business at a number of levels. In this short discussion we have chosen to look at examples of macro-level behaviour towards a specific, and highly significant, topic in a specific industry. In the face of all the pay-related problems that characterise the sector (not least the attraction and retention of employees – hospitality traditionally has the highest rates of labour turnover of all industries) managers consistently fail to address the role of reward in these problems. As long ago as the 1990s, Go and Pine reported that a survey of the 200 largest hotel corporations revealed that in terms of the importance of strategic policies in personnel management, paying 'relatively high wages' and providing both 'attractive benefit packages' and 'incentive programmes' ranked 5th, 7th and 8th on a scale of eight items (1995: 206–210).

At the same time as we make these observations it must be acknowledged that the problems described seem intractable for a very simple reason – despite the low pay, despite the poor conditions of employment, despite the disruptive effects of high labour turnover – the hospitality industry is still largely effective in at least short-term recruitment, and continues to grow as an economic phenomenon. In short, the industry is successful. Why, then, should it concern itself with ethical issues?

Case 6.2.2: Professional behaviour, fairness and ethical standards

Introduction: Meet Rahul and Wendy

Rahul, 27 years old, originally from India, moved to Dubai three years ago to start working in the hospitality industry. He is currently working as a guest service agent in a five-star hotel. Rahul's family, consisting of his parents, sister, his wife and daughter, still live in India. Rahul earns around $700 a month, which is tax-free and includes shared accommodation, transport and three meals at the hotel. To support his family, Rahul sends $500 of his salary home every month. The family uses the money to pay for medical care for Rahul's mother, who has been receiving treatment for cancer.

Wendy, 32 years old, originally from England, moved to Dubai eight years ago to continue her career in the hospitality industry. She is currently working as a front office manager in the same hotel Rahul is working in. Wendy left her family and friends behind in England, but is married to Rob, whom she met in Dubai five years ago. Rob and Wendy live together in an apartment in Dubai Marina. Wendy earns $5000 a month, which is tax-free, includes a live-out allowance, meals at the hotel and a phone allowance.

Rahul and Wendy have been working together for a year and a half now, when Rahul joined Wendy's front office team. Rahul is one of Wendy's favourite employees as he is always on time, polite and friendly with guests. He is also not afraid to 'go the extra mile'. Furthermore, Rahul has shown interest in becoming a Team Leader at the front office. In turn, Rahul likes Wendy's style of leadership. She empowers team members like himself and makes him feel responsible for his own actions. Besides that, Rahul observes that Wendy is working hard to prepare herself for the next step in her career.

A theft or human error?

One day – Wendy was on her day off after working seven days straight – the following incident took place. Rahul started his shift at 3.00 p.m. As always, he prepared his cash float, listened to the briefing of the morning shift and entered the front desk. As the hotel occupancy was not very high that day, Rahul was working together with one other team member who had recently joined the front office team.

There was a group of 20 German guests staying in the hotel who preferred to use the hotel transport service to visit sites in Dubai. The concierge arranged transport for all hotel guests, but just as four people in the group wanted to book another trip, the concierge was busy and couldn't attend to their request. Rahul called them over to the front desk to assist them instead. The guests booked the transport with Rahul and paid for the vouchers, which came to $200 in total. The guests needed the vouchers for transport to prove that they had paid for it already. As Rahul needed to give this money to the

Professional ethics

concierge, who was still busy, he put it in his cash float to hand over later. Rahul's colleague saw that Rahul put the money in his cash float.

The rest of the shift was unexpectedly busy and Rahul needed to stay two hours longer. At the end of his shift at 1.00 a.m., when Rahul was counting his cash float, he found the money of the German guests. Tired and with no concierge present any longer to give the money to, Rahul decided to put the money in the safe, separate from his float. He would hand over the money at his next shift.

Wendy was back in the office after her day off. The security manager called her to inform her that they had found money in Rahul's safe during their weekly spot check. As this was considered theft in the hotel, it meant that Rahul would need to be fired immediately and would be deported from Dubai by law. As Wendy was Rahul's manager, it was her responsibility to deal with the matter.

Questions for discussion

- Without considering the specific legal requirements that may apply, what do you think Wendy should do?
- Which moral arguments can you think of that are in favour of not obeying the law in this case?
- How could these dilemmas be avoided in the future?
- Does professional behaviour always imply living up to ethical codes, regulations and laws? Apply moral arguments in support of your position.
- Build an ethical case – for and against – the three managerial positions towards remuneration in the hospitality industry conveyed in section 6.2.1.1.

6.3 The art of whistle-blowing
Raymond Boland

6.3.1 Introduction to whistle-blowing

The decision facing individuals on whether to blow the whistle on wrongdoing within organisations is a difficult and complex one: difficult because it can lead to personal conflict; and complex because it involves choosing between competing ethical and practical perspectives. This section explores these issues and suggests that greater regulation of organisations and stronger checks on power within organisations can reduce unethical behaviour and the need for whistle-blowing.

Illegal and unethical behaviour in businesses and organisations can potentially involve a range of activities including

> (…) corruption, bribery, receiving and giving gifts and entertainment, kickbacks, extortion, nepotism, favouritism, money laundering, improper use of inside information, use of intermediaries, conflicts of interest, fraud, aggressive

accounting, discrimination, sexual harassment, workplace safety, consumer product safety, and environmental pollution. (Ethics Resource Centre and US Sentencing Commission, as cited in Hoffman and Schwartz, 2015: 771)

Interest rate manipulation at Barclays Bank, Enron's accounting fraud and BP's oil spill in the Mexican Gulf, for example, impact on '...investors, employees, customers, competitors, the natural environment and society in general' (ibid.). Hence, curbing illegal and unethical behaviour is socially and economically desirable.

Unethical behaviour is not limited to private business as it can also occur in charities, aid organisations and nominally non-profit organisations. Aid can be stolen by leaders in wars to fuel their own military. For example food aid enabled both rebel and government armies to continue fighting in Southern Sudan: they both stole it (Polman, 2010: 118–119). Polman (2010) asks her readers to imagine that they, as an aid worker, are in a situation where they see that large amounts of aid are being diverted from their intended purpose. Should the aid worker continue the humanitarian mission on the basis that at least some needy people are still being helped or should she or he stop the mission and blow the whistle as the aid is simply fuelling conflict and corruption and helping make a bad situation worse?

Clearly, witnesses to these situations face a range of options. They can do nothing and 'not rock the boat' as this will usually lead to an easier life and avoid the threat of retaliation for blowing the whistle – either internally from management and colleagues within an organisation or externally through general ostracism within an industry (Park, Rehg and Lee, 2005). They can warn the person or people involved and/or report internally to higher levels of management in the hope that this will stop the wrongdoing. The last and most difficult option is to report externally. This is usually only done when internal mechanisms have failed.

6.3.1.1 Deciding to blow the whistle

The decision to blow the whistle either internally or externally usually involves weighing up conflicting ethical demands. Who does our primary obligation belong to – our employers, our colleagues, our friends and family or to the community at large? How important is our duty of confidentiality? What is the fairest course of action? (Duska, 2015). Essentially, a decision involves choosing to follow one moral responsibility (our sense of obligation, our sense of honesty, our sense of loyalty and our sense of duty) at the expense of the others (Paeth, 2013) (see also Chapter 5).

In situations where ethics conflict, resolution is often attempted by appealing to utilitarian principles, of what action will produce the greatest good, or by ranking morals on a relative scale so that the most weighty moral principle can be followed. However, these attempts to be rational and achieve some sort of generalisable solution are doomed since they ignore the conflict between the mutually exclusive but binding ethical responsibilities described at the end of the previous paragraph. In deciding whether to blow the whistle, one does not choose between an ethical and an unethical action; one chooses between actions which are both ethical and unethical (Paeth, 2013).

Ultimately, an appeal to rationality in ethical decisions is futile. It reduces ethical decision-making to a bureaucratic procedure. Instead, imagination (an ability to put ourselves in someone else's position) is the key to morality and ethical action (Bateman, 2014). Literary fiction is probably the greatest source of this imaginative ability as it allows us to inhabit other worlds and others' minds (Swirski, 2007), so any education for ethical behaviour must include consideration of works of literature.

Moreover, the decision to blow the whistle may well depend on how important specific perspectives are in our choice. From an economic perspective we may well decide to choose the option which maximises our own perceived self-interest. From a legal perspective we will choose the option which best adheres to the law. From an 'ethical perspective' we will choose the option which is the most moral one (MacGregor and Stuebs, 2014: 310). A further consideration concerns 'information credibility' and 'uncertain or imperfect knowledge'. 'Decisions concerning whether to blow the whistle or not are often based on inconclusive or incomplete information in the real world' (MacGregor and Stuebs, 2014: 320). What is credible information, what is rumour, what is second-hand knowledge? Similarly, should we accept a colleague's or superior's explanation when accused of wrongdoing if we cannot be sure they did wrong (ibid.)? Another complicating factor concerns intent and benefit. Should whistle-blowing depend on deciding whether someone intended to break the rules and should someone only be held responsible if he or she benefits from the wrongdoing (MacGregor and Stuebs, 2014: 320)? Similarly, the motivation of the whistle-blower is an important consideration. Is blowing the whistle ethical when the primary motivation is to gain revenge on colleagues or managers for some perceived personal injustice (Hoffman and Schwartz, 2015)?

One way to avoid some of these ethical conflicts is to be proactive and try to ensure that they do not arise (Duska, 2015). A strong internal ethical culture is sometimes believed to be a way of reducing misconduct and the need for whistle-blowing (Hoffman and Schwartz, 2015). However, this is open to question. The gap between hypocrisy, banality and moral pronouncements by multinationals is sometimes not particularly wide (Broughton, 2008). Herve Laroche of the European School of Management shows that in some organisations that prioritise 'core values', faking becomes the standard mode of operation (cited in Gilmore and Pine, 2007: 98).

6.3.1.2 Complicating factors

The last 30 years or so have seen an increasing marketisation of everything (Sandel, 2012). This also includes ethics. Neo-liberalism has a completely ahistorical and quasi-messianic belief in the power of markets and individuals to ensure efficiency and social justice (Gray, 2008). In a way the whistle-blower can be seen as an archetypical neo-liberal construct, as an individual who is made responsible for policing organisations while the potential for collective action by society is ignored. Perhaps a better approach than an appeal to human goodness and the self-regulating power of markets would be to follow Machiavelli (2008 [1515]), who believed that humans are fickle, greedy and self-interested. In this view, fear is the way to promote ethical behaviour. It cannot be denied that humans perform altruistic acts. Nevertheless, it is safe to assume that in most cases they will act to maximise their own perceived self-interest – often with an ethical explanation as in the case of Goldman Sachs' chief executive Lloyd Blankfein's famous claim that he and the investment banks in general were 'doing God's work' (cited in Phillips, 2009).

Individuals and groups will behave badly because of temptation. Greed as an individual vice is often used as an explanation for wrongdoing, as for example in explanations of the causes of the financial crisis which started in 2007/2008 – individual bankers were too greedy and selfish. However, this type of wrongdoing is much more correctly explained by structural factors. Multinational organisations are often effectively free of any real regulation by national governments, and this light-touch regulation is promoted by political parties and neo-liberal ideologues as essential for a good business environment. Taxes on their business operations are low. They are encouraged to pay huge salaries and bonuses to attract the best managers, who then reward themselves handsomely. Short-term profit and shareholder value are what they are judged on and what parts of their reward depend on. None of these are in themselves incentives to socially responsible behaviour.

Rather than relying on whistle-blowers and the mysterious workings of the market, regulation and increased trade union power is an effective means of reducing corporate wrongdoing. Although trade unions are also susceptible to fraud and corruption, they at least provide a counterweight to the unchecked power of managers within organisations. Large multinational corporations which are effectively beyond the democratic control of states and which can sometimes control more wealth than individual countries will not be controlled by appeals to a strong ethical compass alone (Wilkinson and Pickett, 2010).

In the end the decision to blow the whistle is not one that can be made on rational grounds. Rather it is one that requires an imaginative and aesthetic judgement. This can be developed by practice and experience within education, but ultimately it will always be a personal decision based on many factors, both ethical and practical.

The vignette below explores the ethics and pragmatics of whistle-blowing in the tourism industry.

Case 6.3.2: Loyalty and spilling the beans

Introduction: Working for a good company...

Donna is a well-respected professional with a decade-long record of success. She has built an international online tourism booking agency from a start-up to a major player in the field. The head office is located in the capital of a European country. Donna is the managing director of the company, which currently employs approximately 500 people. About 200 employees are based in cities on the European continent, and around 300 in its main destination markets.

The company takes good care of its employees: all posts are paid at above market rates, and staff in developing countries receive excellent education and health insurance benefits for themselves and their families. The business is also highly proactive in promoting women's and minority rights and has an excellent record in promoting staff internally. The company has undoubtedly improved the lives of many of its staff members by providing secure and worthwhile employment. In many ways the company is a fine example of a profitable, socially responsible business with excellent prospects.

One of the employees, working at the head office is Felicity, 24 years of age. She graduated two years ago with a bachelor's degree in tourism. Since then she has been working full-time at the agency. Her main responsibilities revolve around the acquisition of new accommodation, transport and tour-operator services in destinations around the world.

Caught between suspicion and loyalty

Recently at a staff party, Felicity had a brief conversation with a rather drunken member of the senior management team, Doug. He told her that one of the reasons why the company was so successful was that Donna and he himself were very generous with 'payments' to help acquire new business in certain countries. The next day at work Doug sought out Felicity again, and despite not making any specific reference to the content of the previous night's conversation, apologises for his rather 'drunken ramblings' and advises her to not pay attention to what he said as it '... was just the beer talking'.

Although she had never heard of these payments before, Felicity investigated and discovered that 'payments' were made – as Doug called them – and these might include money or special favours given to foreign government officials and/or business partners to, for example, speed up the granting of licences to operate or to influence business decisions. However, the nature of the payments was unclear. In other words, the distinction between legitimate payments and bribes was blurred.

Felicity did some follow-up research which revealed that there was a 'special projects' fund, for which Donna and Doug have exclusive authorisation rights. The official role of this fund was to support local sustainable development projects in developing countries. Nevertheless, Felicity could find no examples of current sustainable development projects or audits for older ones.

Felicity confronted Doug with her suspicions about the 'payments', but he assured her that they were all legitimate and in line with the company's social-responsibility policies. He also referred her to the company's clear no-tolerance policy on bribery. Giving or receiving bribes is illegal in the company's home country.

Felicity was not satisfied with Doug's explanation and felt pressured to make a decision about which action to take in this situation. Something just did not feel right here. Should she approach outside bodies with her suspicions, or try to speak to Donna, or just keep quiet? She feels loyal to the company, because she is paid well, loves her work and is treated humanely and with respect by her superiors. Because she felt settled in this job, she had decided to move to a smaller apartment to have more money available to support her father, who needed extra medical care and could not afford to pay for it. Resigning was not an option for her. Moreover, a quite heavy weight on her shoulders was that Donna and Doug were very supportive and

(continued)

Case 6.3.2: Loyalty and spilling the beans (*continued*)

lenient with her when she first started with the company. Felicity had made a big mistake in her first few days of employment, which had led to the loss of a contract. However, Donna and Doug had accepted the mistake as 'just something that could happen' and had assured her that they valued her work overall and would not hold it against her. The incident was not placed on Felicity's personal record or mentioned again. Yet, she was confronted with a dilemma. What should Felicity do?

Questions for discussion

- What would you do if you were Felicity? Give ethical reasons for your answer.
- Could you identify the main practical, ethical and legal issues facing Felicity? Which issue deserves priority in making a good decision on how to act in this case?
- Which conditions must be met by Felicity before it is justified for her to blow the whistle, i.e. make her suspicions publicly known, for instance via a newspaper?
- Why, do you think, are some employees hesitant to report ethical misconduct in their organisations? Does professional ethics principally require that employees always report suspected wrongdoing?
- What does professional ethics require managers to do in order to ensure dealing with whistle-blowing in a fair and just way? In addition, can you think of personal and professional skills that would be supportive of creating an organisational structure for whistle-blowing?

6.4 Managers' roles in ethical conduct

Jan-Willem Proper

6.4.1 Introduction to managerial roles in ethics

Many organisations currently struggle with questions about how to value and enhance ethics, and it is clear that managers play a crucial role in such discussions and carry a large amount of responsibility for ensuring organisationally ethical behaviour (Hooker, 1996; Kaptein, 2011a; 2011b). Two broad dimensions of organisational ethics can be discerned. 'Business ethics', on the one hand, focusses on how to behave ethically in a competitive environment, balancing corporate goals (e.g. profitability) with moral behaviours while contributing beneficially to society (Caroll and Shabana, 2010; Inoue and Lee, 2011). 'Professional ethics' or 'professional integrity', on the other hand, focusses on the moral attitudes and behaviours of managers and other organisational personnel and can also extend to an organisation's external partners (Clegg and Rhodes, 2006; Fryer, 2015).

Ethics and integrity are frequently viewed as properties of an individual, albeit as mediated by social values, beliefs, experience, culture and education. Yet organisations as entities are increasingly expected to demonstrate ethical behaviours, and the responsibility for such behaviours is vested in leaders and managers. Ethical behaviour in, and of, an organisation emanates from balancing tensions between what we might term the general and specific moral lives of managers (Kaptein, 2003; Paek and Chathoth, 2013). The general focus is on obligations that a manager has as a human being, as a person of integrity. When managers are confronted with a morally ambiguous situation the general response is to ask, 'what should I do as human being?' The specific focus arises out of membership of that category of workers called 'managers', who represent organisational integrity, and may also incorporate additional elements where a manager is also a member of a profession. Here ambiguity generates further questions such as 'what should I do as a professional?' and if there is a conflict between this and the response to 'what should I do as human being?' a third and obvious query arises – 'how should I resolve this?'

6.4.1.1 The ethical character of managers' roles and responsibilities

Usually a distinction is made between leaders and managers. The difference between them is that a leader, in essence, focuses on vision and change and sets directions, while a manager is more oriented towards stability and focuses on planning and results. Yet their roles often overlap in practice. Since both can be united in the same person, and a leader is essentially also a 'manager', the word 'manager' will be used to address both in what follows.

In general, managers have a wide diversity of functions and tasks in terms of roles and responsibilities. The responsibilities of a manager are connected to four essentials (Norman, 2019). *First*, planning involves awareness of challenges, including of issues related to ethics, and deciding where to take a company and selecting steps to get there. Managers re-evaluate their plans as conditions change and make adjustments as necessary. Planning involves allocating resources and accordingly has ethical dimensions. *Secondly*, in order to realise company aims, managers combine 'physical, human and financial resources'. They classify and assign activities to groups or individuals and coordinate the relationships of responsibility and authority within a context of codes of ethical conduct. *Third*, effective managers, in adopting a leadership role, both formally and informally, influence, motivate and communicate their perspectives to employees as well as supervising their work. This includes perspectives on implicit and explicit ethical codes. Managers therefore can influence and even, in theory, change ethical behaviour. Thus an effectively 'amoral organisation' (behaviour is not judged by right or wrong, good or bad, but by productivity and efficiency, for example) can develop to become an 'emergent ethical organisation' and ultimately an 'ethical organisation'. *Finally*, managers have a control function which involves checking whether the company's results match the aims that have been set, to be able to identify sources of deviation and to provide a corrective course of action. This includes measurement of the degree of an organisation's ethical success.

6.4.1.2 Managerial ethics, business and culture

Managerial ethics is about dealing with these four essentials. Managers have to develop their own posture and allocate resources that will enable the organisation to succeed in its business while contributing to a better understanding and establishment of ethical management practices. This is especially challenging in a situation of global interdependency where different cultures often have conflicting expectations of ethical behaviour, and it becomes increasingly difficult to balance such behaviour with organisations' other concerns – particularly, in the case of commercial organisations, the need to make a profit (Trevino and Brown, 2004). Furthermore, resistance to what is perceived as organisational and/or corporate indifference to ethical behaviour has often become highly organised at a global level and not least in areas such as environmentalism, ethical consumerism, product safety, employee safety and welfare, gender and other forms of equality, and poverty.

Managers have both reactive responsibilities, where it is clear when and how they have to take their responsibilities after a negative judgement, and proactive responsibilities, which involve determining the ethical standards to which their organisations should strive to adhere. Establishing the latter can be made more complex by considerations of relativism in cultural values, which challenge any notion of an absolute ethical code. In its crudest form, cultural relativism reminds us that different societies have different ethical beliefs deeply influenced by culture and that what is considered ethical in one culture may not be so considered elsewhere. It is tempting to condone or take advantage of organisational behaviours acceptable in one culture that would be viewed as inexcusable in others, particularly an organisation's 'home' culture. The crudest forms of cultural relativism imply that no single culturally bound moral or ethical code can be deemed superior or inferior to any other (see also Chapter 3). Nevertheless, globally emerging standards promoted by diverse organisations (e.g. the International Labour Organisation; the World Health Organisation; the International Chamber of Commerce), as well as public opinion, are placing increasing pressure on those who would take advantage of possibly harmful practices, however much tolerated these practices may be in certain cultures.

To partially elaborate on these points, in (especially) commercial organisations, business competition will drive managers to look for incentives to do business with overseas partners and suppliers. Although from a cost perspective this might make good business sense, it can also link companies to those elements in society they view as following unethical practices. For example, laws on labour conditions or environmental protection might not be quite as strict in countries where (parts of) a product is manufactured or a service is delivered, compared to where these products or services are consumed. Indeed, one factor contributing to the perception of many businesses as 'unethical' is the perception that 'offshoring' occurs precisely to achieve cost (reduction) advantages. At the same time, there are undoubtedly real instances of where it can be difficult for managers to track working conditions, when, for example, they do not directly engage with second-tier companies that sell to their suppliers.

The key question thus becomes to what extent managers can and should, in such collaborations, be aware of and responsible for unethical practices and their consequences. Here, it is important to acknowledge that an ethical stance need not always be viewed in terms of the avoidance of consumers' negative perceptions. It can also encourage positive associations. Thus, treating customers fairly and honestly can help build an organisation's reputation and brand awareness. Evidencing loyalty and care and a desire to manage in the best interests of customers and society by subscribing to values such as fair trade and practices that entail transparency has the potential to build consumer trust (Badhuri and Ha-Brookshire, 2011).

6.4.1.3 Enhancing organisational and managerial ethics

Given the challenges that managers face, how can they develop and enhance their personal ethics and the ethics of the organisation? The study of business ethics has, in recent decades, reinforced the conviction that businesses have a broad social responsibility as described, for example, in the Brundtland report (United Nations World Commission on Environment and Development (UN-WCED, 1987)). In line with this, the main ethical obligations of managers can be described under three equally important headings.

The *first* is the ethical generation of profit and wealth. Profit and wealth creation are not the same. For example, a case of speculation on land acquisition (especially one that merely 'stores' the land without any form of development) may yield a profit but diminish long-term wealth creation by obstructing the rational use of that land for other purposes that could create alternative forms of economic and social wealth. *Secondly*, for those organisations that create employment there are ethical pressures to ensure the payment of fair wages; the quality and safety of work; and the provision of opportunities to develop employee competences. *Finally*, there is the managerial contribution to social welfare and a sustainable environment. This can be created in different ways – from providing correct information on products and services, to sponsorship, charity or community-building, and also includes taking into account risks to ecological and health-related issues at both individual and global levels.

Ethical awareness of key issues as discussed in the preceding sections represents the primary stage in developing personal and organisational ethical standards (Trevino and Nelson, 2014). The next stage is to establish within an organisation a formal programme or code of ethics that is sufficiently robust to cope with the complexities faced by companies as they develop. Formal systems are intended to regulate and influence behaviour and should be constantly and consistently integrated within an organisation's culture. To achieve this requires organisation-wide understanding of moral imperatives – the what, why, when and how of ethical behaviour. All members of the organisation are the 'who', but managers have a particular responsibility to ensure understanding of a company's ethical culture and to promote ethical behaviour in a clear and consistent manner. Any such system of ethics must embrace concepts of accountability, consider rewards for 'good' behaviours and, of course, consider appropriate sanctions for negative ones. At the same time, it is important to note that unethical behaviour is unlikely to be curbed by formal regulatory systems alone. It demands managers of integrity who not only abide by the codes and laws, but who are also able to assess the ethical necessities and demands of complex situations and have the courage to act according to their own sets of values and also to what could take the ethical character of these situations to a higher level. To borrow a currently fashionable cliché: ethics need to be embedded in an organisation's DNA. How to achieve this is possibly the greatest current challenge facing organisations and their managers.

6.4.1.4 Conclusion

In the aftermath of recent scandals, questions of ethical management and the ethical behaviour of managers have gained more attention. Managers can be required to deal with great complexity in a fast-changing environment. The demands to contribute to the 'bottom line', to be visionary and to inspire and be creative can, as has been suggested, generate potential and actual ethical conflicts.

The ethical issues attendant on managerial decision-making are thus numerous and complex, and increasingly include global public opinion and the activities of diverse transnational organisations – including several representative organisations of business. There can be little doubt that organisational cultures, generally speaking, are at different stages of ethical and moral development. The alignment of shared values, norms and ethical policies and codes both within and between organisations remains, globally speaking, incomplete. A major encouragement to the development of managerial ethical behaviour remains the focus on the benefits of an organisation's financial performance, trust in its products and services, the effects on organisational image and its reputation of being regarded as behaving ethically. At the same time, legal regulation, where present, can serve to guide organisations towards permissible behaviour while discouraging negative practices (Laczniak and Naor, 1985). Within this vast field of moral demands the manager is the person who needs the wisdom to uphold both personal and organisational integrity and responsibility in such a way that neither of those values are jeopardised. This will be explored in the fictitious case below.

Case 6.4.2: Being ethical in the market of medical home products

Introduction: Selling uncertified batteries for medical equipment

Jacques is the general manager of a small and medium-sized enterprise, with its head office in Luxembourg. He works closely with the sales and marketing manager, Henry, and the purchasing manager, Xavier. They form the management team of the company. The company is specialised in medical equipment for use in the increasing market of home medical equipment. The company is constantly looking for new services and products in a very competitive marketplace. It not only has to compete with European suppliers, but also with the e-commerce direct-selling markets in Asia and the United States (US). One of the important components in the home medical equipment the company is selling is rechargeable batteries. These batteries need to comply with the standards of the International Electro-Technical Commission (IEC) – an organisation which, amongst other publications, produces guidelines and standards, for the performance and safety of the whole range of electro-technical equipment across the globe. The CEO, Jacques, visited a medical fair and discovered that most of the suppliers he was doing business with sold batteries

Professional ethics

that did not answer to the IEC standards. This means that the company itself sell uncertified batteries to its clients. He was quite upset by this and when back at the office, he called a meeting with Henry and Xavier in order to discuss the implications for the business.

Conflicting opinions

Jacques introduced the issue to his colleagues and stated that in a very competitive market it was not easy to find new suppliers who do sell IEC-certified batteries. In addition, the costs of cross-checking the updates of the regulation compliances would jeopardise the company's margins. Henry wondered what would happen to the market share and future of the company if these compliance issues became public. In addition, the company needed to be prepared to react to possible future allegations if it turned out that those batteries had put the lives of patients in danger. The market is very sensitive to misleading people that are in need of medical support. Xavier intervened and mentioned that, although no complaints had been filed up to that point, it would be unethical to keep on trading these batteries at the same time as assuring clients on the website that the safety of all its products and services is a top priority. He added that, in light of this discussion, it would be necessary to appoint an ethical compliance officer to make sure these issues would not arise in the future and to uphold the company's image as an honest and fair business.

Jacques got irritated by Xavier's comments and objected that he expected his competitors were in the same situation. To his knowledge, no formal complaints had been filed against them. In addition, Jacques said that he would not be surprised if the manufacturing facilities in the countries where the batteries were made were also failing to answer to the standards of safe working conditions and fair payment. So, why try to be ethical when the whole chain is unethical? Henry agreed with Jacques that the stakes were too high for the company, but added that the organisation would need to keep this quiet for the time being and at the same time gets its story right in case something went wrong in future. The company should stay sensitive to the developments in the market and be ready to take action when it was opportune. But it would just be too detrimental for the company to act right now. Xavier shook his head and left the room.

Questions for discussion

- It is clear from the case that Jacques, Henry and Xavier have different views and ethical principles on how the company should react to the dilemma. Could you describe the way they see their respective managerial roles? Are those roles different from their ethical obligations?
- In solving the dilemma, could you identity the ethical principles that each of these three managers applied? Whose principles, do you think, would

(continued)

> **Case 6.4.2: Being ethical in the market of medical home products (*continued*)**
>
> solve the dilemma best? Is there a better solution than those that these gentlemen proposed? Give reasons for your answer.
> - Could Henry's apparent distinction between a short- and a long-term scenario add to solving this dilemma in a satisfactory way?
> - Integrity is widely regarded as the core characteristic of a manager. How could integrity be made visible in the professional behaviour of these three gentlemen in their roles as a CEO, a sales and marketing manager, and a purchasing manager?
> - Is Xavier's proposal to appoint an ethical compliance officer a realistic option for solving the dilemma? Why? What does this say about managerial responsibility?

6.5 Concluding thoughts

Historically speaking, a profession is seen as a kind of work that is regarded a service to the community and which is underpinned by a body of knowledge and skills, an acknowledged education, codes of conduct and legal acknowledgement. Yet the definition has been broadened over time to encompass any kind of work in which a person uses his/her knowledge to, together with colleagues, deliver a specific service to clients or customers. The focus has turned towards professionalism, depicting an attitude which puts service above gain, and behaviour that is proper and respectful towards the client, the general public and the company itself. Professional ethics, then, entails employees and managers, working at all levels of the organisation and fulfilling different roles, acting from both personal and professional values such as competence, honesty, integrity, respect, loyalty, responsibility and trustworthiness on behalf of the well-being or interests of all stakeholders of the organisation. Responsibility and integrity are often seen as the central values of professional behaviour (see also Chapter 8).

Further reading

Edwards, A. (2010). *Being an Expert Professional Practitioner: The Relational Turn in Expertise.* London/New York: Springer.

Gilbert, J. (2016). *Ethics for Managers: Philosophical Foundations and Business Realities* (2nd ed.). New York/London: Routledge.

Martin, C., Vaught, W. and Solomon, R. (Eds.) (2010). *Ethics across the Professions: A Reader for Professional Ethics.* New York/Oxford: Oxford University Press.

Rendtorff, J.D. (Ed.) (2017). *Perspectives on the Philosophy of Management and Business Ethics: Including a Special Section on Business and Human Rights.* New York/London: Springer.

References

Ambedkar, B.R. (n.d.). B. R. Ambedkar Quotes. In *BrainyQuote.com*. Retrieved 3 September 2015 from http://www.brainyquote.com/quotes/quotes/b/brambedk408662.html#73qEJWQucRrdvlOl.99

Bateman, C. (2014). *Chaos Ethics*. Winchester, UK: Zero Books.

Bhaduri, G. and Ha-Brookshire, J.E. (2011). Do Transparent Business Practises Pay? Exploration of Transparency and Consumer Purchase Intention. *Clothing and Research Textiles Journal*, 29(2): 135–149.

Broughton, P.D. (2008). *What They Teach You At Harvard Business School: My Two Years Inside the Cauldron of Capitalism*. London: Viking.

Caroll, A. B. and Shabana, K. M. (2010). The Business Case for Corporate Social Responsibility: A Review of Concepts, Research and Practice. *International Journal of Management Reviews*, 12: 85–105.

Churchill, W. (n.d.). Winston Churchill Quotes. In *BrainyQuote.com*. Retrieved 14 March 2019 from https://www.brainyquote.com/quotes/winston_churchill_384133.

Clegg, S. and Rhodes, C. (2006). *Management Ethics: Contemporary Contexts*. New York: Routledge.

Dickens, C. (1853 [2003]). *Bleak House*. Harmondsworth: Penguin.

Duska, R. (2015). Acting Ethically Is Not Always Easy – Some Tough Questions for Estate Planners. *Journal of Financial Service Professionals*, 69: 22–25.

Einstein, A. (n.d.). Albert Einstein Quotes. In *BrainyQuote.com*. Retrieved 30 June 2017 from https://www.brainyquote.com/quotes/quotes/a/alberteins125365.html.

Friedman, M. (1970). The Social Responsibility of Business is to Increase Its Profits. *New York Times Magazine*, September 13: 32–33 and 122–124.

Fryer, M. (2015). *Ethics Theory: Business Practice*. London: Sage.

Ghiselli, R. F. (1999). The Ethical Inclination of Foodservice Managers and Hospitality Students. *Journal of Hospitality and Tourism Education*, 11: 92–98.

Ghoshal, S. (2005). Bad Management Theories Are Destroying Good Management Practices. *Academy of Management Learning and Education*, 4: 75–91.

Gilmore, J.H. and Pine, B.J. (2007). *Authenticity: What Consumers Really Want*. Boston, MA: Harvard Business School Press.

Go, F. and Pine, R. (1995). *Globalization Strategy in the Hotel Industry*. London: Routledge.

Gray, J. (2008). *Black Mass: Apocalyptic Religion and the Death of Utopia*. London: Penguin Books.

Hall, J. (2013, 6 August). They Won't Be Lovin' It: McDonald's Admits 90% of Employees Are on Zero-Hours Contracts Without Guaranteed Work or a Stable Income. In *The Independent*. Retrieved 12 August, 2014, from http://www.independent.co.uk/news/uk/home-news/they-wont-be-lovin-it-mcdonalds-admits-90-of-employees-are-on-zerohours-contracts-without-guaranteed-work-or-a-stable-income-8747986.html.

Heseltine, M. (n.d.). Quoted in 'Business Ethics Quotes'. In *12Manage: The Executive Fast Track*. Retrieved 3 September 2015 from http://www.12manage.com/quotes_er.html.

Hickman, M., Usborne, S. and Grice, A. (2008, 15 July). Revealed: How the Restaurant Chains Pocket Your Tips. *The Independent*. Retrieved 15 September 2013 from http://www.independent.co.uk/news/uk/home-news/revealed-how-the-restaurant-chains-pocket-your-tips-867634.html.

Hoffman, W.M. and Schwartz, M.S. (2015). The Morality of Whistle Blowing: A Commentary on Richard T. De George. *Journal of Business Ethics*, 127: 771–781.

Hooker, J.N. (1996). Toward Professional Ethics in Business. Pittsburgh, PA: Carnegie Mellon University. Retrieved 10 March, 2019, from http://public.tepper.cmu.edu/ethics/bizethic.pdf.

Inoue, Y. and Lee, S. (2011). Effects of Different Dimensions of Corporate Social Responsibility and Corporate Financial Performance in Tourism-Related Industries. *Tourism Management*, 32: 790–804.

Kaptein, M. (2003). The Diamond of Managerial Integrity. *European Management Journal*, 21: 99–108.

Kaptein, M. (2011a). Understanding Unethical Behaviour by Unravelling Ethical Culture. *Human Relations*, 64: 843–869.

Kaptein, M. (2011b). Towards Effective Codes: Testing the Relationship with Unethical Behaviour. *Journal of Business Ethics*, 99: 233–251.

Khurana, R. and Nohria, N. (2008). It's Time to Make Management a True Profession. *Harvard Business Review*, 86(10): 70–77.

Laczniak, G.R. and Noar, J. (1985). Global Ethics: Wrestling with Corporate Conscience. *Business*, July–September, 3–10.

Lee, Y-K., Choi, J., Moon, B-Y. and Babin, B. J. (2014). Codes of Ethics, Corporate Philanthropy, and Employee Responses. *International Journal of Hospitality Management*, 39: 97–106.

Liebermann, K. and Nissen, B. (2013). *Ethics in the Hospitality and Tourism Industry* (2nd ed.). Lansing, MI: Educational Institute of the American Hotel and Lodging Association.

MacDonald, K. M. (1995). *The Sociology of the Professions*. London: Sage.

MacGregor, J. and Stuebs, M. (2014). Whistle While You Work: Whistle Blowing in the Presence of Competing Incentives and Pressures. *Accounting Perspectives*, 13: 309–324.

Machiavelli, N. (2008 [1515]). *The Prince* (Trans. P. Bondanella). Oxford: Oxford University Press.

Norman, L. (2019). What are the Four Basic Functions That Make Up the Management Process? *Chron*. Retrieved 10 March 2019 from https://smallbusiness.chron.com/four-basic-functions-make-up-management-process-23852.html.

Paek, S. and Chathoth, P. K. (2013). Multiple Levels of Ethics Management: A Case of Airline and Hotel Firms. *Tourism Planning and Development*, 10: 388–415.

Paeth, S.R. (2013). The Responsibility to Lie and the Obligation to Report: Bonhoeffer's "What Does it Mean to Tell the Truth?" and the Ethics of Whistle Blowing. *Journal of Business Ethics*, 112: 559–566.

Park, H., Rehg, M.T. and Lee, D. (2005). The Influence of Confucian Ethics and Collectivism on Whistle Blowing Intentions: A Study of South Korean Public Employees. *Journal of Business Ethics*, 58: 387–403.

Phillips, M. (2009, 9 November). Goldman Sachs' Blankfein on Banking: Doing God's Work. *The Wall Street Journal*. Retrieved 10 July 2015, from https://blogs.wsj.com/marketbeat/2009/11/09/goldman-sachs-blankfein-on-banking-doing-gods-work/.

Polman, L. (2010). *War Games: The Story of Aid and War in Modern Times* (Trans. L. Waters). London: Viking.

Profession. (n.d.). In *Wikipedia*. Retrieved 14 March 2019 from http://en.wikipedia.org/wiki/Profession.

Roddick, A. (n.d.). Quoted in 'Business Ethics Quotes.' In *12Manage: The Executive Fast Track*. Retrieved 3 September 2015 from http://www.12manage.com/quotes_er.html.

Sandel, M. (2012). *What Money Can't Buy: The Moral Limits of Markets*. London: Penguin.

Swirski, P. (2007). *Of Literature and Knowledge: Explorations in Narrative Thought Experiments, Evolution and Game Theory*. Abingdon, UK: Routledge.

Trevino, L.K. and Brown, M.E. (2004). Managing to Be Ethical: Debunking Five Business Ethics Myths. *Academy of Management Perspectives*, 18: 69–81.

Trevino, K. and Nelson, K. (2014). *Managing Business Ethics: Straight Talk About How To Do It Right* (6th ed.). New York: Wiley.

UN-WCD. (1987). *Report of the World Commission on Environment and Development: Our Common Future.* Retrieved 1 June 2016 from www.un-documents.net/our-common-future.pdf.

Wilkinson, R. and Pickett, K. (2010). *The Spirit-Level: Why Equality is Better for Everyone.* London: Penguin Books.

Williams, S., Adam-Smith, D. and Norris, G. (2004). Remuneration Practices in the UK Hospitality Industry in the Age of the National Minimum Wage. *The Service Industries Journal,* 24: 171–186.

Wood, R. C. (2015). *Hospitality Management: A Brief Introduction.* London: Sage.

Wright, F.L. (n.d.). Frank Lloyd Wright Quotes. In *BrainyQuote.com.* Retrieved 30 June 2017 from https://www.brainyquote.com/quotes/quotes/f/franklloyd127699.html.

Chapter 7

Organisational ethics

Celiane Camargo-Borges, Liliya Terzieva,
Jalal Atai, Johan Bouwer and Mata Haggis

7.1 Introduction to organisational ethics

Celiane Camargo-Borges

7.1.1 The changing world and implications for organisational ethics

The present section argues that the classical theories of organisational ethics, that often provide a set of universal codes and normative prescriptions about how organisations should operate and how professionals should behave in their daily working life, are not up to date with the needs and demands presented by contemporary society and organisations.

Globalisation and the technological revolution, amongst other phenomena, are transforming the global economy in that there is less need for manufacturing organisations. Instead, there is an expansion of digitalised and interconnected organisations, which in turn, generate new institutional demands (Camargo-Borges and Rasera, 2013). In this transition, such social-technological advancements provoke new forms of practice, and new interactional and behavioural expectations. In addition, these new patterns of relating call into question the existing foundational ethical rules. This has created a clash between theorising about what organisations and people should do and what is really happening within the ever-changing organisational contexts.

The classical theories of organisational ethics, also called prescriptive ethics (Kotze, 2002), are based on general laws, that emerged within the classical Western tradition. Prescriptive ethics places major emphasis on the individual as the main decision-maker and the responsible agent for what happens in organisations (Kotze, 2002). Such approaches are in danger of becoming obsolete, since their understanding of ethics seems close to the model that views organisations as machines (Suchman, 2011; Gergen, 2016). This 'machine' metaphor has its roots in the Industrial Revolution, when factories offered the model for prediction and control. The working style of an organisation as a machine has been investigated by many authors and presupposes an organisation that is taken as a closed system, with a linear way of performing. It is also supportive of a workplace that subscribes to a command-and-control approach, where the leadership model is hierarchical and focussed on one person (the boss) and where ideas flow from the top (experts) down to those who should operationalise them. Looking at an organisation as a closed system centralises the physical space, so that the roles and tasks of facilities and departments are emphasised over people and their relationships. According to Suchman (2011), this approach to organisations is not aligned with the latest needs of our fast-changing world.

Suchman (2011) suggests a shift from looking at an organisation as an entity (e.g., a physical place) to looking at it as a conversation. Viewing an organisation as a conversation opens us to embrace the notion that such an entity is a complex system in which people are in constant interaction. It is a place in which the way professionals perceive themselves, their roles and their teams will directly affect and create the reality of the organisation.

7.1.2 Organisations as open complex systems

An organisation, according to Ford (1999), is a network of conversations, as both the medium and product of reality. Change in an organisation therefore starts with change in conversations, in how people behave, how they relate, how they are responsive and how they address each other. New conversational realities will produce new meanings, which in turn open up opportunities for new actions. According to Ford (1999) the benefit of embracing organisations as a network of conversations is that it brings more alignment and therefore more investment in the collective. Within this approach, people are at the centre of the organisation and change is an outcome of coordinated conversations.

To understand the organisation as a network of conversations is to embrace it as an open complex system. As an open system, the organisation is seen as a living human construction whose focus is not on keeping order and structure but embracing the dynamics between structure, relationships, and their full complexity.

An organisation as a complex open system invites one to look at situated organisational practice and also to explore the expectations and values that participants bring to a specific context. In the context of ethics, this means that everyone should be engaged in a certain organisational matter. This gives people the opportunity to not only participate in the discussion of a particular norm (by providing their own opinion), but also to have a better understanding of the process itself whereby decisions are made and why certain norms are sustained. Furthermore, inclusive decision-making often fosters broad-based understanding and commitment.

This approach invites one to understand ethics from a relational perspective and it shifts members' stance from a prescriptive ethic, in which protocols and universal codes define the organisational behaviour, to an ethic of responsivity, which entails awareness and sensitivity towards the context, to what people talk about and to the values at stake in a particular case.

7.1.3 Relational ethics

A relational ethic draws on systems thinking and relational theories, such as social constructionism, embracing the perspectives of people as meaning makers and inescapable participants of a larger system (Haslebo and Haslebo, 2012). This orientation is concerned with the ways in which knowledge is historically situated and embedded in cultural values and practices (Gergen and Gergen, 2004; Gergen and Gergen, 2012). That means that the understanding of good and bad is not derived from the world itself, but from our immersion within a tradition of cultural practices of which the production is an outcome of interactive exchanges amongst people in their relational processes (Gergen, 2009). In simple words, meaning emerges in what people do together. According to social constructionism, the validity and sustainability of knowledge is maintained throughout time not by its empirical truth but within social processes (Burr, 2015). That means that people keep acknowledging and accepting what they have created through history within their cultural and interactive practices. Thus, according to social constructionism, there is a need to focus on what people do together since this is the source of change and maintenance of organisational behaviour patterns, not abstract ethical codes.

According to social constructionist epistemology, ethics is not universal in a foundational sense. Rather, ethics is constructed in very specific historical, political and social moments (Haslebo and Haslebo, 2012). If this epistemological assumption is embraced, it means that one starts to acknowledge that there are always alternatives to any given ethical stance. This is not to claim that 'anything goes', but to note that what is 'ethical' is always tied to the particular interactive moment and requires participants to coordinate their actions in such a way that any given ethic is maintained. Therefore, if participants shift their form of action, it is likely that an alternative – situationally crafted – ethic will emerge (McNamee, 2015). In other words, any situation could change depending on how people, in their interaction, might construct local contextual ethics. Social construction therefore moves ethics to a new centrality, as a relational endeavour that is not timeless, but formulated in a specific context, which invites a close examination of this context.

On the opposite spectrum of relational ethics is prescriptive ethics. Haslebo and Haslebo (2012) describe prescriptive ethics as 'common-sense morality' suggesting that, with this approach, 'we often see the world in black and white, opposites, conflicts, and good versus bad, and we hold each other to account, make others see the error of their ways, assign guilt and blame – all in the hope of making other people wiser and better human beings' (Haslebo and Haslebo, 2012: 28). This prescriptive approach to ethics creates, as the authors suggest, isolation because all is summarised into prizing, blaming and individual responsibility for actions. A sense of organisational coherence, team-collaboration and trust is lost.

The relational approach to ethics can be very powerful in creating engagement in organisations. It invites an open-mindedness in examining different assumptions and invites everyone to question their own assumptions, thereby bringing awareness to their own biases (Haslebo and Haslebo, 2012). McNamee (2015) goes a step further by suggesting that a relational ethic can direct people's attention towards creating opportunities for different conversations, which search for local coherence and local values and avoid abstract judgements. This leads to the intriguing question: '(...) can we attempt to coordinate multiple moral orders and imagine a future that is relationally sensitive?' (McNamee, 2015: 432).

7.1.4 Implications for practice

Organisational ethics taken from a relational perspective has certain implications for practical behaviour. That means that embracing this kind of ethics will trigger conversations, but also function as a guideline for enacting the possibility for people to work together.

In advocating a movement from theorising to practising ethics, McNamee (2016) recommends the work of John Shotter. According to Shotter, modernist culture aspires to search for universals, for the truth. Doing so invites professionals to adopt what Shotter calls 'aboutness' thinking. Aboutness thinking is a way of being in the world that positions individuals in opposition to one another – as the 'other'. The 'other' becomes an object 'about' whom one makes claims, based on subjective observations. As an alternative, Shotter proposes to move into what he calls 'withness' thinking. Withness thinking presupposes the coordination of activities together with others and the environment. This coordination enhances tolerance of difference and, as a by-product, it is more likely that engagement can transpire. In more specific terms, participants explore organisational topics together in order to collectively generate meaning, ultimately engendering new knowledge and actions. There is an invitation to negotiate new forms of understanding.

How can this be done? There is a concept from the creative industries that could be useful as a practical resource for charting a relational ethic: co-creation. Co-creation is a buzzword in the creative industries. Many authors have argued that, in times of a globalised interconnected society, value co-creation needs to take place at the strategic level of an organisation and needs to be at the centre of what employees should learn when creating value together (Lusch, 2007; Vargo and Lusch, 2008; Prahalad and Ramaswamy, 2004). Co-creation stresses that human beings are co-creators of life and society. It is therefore more than a concept. It is a resource, which can help to activate ethics as an activity (it is a form of *practice itself*), not simply a set of codes and norms. As a practice, it is a creative tool that brings people together in finding common ground and in creating a collective project, idea, or intervention in an organisation (Camargo-Borges and Rasera, 2013). In addition: as a resource, co-creation also focuses on what people are doing together and how this makes sense to them. Everyone is engaged in the process of reflecting. In co-creation, questions and reflections are the core elements of action. Reflective practices encourage employees to reflect on their own actions and perspectives, and also invite them to think of their own professional role in their organisation (Schön, 1983).

The art of asking questions is also at stake. In order to stimulate co-creation in practice, one needs to invite people to sit together and ask open, reflexive and imaginative questions in order to expand understanding and elicit different perspectives on the same matter. Questions encourage employees to expand their thinking and to examine multiple descriptions of one single situation, thereby amplifying the possibilities for imagining and co-creating multiple solutions. Asking questions is a good way to problematise assumptions. Questions such as 'whose standards are we using in judging this case?' become critically useful. Being curious and asking questions can encourage participants to consciously draw upon new discourses that, in turn, contribute to a greater understanding. Without curiosity and questioning, participants remain exclusively focussed on the established understanding or agreement. Furthermore, it is important to also consider (prior to asking) whether the manner in which questions are asked will lead to the creation of a more useful interaction in the organisation. One can also ask reflexive questions such as, 'is my behaviour enabling the organisation to flourish? Is my behaviour in this specific situation respectful and mindful of others?' Furthermore, the distribution of authority and responsibility also enables co-creation, which, in turn, increases organisational capacity and produces more bottom-line results.

Co-creation, as a resource for ethical action, can be viewed as an attempt to achieve coordinated respect through exercising other forms of interaction on a given topic. When people become co-designers of something, they become responsible for what they create, and engagement with the creation and each other is more likely. Co-creation as a practice can help guide an ethical posture in organisations by inviting the organisation and its members to come together and examine their situated ethics with a more collaborative stance, generating relationally responsible actions (McNamee and Gergen, 1999), which will, in turn, enhance forms of interchange and meaningful action.

In situations where adversities are high and topics are too sensitive, it is advisable to invite individuals who have different perspectives and opinions to first come together and envision in advance a workable communication format that will govern the co-creation interaction. That means to first conduct some individual interviews to understand better what is at stake and how sensitive a topic is – before starting. Only after having done this preparation will the way be clear to come together and respectfully co-create.

7.1.5 In conclusion

Times are changing rapidly, and organisations are confronted with challenges that have never before been predicted or expected. Organisational ethics, as it is mainly practised today, needs to adapt in order to properly address the demands of the contemporary world. This chapter offers an alternative approach to ethics – a relational ethic – which is quite different from traditional, prescriptive ethics. As articulated above, traditional, prescriptive ethics often focus on decontextualised morals and codes, thereby leaving no opportunity for a practical, *situated* ethics.

The rationale here is not to dismiss the idea of professional codes of conduct and professional ethics. These elements are quintessential building blocks in producing a consistent professional practice, helping organisations to protect their people and clients. The invitation here, inspired by relational theories such as social constructionism, is to challenge the universal taken-for-granted formats where one size fits all and, instead, move into a more dynamic, practical approach to ethics. Organisational ethical codes can be very important but should not overrule locally crafted moral orders and violate the responsivity and the local ethics that are very much a part of an organisation's daily life.

Co-creation is one approach from the creative industries that could be useful in rethinking the understanding of ethical practices. As a practical tool it takes a relational and practical orientation to ethics, and invites a reflective approach, which entails asking unsettling questions such as 'Whose codes or ways of being are these anyway?', 'Who benefits from having these specific guidelines in practice?', 'Who gets excluded from the process?' and 'What other ways of looking at this could be useful for the organisation?'

According to social construction, ethics is a relational phenomenon that is co-created and institutionalised in everyday patterns of communication. Thus, it can be deconstructed through reflection and curious questioning, allowing participants to reconstruct an ethic that is sensitive to and aligned with the contemporary demands presented. Relational ethics therefore invites responsiveness to the other and opens an organisational stance that offers new forms of action, thereby making possible the creation of new meaning and new forms of understanding. This, in turn, engages participants to act upon what is needed, together.

In the remainder of this chapter, three discussions with aligned cases, reflecting moral issues and ethical dilemmas, are presented. These stories demonstrate how everyday events present organisational challenges and can be handled from different perspectives and approaches. The first case is about leadership – a topic that has provoked much academic research over time. Terzieva introduces a case on the role of a director of a library in the Netherlands who urgently needs to initiate change in the organisation while at the same time there is resistance from the employees to changes in what they feel their roles to be. The case introduces the concept of dynamic leadership proposing an innovative way to lead in complex and continuously changing times, showing how a leader can embrace strategic directions that do not impose on the employees but on the contrary, co-create with them, so that at the end everyone can claim ownership on what is being proposed. Secondly, Atai and Bouwer discuss the relationship between good corporate governance and fraud, and argue that a company should have effective internal control mechanisms in place in order to prevent internal fraudulent behaviour. They demonstrate in their case how the Fraud Triangle could help to deter fraud in the front office of a Bangalore hotel. The third discussion revolves around the theme of responsible business in the video-game industry. Haggis mainly focusses on the working conditions under which game designers function. His case study elaborates on the ethics of employer responsibilities.

7.2 Effective leadership in the context of libraries

Liliya Terzieva

7.2.1 Introduction to effective leadership

7.2.1.1 *Leadership theories in the evolution and diffusion of effective leadership*

Research shows that various approaches to and definitions of leadership exist. The following paragraphs aim to introduce an overview of existing understandings of leadership and their development.

In terms of the overall development of research in this area, leadership was first understood as a quality individuals were born with, referring to the trait theory (Colbert et al., 2012). Over the course of time, researchers focussed more on mental traits like intelligence, charisma, dominance and decisiveness, but this theory did not satisfy the critics, because people without leadership positions could also have these traits (Stanislavov and Ivanov, 2014).

More recently, academia has concentrated on behavioural theory (Conger and Kanungo, 1987), which focusses on the way things are done and suggests that leaders can be trained. This theory elaborates on Kurt Lewin's theory of the three leadership styles: autocratic, democratic and laissez-faire leadership behaviour (Lewin, Lippitt and White, 1939). The distinction drawn by Lewin was in fact the starting point for further research oriented towards what defines effective and ineffective leadership, which has led to distinctions being made between styles such as 'task-oriented', 'relations-oriented' and 'participative' leadership (Yukl, 2010: 72–74; 520–521; 87–94). In the 1960s, researchers coined the distinction between 'need for power', 'need for affiliation' and 'need for achievement' (McClelland and Burnham, 1976: 247–270).

During the third stage of leadership research, scientists set their focus on situational and context-based leadership variations and styles; this is known as the contingency theory (Fiedler, 1967). In this view, leadership is seen as being more flexible, meaning that different leadership styles are applied at different times depending on the context. The theory suggests that leadership is not a fixed series of characteristics that can be transposed into different contexts. Fiedler (1967) highlights that leaders change their behaviour according to the situation they are facing and for their personal benefit. Hersey and Blanchard (1969) took leadership science further, developing a theory which supports the view that leaders need to estimate the maturity of their followers and, based on that, adapt their leadership style. This is called the situational theory. The fundamental underpinning of the situational leadership theory is that there is no single 'best' style of leadership. Effective leadership is task-relevant, and the most successful leaders are those who adapt their leadership style to the maturity of the individual or a group they attempt to lead or influence, thereby expressing 'the capacity to set high but attainable goals, willingness and ability to take responsibility for the task, and relevant education and/ or experience for the task' (Hersey and Blanchard, 1972: 50). Effective leadership varies, not only with the person or group that is being influenced, but also don the task, job or function that needs to be accomplished.

In 1978, Burns took a further step, publishing his theory about transformational leadership, which proposed that leaders have the competence to transfer a vision that inspires others and thereby fosters their motivation and moral values. Bass (1985: 31) further built on the transformational leadership theory by articulating the four main aspects of 'inspiration', 'charisma', 'intellectual stimulation' and 'consideration'. Transformational leadership is often compared to the transactional theory of leadership, which focuses on the management of an organisation, procedures and efficiency and working rules and contracts, as well as managing current issues and problems. In comparison to transformational leadership, transactional leadership is highly focussed on hard factors, and neglects, for example, an issue like intrinsic motivation. It is therefore only partially relevant in today's culture.

Alongside the developments in leadership, research has also focussed on intelligence and different kinds of thinking, which add up to leadership effectiveness (Stanislavov and Ivanov, 2014). Edward Thorndike differentiated between mechanical, social and abstract intelligence (Thorndike, 1921). Mayer and Salovey

(1997) worked on the above concepts and developed the framework of 'emotional intelligence'. Stanislavov and Ivanov (2014) further elaborated on this, taking into account the recognition of emotions, its application in facilitating thinking processes, and the understanding of emotions and how to use them positively for personal growth. Goleman was the first researcher who linked 'emotional intelligence' to leadership efficiency and the work-related environment (1995). In his view, 'emotional intelligence' can lead to highly beneficial performances and a higher level of effective leadership.

Goleman also defined the framework of the six leadership styles, which he referred to as the coaching, affiliative, democratic, pace-setting, coercive and authoritarian leadership styles (Goleman, 2000). He holds that in order for leadership to be effective, at least four styles should be used, depending on the context and setting (Goleman, 2000). Furthermore, Goleman's position gave room for other leadership styles, such as spiritual, ethical and authentic leadership. All the emerging leadership types described above follow the idea that aspects such as integrity, rationality, values and characters, morals and ethics should be included as part of leadership. Later on, Killian (2007: 3) focussed on the assumption that leadership increasingly draws on the leader's personal characteristics. His research therefore encompasses aspects such as:

- Authenticity and ethics in leadership.
- Emotional bonds in relationship and how to sustain these.
- Different thinking styles of leaders.
- Leading a diversity of people.
- Leading staff regardless of their geographic location.
- Leading staff in changing times.

Within Bouwer's (1971) research, the two identities of a leader, the professional and the personal, are explored. The *professional* identity is described as an open-minded authority who is unbiased in his/her judgement. It also encompasses a critical and creative imagination and taking responsibility for others and the job (Bouwer, 1971). The *personal* identity of a leader regards the surrounding context: it explores spiritual growth and cognition, and considers feelings and differences in behaviour. According to Bouwer (1971), both identities partly overlap and can be integrated in one person.

The most recent developments in leadership take the theory of complexity into consideration. They propose a new type of effective leadership, namely dynamical leadership (Quade and Holladay, 2010). Dynamical leadership acknowledges the existence of complex adaptive systems and therefore builds upon the adaptive capacity model, proposing a way in which organisations can be led in complex and continuously changing times. Quade and Holladay refer to complex adaptive systems 'as a group of semi-autonomous agents interacting in interdependent ways such that they create system-wide patterns' (2010: 30), and which, in turn, influence the behaviour of agents within the system. Semi-autonomous agents are people, who have the freedom of making choices and the freedom to interact however they like. Furthermore, interdependent agents' actions initiate reactions, which depend on one another and therefore pave the way for system-wide patterns, which are repeated, connected and observable. They impact on overall behaviour as well as the actions taken by the individuals within a system (Quade and Holladay, 2010). Over time, this repeated behaviour and actions develops into a pattern of expectations, norms and even practices. Quade and Holladay (2010) claim that leaders, being aware of complex adaptive systems, understand that they cannot control or estimate patterns. However, they have the ability to recognise patterns of behaviour for setting up strategies influencing those organisational patterns in order to achieve adaptation, sustainability and effectiveness. To understand the model of adaptive capacity, the following three questions need to be tackled (Quade and Holladay, 2010):

- What makes an adaptive leader?
- What is important in the work?
- How are resources and information shared?

One of the most significant challenges for leaders within organisations is to prepare that organisation for the future, thereby orchestrating interventions for initiating change and for strategically implementing it (Battilana et al., 2010). Battilana studies task-oriented and person-oriented behaviour. He states that task-oriented behaviour is represented through organisational structure, design and control, and also through routines aiming at following the organisational goals and changing developments (Battilana et al., 2010). With regard to person-oriented behaviour, aspects like interaction, collaboration, a social and supportive climate and equal treatment are represented throughout the workforce. In particular, the above-mentioned intrapersonal qualities are highly important, as they create further motivation for leaders and also teach them how to act in a leadership position (Battilana et al., 2010).

Considering the various different types of leadership styles (and the ways in which they have developed), it can be stated that in general the most relevant type of leadership will be the one that best fits the organisation itself. However, when one focusses on today's changing society and the complexity that comes with it – especially with regard to the topic of cultural change – complementary recommendations have to be made that such leadership should also:

- Be participative (meaning that it co-creates, incorporating people's ideas, energy, talents and criticism).
- Be systemic (avoiding automatic or mechanical procedures of work allocation).
- Be representative of emergent leadership *behaviour* (embracing uncertainty instead of ignoring it and actively working with it).

7.2.1.2 The translation of effective leadership to the creative industries' sector

Modern-day creative industries operate in a turbulent environment with factors that are beyond their control. They operate in a highly competitive landscape (O'Connor, 2014) that is part of a realm defined as 'world 2.0' (Karakas, 2009: 23–30). In this context, effective leadership becomes more and more crucial for an organisation's survival. Karakas describes this world as:

An interactive, hyper-connected, immersive, virtual, digital online ecosystem or mega-platform where users create and share knowledge, innovate and collaborate together, have fun and entertainment, interact, network or connect with each other, design new products or buy and sell merchandise, connect and communicate globally with mobile devices, write reflection blogs, share their photos, podcast their presentations or make creative films, develop projects, and express themselves to the world. (2009: 25)

The above shift in the world goes hand in hand with the trend of 'digital natives'. Digital natives is Prensky's (2001: 1) term for people that were born in a digital world (after the year 1980). They work in a different way than those who were born before the digital age. 'Digital natives have grown up with internet access and depend heavily on mobile devices, are heavy consumers of social networking services, consider speed to be amongst the most important characteristics of digital products and services, and multitask across devices and between work and entertainment' (Prensky, 2001: 2). To fulfil the needs and expectations of digital natives, creative industries need to adapt their services. But even though these industries tend to embrace technology to its fullest potential, it has to be noted that the consumer still needs physical encounters with either the creative people or other consumers to feel part of a community. This complex aspect in particular has to be addressed in the leadership model applied within the creative sector.

Another shift in the direct environment of creative industries and the way they are being led is the importance of networking, stimulated by modern communication techniques. Creative industries' organisations have more and more transformed into relational businesses. These new relationships and collaboration need to contribute to the innovation of the organisation itself as well as to its partnership network. In his article Karakas explains how 'collaboration', 'connectivity', 'convergence' and 'community' are considered to be four of the five important shifts in world 2.0 – especially when it comes to creative industries and the call for reframing their role in relation to business (2009: 28). The other shift he mentions is 'creativity', which is the core element of the creative industries in terms of their meaning and understanding. Creativity is actually becoming more important in business platforms. Ed Catmull (2008), for example, refers in his article to the way a big company endorses creativity and what it means for a large number of people to work together within the framework of a creative process. He refers to this process as 'collective creativity' (Catmull, 2008: 64–72). The importance of collective creativity is also stated by Marion and Uhl-Bien, who argue that people who are encouraged to innovate and network produce far more than do single individuals by themselves. This, therefore, has to be the basis for the new type of leadership creative industries are now tending to adopt (2001). This point will be demonstrated by the case in the next section.

The case looks into the role libraries play in today's society. It explores their reframed nature as multifunctional leisure organisations and investigates how leadership within libraries carry out this logical transformation. The case unfolds the dilemmas an 'ethical leader' faces when networking with stakeholders; when applying the concept 'from collection to connection' in practice; and with 'translating creativity' in the daily interactions with his/her colleagues/employees and customers.

Case 7.2.2: Effective leadership in the library

Introduction: Strategies for library survival

In order to survive, libraries today need to come up with creative strategies towards funding and stakeholder interaction, which at the same time demands a new type of effective leadership. In doing so, the director of a library in North Brabant (Netherlands), a very dynamical leader, decided to implement the following two strategic interventions:

- Reframe the roles of the librarians as networkers and, in order to increase new funding sources and raise more awareness, ask them to approach existing and new stakeholders by using presentations and organising meetings and special visits.
- Open up the library for new initiatives such as 'joint book (themed) reading sessions', '3-D printing (Maker-clubs)'; 'school interaction'; 'business workshops', 'senior expert sessions', 'inter-generational expeditions', etc., which required both the management and the librarians to completely change their mindset, behaviour and attitudes.

Neither strategic direction was imposed on the employees but, on the contrary, they were shared, discussed and even further developed together with the employees. The purpose was that everyone would be able to claim ownership of what had been proposed, and that collective creativity could emerge in the end.

Resistance and acceptance

As a result of the strategic process that had been introduced, most of the employees showed resistance to the changes. Several even stated: 'we have been working here for more than 20 years and have educated ourselves to be knowledgeable about the books and collections that we have. People need to come to us and not the other way round. We are not salesmen and cannot humiliate ourselves to go to our partners and ask for money!'

However, several of the recently employed librarians – the youngest were between 25 and 35 years old – said the following: 'we actually do not find the strategy bad at all since we have difficulties in explaining to our friends and stakeholders why our library exists and how it contributes to society. We need to start opening up and searching for our new future. Of course we need to be the ones showing the value of what we do, even if it means that we can no longer sit in front of the computer or in the library itself all day!'

The schools as well as some of the business organisations in the region – once they understood the changes that were being made – immediately stated: 'we've been trying for so long to convince the library about the potential it has for facing the challenges of our times. We are more than willing to be part of its further development. This type of creativity was exactly what we were expecting and here it comes. Great strategy!'

> ## Questions for discussion
> - Do you regard the behaviour as well as the 'creative strategy' of the leader (the director) as ethical? Explain your position.
> - Can you think of actions taken by the director that were ethical, but not effective?
> - Could the director have done more to persuade all the employees to go along with necessary changes? If yes, what would this entail?
> - What is the best way for an ethical leader to deal with the resistance created by the transformations in an organisation?
> - Taking into consideration this particular case and the issue of ethics, what are your reflections on the trends of translating effective leadership in the sectors of the cultural and creative industries?

7.3 Good corporate governance and fraud

Jalal Atai and Johan Bouwer

7.3.1 Introduction to good corporate governance and fraud

The world has known a series of major corporate ethical scandals from the turn of the 20th to the 21st century onwards. Think about the infamous collapses of Enron and Arthur Andersen due to accounting scandals, which were followed by an incessant stream of incidents. DesJardins gives a summary of those scandals: 'in just the first five years of the twenty-first century, a wave of ethical scandals swept through the corporate world as fraudulent and dishonest practices were uncovered at such firms as WorldCom, Tyco, Adelphia, (…), Parmalat, Marsh and McClennen, (…) and even the New York stock exchange itself' (2014: 4). The list is endless. Fraudulent practices have led to people, businesses, financial institutions and even governments losing a lot of money and also their trust in business and financial institutions. Consumers, employees and ordinary citizens have become more and more aware of the fact that their lives are affected by the decisions made within business organisations (Hartman et al., 2014: 8), which, in turn, places the leadership of companies under the spotlight.

This evokes the question of the way executives govern their companies, and the structures and principles that are in place in ensuring that a company is steered well. In particular, the accounting scandals mentioned above increased the interest of regulators, investors, scholars, practitioners and policymakers in governance mechanisms. Amongst their other functions, government strategies are meant to make sure that those in power do not act in ways that are unethical, illegal or inappropriate (Malagueño et al., 2010). As governance mechanisms seek to enhance 'formal systems of accountability, oversight, and control' (Ferrell, Fraedrich and Ferrell, 2015: 52), they are, consequently, perceived to make fraudulent acts more difficult. This also applies to the behaviour and attitudes of the employees of a company. Governance mechanisms should also create opportunities for employees to make unethical decisions obsolete.

The interactions between good corporate governance and the prevention and eradication of fraud will be made clearer in the exploration of a case at the end of this section, which is related to the hospitality industry. But first, the leading constructs of 'good corporate governance' and 'fraud' in this article will be elaborated upon, followed by the description of the Fraud Triangle (FT) – a tool that is commonly used to deter fraudulent practices in companies, and which will also feature in the case at the end of this section.

7.3.1.1 The concepts

7.3.1.1.1 GOOD CORPORATE GOVERNANCE

The term 'corporate governance' – as indicated above – relates to a system by which organisations are controlled and directed (Rhodes, 1996). It refers to the establishment and continuous monitoring of policies by the members of the governing body of an organisation. Ferrell, Fraedrich and Ferrell distinguish between two kinds of corporate governance: the shareholder model, which solely caters for the interests and benefits of the shareholders of a company, and the broader shareholder model, which holds the purpose of business to be reckoning with the interests of all stakeholders (2015: 52). The model pursued by a company obviously reflect its views and determines its behaviour. The first, the shareholder model, is mainly directed towards making profits for the shareholders, while the second, the broader shareholder model, is more relational and inclusive. In both cases the board of directors are legally responsible for the behaviour and decisions taken by the company and can therefore be held accountable. The members of the board are also expected to be transparent and independent in their decision-making (Ferrell, Fraedrich and Ferrell, 2015: 53).

In order to assist and support good corporate behaviour and decision-making, several documents have been produced. Examples of principles and/or codes guiding the governing functions of executives are the Cadbury Report, adopted in the United Kingdom (UK) in 1992; the Principles of Corporate Governance, developed by the Organisation for Economic Cooperation and Development (OECD) (2015); the United Nations (UN) Global Compact (2009), and the Sarbanes-Oxley Act which was passed in 2002 in the United States. These documents regulate governing issues such as internal control procedures, balance of power and remuneration, but also takeovers, debt covenants and the integrity of financial statements ('Corporate Governance', n.d.).

The placing of the adjective 'good' in front of 'corporate governance' refers to the moral and ethical foundations underlying the efficiency and integrity of an organisation and the way the company relates to society, or the context it is operating in. 'Good corporate governance' also describes how public institutions conduct public affairs and manage public resources. It assures, amongst other things, that fraud is minimised. Bad or poor corporate governance, on the other hand, is increasingly regarded as one of the root causes of fraud within businesses and our societies (UNESCAP, 2009). Moreover, bad governance, and especially fraud, can cause large corporate firms to collapse.

7.3.1.1.2 FRAUD

'Fraud' is often contrasted with 'corruption'. However, some scholars do not make any distinction between fraud and corruption: corruption is seen as a form of fraud. A closer look at the way these concepts are used in literature points out that – although there is some overlap in their fields of meaning (both have to do with dishonesty and behaving without integrity) – they are not identical. Whereas 'corruption' is seen as a state of affairs in which a person or a company does not fulfil his/her/its purpose as a result of not performing 'as it was intended to perform' (Bowie, 2013: 152), 'fraud' can be defined as the misrepresentation of information or/and misappropriation of assets. Corruption, when applied to personal behaviour, can also be seen as the misuse of (public) power. In this sense it is mainly a governmental (public) phenomenon. Fraud, on the contrary, in the sense defined above, can be related to both the private and governmental (public) sector. Besides, corruption is different from fraud as it does not leave any trace in the records of an organisation and the auditors (Dye and Stapenhurst, 1998).

7.3.1.1.3 GOOD CORPORATE GOVERNANCE, FRAUD AND RISK ASSESSMENT

As far as the relationship between good corporate governance and fraud is concerned: the former specifically embraces accounting, auditing and internal control mechanisms and provides excellent tools for policymakers to mitigate, if not eliminate, fraud and corruption risks (Atai, 2015). Since 'risks' can be defined as 'conditions or behaviours that can affect a company either beneficially or detrimentally' (Rossouw and van Vuuren, 2017: 234), good corporate governance manages both the financial risks, that are likely to prevent businesses from reaching their goals, and the operational risks that could highly influence business risks through loss of stakeholder trust, reputation, human capital and the like (Rossouw and van Vuuren, 2017: 235). Risk assessment, in the case of fraud, entails the identification of those factors that could threaten good corporate governance, or more specifically, incite bad and unethical corporate behaviour.

Different tools have been developed to help companies to either prevent or eliminate fraud. Examples are the SAS99 (Statement on Auditing Standards No. 99), the COSO model (describing five components for internal control) and the FT (for removing causes in deterring fraud) ('Fraud Deterrence', n.d.). The FT will be described next.

7.3.1.2 Deterring fraud: The Fraud Triangle model

The Fraud Triangle (FT) model enables companies to assess why people commit fraud. The *idea* of the FT was coined by Donald Cressey. Cressey holds that three factors must be present at the same time in order for an individual to be able to commit fraud. These factors (dimensions or branches) are (a) opportunity, (b) rationalisation and (c) pressure (Cressey, 1953). In order for fraud to take place the agent should, at least, be under pressure (e.g., financial or non-financial), the opportunity gateway should have been left open (e.g., non-existent or weak governance mechanisms) and the agent is able to rationalise his/her fraudulent actions (e.g., reducing the moral impact due to low integrity).

When the FT model and the (sub)factors associated with each dimension are examined more closely, the following pattern will emerge. Firstly, the opportunity dimension (a) tends to be mainly governance-oriented, which implies that non-existent or weak governance mechanisms may create the opportunity of fraud (Dye and Stapenhurst, 1998; Farber, 2005). This enables the agent to conceal fraudulent acts committed with regard to, for example, accounting and auditing services, government effectiveness and the rule of law. Secondly, the rationalisation dimension (b) tends to be culturally, socially, and politically oriented, which implies that the incentives for committing fraud are affected by an individual's beliefs, attitude, integrity and political environment, such as ethnical fractionalisation (polarisation), religion and press freedom (Vona, 2008). Thirdly, the pressure dimension (c) seems to be more economically oriented, which means that mostly economic incentives (related to the financial-economic or non-financial obligations of the agent, and wages, GDP growth and inflation) cause the pressure to committing fraud (Murdock, 2008; W.S. Albrecht, 2008; C.T. Albrecht, 2010).

Cendrowski et al. pointed out that the FT, in reducing (the opportunity for) fraud in a company, should actually be 'broken' in order to be effective – meaning that one of the dimensions or sides should actually be 'removed' from the triangle. They state: 'Of the three elements, removal of *opportunity* is most directly affected by the system of internal controls and generally provides the most actionable route to deterrence of fraud' (2007: 41).

Despite of its extensive usage by regulators, professionals and academics, the FT model also has its shortcomings; these relate mainly to (a) its inability to *explain* fraud satisfactorily, because the other two factors (pressure and rationalisation) are not observable in advance but (b) also the fact that other important factors, such as the capabilities of the agent, are not taken into account (Kassem and Higson, 2012).

How the FT could be used to assess fraud will be demonstrated by the case below. This case is fictional, but is inspired by a case titled 'Managing fraud, bribery and corruption risks in the hospitality industry', which was published in a report by Ernst & Young in 2016 (Ernst & Young LLP).

Case 7.3.2: Deterring fraud in the hotel industry

Introduction: Assessing loss of revenue in prosperous times

Globally, people are earning more money, which enables them to spend more on luxury goods or travel to exotic and culturally rich countries. In order to answer this increasing demand, and of course to increase revenue, the hospitality and tourism industry are working quite hard on their business cases in order to be able to seduce potential customers with attractive packages and keep them satisfied with splendid facilities. In India, for example, which has a rich history, different cultures and beautiful landscapes, the flow of international tourists is ever increasing. Hotels offer all kinds of packages such as, for example 'healthy holidays' featuring yoga tutors, yoga books, Ayurvedic massages, special meals and much more.

Yet there is a flipside to this apparently optimistic picture. The competition is severe and the profit margins are quite slim. In addition, the Indian government has enforced requirements for effectively regulating activities within the hotel industry, such as the commissioning and construction of hotels, their operation and management, and compliance with regard to taxes and the regulations. These circumstances make hotels and tour operators vulnerable to fraud and corruption, as will be demonstrated next.

One of the hotels of an international hotel chain, situated in the centre of the commercial district of Bangalore near to shopping centres and tourist attractions, and which offered very luxurious services and amenities, was, despite its popularity, facing continuing losses – especially with regard to the income made from room sales. The executive board decided to approach an internationally well-known accountancy firm, called HoBiz Solutions, and commission them to undertake an investigation.

Salman and Anjika, the consultants who did the investigation, talked to all the members of staff who were working in the front office. They hypothesised that, since the losses were related to room sales, something might be wrong there. In addition, they talked to a few guests, randomly selected over a period of one month, and also consulted a number of potential tourists they approached via the database of a bona fide tour operator, and whose consent had been asked first. They presented their final report at a special meeting of the executive board. Advay, the president of the executive board, welcomed them and gave them the floor.

Causes and solutions to fraudulent practices

Anjika described the way she and Salman worked, the people they had talked to and also mentioned that their analysis was based on the FT. Here are their main findings:

Anjika: 'Our first three observations are specifically related to the way the staff of the front office worked. Firstly, in one case, the front office manager effectively accounted for only one room, while two rooms were used by two guests. Here is how it works: The computer adds a room charge for the stay of, say, Mrs O'Connor. But the manager collects this room charge in cash and does not show settlement in her folio. Instead he transfers the room charge to the folio of another guest, say, Mr Lipmann, who paid with his credit card. Secondly, the manager offers, in another case, a category "B" room to "walk-in" guests for $200. When the guest asks for an upgrade to a higher category room, the manager offers him/her a category "A" room for $300, but if he/she pays $50 in cash, then he/she could get the room for the same rate as the category "B" room ($200). This contributes greatly to the reduced income for the hotel. Thirdly, we also discovered that rooms that were out of order were rented for cash, and were therefore not accounted for as income.'

(continued)

Case 7.3.2: Deterring fraud in the hotel industry (*continued*)

Salman: 'We have three more general observations to make. You can see them as points of attention when working towards changing this situation, because they reflect the rationalisations three different categories of people make when considering whether they would go with the flow of committing fraud or not. Firstly, with regard to your own employees: they are open to fraud because they see everyone doing it; they feel that they will never be caught and that hotels with such a standing will not feel the pinch. Secondly, with regard to your guests: they have the money to convince staff through tipping to do something "special" for them and they know that no one will dare question them. And then last, but not least, "third parties" – those people who are not directly involved, but who could benefit from knowing what is going on. They say to themselves: "The hotel makes a huge revenue, I should also benefit. They will not check my backgrounds and besides, I have the affiliation of the purchase manager."'

Advay asked: 'What did you learn from the Fraud Triangle?'

Anjika answered: 'The opportunity for committing fraud was created by the weak and apparently non-existent control mechanisms. And the employees rationalise their acts by telling themselves that the guests are rich, and that the hotel makes a lot of money, while they themselves are poor and in need of more money. Besides, everyone does it. It is an interplay of economic and socio-cultural forces that "pressurise" them to commit fraud.'

Advay sighed: 'Where do we start?'

Salman replied: 'My advice would be to pay attention to the cash transactions and the internal control mechanisms. It seems that there was no independent verification of data or transactions-all schemes. To be brief: remove all opportunities for fraud, work on changing your staff's attitudes towards fraud and eradicating all pressures that could result in fraudulent behaviour.'

Advay: 'Thanks to you both and also to HoBiz Solutions. It seems that we have a lot of work to do.'

Questions for discussion

- Can you think of factors other than opportunity, rationalisation and pressure which could pave the way for committing fraudulent behaviour?
- If you were Advay, how would you address the culture of fraud that exists in the front office of the hotel?
- Does underpayment legitimise fraud? Explain your answer.
- Could you describe the behaviour of the executive board of this hotel as 'good corporate governance'? Explain your answer.
- Which ethical principles are in play when we have to distinguish between fraud and corruption?

7.4 Responsible business in the video-game industry

Mata Haggis

7.4.1 Introduction to responsible business in the video-game industry

This section will discuss organisational ethics, more specifically responsible business, amongst mid-to-large developers in the mainstream entertainment sector of the video-game industry. There are many small businesses that also work in this sector, often referred to as 'indie' developers, and some face similar challenges, but the issues discussed in what follows are most prevalent in larger companies. Both organisational treatment of the workforce and decision-making processes regarding the content of video games will be examined. The main theme is that the vast majority of decisions in the high-end games industry are made for reasons associated with profit margins, and those that appear motivated by ethical concerns are ultimately taken because they are compatible with a profitable business model.

7.4.1.1 'Fun' versus pressure for success

The games industry has two facets reflected in its name: 'games' suggests fun, entertainment, and perhaps an element of childishness in the content, and 'industry' reflects the business of creating products for a wide audience. The games business has grown rapidly in the 21st century to become financially the largest single entertainment media, and it is has a wide appeal to many young people who wish to work on creating the games that they enjoy playing. Like many sectors discussed in this book, the games industry does not have problems with the number of applicants for recruitment and, as with these other industries, there is thus little impetus for firms to change in the treatment of their workforce.

It would be easy to assume that the creative element of games automatically translates into a playful and informal workplace, and to some extent there is accuracy in this, but it is nonetheless the case that game development is also a full-time job with quality standards, deliverables and many standard office-work expectations. The size of the industry means that many large games have development budgets of tens, or even hundreds, of millions of dollars and can double or triple this budget with marketing. For example, Activision's 2014 *Destiny* is estimated to have 'cost half a billion dollars to produce and market' (Curtis and Hoggins, 2014). The risk of such investments is similarly large, with games that fail to pay back their investment, or not fulfilling their full potential at market, often forcing studios to close (Alexander, 2009). Although the reputation for playfulness in game-development studios does have some merit, there is also unquestionable pressure for success.

In 2004, an initially anonymous blog post started a heated discussion about the working conditions that resulted from the high-pressure industry atmosphere. It focussed on the major games publisher and developer Electronic Arts, also known as 'EA', but it raised issues that were near-universally recognised across the games industry. The writer, under the pen name 'EA Spouse', argued 'this company is not strapped for cash; their labour practices are inexcusable' (Hoffman, 2004). At greater length, it explained that EA was unconcerned at the time by the accusations of unfair employee treatment:

> EA's attitude toward this – which is actually a part of company policy, it now appears – has been (in an anonymous quotation that I've heard repeated by multiple managers): 'If they don't like it, they can work someplace else.' Put up or shut up and leave: this is the core of EA's human resources policy. The concept of ethics or compassion or even intelligence with regard to getting the most out of one's workforce never enters the equation: if they don't want to sacrifice their lives and their health and their talent so that a multibillion dollar corporation can continue its Godzilla-stomp through the game industry, they can work someplace else (Hoffman, 2004).

Although Hoffman's piece was written in 2004, over a decade later there are still notable similarities in workplace conditions.

7.4.1.2 'Crunch'

The primary point of complaint about the industry is 'crunch': this is where employees work long hours, frequently late into the night and at weekends, in order to meet deadlines for the game that they are creating. These deadlines may be externally set, such as from companies that have a window of production for a physical disk, but other deadlines may be internal milestones. These are closely related, with each milestone deliverable creating progress towards the final deliverable, but the structure and content of these deadlines, and the final game deliverable, are set early in production and controlled by the companies involved. If a developer is working for a publisher, the publisher will often hold back payments until the milestone is met, and too many missed milestones will mean financial difficulties for the developer. To avoid financial instability for their employer when these deadlines appear unlikely to be met, staff often work extra hours in order to meet the required standards.

It is argued that the necessity of crunch is part of inadequate planning by the games industry, which by the nature of only being a few decades old has not yet evolved sufficient skills in project management, but others do not believe that this assessment is accurate:

> It's easy enough to understand how small indies with their limited resources may recourse to crunch in this way. But why are the large companies the biggest offenders? If we're to accept the young industry theory of crunch, big studios should have the resources – if not the management acumen – to address the problem. The answer [...] is that the big players don't address it because it's in their economic interests not to (Williams, 2015).

Crunch, the exploitation of workers, is tolerated as part of the job, but there is a common sentiment that it could be heavily mediated if there were sufficient industry interest in actually doing so.

Organisational ethics

The practice of crunch relies on several factors. The milestones that are set are an initiating factor, but it is sustained by other factors, such as an eager aspirational workforce that want to join the industry, which gives a sense of insecurity to many roles; the relatively young workforce, who have a lower number of dependents than an older population; the high need for geographical mobility amongst staff, meaning low numbers of social ties outside of the game-development studio; and that the personality types often attracted to game development can be highly dedicated to delivering the best possible version of their game. Although crunch is rarely welcomed, it is also often accepted as an inevitable part of game development which staff sometimes feel that they have volunteered to participate in, and consequently feelings about it amongst staff are not universally negative.

7.4.1.3 Implications for staff

Crunch can be made worse by industry practices of hiring and firing according to changing requirements for workers. Staff can be hired for the increase in workload towards the end of a game-development project, where they work crunch hours for a year, and they are then laid off when the game is finished. Staff are often unaware that this is the plan for them until it happens, and relocation is usually necessary to find another job in the games industry. There is a possibility that the next studio that employs the worker will also be engaging in the same practice, and so a person can move between crunching studios several times in a row. The impact on the worker's personal life and health can be very high, and may be a significant contributing factor to the number of staff who leave the game-development industry after less than a decade (Edwards et al., 2014: 17–18). There have been some positive responses to this situation, such as an increase in contract work, which explicitly identifies the period of employment and allows a staff member to plan for their future, and there are negative responses, such as managers who are hired for their ability to push staff to crunch to meet deadlines, even if it is against the best interests of the individual workers.

7.4.1.4 Profit and game content

Just as profit drives human resource decisions, it is often the deciding factor in the content of games. The content of games is frequently not attuned to societal developments, such as equal opportunities and respect for minorities and marginalised groups, and instead often returns to content that would be considered immature or offensive in many other forms of creative media. The press is divided on the value of highlighting these issues and their impact on evaluating the quality of a game, for example in their review of *Grand Theft Auto V*, the major gaming website *GameSpot* stated the following:

> Characters constantly spout lines that glorify male sexuality while demeaning women, and the billboards and radio stations of the world reinforce this misogyny, with ads that equate manhood with sleek sports cars while encouraging women to purchase a fragrance that will make them 'smell like a bitch'. Yes, these are exaggerations of misogynistic undercurrents in our own society, but

not satirical ones. With nothing in the narrative to underscore how insane and wrong this is, all the game does is reinforce and celebrate sexism. The beauty of cruising in the sun-kissed Los Santos hills while listening to 'Higher Love' by Steve Winwood turns sour really quick when a voice comes on the radio that talks about using a woman as a urinal (Petit, 2013).

This content sounds damning, and in a film review would likely mark the product out as highly unacceptable for a general audience, but this game is one of the highest-selling titles in history, and *GameSpot*, at the end of this review, awarded it a rating of nine out of ten. Despite its having content that is unethical, reviewers of the game are almost unanimous in their overall praise, and the financial success of *Grand Theft Auto V* means that the developers will not be discouraged from exploring their specific idea of 'being masculine' (Hill, 2013) in future games in the series.

7.4.1.5 Ethics and game content

As in other media industries, ethical issues in regard to the content of video games have been subject to increasing analysis and criticism in the 21st century, and passionate defences against accusations of racism, misogyny and more, have also emerged. This is an ongoing debate amongst the community of players, critics and developers, but the content of games is slowly reflecting changing social values. As in the film industry, there appear to be small shifts occurring in the content of games, with more women protagonists being seen in the new titles announced in 2015 than in 2014 (Mueller, 2015). There is a lot of room for progress in terms of equal treatment for minorities and all genders, both in wider society and in video games, but this shift is unlikely to accelerate unless the business model is proven, and risks stalling if the results of these tentative steps are not financially positive.

The indie game-development community is often ahead on ethical content development, with games featuring lead characters that are gay (*Gone Home*), or attempting to tell stories about everyday mental illness (*Depression Quest*), or topics such as the death of a child from cancer seen from the perspective of a parent (*That Dragon, Cancer*). However, the indie development community is rarely referred to as an 'industry', and more commonly given the title of 'community' or 'scene', partly due to the limited commercial impact of its subject matter. Equally, for all the liberal values that some indie games show, others are expressly marketed on their lack of ethical concerns, such as *Hatred*, where the player controls a sociopath on a graphic and extremely violent killing spree, attacking innocent civilians. Both of these extremes are considered non-commercial when compared to the appeal of *Grand Theft Auto V*, and in many regards it is the commercial viability that delineates the mainstream game developers from the indie scene.

7.4.1.6 Wrapping up

The games industry is large, complex, and relatively young. It has emerged during a tumultuous time in the evolution of entertainment media, and there are numerous uncertainties about the ethical standards in game development. Alongside the issues of the health of the workplace in the games industry, there are many further

Organisational ethics

discussions that are possible about the content of video games and how they are created: the ongoing discussions of the representation of violence in games; the issue of the use of sexual imagery in advertising and content; or the question of the exploitation of addiction in both mainstream titles and the emerging 'free to play' business model, to name only a few. The overriding guiding principle of the games industry remains focussed on profit, where strong sales are interpreted as social and cultural endorsement for both workplace and content decisions. As the industry matures, it is possible that a more nuanced business model may evolve that reflects the needs of both developers and society, but this point has not been reached yet.

Case 7.4.2: Employee crunch versus making profits

Introduction: Completing the game on time...

A large video-game development studio, with shareholders, is nearing the end of a game project. They have been creating the game for two years, which is a somewhat unusually long period of time for the genre. They have been working on implementing innovative ideas, and those ideas have pushed the team to create many iterations to improve the feel of the game. The project is behind schedule and should be approximately ten months from completion, so the company needs extra staff to fulfil the time-consuming task of implementing the designed interactions across the virtual world, otherwise they will have to delay the release of the game (with associated costs).

Employee crunch versus profits

The team working on the game consists of 100 people and the company hires an extra 15 staff to help finish it; most of those new hires need to relocate to the city where the studio is based. The new staff are enthusiastic and for many it is their first job in the games industry. After an initial period of training for two weeks, the new staff are expected to meet tough deadlines to implement their content into the game. Development managers regularly walk around the studio to check on progress. 'Curry nights' are implemented as a reward for staff working in the evenings, but the food is ordered late, meaning the staff are often working even longer hours than they usually would.

If staff leave on time, the development managers ask them if they are up to date on their tasks before they leave. If they are on track, they are asked if there is anything else they could be helping with, and long hours become the expected behaviour. There are discussions about TOIL (Time Off in Lieu - extra holiday or payment for the overtime), but these do not result in any clear ruling and there is no obvious attempt to track hours worked. Few holidays are taken in the months before releasing the game.

(continued)

Case 7.4.2: Employee crunch versus making profits (*continued*)

The company does not have fully developed plans for a game to follow their large release, and so will not need all of the team once the current game is finished. Most of the new staff will be laid off within three months following its release, usually with no or little consideration for extra TOIL payment, and several of the less essential existing team will likely be laid off too. The game is released to generally high review scores, it sells quite well and it makes a strong addition to the CV of everyone involved.

Questions for discussion

- If you were the director of this company, what factors would you be addressing in addition to the well-being of your staff?
- Is it the duty of a company director to protect the long-term stability of the work environment for the core team of employees, or does the director have other duties?
- What problems is this company causing for the core team of staff, and are there different problems for the newly hired staff?
- The game contains the possibility of violent interactions. Is the company liable if their violent video game appears to induce a player to commit acts of violence in the physical world? If so, who is responsible: the developer or the CEO, or some other person/group?
- Does responsible business imply that every kind of product can be developed so long as there is a market for it?

7.5 Concluding thoughts

Organisational or corporate ethics comprises those principles that steer the behaviour of all personnel, including that of the CEO. Organisational behaviour entails treating both employees and external stakeholders with integrity, responsibility, fairness, transparency and respect at all levels of activity related to economics, human rights, and the environment. Corporate ethics is about more than ensuring businesses comply with the law and their own corporate codes of ethics only. This would imply that the organisation is merely trying to avoid doing or causing any harm. Ethics within and the ethics of an organisation also entails working for the greater good through business activities, both inside (employees, e.g.) and outside the organisation (e.g. suppliers, customers, society, etc.). This implies that the organisation is (pro)actively pursuing the well-being of all its stakeholders.

Thinking about organisational or corporate ethics also includes reflection on the way a company is steered and led. This is called corporate governance. Corporate governance entails a long-term corporate culture of accountability towards all of the company's stakeholders through a system of checks and balances with regard to all of its business activities. It is therefore about monitoring the business's policies (including codes of ethics and responsible behaviour), the decisions taken and the activities of all involved, in order to thereby ensure that the company enjoys the trust of authorities, business partners, customers and the general public (see also Chapters 6 and 8).

Further reading

Amann, W. and Stachwicz-Stanusch, A. (Eds.) (2013). *Integrity in Organizations: Building the Foundations of Humanistic Management.* New York/Basingstoke: Palgrave Macmillan.
Boaks. J. and Levine, M.P. (Eds.) (2017). *Leadership and Ethics.* London/New York: Bloomsbury.
Clark, T. and Branson, D. (Eds.) (2012). *The Sage Handbook of Corporate Governance.* London/Thousand Oaks, CA: Sage Publications.
Collins, D. (2012). *Business Ethics: How to Design and Manage Ethical Organizations.* Hoboken: John Wiley & Sons.
Flynn, G. (Ed.) (2008). *Leadership and Business Ethics.* London/New York: Springer.
Haslebo, G. and Haslebo, M.L. (2012). *Practicing Relational Ethics in Organizations.* Chagrin Falls, OH: Taos Institute Publications.
Solomon, J. and Solomon, A. (2004). *Corporate Governance and Accountability.* Chichester, UK: John Wiley & Sons.

References

Albrecht, C.T. (2010). The Relationship Between South Korean Chaebols and Fraud. *Management Research Review,* 33(3): 257–268.
Albrecht, W.S. (2008). Current Trends in Fraud and its Detection. *Information Security Journal: A Global Perspective,* 17(1): 2–12.
Alexander, L. (2009, 12 August). Swedish Developer GRIN to Close its Doors. *Gamasutra,* Retrieved 10 July 2015 from http://www.gamasutra.com/php-bin/news_index.php?story=24818.
Atai, J. (2015). Accounting, Auditing and Corruption: Is Accounting and Auditing Quality Associated with Corruption? Unpublished master thesis. Erasmus School of Economics, Erasmus University, Rotterdam, the Netherlands.
Bass, B. M. (1985). *Leadership and Performance beyond Expectation.* New York: Free Press.
Battilana, J., Gilmartin, M., Sengul, M., Pache, A.-C. and Alexander, J. A. (2010). Leadership Competencies for Implementing Planned Organizational Change. *The Leadership Quarterly,* 21: 422–438.
Bouwer, P.J. (1971). The Power to See Ourselves. In Bursk, E.C. and Blodgett, T.B. (Eds.), *Developing Executive Leaders.* Cambridge, MA: Harvard University Press.
Bowie, N. (2013). *Business Ethics in the 21st Century.* New York/London: Springer.
Burns, J. M. (1978). *Leadership.* New York: Harper & Row.
Burr, V. (2015). *Social Constructionism* (3rd ed.). New York: Routledge.
Camargo-Borges, C. and Rasera, E.F. (2013). Social Constructionism in the Context of Organisation Development Dialogue, Imagination and Co-Creation as Resources of Change. *Sage Open* 3(2): 1–7.
Catmull, E. (2008). How Pixar Fosters Collective Creativity. *Harvard Business Review,* 86(9): 64–72.
Cendrowski, H., Martin, J.P. and Petro, L.W. (Eds.) (2007). *The Handbook of Fraud Deterrence.* Hoboken, NJ: John Wiley & Sons Inc.

Colbert, A., Judge, T., Choi, D. and Wang, J., (2012). Assessing the Trait Theory of Leadership Using Self and Observer Ratings of Personality: The Mediating Role of Contributions to Group Success. *The Leadership Quarterly*, 23: 670–685.

Conger, J.A. and Kanungo, R.N. (1987). Toward a Behavioural Theory of Charismatic Leadership in Organizational Settings. *The Academy of Management Review*, 12(4): 637–647.

Corporate Governance. (n.d.). In *Wikipedia*. Retrieved 9 May 2017 from https://en.wikipedia.org/wiki/Corporate_governance.

Cressey, D. (1953). *Other People's Money: A Study in the Social Psychology of Embezzlement*. Glencoe, IL: Free Press.

Curtis, S. and Hoggins, T. (2014, 9 September). Is Destiny the Most Expensive Video Game Ever Made? *Daily Telegraph*. Retrieved 10 July 2015 from http://www.telegraph.co.uk/technology/video-games/11084023/Is-Destiny-the-most-expensive-video-game-ever-made.html.

DesJardins, J. (2014). *An Introduction to Business Ethics* (5th ed.). New York: McGraw-Hill.

Dye, K.M. and Stapenhurst, R. (1998). *Pillars of Integrity: The Importance of Supreme Audit Institutions in Curbing Corruption*. Washington, DC: Economic Development Institute of the World Bank.

Edwards, K., Weststar, J., Meloni, W., Pearce, C. and Legault, M.-J. (2014). *Developer Satisfaction Survey 2014: Summary Report*. International Game Developers Association (IGDA). Retrieved 11 March 2019 from https://static1.squarespace.com/static/551ac4c9e4b0038a33ecc74e/t/551b223ee4b0ae1f4a708171/1427841598800/IGDA+DSS+2014-Summary+Report_released.pdf.

Ernst & Young LLP (2016). *Managing Fraud, Bribery and Corruption Risks in the Hospitality Industry*. Kolkata: Ernst & Young LLP.

Farber, D. B. (2005). Restoring Trust After Fraud: Does Corporate Governance Matter? *The Accounting Review*, 80(2): 539–561.

Ferrell, O.C., Fraedrich, J. and Ferrell, L. (2015*). Business Ethics: Ethical Decision Making and Cases* (10th ed.). Stamford, CT: Cengage Learning.

Fiedler, F. E. (1967). *A Theory of Leadership Effectiveness*. New York: McGraw-Hill.

Ford, J. D. (1999). Organizational Change as Shifting Conversations. *Journal of Organizational Change Management*, 12(6): 480–500.

Fraud Deterrence. (n.d.). In *Wikipedia*. Retrieved 9 May 2017 from https://en.wikipedia.org/wiki/Fraud_deterrence.

Gergen, K. (2016). From Commands to Conversations: Identity in the Coming Organizational Culture. *Gruppe. Interaktion. Organisation. Zeitschrift für Angewandte Organisationspsychologie*, 47(1): 31–34.

Gergen, K.J. (2009). *Relational Being: Beyond Self and Community*. Oxford: Oxford University Press.

Gergen, K.J. and Gergen, M. (2004). *Social Construction: Entering the Dialogue*. Chagrin Falls, OH: Taos Institute Publication.

Gergen, K.J. and Gergen, M. (2012). *Playing with Purpose: Adventures in Performative Social Science*. New York: Routledge.

Goleman, D. (1995). *Emotional Intelligence*. New York: Bantam.

Goleman, D. (2000). Leadership That Gets Results. *Harvard Business Review*, 78: 82–83.

Hartman, P., DesJardins, J. and MacDonald, C. (2014). *Business Ethics: Decision Making for Personal Integrity and Social Responsibility* (3rd ed.). New York: McGraw-Hill.

Haslebo, G. and Haslebo, M.L. (2012). *Practicing Relational Ethics in Organizations*. Chagrin Falls: Taos Institute Publications.

Hersey, P. and Blanchard, K. H. (1969). Life Cycle Theory of Leadership. *Training and Development Journal*, 23(5): 26–34.

Hersey, P. and Blanchard, K. (1972). *Management of Organizational Behaviour: Utilizing human resources* (2nd ed.). Englewood Cliffs, NJ: Prentice-Hall, Inc.

Hill, M. (2013, 7 September). Grand Theft Auto V: Meet Dan Houser, Architect of a Gaming Phenomenon. *The Guardian.* Retrieved 10 July 2015 from: http://www.theguardian.com/technology/2013/sep/07/grand-theft-auto-dan-houser.

Hoffman, E. (2004). ea_spouse – EA: The Human Story. In *EA Spouse.* Retrieved 10 July 2015 from http://ea-spouse.livejournal.com/274.html.

Karakas, F. (2009). Welcome to World 2.0: The New Digital Ecosystem. *Journal of Business Strategy,* 30(4): 23–30.

Kassem, R. and Higson, A. (2012). The New Fraud Triangle Model. *Journal of Emerging Trends in Economics and Management Sciences,* 3(3): 191–195.

Killian, S. (2007). *The ABC of Effective Leadership.* Melbourne: Australian Leadership Development Centre.

Kotze, D. (2002). Doing Participatory Ethics. In Kotze, D., Myburg, J. Roux, J. and Associates, *Ethical Ways of Being.* Pretoria: Ethics Alive.

Lewin, K., Lippitt, R. and White, R.K. (1939). Patterns of Aggressive Behaviour in Experimentally Created Social Climates. *Journal of Social Psychology,* 10: 271–301.

Lusch, R.F. (2007). Marketing's Evolving Identity: Defining Our Future. *Journal of Public Policy and Marketing,* 26(2): 261–268.

Malagueño, R., Albrecht, C., Ainge, C. and Stephens, N. (2010). Accounting and Corruption: A Cross-Country Analysis. *Journal of Money Laundering Control,* 13(4): 372–393.

Marion, R., and Uhl-Bien, M. (2001). Leadership in Complex Organizations. *The Leadership Quarterly,* 12 (4): 389–418.

Mayer, J.D. and Salovey, P. (1997). What is Emotional Intelligence? In Salovey, P, and Sluyter, D. (Eds.), *Emotional Development and Emotional Intelligence: Implications for Educators* (pp. 3–31). New York: Basic Books.

McClelland, D. C. and Burnham, D. H. (1976). Power is the Great Motivator. *Harvard Business Review,* 54: 100–110.

McNamee, S. (2015). Ethics as Discursive Potential. *The Australian and New Zealand Journal of Family Therapy,* 36: 419–433.

McNamee, S. (2016). The Ethics of Relational Process. John Shotter's Radical Presence. In Corcoran, T. and Cromby, J. (Eds.), *Essays in Honour of John Shotter.* London: Routledge.

McNamee, S, and Gergen, K. J (Eds.) (1999). *Relational Responsibility: Resources for Sustainable Dialogue.* Thousand Oaks, CA: Sage.

Mueller, S. (2015, 19 June). E3 2015: Female Gamers Are Finally Getting the Badass Characters They Deserve. *International Business Times.* Retrieved 10 July 2014 from: http://www.ibtimes.com/e3-2015-female-gamers-are-finally-getting-badass-characters-they-deserve-photos-1975636.

Murdock, H. (2008). The Three Dimensions of Fraud: Auditors Should Understand the Needs, Opportunities, and Justifications that Lead Individuals to Commit Fraudulent Acts. *Internal Auditio,* 65(4): 81–83.

O'Connor, S. (2014). Leadership for Future Libraries. *Library Management,* 35(1/2): 78–87.

Petit, C. (2013, 17 November). Grand Theft Auto V Review: City of Angels and Demons. *GameSpot.* Retrieved 10 July 2015 from http://www.gamespot.com/reviews/grand-theft-auto-v-review/1900-6414475/.

Prensky, M. (2001, October). Digital Natives, Digital Immigrants. In *MarcPrensky.com.* Retrieved 25 May 2016 from http://www.marcprensky.com/writing/Prensky%20-%20Digital%20Natives,%20Digital%20Immigrants%20-%20Part1.pdf.

Quade, K. and Holladay, R. (2010). *Dynamical Leadership: Building Adaptive Capacity for Uncertain Times.* Apache Junction, AZ: Gold Canyon Press.

Rhodes, R.A. (1996). The New Governance: Governing Without Government. *Political Studies*, 44: 652–667.

Rossouw, D. and Vuuren, L. van (2017). *Business Ethics* (5th ed.). Cape Town: Oxford University Press.

Schön, D. (1983). *The Reflective Practitioner.* London: Ashgate.

Stanislavov, I. and Ivanov, S. (2014). The Role of Leadership for Shaping Organizational Culture and Building Employee Engagement in the Bulgarian Gaming Industry. *Tourism*, 62: 19–40.

Suchman, A.L. (2011). Organizations as Machines, Organizations as Conversations: Two Core Metaphors and their Consequences. *Medical Care. Emerging Perspectives,* 49(12): 43–48.

Thorndike, E.L. (1921). Intelligence and Its Measurement: A Symposium. *Journal of Educational Psychology*, 12: 123–147; 195–216; 271–275.

Vargo, S.L. and Lusch, R.F. (2008). Service-Dominant Logic Continuing the Evolution. *Journal of the Academy of Marketing Science*, 36: 1–10.

Vona, L. W. (2008). *Fraud Risk Assessment. Building a Fraud Audfit Program.* Hoboken, NJ: John Wiley & Sons, Inc.

UNESCAP. (2009).What is Good Governance? *UNESCAP.* Retrieved 25 April 2017 from http://www.unescap.org/sites/default/files/good-governance.pdf.

Williams, I. G. (2015, 18 February). Crunched: Has the Games Industry Really Stopped Exploiting its Workforce? *The Guardian.* Retrieved 10 July 2015 from http://www.theguardian.com/technology/2015/feb/18/crunched-games-industry-exploiting-workforce-ea-spouse-software.

Yukl, G.A. (2010). *Leadership in Organizations* (7th ed.). Upper Saddle River, NJ: Prentice Hall.

Chapter 8

Corporate social responsibility

Marisa de Brito, Jan-Willem Proper, Han Verheijden and Françoise van den Broek-Serlé

8.1 Introduction to corporate social responsibility

Marisa de Brito

8.1.1 Definition and meaning of corporate social responsibility

There is no universal definition of corporate social responsibility (CSR). A recent analysis of the definitions coined since 1953 reveals that the words that are mostly associated with CSR have also changed over time (Sarkar and Searcy, 2016). In the first 30 years after the term was coined, definitions tended to emphasise the legal, but also extended to the obligations of profit organisations in terms of voluntarily meeting the expectations of society. Over the following 20 years, new terms entered the glossary of CSR, such as stakeholders, and sustainability. This is not a coincidence. After all, stakeholder theory, as the popularised concept of sustainable development, also came into being in the 1980s (Freeman, 1984; WCED, 1987). Calls for businesses to behave in an ethical manner also intensified in this period. In the last ten years there has been an acceleration of debates and published material around CSR – both academic and non-academic. Again, this is not surprising, especially when we consider that in the early 2000s the Internet bubble burst, businesses faced recession and scandals like Enron were high profile in the media. A global analysis of the core elements of the definitions of CSR (Sarkar and Searcy, 2016) reinforces the call for the triple-p baseline (profit, people, planet), which balances profits with social well-being and environmental value. In addition, the emphasis on ethical behaviour steers the repeated call for openness, transparency and voluntary accountability.

And as far as sustainable development, which will be explored more closely in Chapter 9, is concerned: its ambition (meeting our needs today without impairing the ability of future generations to satisfy their own needs) is inherently related to the willingness of businesses to go beyond their financial obligations to their stockholders, to the point of taking into account the needs of a diversity of stakeholders. The father of stakeholder theory said: 'a stakeholder can be anyone who affects or is affected by operations of a company' (Freeman, 1984: 46). Employees, suppliers and customers, but also local communities, competitors, the media and both governmental and non-governmental institutions are some of the generic stakeholder groups of every corporation. However, since exerting influence may be just a click away today (e.g. by posting or tweeting), global communities, society in general and also future generations may be regarded as stakeholders as well. So, CSR can be defined as 'the continuing commitment by business to contribute to economic development while improving the quality of life of the workforce and their families as well as of the community and society at large' (Watts and Holme, 1999: 3). But, although this definition may be rigorously correct, it poses a practical challenge to businesses: how should they create focus and prioritise concrete actions towards taking responsibility?

8.1.2 Business responsibility and stakeholders

Several frameworks have been put forward over time to help businesses prioritise their stakeholders. These include simple approaches such a discriminating between two groups (e.g. identifying primary versus secondary stakeholders, and stakeholders who are against versus for); a double classification, such as the power–interest matrix (Gardner, Rachlin and Sweeny, 1986); or the three circles of Mitchell, Bradley and Wood (1997), which categorise stakeholders not only according to power, but also regarding legitimacy and urgency. For more of this, see the work of Poplawska et al. (2015), who not only review previous frameworks but also introduce a dynamic framework to prioritise stakeholders using fuzzy logic.

The original theories on how businesses should deal with stakeholders took a managerial approach. Accordingly, actions like 'keep informed', 'keep satisfied', or use 'minimal effort' are suggested in the original power–interest stakeholder's matrix of Gardner et al. (1986). However, Gardner's matrix assumes one-way communication from the corporations to their stakeholders. This is currently no longer the case, as stakeholder groups or individuals can easily voice their expectations, needs or demands in chat rooms, websites and so on. Although it depends on the CSR maturity of each corporation, the stakeholder management approach is evolving into stakeholder engagement. Thus, concepts like 'building trust' and being 'inclusive' have become commonplace in the new frameworks (Jeffery, 2009).

Taking responsibility as a business, and towards a diversity of stakeholders, is the crux of CSR. However, what does responsibility entail? Carroll (1991) identifies four types of responsibilities for businesses: economic, legal, ethical and philanthropic. This means that businesses are required to make a profit and to operate within the law. In addition, society expects businesses to exert ethical behaviour, and also expects businesses to go a step further by giving back to society. When applied to sustainability, this would mean companies should not only do the minimum by not harming the environment or society, but also look for ways to generate a social and environmental surplus.

A recent study shows that consumers are able to distinguish between the different dimensions of CSR responsibility (Palihawadana, Oghazi and Liu, 2016). Corporations face a consumer that:

- Wants to consume ethically (Yeoman, 2013; Cavagnaro, Postma and de Brito, 2016).
- Is more demanding and impatient than ever before (Calvo-Soraluze, de Brito and San Salvadore del Valle, 2015).
- Pays attention to how the corporation operates.

Companies in the creative, cultural and lifestyle service industries have a lower CSR threshold, and since the consumer is more exigent, they are therefore more vulnerable to failures (Werther and Chandler, 2011).

A corporation can express responsibility in words (e.g. in its mission, by setting CSR goals) and can take responsibility by undertaking concrete CSR activities or initiatives. One type of activity is active engagement with stakeholders (through debates, forums and brainstorming sessions; by teaming up with partners, joining committees or by networking) or tailor-made actions towards an environmental or social goal. Some goals or initiatives might be short term, while others may only be achieved in the medium/long term. Given that CSR needs to be a 'continuing commitment' (Watts and Holme, 1999: 3) the likelihood of success is higher if CSR is embedded in corporate strategy (see also Chapter 9).

8.1.3 Corporate strategy and CSR motivation

Corporate strategy can be defined as 'the overall scope and direction of a corporation and the way in which its various business operations work together to achieve particular goals' ('Corporate Strategy', n.d.). Thus, in establishing (new) businesses, achieving particular goals implies the establishment of goals in the first place and only then delineating *how* to deal with them in the marketplace and how to compete. Businesses ought to reflect first on the desired future and what the business is really about (in the form of a vision and mission), if their strategy is to be well rooted. Particularly in emerging markets, it works in companies' favour if they communicate their ethical standing before getting involved with CSR-related activities (Karaosmanoglu, Altinigne and Isiksal, 2016). In other words: embracing CSR should go hand in hand with a strong ethical identity.

Companies may engage in CSR for a myriad of reasons (Coles, Fenclova and Dinan, 2013). Putting it plainly: companies may either expect to benefit from CSR (directly or indirectly – see Weber, 2008) or there may be an inherent moral driver, which impels leaders to practise good corporate citizenship based on 'ethical values and moral leadership' (Dhanesh, 2015). The push towards engaging in CSR may also be an external one, due to regulatory or stakeholders' pressure. Companies' CSR strategies will generally relate to two categories (Kramer and Kania, 2006):

- Being defensive or reactive (trying to avoid targeted attacks by environmental organisations and avoid further criticism).
- Being offensive or proactive (thinking ahead on how to create environmental and social value and by making it into a competitive advantage). As Saeed and Arshad put it: 'CSR as an area of practice is moving toward responsible competition' (2012: 220).

A competitive edge might be expected in areas such as brand differentiation, building reputation, increasing customer loyalty (Rashid, Khalid, and Abdul-Rahman, 2015), increasing employee attachment (Gardiner, Rubbens and Bonfiglioli, 2003) or financial returns (Lee, 2008). For instance, a review of companies approaching CSR through sponsoring (Djaballah, Hautbois and Desbordes, 2016) shows that some of the objectives of such action are: creating an image of community involvement; increasing brand awareness; developing public relations; making products known to a wider public; giving perks to employees (e.g. tickets for matches); increasing direct sales; and creating competitive differentiation.

Some companies may start with an attitude of dismissal of CSR, then proceed to (minimum) compliance and finally move towards a more strategic approach towards it (Zadek, 2004; Maon, Lindgreen and Swaen, 2010). Successful implementation of CSR will depend on factors such as organisational culture and structure, control mechanisms, employee motivation and capabilities, leadership, and communication (Engert and Baumgartner, 2016). Companies may choose a stepwise approach by putting a CSR officer in place, aligning rewards with the CSR goals, implementing a code of conduct and then reporting on their activities and performance. For the medium and long term, companies can proceed to further engagement with stakeholders, go on to professionally manage the CSR message and perhaps to embrace corporate activism in the form of a cause (Werther and Chandler, 2011).

Embracing a cause, as a company, may call for the establishment of a partnership with a civil society organisation (CSO). In forming such an alliance, the company may either lead the cause or lean on a cause. This can be illustrated by the following two examples: Firstly, ID&T, a Dutch entertainment company specialising in electronic music and dance events recently adopted the cause 'water... our fundamental right' (ID&T – Choose Tap Water, 2014). They started to offer water for free at their outdoor festivals, such as Welcome to the Future and Mysteryland. It took only a few months, and several incidents at another festival, for the mayor of Amsterdam to issue a bill requiring that water should be made available for free at outdoor festivals (van Ooijen, 2014). Secondly, it is more common and effective to enter into a partnership with an organisation that is already fighting for a cause. For instance, the Intercontinental Hotel Group (IHG), amongst the largest hotel groups in the world, has worked on several projects with UNICEF for the education of children around the world.

Such partnerships work rather well when the causes of the CSO are well known and in some way fit the company's purpose (Rim, Yang and Lee, 2016). De Brito and Terzieva's design model for environmental and social value supports this finding (2016). Their model proposes, first, a discover-phase, in which the vision of the company and its values are clarified. This is followed by a develop-phase, which comprises forging the right partnerships, with a strong customer orientation. It ends with a deliver-phase, which embraces environmental or social innovation.

Along with setting CSR objectives, companies measure their performance, and increasingly use both in their communication. The practice of CSR reporting is nowadays a global one (Vartiak, 2016). If done internally, it is a tool in the performance management cycle and can lead to organisational learning (Gond and Herrbach, 2006). If used externally, it can be a tool for managing reputation (Hooghiemstra, 2000). Yet, managing the CSR message is sensitive, as diverse stakeholders are sceptical of corporations' CSR motives (Lock and Seele, 2016). Acknowledging both self-benefit and societal benefit seems to soothe consumers' doubts about companies' motives (Kim, 2014). Manente, Minghetti and Mingotto (2014) put forward four criteria to use in order to improve CSR reporting, for example in tourism. CSR reports should reflect on

- The degree of coverage given to the three pillars of sustainability
- Whether or not there is active engagement with a diversity of stakeholders (with a special focus on host communities)
- Transparency and accountability – especially in the nature of the auditing
- Whether or not standards and criteria are supportive of all companies – also of small and medium-sized enterprises which lack the resources of large enterprises.

Transparency and credibility in CSR is expected to increase when a company goes from self-reporting to ratification by the applicable industry association (or ideally an audit by an independent agency). The Global Reporting Initiative (GRI) is one such organisation, and promotes the use of sustainability reporting as a common practice, by producing standards and guidelines and providing external assurance. However, recent research shows that companies which adopt GRI are not more balanced or precise in reporting when compared with companies that produce stand-alone reports (Michelon, Pilonato and Ricceri, 2015). A longitudinal study of CSR reporting (1997–2006) identifies three phases in CSR reporting (Shabana, Buchholtz and Carroll, 2016):

- Phase 1 is basically about companies trying to meet stakeholders' expectations (the 'ought to do').
- Phase 2 is much more about letting the company's own internal CSR objectives take the lead.
- Phase 3 is more oriented towards seeking industry consistency by imitating (to some degree) peer companies.

In dealing with strategic, and even practical, issues such as defining sustainability, prioritising stakeholders, establishing partnerships, embracing causes, dealing with an eager consumer, and deciding on which standards to adopt and on what to report, there will always be trade-offs. Melnyk et al. make salient 'the need to better understand and manage risk and performance together' (in as much as they can be managed) at the same time as acknowledging that risk and performance are bound to be influenced by organisational culture, as well as the external environment (2014: 184). As the world grows more interconnected and interdependent, as information flows accelerate and as the mobility of manufactured goods, resources and human and financial capital increases, the external environment that affects a company nearly encompasses the entire globe. Thus, practising CSR becomes inherently more complex because of the proliferation of issues, stakeholders, the mingling of cultures and backgrounds, and different needs and views. More trade-offs are made at a faster pace, since different stakeholders are continuously being affected by companies' decisions in different ways. With this in mind, movements against globalisation may well be mislabelled, since fighting the enlarged connectivity of the world seems more like a (desperate) attempt to actually fighting the inequality of its impacts. One could say that to call for ethical globalisation instead would be conceptually more precise. In practice, this would entail raising awareness about those uneven impacts (whereby some stakeholders benefit, while others experience worsening conditions), and pursuing alternative forms of globalisation by means of which adverse effects could be mitigated.

8.1.4 In conclusion

The principle of CSR has come a long way from its conceptual inception in the 1950s. It generally refers to business activities that realise a balance between economic gains and societal and environmental well-being. Freeman's stakeholder theory has led to companies recognising that they have more stakeholders than just their stockholders alone. They have to consider their employees, customers, suppliers, competitors, the media and society at large as well. The idea of CSR is more than just abiding by the law: it is an ethical endeavour that focusses on transparency, responsibility and the conditions for well-being for generations to come. It should always be embedded in a corporate strategy detailing the overall purpose, goals and values of an organisation. Yet the drivers for pursuing CSR can be both intrinsically and extrinsically motivated. In order to convince the critical customer of their noble efforts (and thus that they are intrinsically motivated), companies need to pursue a clear cause which is embedded in corporate strategy, and show readiness to not only write an annual and honest CSR report, but also to be ratified by an 'accreditation' institution. However, since different stakeholders are affected in different ways by companies' decisions, there will always be complex situations in which ethical dilemmas are unavoidable. This will be demonstrated in the rest of this chapter.

Three discussions are put forward that prelude three cases. These reflect on ethical dilemmas that (could) emerge with regard to the supply chain, within the themes of productivity, effective and efficient organisations, and ethical sourcing and waste management. The first discussion is introduced by Jan-Willem Proper, and focusses on supply-chain integrity, depicting the goal of minimising the risk of unethical corporate behaviour by aligning all parties with regard to compliance, ethics and CSR. His case reflects on ethical dilemmas that could emerge from doing business in a foreign country when there seems to be a discrepancy between the positive and negative impacts for different stakeholders in the supply chain. The second theme, productivity, here conceived of as meaning effective and efficient operations, is introduced by Han Verheijden. He points out that, especially in the leisure and hospitality sectors, capital productivity is exposed to higher risk than labour productivity and illustrates in his case how the interactions between profit, productivity and CSR could lead to dramatic challenges for young entrepreneurs. Françoise van den Broek-Serlé closes with a reflection on how organisations can make their CSR visible through taking extended responsibility for ethical sourcing and waste management – an issue with a global impact. Her case deals with the intriguing question of how 'fair' the manufacturing of a 'fair' mobile phone fundamentally is when we consider the consequences and impacts of retracting business from the developing countries where e-waste was previously dumped, but where this had enabled many poor families to make a living.

8.2 Supply-chain integrity
Jan-Willem Proper

8.2.1 Introduction to supply-chain integrity

8.2.1.1 Supply-chain integrity

Supply-chain integrity is a relatively new business practice that enables companies to manage their supply-and-demand relationships through strategies, operations and metrics that align overall business conduct (Brandenburg et al., 2014). One of the goals is to reduce the overall risk of integrity failure in the supply chain by ensuring the alignment of all involved parties in three major areas: compliance, ethics and corporate responsibility.

The supply chain is an area of focus for value creation and cost reduction. In essence, supply-chain management (SCM) integrates supply-and-demand management within and across companies. It encompasses the design, planning and operational management of all activities involved in sourcing and procurement, conversion, and all logistics-management activities ('Supply Chain Management', 2017). It is most often referred to as an essential element in operational efficiency (Christopher, 2008; Pienaar and Vogt, 2012).

Clearly, the impact that SCM has on business is also significant for customer satisfaction. It can be increased by making sure that the right product or assortment and the right quantity are delivered in a timely fashion at the desired location. Customers should also receive quality aftersales customer support, which includes a recall system they could rely on, if needed. With an increasing importance placed on transparency, consumers look beyond company practices to ensure that organisations uphold adequate supply-chain ethical decision-making. Sople states:

> Consumers, investors, business partners, regulators, and media organisations now expect a company and its entire supply chain to be ethical. The supplier-generated ethics scandal is probably one of the biggest (and least foreseen) business risks most leading companies face today. The damage can be great, and protective measures can and should be adopted immediately (2012: 438).

When managers perform risk assessments, it is important to include an evaluation of suppliers, vendors and any other points of contact within the physical supply chains and organisational networks (Dawson et al., 2016). This is to decrease the risks, and includes examining culture, ethics and compliance practices adopted by the partners. It helps managers to make informed decisions in selecting suppliers that 'fit' with their existing culture and practices.

Efficiency developments in supply chains are ongoing, and are caused by severe competition at the level of both products and brands. These developments also impact discussions about integrity areas in decision-making processes. Management decisions on supply chains touch upon major trends such as global expansion, the growth of multinational corporations and strategic partnerships. They also cover corporate social responsibility and environmental concerns, as well as the impact of regional differences from a business ethics perspective (Crane and

Matten, 2010: 20–24). Managers usually focus on future resource scarcity, and many are embarking on initiatives to reduce emissions, cut waste and develop other sustainable business practices. There is a continuous focus on optimising supply chains by using modern information technology (IT) and supply-chain finance, which affects cash flow and profits.

These issues affect the supply-chain strategy and bottom-line decisions of organisations, and induce reflection on the importance of professional and organisational ethics in this domain (Griseri and Seppela, 2010). In this context, professional ethics in supply chains, for example, is not only relevant to the board and directors of the organisation, but also to all other professionals who are in control of the supply chain and in touch with their external partners (Clegg and Rhodes, 2006; Fryer, 2015). Collaboration between channel partners is all about managing and optimising supply chains and is mostly a process of multi-organised coordination and cooperation. Although one of the channel partners is usually more dominant in the design of the supply, the operations are performed as part of a multi-organisational effort.

Since the early 1980s, a growing body of academic research has emerged, which addresses various environmental, social and ethical issues in supply chains (Quarshie, Salmi and Leuschner, 2016). Challenged by political and non-governmental organisation (NGO) discussions, for example the World Commission on Environmental Development (WCED), umbrella concepts like 'sustainability' and 'corporate social responsibility' have been increasingly used in communication and reflection. As indicated in the introduction of this chapter, numerous definitions and interpretations of sustainability and CSR exist, which means they are also 'contested'. In the following sections of this chapter, following the concepts of the 'pyramid of social responsibility' (Schwartz and Carroll, 2003) and the 'triple bottom line' of Elkington (Willard, 2002), the focus will be on managerial integrity within the context of the supply chain.

8.2.1.2 Managerial integrity in supply chains

Management decision-makers face different supply-chain risks: regulatory risks, brand erosion, and social compliance. Any one of these issues could lead to the loss of profits, product recalls and/or customer erosion. At the same time, the longer the supply chain – with more levels of suppliers, disparate geographies and other middlemen – the more complex and challenging compliance becomes (Wheelen, 2015). The role of management in dealing with possible risks is to create a supply-chain integrity approach. A global integrity approach, for example, should provide all decision-makers with a guide to acting on and obeying all applicable laws and regulations while conducting business around the world. This implies acting with integrity and making ethical decisions, because trust and confidence are critical for success in business, and more specifically, for maintaining structural relations with shareholders, employees and consumers. First of all, a direction statement on how to develop and operate with integrity is needed. Elements of this structural approach include decisions on a code of conduct which focusses on the personal responsibility that every employee in the supply chain has in ensuring that their companies conduct business in a legal and ethical way. The code of conduct needs to be transparent and clear and distributed around the world to all supply-chain partners. In addition, an integrity programme needs to be developed as part of the organisational culture. This might include appointing supply-chain integrity officers who work with senior management in implementing the programme, and offering (online) training programmes in understanding legal and ethical business practices. A programme for 'listening, investigating and acting', an audit committee and a reporting structure for informing supply-chain managers about the compliance of actions with the law and ethics will clearly support this endeavour.

In conclusion, it is important that the manager – with regard to 'supply chain integrity' – keeps the overview, is realistic and understands the complexities surrounding this issue. Especially in the global context, supply chains have multicultural links and involve many primary and secondary partners (the supplier of the supplier, the customer of the client), which makes this a big challenge. The costs of failure and of brand image damage need to be weighed against the appraisal and prevention costs.

8.2.1.3 Empowering integrity in supply chains

Managing a global supply chain with integrity could have huge benefits, since it generates animated discussions about the responsibilities organisations have with regard to creating opportunities and a climate that can strengthen the relationships and reputations on which companies' success depends. Complexity can never be used as an excuse for not acting with integrity. Therefore management needs to empower sustainable and ethical supply chains by driving performance improvements. This can be done through business practices in key areas like labour standards, health and safety and environment impacts. In addition, supply-chain managers need to focus on the following issues:

- *Prevention of the intention and appearance of unethical or compromising conduct.* This indicates an early focus on integrity issues when developing more sustainable supply chains, which can be done by concentrating on holistic solutions. At a minimum, this should involve the integration of ethical considerations into technical solutions by selecting partners with strong ethical values and compliance policies. This approach also emphasises considering partnerships critically, as the process and importance of establishing integrity in SCM must be created early in the contractual negotiation stage.
- *Championing ethical and sustainability practices in supply management.* The sustainable growth and integration of ethics in supply chains involves continuous debate amongst all partners about the managerial decisions to be taken on the quality and quantity of products and services, and also the process of transference from supplier to customer, as the operations expand.
- *Avoidance of behaviour or actions that may or might negatively influence supply-management decisions.* This includes managing and developing a stronger ethical culture by training beyond compliance, with links to product safety and customer safety and instilling a deeper ethical sense in all decision-makers involved in the supply chain. This will support companies when recalls are required and

will create trust amongst partners that will enable them to find the right solutions in case of a safety scandal, for example. This approach covers, in addition to supply-chain technical skills, the need for organisations to attract future decision-makers who are devoted to integrity in the supply-chain business, and to discuss their ethical ingenuity and professional and personal integrity.

- *Conducting business in such a way that competence is demonstrated and the supply-management profession is promoted.* Integrity awareness is increased by both strengthened regulatory enforcement and higher expectations amongst consumers. Bearing in mind some of the service- and product-safety scandals which have drawn much public attention during the last few years, supply-chain managers need to ensure quality and ethical conduct throughout the supply chain. This will push supply-chain managers to address these issues more effectively with their directly connected suppliers and distributors. In addition, by sharing information in the sector and with other sectors like NGOs and research organisations, the supply-chain sector can collaboratively, strategically and resourcefully apply best practices of integrity to SCM in order for their business to perform well in the long term, to harness internal and external resources and skills, and to achieve committed supply-chain organisations and employees (Glover et al., 2014; Amaeshi, Osuji and Nnodim, 2008; Gimenez, Sierra and Rodon, 2012). As Novak stated: 'Professional development requires continuing education' (2008: 9).

Implementing integrity in SCM practices and making quick, effective and transparent improvements is quite hard – certainly for larger organisations, which in some cases have hundreds of partners. A credible supply-chain manager places integrity policy and performance in supply-chain processes and practices at the heart of the company's business, and looks beyond the lowest price and bottom line. This manager buys the best, safest and most suitable products in accordance with the integrity policies of the company and seeks assurance that the company's partners have equally sound policies and performances. Sustainable and ethical SCM is not about appearances, marketing or sales, but about building a level of trust into the supply chain for all partners.

It is quite complicated to ensure that a supply chain fully adheres to environmentally and ethically sound standards. To deliver on the promises made in integrity policies, companies need to effectively monitor all performance. But often, there is a disconnect between intentions and actions. Many managers do not have structures in place to ensure that their supply chains achieve standards, and many companies rely on the self-auditing of their own suppliers. A company may claim to have a sustainable supply chain, but if it is not auditing its suppliers, how can it back up its statements? While the costs of setting up an auditing process need to be taken into consideration, these also needs to be weighed against long-term benefits, such as avoiding becoming entangled in an all-consuming web of legal proceedings and instilling a sense of shared accountability amongst employees.

How these challenges are perceived and met by customers and the general public will be demonstrated in the fictitious case presented below.

Corporate social responsibility

Case 8.2.2: Selling solar TVs in Benin City

Introduction

During a board meeting of a large company with 830 employees and a head office in Belgium, which mainly does business in African countries, the CEO announced that a very lucrative opportunity was at hand to deliver their main product (solar TVs) to a new market in Nigeria. Profits could be tripled, which would give the company's growth a much needed boost. It was on the verge of laying off about 10 per cent of its workforce. The project will be successful if 20 of the company's employees are stationed in Benin City in Edo province to oversee the production process. Local people will be trained and employed according to local labour conditions.

Conflicting interests

After the CEO has ended his presentation, the newly appointed ethical compliance officer, Martin, asked whether the supply-chain integrity would be guaranteed, since it is known that corruption is a big issue in Nigeria. The CEO said that bribes will inevitably be paid in order to get things done, but that this had been budgeted for and would cause very few problems. Sally intervened and said that it did not feel good, since the company had decided a month before that it wanted to do fair business and be ethical in its actions, and also expected its suppliers to comply. It was quiet for a while and then the CEO said: 'There is something else you should know: the cables and connectors of the solar panels will be imported from India, where they are fabricated by children. But since children and their families will die from hunger if they don't work, it seems right to me if we proceed. These children and their families will be able to make a living, about 200 families in Nigeria will be supported by family members who will be appointed by us, and our company will be put back on track with this much needed growth. It will enable us to invest in new products, and by the way, we will take care that the environment in Benin City will not be spoilt or harmed by the production.'

Neither Martin and Sally were amused, stating, 'We are violating our decision to keep our supply chain "clean" from unethical behaviour – both on our side and that of our suppliers.' The board was divided in its opinion: about a third of the board felt that they should not proceed, while the majority (two-thirds) felt that this was a one-time opportunity and the company should not miss out on it.

Questions for discussion

- The board is divided with regard to the question of whether the company should proceed with this project or not. Could you tease out the moral arguments of both the minority and majority positions amongst the members of the board?

(continued)

> **Case 8.2.2: Selling solar TVs in Benin City (*continued*)**
>
> - On which ethical principles do Martin's and Sally's objections rest?
> - While child labour is globally regarded as an offence against human rights, their labour in the case above will benefit the child workers and their families in India, the local employees and their families (200) in Benin City, keep 10 per cent of the employees of the company from losing their jobs, ensure that the profits of the company will be tripled, and last but not least, will not impact negatively on the environment. Is it morally sound to continue business activities when it is clear that the positive consequences outweigh the negative ones?
> - Could you think of a business case that would satisfy the minority of the board and get them to support the decision to proceed?
> - How, in general, can a company balance the principles of fair business, including a supplier code of conduct, with the interests of all stakeholders?

8.3 Productivity: Effective and efficient operations

Han Verheijden

8.3.1 Introduction to productivity

8.3.1.1 The relevance of productivity has increased over time

In the 1960s to the 1980s, leisure entrepreneurs, who will be the focus of reflection in this section, spectacularly increased their scale as well as their revenues and profits. Many companies in this sector have, during the last few decades, invested heavily in improving the quality of their products and of the organisations themselves. Leisure entrepreneurs have been transformed from pioneers into professional entrepreneurs.

Since 2005, the sector has known dramatic changes. For example, the Internet and globalisation created more potential markets on the one hand, but also more competition on the other. It was not always in a fair level playing field. In addition, the credit crunch of 2008 caused decreases in demand, revenue and profitability. Especially in Northern European countries, such as Belgium, the Netherlands, Denmark, Germany and Luxembourg, leisure companies suffered a great deal. They were (for the first time!) confronted with overcapacity, and thus with fiercer competition.

Because of all these developments, productivity, defined as 'effective and efficient operations', became a hot issue in the leisure industry. Instruments such as yield management, flexible labour management, multitasking and outsourcing have become standard procedures in organisations. And although the economic situation has improved lately, the need for efficiency will remain a standard factor in almost all leisure sectors. One could say that the leisure sector has entered a phase which places it on the same level as industry, transportation, retail and even services like healthcare.

Corporate social responsibility

8.3.1.2 Productivity instruments and strategies in both capital and labour

The leisure sector is both labour and capital intensive. Many companies and organisations tend to focus on labour costs in order to make 'quick wins' (improving productivity on the short term). The instruments that make an organisation more efficient include, amongst others, multitasking, outsourcing and flexibility – as indicated above.

Multitasking is quite often positively embraced by employees. After all, many tasks tend to grow into quite simple 'manual jobs' over time and thus become boring for highly educated people. Therefore, extra tasks and responsibilities often increase employees' job satisfaction.

However, outsourcing can cause damage for some workers. Especially older people, who regard themselves to have been loyal to the company for many years, feel offended and deserted. Younger employees are often more flexible and can be transferred to a new employer more easily and have a greater chance of pursuing a better career in a new situation.

Of the three productivity instruments mentioned above, flexibility is the highest source of stress – especially when it leads to uncertainty about income. Fortunately, the bottlenecks with regard to labour satisfaction that it causes, are not too severe. Many employees even prefer to work either part-time or as freelancers. It gives them more freedom and enables them to, for example, improve their household planning. Because many jobs in leisure (including hospitality) are occupied by young people and married women, this new operational approach encompassing more flexibility has been highly appreciated.

8.3.1.3 Lack of capital productivity is highly problematic

As stated before, the leisure (and hospitality) sector is also capital intensive. For example, purchasing or leasing luxurious touring cars or aeroplanes, and investing in apartments in resorts and attractions in theme parks is very expensive. Actually, capital productivity in leisure is more problematic than labour productivity. This phenomenon is caused by the following factors:

- The average occupancy of the assets is low, compared to industry-related services such as energy/power provision. This low grade of occupancy is related to the concentration of demand over time (season, evening, weekend etc.).
- The facilities are very inelastic, while the client is very elastic. The client can travel anywhere and looks for the lowest price, while the facilities are context-bound.
- Leisure is more cyclical than many other services like supermarkets or healthcare, since it is bound to recurring 'trends'.

As a result, many investors and banks are hesitant to get involved in the leisure industry. And many entrepreneurs consider these capital risks as being too high for them.

8.3.1.4 Shift of capital risk to non-professionals as a strategy

In many branches of the leisure sector entrepreneurs try to 'get rid' of the capital-intensive parts of the company. Many years ago American hotels chains, such as

Hilton and Holiday Inn, did the same. They assessed the situation and found that the investments in, for example, staff, marketing and automation were much more profitable than the return on investment (ROI) in buildings or land. Therefore, they created joint ventures between themselves and local investors. The local investor was to invest in the location, building and equipment while the hotel company focussed on the operations. Depending on the perceived market potential the hotel company opted for either a lease (including operational risks) or management contract (without any risk).

The success of this approach as followed by the hotel chains has inspired similar companies, such as holiday resorts, to follow the same strategy. The builders and/or operators who developed these resorts (by building apartments or vacation houses) could not – due to a lack of credible forecasts for return on investment – find one professional investor who was interested. Thus they sold these units to private families (sometimes in a timeshare format).

At the time of writing, this shifting of capital risks has become more or less the norm. Fast-food chains, restaurants, small hotels and the like try to find people who are willing to take over the capital risks. This has even become a specialty for real-estate developers who see an opportunity to make 'quick money'. They buy old resorts, camping grounds or hotel groups, split the assets into individual shares or plots and sell these with high margins to private families. Even corporate finance consultants create financial constructions which allow for investments in new concepts (for example, bars and fast-food establishments) and afterwards transfer the assets and operations to less professional entrepreneurs.

8.3.1.5 Shift of capital risk creates victims

Non-professionals often have the illusion that they can raise the same wealth as all successful entrepreneurs. This illusion is often fed by the providers of the business formats mentioned above ('make your dream come true'). People tend to be very optimistic about the profitability of their own plans, especially when these are confirmed or delivered by reputable accountants. In practice, they can lose a lot of money or even go bankrupt, which results in their suffering for the rest of their lives. Human dramas like these often lead people to feel ashamed and consider the disappointing results as a personal failure. Many entrepreneurs within the leisure and hospitality industry have suffered the same fate. It is therefore important to consider replacing these kinds of business models with new, more sustainable ones that concord with the ideal of CSR. Strategies for improving productivity, and therefore effectiveness and efficiency of operations, should be monitored by all relevant stakeholders in the industry. Banks, accountants and – last but not least – the providers of leisure and hospitality services themselves should sit together and draw up a viable and sustainable business plan which makes a clear distinction between effectiveness and efficiency. It is not about making (short-term) profits at all costs, but about transparent and honest communication and co-creating value that exceeds profit alone, as well as considering the long-term outcomes and benefit for all involved.

In the case below, an example is given of how the close relationship between low capital productivity and the shift of capital risk in the leisure sector could lead to the dramatic and tragic victimisation of two young entrepreneurs.

Case 8.3.2: Profits, productivity and corporate social responsibility

Introduction: Pursuing capital productivity

Jan and Ilona (both Polish citizens and 35 years old) are married and met each other while studying at a middle-management hospitality school in Poland. They both are very enthusiastic cooks and consider themselves to be professionals in both catering and general hospitality services. They are good at multitasking, quite flexible and always work overtime without claiming extra wages. Despite 15 years of hard work in different hotels and restaurants, all over Europe, they had not built up much of a career. They noticed that other employees have moved quite rapidly to senior management positions, while they remained on the same level. They felt that their hard work and self-sacrifice have unjustly passed over for reward. Jan and Ilona decided to start their own business. They think of starting a restaurant, bar or small hotel. They have ample experience after all, and have saved capital to the amount of €150,000. They decided to contact an agency in the catering industry.

The catering agency Jan and Ilona contacted is called Midlands Premium. It is a young company with relatively high costs because of its prestigious office location. The company earns its money through intermediate services between buyers and sellers on a 'no-cure-no-pay' basis. Its earning model requires signed contracts. The agent Jan and Ilona talked to was called Michael. He is an assertive, almost aggressive man with a lot of charm and strong sales competence. It just so happened that Michael was dealing with an order for a local estate group (GDC) which had developed a commercial golf club with a total investment of € 5.5 million. It wanted to sell 800 'shares' (at a price of €9,000 each), which would create a situation whereby the whole project was funded, with a development margin of €1.7 million. Furthermore, GDC has to create a clubhouse, including a restaurant-bar and shop. The costs have been estimated at €0.5 million. The group has tried to sell this complex to local professional catering entrepreneurs, who do not believe that they will make a sound profit, since the operational costs are quite high and the expenditure of the golf players is uncertain. The company GDC has promised all participants that the clubhouse would be open seven days a week, twelve hours a day. Yet the expectation was that the turnover would not be profitable. The owner of the golf club does not want to lose a part of his margin and insists on selling all capital assets, including the clubhouse. Michael has to find a buyer/operator as soon as possible.

The risk implodes: Collapse of a dream

Michael saw an opportunity to match Jan and Ilona's dream of starting their own business with GDC's the assignment of GDC and advised them to buy the clubhouse. He provided them with a report from a highly reputable

(continued)

Case 8.3.2: Profits, productivity and corporate social responsibility (*continued*)

accountant who states that a revenue of €1.5 million per annum is feasible. The operational profits had been forecast at approximately €300,000. The investment of €500,000 could easily be earned back within a few years. Michael suggested having lunch with a senior account manager of the bank, who was a golf and catering expert himself, and might be willing to lend the €350,000 which Jan and Ilona need to buy the clubhouse. It all worked out well and the deal was cut. GDC promised to include furniture and decoration in the price. Money for the food and beverage supply could be borrowed from a local brewery. GDC charged a reasonable interest of only 8 per cent on their (extra) loan of €30,000 for this purpose. Jan and Ilona opened the doors of their new establishment five months later and celebrated with a party which cost € 3000. They assumed that GDC would pay for the event.

But then the nightmare started. Within the first week after opening, they learned that GDC was not willing to pay the bill for the opening party; they had to pay Michael €7500 for mediation fees, having expected that the seller would do that; the bank charged them another €5500 in administration costs for their loan; and the notary sent his invoice for transfer tax and service costs in the amount of €7,899. Suddenly their total debt was €404,000 and the redemption and interest costs were fixed at €2,200 per month.

Jan and Ilona worked very hard right from the beginning, but earned very little. The club members' expenditure appeared to be very poor. Many golf players did not spend anything at all and on rainy days only a few players showed up. The revenues of one month amounted to no more than €7,230. The operational costs (such as energy, purchase, maintenance contracts, repair and cleaning staff) were found to be much higher than expected: €5,240! This meant that Jan and Ilona could not pay the interest and redemption on their loans, let alone their own salary. A few months later, earnings had increased a bit, but so had the debts – because of the high monthly charges. Four months later, neither Michael's bill nor the notary's invoice had yet been paid.

Michael filed for bankruptcy. The notary and the brewer insisted that their bills should be paid. In a meeting with the department for bank default it became clear that bankruptcy was inevitable. The bank would apply mortgage law. The bank had already ordered Midlands Premium to find a new buyer or a tenant. Jan and Ilona were summoned to pay back all their debts (at that stage amounting to €435,000). Parts of their future salaries would be withheld by the liquidator for a period of 15 years. After this meeting, Jan and Ilona tried to contact Michael, Jack, the CEO of GDC and the accountant, but no one could be reached.

Questions for discussion

- How is productivity defined by the main parties in this story? Which party was the most 'moral' in their definition?
- Capital productivity is very hard in leisure and hospitality. How should productivity in the sense of effectiveness and efficiency be implemented or applied to this case in order to optimise benefits for all parties involved?
- Which party in this case most lived up to the ideal of CSR? How do you see the relationship between ethics and CSR?
- Do you think that Jan and Ilona are themselves responsible for this failure? After all, they failed to investigate the business case thoroughly (GDC's proposal) and started a company in a market in which they had no experience. If yes, why and if no, why not?
- What is the professional and moral responsibility of all other actors (GDC's CEO Jack, Michael, the bank, the brewer, the accountant)? Who should take the most responsibility and why?

8.4 Ethical sourcing and (electronic) waste management

Françoise van den Broek-Serlé

8.4.1 Introduction to ethical sourcing and (electronic) waste management

8.4.1.1 CSR, ethics and sustainable thinking

Environmental and social considerations have become more important in corporate decision-making in recent years. Companies increasingly deem a well-implemented and strongly enforced CSR policy necessary in order to facilitate their contribution to sustainable development (McKinnon et al., 2015: 107). Holmes and Watts define CSR as 'the continuing commitment by business to behave ethically and contribute to economic development while improving the quality of life of the workforce and their families as well as of the local community and society at large' (2000: 8). More specifically, CSR, within the framework of sustainable thinking, is important since the resources businesses use, the products they make and the resulting waste streams pose enormous challenges for future generations. Considering the fate of future generations, CSR could be seen as a matter of justice and therefore as an essential part of sustainable thinking. It includes 'the broad moral order within which all trends of inequality or exploitation are contextualised' (Jacques, 2015: 121).

As far as environmental issues are concerned, the reduction of greenhouse gas (GHG) emissions from logistic activities appears to be one of the most prominent aspects of CSR discussed in recent academic literature. The rise in environmentally responsible logistic operations has been a 'result of governmental regulations, economic considerations and increasingly strong market signals from environmental conscious consumers' (Goldsby and Stank, 2000: 187–208). In addition, scholars increasingly point out that there is an environmental dimension to sustainability ethics (Kibert et al., 2011: 95–118).

It is important not to ignore or neglect the social element in CSR. McKinnon et al. (2015: 117) incisively point out that the main social sustainability aspects covered in logistics research include the following issues:

- Labour and human rights.
- Employment (contracts, wages and compensations).
- Working conditions, and occupational health and safety.
- Job satisfaction, working hours, and the time workers stay away from home.
- Ethics.
- Workforce diversity.

McKinnon et al.'s position shows that CSR can essentially be regarded an ethical issue, which also applies to the responsibility companies have towards managing their supply chains in a sound way.

8.4.1.2 Supply chains and globalisation

Since the 1970s, the pace of globalisation has increased rapidly. It has had a major effect on the development of logistics. Major factors in this have been the 'widespread adoption of the standard shipping container, international trade liberalisation, the expansion of international transport infrastructure such as ports, roadways and railroads, and production and logistics cost differentials between developed and developing countries' (Grant, Trautrims and Wong, 2013: 12). The geographical length of supply chains has increased and environmental issues of fuel, emissions and responsibilities have become more and more complex. In particular, the production locations and sales markets of fast-moving consumer goods and electronics have internationalised at a very high pace.

This means that a customer base can be expanded quite effectively through the extension of the supply chains to places all over the world. In addition, companies have also gained access to less expensive labour and materials. However, Grant, Trautrims and Wong put forward that, due to global sourcing and distribution, globalised supply chains face greater risks and ethical dilemmas despite the economic benefits, because it sometimes 'is inevitable to source raw materials and products from countries facing more frequent natural disasters or man-made production' (2013: 175). This can cause a 'reputational risk' for the companies involved, as has often been revealed by non-governmental organisations (NGOs) such as Greenpeace, the World Wildlife Fund and Save the Children.

8.4.1.3 Product life cycle and waste

Research into sustainable distribution of goods has mainly focussed on the improvement of product delivery from manufacturer to end consumer. There was a need to understand how the various supply chain operations function at local, regional and global levels (McKinnon et al., 2015: 338). It was found that the reverse or return networks and systems were significantly underdeveloped (Grant et al., 2013: 16). The logistic activities associated with these developments have drawn the attention of businesspeople because cost reduction and the maximisation of efficiency within the distribution sector is financially quite attractive. However, not only have the economics related to the development of reverse logistics gained importance: the product life cycle has also caught the eye of companies.

The standard linear approach to the product life cycle is often referred to as 'take, make, waste/dispose' or 'cradle-to-grave' (McDonough and Braungart, 2002). The linear model draws on big quantities of resources and energy that are easily accessible. As such this model becomes increasingly obsolete, because it generates scarcity, waste and pollution, and is not in line with sustainable thinking. As far as waste is concerned, Grant et al. state that 'waste is generated when a product is no longer functional, needed or fashionable, and which its owner wants to dispose or discard. Waste may also be generated during the extraction of raw materials, the processing of raw materials into intermediate and final products, and the consumption of final products' (2013: 149). In addition, materials discarded by municipalities, electrical and electronic manufacturers, and industrial companies and new, or counterfeit (fake or illegal) pesticides developed by agricultural businesses, could also be labelled as 'waste'. Decommissioned ships, mobile phones and used car tyres can also be added to this list (Rucevska et al., 2015). More than ever before, it seems important that mankind comes to learn how to manage waste effectively. The future of the planet depends on it.

Robertson describes how companies dealt with waste until the beginning of the twentieth century. It was put into 'dumps', meaning that it was put in a hole in the ground or piled up on top of the ground. The waste was left uncovered and exposed to the elements. But in the twentieth century, he goes on, 'the technology of the sanitary landfill was developed. This type uses methods intending to keep surroundings clean by preventing leaks into soil and water. Landfills do not treat waste; they provide long-term storage' (2014: 270). Approximately 64.5 per cent of the waste produced by municipalities in the United States is sent to landfill; the remaining 35.5 per cent is incinerated. Incineration can be thought of as a method of reducing the volume of landfill waste. The ashes must be landfilled. Ash left over from incineration contains heavy metals, dioxins, and other toxic pollutants, which become concentrated. When the ash is stored in a landfill site, these toxins can become mobile in leachate and enter soil and groundwater (Robertson, 2014: 271). In the Netherlands, landfilled waste decreased until 2009 after which it stabilised at about 2.4 million metric tons (Mt) in 2013 (*Afvalverwerking in Nederland, Gegevens 2013*, 2014: 5).

Yet a special kind of waste should be mentioned here, since it will become more and more relevant in the current digital and electronic age. It is electronic waste (e-waste).

8.4.1.3.1 ELECTRONIC WASTE

The term electronic waste refers to denotes discarded electronics and electrical appliances such as computers, cell/smartphones, televisions and refrigerators (Robertson, 2014: 276). It is

> Largely categorized as hazardous due to the presence of toxic materials such as mercury, lead and brominated flame retardants. E-waste may also contain precious metals such as gold, copper and nickel, and rare materials of value such as indium and palladium making it an attractive trade. In practice, many shipments of e-waste are disguised as second hand goods. (Rucevska et al., 2015: 8)

Maczulak estimates that 'up to 80% of America's e-waste is exported to developing countries, where environmental and worker protection laws and enforcement are less strict (2010: 36). Sims (2010) adds that low-wage workers (including children) in those countries do not wear protective clothes but have to burn that waste, 'soak them [sic] in acid baths to separate small amounts of resalable materials, breath [sic] dioxin-filled smoke, and disassemble lead- and mercury-laden parts with their hands'. In addition, 'contaminated water is poured into lakes and rivers and contaminated solid waste is dumped in huge piles near villages, where toxins continue to leak into soil and water supply' (as cited in Robertson, 2014: 277).

The latest research on e-waste estimates that about 41.8 Mt of e-waste was generated in 2014 (as much as US$18.8 billion annually). This number have increased to 50 Mt by 2018 (Baldé et al., 2015: 8). According to various calculations, the amount of e-waste properly recycled and disposed of, ranges between 10 and 40 per cent (UNODC, 2013). Rucevska et al. point out that 'the presence of the informal economy (including illegal handling) makes solid estimates of the value for the sector difficult' and suggest that the monitoring and governing of e-waste and illegal behaviour will increase if structures of sustainable management are not implemented. In addition, attempts to public health of people and protecting the environment will be undermined (2015: 7; 4).

Examples of serious crimes in the (international) e-waste chain are the following:

- Exposing populations to toxic material through improper handling and disposal.
- Falsification of customs forms, tax fraud through over- or under-invoicing costs and incomes or money laundering.
- Bypassing environmental legislation and tax laws for profit.
- Deliberately classifying e-waste as other items to deceive law-enforcement authorities (using product codes for hazardous waste).

Key destinations for large-scale shipments of hazardous waste, such as electrical and electronic equipment, include Africa and Asia – for example, China, Hong Kong, Pakistan, India, Bangladesh and Vietnam (Rucevska et al., 2015: 8).

The most important incentive for the illegal shipping of waste to destination countries is the profit made from payments made for the safe disposal of waste. The beneficiaries of the profit usually consist of exporters, middlemen and informal recyclers. 'Their activities are usually structured along a legal chain of operations, albeit where the players take advantage of loopholes in control regimes and actual control capacities' (Rucevska et al., 2015: 8). In reality, the destination countries either dump most of the waste, or recycle it in an unsafe manner. Some profits might indeed be made from the recycling of certain components, but while this aspect seems to be positive, the overall outcome of these activities is that an environment is created which is very dangerous to the health of the local people.

Most US states have legislation which mandates the recycling of e-waste. Some electronic manufacturers have instituted voluntary take-back programmes which allow consumers to return old electronics to those manufacturers for recycling when they buy new ones. The last decade has shown increasing interest in new ways of dealing with waste, such as recycling, reverse logistics and, on macro level, the introduction of a circular economy. It seems that more and more people feel that the entire operating system should be changed (*Delivering the Circular Economy*, 2015).

8.4.1.4 Recycling, reverse logistics and circular economies (closing the loop)

Reverse logistics and recycling play important roles in sustainable logistics and SCM. They take care of the end-of-life phase of the chain. Recycling is a method of disposal that is better than landfilling and incineration, since materials are extracted from the waste stream and processed for reuse in some way or another (Robertson, 2014: 272). Recycled materials used in manufacturing new products 'almost always use less water and energy, release less pollution and emit less carbon dioxide than manufacturing with virgin materials' (Robertson, 2014: 275–276). McKinnon et al. hold that end markets are of paramount importance for reverse logistics networks that handle recycled material. The absence of these markets has long been regarded as a barrier to recycling. To change this, the Waste and Resources Action Plan (WRAP) was established in 2000. It embraces a vision that opts for the creation of stable markets for recyclable materials (2015: 346).

Reverse logistics is central to a closed-loop supply chain, which typically comprises both a forward flow of materials from suppliers to end customers, and a backward flow of products to the manufacturing or distribution supply chains. 'Reverse logistics prevents the disposal of end-of-life products in less environmental friendly channels such as landfill and incineration' (Grant et al., 2013: 152) and, in addition, it 'impacts the profitability and any closed-loop chain' (Fleischmann, 2001: 18).

8.4.1.4.1 REVERSE LOGISTICS, RECYCLING AND REGULATIONS

The effectiveness of reverse logistics and recycling systems depends partly on regulations. The development and implementation of European Union (EU) waste policy and legislation takes place within the context of several wider EU policies and programmes – including the Seventh Environment Action Programme, the Resource Efficiency Roadmap and the Raw Materials Initiative (European Commission, n.d.). These initiatives and regulations set up by the European Commission were meant to drive the reverse and recycling movements in Europe and give sustainability thinking and CSR a boost (Grant et al., 2013: 171).

8.4.1.4.2 ENVIRONMENTALLY FRIENDLY, RECYCLABLE PRODUCTS AND MATERIALS

The high costs of the disposal of dangerous waste, weak regulations regarding the environment, poor enforcement and low environmental awareness, and the illegal transportation of dangerous waste from developed countries to developing countries (destination countries) have raised great global concern.

There are several ways in which action could be taken. It is obvious that the uncontrolled disposal of electronic waste must stop and that clever methods and techniques for cleaning up the mess should be implemented. Safeguarding drinking water for local communities is an ongoing battle given that current solutions such as chlorination, distillation, boiling and high-tech filtration are very often reliant on fossil fuels. A new filtering device designed by eighteen-year-old Perry Alagappan removes 99 per cent of heavy metals from water that passes through it. And it costs a mere $20 to make, which is five times less than the existing technology used. For his invention, Alagappan was awarded the Stockholm Junior Water Prize at 2015's World Water Week. He announced that he would not patent his groundbreaking water-cleaning technology, but would share it with the world (Mathiesen and Riley, 2015).

Figueredo and Guillén calls for an intensification of the production of environmentally friendly materials and products, and the reuse of waste to counter the negative impact of waste disposal. They point out that currently about 80 to 90 per cent of end-of-life electronic products are still being sent to landfill sites, and advocates a design for recycling (DFR) technologies in order to change this situation. They argue that, through DFR, two goals can be reached: first, the use of 'hazardous or toxic materials that may present a grave danger to the environment or put recycling workers in jeopardy' could be eliminated or reduced and, secondly, it could 'discourage the use of materials that are not recyclable or manufacturing techniques that make a product non-recyclable using current techniques' (2012: 6).

Last, but not least, action should be taken to somehow 'enforce' ethical behaviour through the introduction of codes of conduct, for example, to suppliers. This is especially important for the electronics sector and will be addressed next.

8.4.1.4.3 SUPPLIERS' CODES OF CONDUCT IN THE ELECTRONICS INDUSTRY

Global original equipment manufacturers (OEMs) have traditionally sourced the production of components from manufacturers in other countries than their own. This has been mentioned above. Health, safety and working conditions are critical issues for companies such as Hewlett-Packard (HP), Apple, Dell and IBM. The social and environmental performance of these companies can only be assured with the involvement and cooperation of their suppliers. The Electronic Industry Code of Conduct (EICC) was developed by, amongst others, these aforementioned companies and the electronic manufacturers Solectron, Sanmina-SCI, Flextronics, Celestica and Jabil (Grant et al., 2013: 197). The EICC Group entered a partnership with the Global eSustainability Initiative (GeSI) in 2005, which represents information and communications technology companies in Europe, North America and Asia. However, only a few companies appreciate these efforts to increase CSR and sustainability, and with it their competitive advantage. Although damage to the environment caused by their supply chains could lead to reputational damage and reduction of profits, still, many companies tend to see regulations as merely an extra cost (Grant et al., 2013: 197–199). Many purchasers are currently still rewarded if they sustain lower costs – independent from the environmental costs of their activities.

Progress can only be made when social responsibility is not viewed as an obligation, but as part of the values of a company. The following case addresses this issue within the context of developing a 'fair mobile phone'.

Case 8.4.2: The mobile phone as a change agent?

Introduction

For quite some time, developed countries have shipped tons of obsolete mobile phones and other electronic devices to developing countries. Neither the developed nor developing countries were aware of the environmental disaster this could cause. In particular, many poor children were attempting – and still do attempt – to make a living for their families by collecting valuable components from the devices through a process of incineration. Not only does this cause a lot of pollution, but also, as the children do not wear protective gear, it causes illness and disease.

Gradually, the developed world came to realise that these devices contain many valuable materials, which could be exploited by themselves. Therefore, developed countries no longer dispose of this kind of waste by sending it to poor and developing countries. The concept of 'extended producer responsibility', meaning that a producer is held responsible for the post-consumer stage of a product's life cycle, is gaining global popularity. There are signs that these developed countries even want to excavate their municipal rubbish dumps, which came into being in the 1950s.

Partly against this background, the 'Fairphone' initiative was launched a couple of years ago. It started with the idea of raising awareness of so-called 'conflict minerals' in electronics and has grown into a social enterprise that actively pursues 'fairer products and a fairer supply chain as well as giving people the possibility to buy as a political act' (Wiens, 2014). The company has an ambitious agenda. It 'aims to produce the world's first fair mobile phone: a mobile device that is being designed and produced while doing minimal harm to human beings or the environment' ('The Mobile Phone as Change Agent', 2012). Fairphone, according to its founder Bas van Abel, seeks to advocate and encourage mining systems that are fair, to work towards improvement in production and working conditions, to pursue 'smart design' that is sustainable, to promote the recycling and reuse of products and to uphold transparency in doing business ('The Mobile Phone as Change Agent', 2012). By doing business in this way, the company's activities – across the entire product life cycle, from the extraction of minerals up to its destruction – will be steered by choices that are fundamentally sustainable.

How 'fair' is 'fair'?

'Fairphone' has created the world's first ethical smartphone, and initially sold 25,000 mobile phones – which could by no means be compared with Apple's record of selling 9 million iPhone 5S in one weekend, but could still be regarded a relatively powerful achievement for a company that had no track record at that time. It indicates that people are ready for change if the

(continued)

Case 8.4.2: The mobile phone as a change agent? (*continued*)

alternatives are qualitatively competitive and reasonable. However, there are still a few issues that need reflection.

Firstly, Fairphone is just like other manufacturers of mobile phones, as it is confronted with all the complexities that the production process of mobile phones and the supply chain entail. Smartphones, for example, are quite complicated to build. Wiens relates that they are composed of 'anywhere from 500 to 1,000 individual component materials – from heavy metals to chemicals' (2014). These supply chains run all over the world and it is therefore very difficult to track down these materials, which have passed through the hands of miners, middlemen, distributors and factories many, many times before ending up in a mobile telephone. Can the 'fair trade' of materials be fully guaranteed?

Secondly, by taking the end-of-life cycle of a product into account at the very beginning, the mobile phone's design could allow its components and materials to be reused when producing or assembling new electronic products – something which Fairphone is doing. This causes less environmental damage, depletion of raw materials and pollution, and offers more transparent value chains and proper jobs, all of which are the right things to do. But the other side of the coin is that the manufacturing of fair smartphones in developed countries could have an adverse impact on people in developing countries who depend for their living on the dismantling of obsolete smartphones. As indicated above, developed countries are starting to see the value of reusing or recycling electronic waste, which will leave developing countries to encounter a loss of income when the disposal of electronic waste in these countries stops. These countries will be left behind with highly polluted sites such as the burning platforms and the population will be thrown back into a poverty that will be worse than before. Not to mention the impact thereof on the economies of these countries.

Therefore, can the development of a 'fair' mobile phone be a change agent given the complexity of the playing field?

Questions for discussion

- The title of this case suggests that a fair mobile phone could serve as a change agent for sustainability thinking and integrating CSR into the very DNA of a company. Yet the question mark indicates doubt. Could you – considering this case – identify the ethical dilemma(s) that is/are expressed by its title?
- Does advocating sustainability as the main focus of CSR imply ignoring or downplaying the social side of CSR? Give ethical reasons for your position.
- Try to identify the ethical principles that are in play when a company designs, produces, stores, distributes, uses, disposes or reuses products. Which principle do you regard as the most important?

- In which way should a circular economy take the social and environmental impacts of business into account, such as the retrieval of electronic waste from countries which heavily depend on it for income?
- Can you think of other change agents in the realm of social business which testify to the ideal of CSR? How do the ethical values and principles that steer them compare with the ethical values and principles that 'Fairphone' holds in high regard?

8.5 Concluding thoughts

Corporate social responsibility (CSR) is seen as part of the core business of enterprises. However, no uniform and globally accepted definition of it yet exists. It is theoretically and conceptually often used as a synonym for business ethics and/or sustainability, maybe because CSR is not really new to business. Business has always had a connection with stakeholders, governments, owners, and also a social, environmental and economic impact. As a 'technical term' CSR can be regarded as a common denominator for issues like social investment, community involvement, philanthropy, social responsibility and performance, stakeholder orientation, the triple bottom line and lately also the phenomenon of social entrepreneurship (see also Chapter 11). Some people see CSR as an issue that focusses on the good things that a company does, while seeing business ethics as an issue that focusses on the unethical behaviour of companies. Others deem sustainability to be the core of CSR. However, business ethics is arguably the most foundational layer of both sustainability and CSR, because it reflects the values, norms and principles that permeate the mission, vision, strategy and activities of the company in such a way that harmful and unethical business behaviour is addressed and corrected, and at the same time reflects on ways to do good and responsible business.

Therefore, in practice, CSR refers to the concrete manifestations of a company's basic ideas and approaches to business, such as written codes, training of employees on ethical issues, and reports on (ethical) performance on the one hand, and the way decisions are taken with regard to concrete business plans and activities on the other. This is to say that CSR is expressed in the choices a company makes, and becomes visible in the way it lives up to its own views of the (social) responsibility it has – within its regular, daily practices. CSR anno 2019 is still a voluntary endeavour which, broadly taken, reflects the way in which social and environmental concerns and stakeholder interaction are integrated within a company's business model.

Further reading

Aras, G. and Crowther, D. (2016). *A Handbook of Corporate Governance and Social Responsibility*. Abingdon, UK/New York: Routledge.

Freeman, R.E., Harrison, J.S., Wicks, A.C. Parmar, B.L. and De Colle, S. (2014). *Stakeholder Theory: The State of the Art*. Cambridge: Cambridge University Press.

Hemingway, C.A. (2013). *Corporate Social Entrepreneurship: Integrity Within*. Cambridge: Cambridge University Press.

Visser, W. (2014). *CSR 2.0: Transforming Corporate Sustainability and Responsibility*. London/New York: Springer.

References

Afvalverwerking in Nederland: Gegevens 2013 (2014). Utrecht: Rijkswaterstaat. Retrieved 25 May 2017 from https://www.verenigingafvalbedrijven.nl/fileadmin/user_upload/Documenten/PDF2014/Werkgroep_Afvalregistratie_Afvalverwerking_in_Nederland_gegevens_2013_1.1_december_2014.pdf.

Amaeshi, K.M., Osuji, O.K. and Nnodim, P. (2008). Corporate Social Responsibility in Supply Chains of Global Brands: A Boundary Less Responsibility? Clarifications, Exceptions and Implications. *Journal of Business Ethics*, 81: 223–234.

Baldé, C.P., Wang, F., Kuehr, R., and Huisman, J. (2015). *The Global E-waste Monitor 2014: Quantities, Flows and Resources*. Tokyo/Bonn: United Nations University.

Blewitt, J. (2008). *Understanding Sustainable Development*. London/Sterling: Earthscan.

Brandenburg, M., Govindan, K., Sarkis, J. and Seuringa, S. (2014). Quantitative Models for Sustainable Supply Chain Management: Developments and Directions. *European Journal of Operational Research*, 233(2): 299–312.

Calvo-Soraluze, J., de Brito, M.P. and San Salvador del Valle, R. (2015, September). *Making waves in events: From trends to future competences*. Paper presented at: Making Waves in Macao: The 3rd International Conference on Events (ICE2015), 7–9 September, Institute for Tourism Studies, Macao, China.

Carroll, A.B. (1991). The Pyramid of Corporate Social Responsibility: Toward the Moral Management of Organizational Stakeholders. *Business Horizons,* 34(4): 39–48.

Cavagnaro, E., Postma, A. and de Brito, M.P. (2016). Events: The Sustainability Agenda. In Ferdinand, N. and Kitchin, P.J. (Eds.), *Events Management: An International Approach* (2nd ed.). London/Thousand Oaks: Sage.

Christopher, M. (2008). *Logistics and Supply Chain Management: Creating Value-Adding Networks*. Dorchester: Prentice Hall.

Clegg, S. and Rhodes, C. (2006). *Management Ethics: Contemporary Contexts*. New York: Routledge.

Coles, T., Fenclova, E. and Dinan, C. (2013). Tourism and Corporate Social Responsibility: A Critical Review and Research Agenda. *Tourism Management Perspectives*, 6: 122–141.

Corporate Strategy. (n.d.). In *Business Dictionary*. Retrieved 15 March 2019 from www.businessdictionary.com.

Crane, A. and Matten, D. (2010). *Business Ethics* (3rd ed.). Oxford/New York: Oxford University Press.

Crane, A. and Matten, D. (2015). *Business Ethics: Managing Corporate Citizenship in the Age of Globalization* (4th ed.). Oxford/New York: Oxford University Press.

Dawson, R.J., Thompson, D., Johns, D., Gosling, S., Chapman, L., Darch, G., Watson, G., Powrie, W., Bell, S., Paulson, K., Hughes, P., and Wood, R. (2016). *UK Climate Change Risk Assessment Evidence Report: Chapter 4, Infrastructure*. Report prepared for the Adaptation Sub-Committee of the Committee on Climate Change, London.

De Brito, M.P. and Terzieva, L. (2016). Key Elements for Designing a Strategy to Generate Social and Environmental Value: a Comparative Study of Festivals. *Research in Hospitality Management*, 6(1): 51–59.

Delivering the Circular Economy: A Toolkit for Policymakers (2015). The Ellen MacArthur Foundation. Retrieved 28 August 2016 from https://www.ellenmacarthurfoundation.org/assets/downloads/publications/EllenMacArthurFoundation_Policymaker-Toolkit.pdf.

Dhanesh, G.S. (2015). Why Corporate Social Responsibility? An Analysis of Drivers of CSR in India. *Management Communication Quarterly*, 29(1): 114–129.

Djaballah, M., Hautbois, C. and Desbordes, M. (2016). Sponsors' CSR Strategies in Sport: A Sense Making Approach of Corporations Established in France. *Sport Management Review*, 20(2): 211–225.

Engbert, S. and Baumgartner, R.J. (2016). Corporate Sustainability Strategy – Bridging the Gap between Formulation and Implementation. *Journal of Cleaner Production*, 113: 822–834.

European Commission. (n.d.). *Seventh Environment Action Programme, the Resource Efficiency Roadmap and the Raw Materials Initiative*. Retrieved 19 August 2015 from http://ec.europa.eu/environment/waste/index.htm.

Figueredo, J.N. de, and Guillén, M.F. (2012). *Green Products: Perspectives on Innovation and Adoption*. Boca Raton, FL: Taylor & Francis.

Fleischmann, M. (2001). *Reverse Logistics Network Structures and Design*. ERIM Report Series Research in Management. Rotterdam: Erasmus Research Institute of Management. Retrieved 25 May 2017 from https://pdfs.semanticscholar.org/8158/62422d-9fee6a06123b556703e52ff68f9b14.pdf.

Freeman, R.E. (1984). *Strategic Management: A Stakeholder Approach*. Boston, MA: Pitman.

Fryer, M. (2015). *Ethics Theory: Business Practice*. London/Thousand Oaks, CA: Sage.

Gardner, J.R., Rachlin, R. and Sweeny, H.W.A. (1986). *Handbook of Strategic Planning*. Hoboken, NJ: John Wiley & Sons.

Gardiner, L., Rubbens, C. and Bonfiglioli, E. (2003). Big Business, Big Responsibilities. *Corporate Governance*, 3(3): 67–77.

Gimenez, C., Sierra, V. and Rodon, J. (2012). Sustainable Operations: Their Impact on Triple Bottom Line. *International Journal of Production Economics*, 140(1): 149–159.

Glover, J.L., Champion, D., Daniels, K.J. and Dainty, A.J.D. (2014). An Institutional Theory Perspective on Sustainable Practices across the Dairy Supply Chain. *International Journal of Production Economics*, 152: 102–111.

Goldsby, T.J. and Stank, T.P. (2000). World-Class Logistics Performance and Environmentally Responsible Logistics Practices. *Journal of Business Logistics*, 21(2): 187–208.

Gond, J. and Herrbach, O.J. (2006). Social Reporting as an Organizational Learning Tool? *Journal of Business Ethics*, 65(4): 359–371.

Graham, L. (2015, 8 July). Apple Watch Online Sales Plunge 90% in US: Report. *CNBC*. Retrieved 19 August 2015 from http://www.cnbc.com/2015/07/08/apple-watch-online-sales-plunge-90-in-us-report.html.

Grant, D.B., Trautrims, A. and Wong, C.Y. (2013). *Sustainable Logistics and Supply Chain Management: Principles and Practices for Sustainable Operations and Management*. London/Philadelphia: Kogan Page Limited.

Griseri, P. and Sepella, N. (2010). *Business Ethics and Corporate Social Responsibility*. Andover, UK: Cengage Learning.

Holmes, L. and Watts, R (2000). *Corporate Social Responsibility: Making Good Business Sense*. Conches-Geneva: World Business Council for Sustainable Development.

Hooghiemstra, R. (2000). Corporate Communication and Impression Management: New Perspectives Why Companies Engage in Corporate Social Reporting. *Journal of Business Ethics*, 27: 55–68.

ID&T – Choose Tap Water. (2014). Video. Delight Agency. Retrieved 20 May 2016 from http://www.delightagency.nl/2014/05/idt-choose-tap-water/.

Jacques, P. (2015). *Sustainability: The Basics*. London: Routledge.

Jeffery, N. (2009). *Stakeholder Engagement: A Road Map to Meaningful Engagement*. Cranfield, UK: Doughty Centre, Cranfield School of Management. Retrieved 12 March 2019 from https://www.fundacionseres.org/lists/informes/attachments/1118/stakeholder%20engagement.pdf.

Karaosmanoglu, E., Altinigne, N. and Isiksal, D.G. (2016). CSR Motivation and Customer Extra-role Behaviour: Moderation of Ethical Corporate Identity. *Journal of Business Research*, 69: 4161–4167.

Kibert, C.J., Monroe, M.C., Peterson, A.L., Plate, R.R. and Thiele, L.P. (2011). *Working Towards Sustainability: Ethical Decision Making in a Technological World*. Hoboken, NJ: John Wiley & Sons.

Kim, Y. (2014). Strategic Communication of Corporate Social Responsibility: Effects of Stated Motives and Corporate Reputation on Stakeholder Responses. *Public Relations Review*, 40: 838–840.

Kramer, M. and Kania, J. (2006). Changing the Game: Leading Corporations Switch from Defence to Offence in Solving Global Problems. *Stanford Social Innovation Review*, 4(1): 20–27.

Lee, M-D. P. (2008). A Review of the Theories of Corporate Social Responsibility: Its Evolutionary Path and the Road Ahead. *International Journal of Management Reviews*, 10(1): 53–73.

Lock, I. and Seele, P. (2016). The Credibility of CSR Reports in Europe. Evidence from a Quantitative Content Analysis in 11 countries. *Journal of Cleaner Production*, 122: 186–200.

Maczulak, A. (2010). *Environmental Engineering: Designing a Sustainable Future*. New York: Facts on File.

Manente, M., Minghetti, V. and Mingotto, E. (2014). Corporate Social Responsibility in the Tourism Industry: How to Improve CSR through Reporting System. In Keller, P., Smeral, E. and Penchlaner, H. (Eds.), *Tourism and Leisure: Current Issues and Perspectives of Development* (pp. 307–322). Wiesbaden: Springer.

Maon, F., Lindgreen, A. and Swaen, V. (2010). Organizational Stages and Cultural Phases: A Critical Review and a Consolidative Model of Corporate Social Responsibility Development. *International Journal of Management Reviews*, 12(1): 20–38.

Mathiesen, K. and Riley, T. (2015, 27 August). Texas Teenager Creates $20 Water Purifier to Tackle Toxic E-Waste Pollution. The Guardian. Retrieved 8 October 2015 from https://www.theguardian.com/sustainable-business/2015/aug/27/texas-teenager-water-purifier-toxic-e-waste-pollution.

McDonough, W. and Braungart, M. (2002). *Cradle to Cradle: Remaking the Way We Make Things*. New York: North Point Press.

McKinnon, A., Browne, M., Piecyk, M. and Whiteing, A. (2015). *Green Logistics: Improving the Environmental Sustainability of Logistics*. London/Philadelphia: Kogan Page.

Melnyk, S., Bititci, U., Platts, K., Tobias, J. and Andersen, B. (2014). Is Performance Measurement and Management Fit for the Future? *Management Accounting Research* 25(2): 173–186.

Michelon, G., Pilonato, S. and Ricceri, F. (2015). CSR Reporting Practices and the Quality of Disclosure: An Empirical Analysis. *Critical Perspectives on Accounting*, 33: 59–78.

Mitchell, R.K., Bradley, R.A. and Wood, D.J. (1997). Toward a Theory of Stakeholder Identification and Salience: Defining the Principle of Who and What Really Counts. The *Academy of Management Review*, 22(4): 853–886.

Novak, P. (2008). *Principles and Standards of Supply Management Conduct: With Guidelines*. Tempe, AZ: Institute for Supply Management. Retrieved 3 May 2017 from https://www.instituteforsupplymanagement.org/files/Pubs/Proceedings/09ProcCD-Ethics.pdf.

Ooijen, M. van (2014). Free Water at Festivals Enforced by the Amsterdam Mayor. *Deep House Amsterdam*. Retrieved 20 May 2016 from http://www.deephouseamsterdam.com/free-water-at-festivals-enforced-by-amsterdam-mayor/.

Palihawadana, D., Oghazi, P. and Liu, Y. (2016). Effects of Ethical Ideologies and Perceptions of CSR on Consumer Behaviour. *Journal of Business Research*, 69: 4964–4969.

Pienaar, W.J. and Vogt, J.J. (2012). *Business Logistics Management: A Supply Chain Perspective*. Cape Town: Oxford University Press.

Poplawska, J., Labib, A. Reed, D.M. and Ishizaka, A. (2015). Stakeholder Profile Definition and Salience Measurement with Fuzzy Logic and Visual Analytics Applied to Corporate Social Responsibility Case Study. *Journal of Cleaner Production*, 105: 103–115.

Quarshie, A.M., Salmi, A. and Leuschner, R. (2016). Sustainability and Corporate Social Responsibility in Supply Chains: The State of Research in Supply Chain Management and Business Ethics Journals. *Journal of Purchasing & Supply Management*, 22(2): 82–97.

Rashid, N.R.N.A., Khalid, S.A. and Abdul-Rahman, N.I.A. (2015). Environmental Corporate Social Responsibility (ECSR): Exploring its Influence on Customer Loyalty. *Procedia Economics and Finance*, 31: 705–713.

Rim, H., Yang, S-U, and Lee, J. (2016). Strategic Partnerships with Nonprofits in Corporate Social Responsibility (CSR): The Mediating Role of Perceived Altruism and Organizational Identification. *Journal of Business Research*, 69: 3213–3219.

Robertson, M. (2014). *Sustainability: Principles and Practice*. London: Routledge.

Rucevska, I, Nelleman, C., Isarin, N., Yang, W., Liu, N., Yu, K., Sandnaes, S., Olley, K., McCann, O., Devia, L. et al. (2015). *Waste Crime: Low Risks – High Profits. Gaps in Meeting the Global Waste Challenge*. A Rapid Response Assessment. UNEP. Retrieved 18 October 2016 from http://hdl.handle.net/1854/LU-6861717.

Saeed, M.M. and Arshad, F. J. (2012). Corporate Social Responsibility as a Source of Competitive Advantage: The Mediating Role of Social Capital and Reputational Capital. *Journal of Database Marketing & Customer Strategy Management*, 19(4): 219–232.

Sarkar, S. and Searcy, C. (2016). Zeitgeist or Chameleon? A Quantitative Analysis of CSR Definitions. *Journal of Cleaner Production*, 135: 1423–1435.

Schwartz, M.S. and Carroll, A.B. (2003). Corporate Social Responsibility: A Three-Domain Approach. *Business Ethics Quarterly*, 13(4): 503–530.

Shabana, K.M., Buchholtz, A.K. and Carroll, A.B. (2016). The Institutionalization of Corporate Social Responsibility Reporting. *Business & Society*: 1–29.

Sims, M. (2010). Waste. In Jenkins, W. (Ed.), *Berkshire Encyclopaedia of Sustainability: The Spirit of Sustainability* (vol.1). Great Barrington, UK: Berkshire Publishing Group.

Sople, V.V. (2012). *Supply Chain Management: Text and Cases*. Delhi/Chennai: Pearson.

Supply Chain Management. (2017). In *CSCMP Directory*. Retrieved 2 February 2017 from http://cscmp.org/CSCMP/Educate/SCM_Definitions_and_Glossary_of_Terms/CSCMP/Educate/SCM_Definitions_and_Glossary_of_Terms.aspx?hkey=60879588-f65f-4ab5-8c4b-6878815ef921.

The Mobile Phone as Change Agent: Design Activism at the Heart of the Production Process. (2012, 23 April). *The Beach*. Retrieved 17 October 2015, from https://www.thebeach.nu/en/page/471/the-mobile-phone-as-change-agent.

UNODC. (2013). *Transnational Organised Crime in East Asia and the South Pacific: A Threat Assessment* Bangkok/New York: UNOD.

Vartiak, L. (2016). CSR Reporting of Companies on a Global Scale. *Procedia Economics and Finance*, 39: 176–183.

Watts, P. and Holme, R. (1999). *Corporate Social Responsibility: Meeting Changing Expectations*. World Business Council for Sustainable Development. Geneva: WBCSD Publications.

WCED. (1987). *Report of the World Commission on Environment and Development: Our Common Future.* Oxford: Oxford University Press.

Weber, M. (2008). The Business Case for Corporate Social Responsibility: A Company-Level Measurement Approach for CSR. *European Management Journal*, 26: 247–261.

Werther, W.B. and Chandler, D.B. (2011). *Strategic Corporate Social Responsibility: Stakeholders in a Global Environment.* London/Thousand Oaks, CA: Sage.

Wheelen, T. L. (2015). *Strategic Management and Business Policy: Globalization, Innovation and Sustainability* (14th ed.). Harlow, UK: Pearson Education.

Wiens, K. (2014). I Don't Want a Smartphone, I Want a Fairphone. In *IFixitOrg*. Retrieved 8 October 2015 from http://ifixit.org/blog/6403/fairphone/.

Willard, B. (2002). *The Sustainability Advantage: Seven Business Case Benefits of a Triple Bottom Line.* Gabriola Island, Canada: New Society Publishers.

Yeoman, I. (2013). A Futurist's Thoughts on Consumer Trends Shaping Future Festivals and Events. *International Journal of Event and Festival Management*, 4(3): 249–260.

Zadek, S. (2004). The Path to Corporate Responsibility. *Harvard Business Review*, 82(12): 125–132.

Chapter 9

Sustainability and business

Frans Melissen, Ko Koens, Paul Peeters and Jeroen Nawijn

9.1 Introduction to sustainability and business
Frans Melissen

9.1.1 Challenging 'unsustainability'

Today, more and more people see business as one of the main causes for the unsustainable course of our societies; a course that means we will not only run out of resources like oil and gas, but also a course that results in problems such as climate change – which in turn leads to rising sea levels, flooding and droughts and a breakdown of our food production systems, various health problems, habitat and thus biodiversity loss, and an unequal division of wealth across our globe and across groups of people. Within this context, business is currently seen as making money at the expense of (other people's) social, environmental and economic problems, and thus aggravating unsustainability. Consequently, the social licence of (many) businesses to operate is under threat. In fact, some even feel that our whole capitalist system is under threat.

9.1.2 Shared value: Solution or nonsense?

That is why Porter and Kramer, in their influential paper entitled 'Creating shared value' (2011), state that business must bring the business world and society back together. The solution suggested by them is to focus on the principle of shared value: doing business by creating economic value in such a way that it simultaneously creates societal value through addressing specific problems or satisfying specific needs. Ultimately, this should allow for creating a positive relation between company profits and prosperity of people and communities, which Porter and Kramer label as 'a higher form of capitalism' (2011: 75).

The fact that business and the way it (currently) operates are part of the problem when it comes to striving for sustainable development is now, more or less, commonly accepted. Many companies use a lot of (non-renewable) resources to create their products and services, and the manufacturing processes that are applied to do so often result in emissions of CO_2 and other hazardous substances into air, water and ground. What is more, the profits that result from selling products and services to consumers are rarely distributed beyond an inner circle of investors, shareholders, upper-level management and owners.

The answer to the question of how to turn this around, however, is much more contested. A number of companies have listened carefully to Porter and Kramer's advice and have embraced the shared value concept as a means to link corporate social responsibility (CSR) to the strategic direction and targets of the company as a whole. However, some have questioned whether this approach actually solves some of the underlying problems that have minimised the (positive) impact of CSR programmes and initiatives thus far. In fact, Crane, Palazzo, Spence and Matten (2014) claim that the shared value concept is not only unoriginal – stating that it is simply a fancily worded version of existing concepts such as CSR, stakeholder management and sustainable (social) innovation, but also suffers from some major shortcomings. The main shortcoming identified by these authors is that, despite its undeniable attraction as a result of highlighting possible win–win scenarios, the concept does not actually address the almost omnipresent tension between social and economic goals. In addition, Crane et al. state that many of the potential win–win situations referred to by Porter and Kramer will actually amount to ethical dilemmas in a real-life context, because real life is still dominated by the rules of the game called capitalism. They refer to slave labour involved in the production of cocoa as a typical example. Obviously, a company that claims to create economic value through creating social value cannot afford to get involved with suppliers that allow slave labour. Simultaneously, using suppliers that do not resort to slave labour is usually more expensive, which makes it extremely difficult to compete with companies that have no moral objectives to using suppliers that do resort to slave labour. The reasoning applied by the second category of companies is often that slave labour is still better than no labour at all since it prevents people from starving (2014). Similar problems can arise in various other areas, with microfinance representing a well-known and typical example of a field in which many companies have actually tried to join social and financial goals but often resulting in having to give up on some of the initial social goals as a consequence of financial problems. What is more, what if a company's current product or service does not address a specific social problem? How do they then turn their operations into a way of doing business that truly creates economic returns through creating social value? Ultimately, in today's marketplace, success and, more importantly, survival are based on financial performance, not on social performance. According to Crane et al., the shared value concept does not change the rules of this game and, thus, does not change the role of business in our society (2014). Stressing the need for creating economic value through creating social value still means adhering to the 'logic' of, or, more precisely, legitimising self-interest as an underlying principle for doing business. As such, this so-called CSR 2.0 or 'higher form' of capitalism probably does not provide the solution to the problem we were trying to address. In fact, it might even make it more difficult to truly pursue sustainable development based on principles such as equality and inclusiveness (see also Chapter 8).

9.1.3 Capitalism versus virtues

A very interesting study, in light of the above, is one that was conducted by Graafland (2009). In his paper, Graafland refers to Hirschman's seminal paper (1982) which introduces two opposing hypotheses on the influence of operating on markets, within a system based on capitalism and neo-liberalism, on human manners and virtues, such as generosity, diligence, temperance, sociability and envy. The first hypothesis is the so-called 'doux commerce' thesis, which suggests that operating on markets has a positive effect on those virtues. In contrast, the 'self-destruction' hypothesis states that functioning on markets and, thus, having to adhere to the rules of the game played in that market, actually has a negative effect on those virtues and, ultimately, undermines the type of behaviour that is essential to the proper functioning of that same market. Over the years, practitioners as well as scientists have tended to take sides with one of the two hypotheses and have used them both as a reference point and legitimisation of their arguments and actions. Interestingly though, as pointed out by Graafland, many do so without actually providing empirical evidence for the assumed positive or negative effects of operating in markets. He indicates that this has resulted in a rather fruitless stand-off where roughly 50 per cent of theoretical studies claim that the 'doux commerce' hypothesis is correct, whereas the other 50 per cent is certain that the 'self-destruction' hypothesis is correct. However, and this is what makes Graafland's analysis so interesting, he points out that if one only looks at actual empirical studies and real-life case studies, the overall picture is actually not as balanced as that stand-off suggests. In about 70 per cent of these studies, the negative impact of operating in markets clearly outweighs any positive effects. Therefore, it seems that the positive effects that are often ascribed to our capitalistic system are much more based on ideology than on fact.

Maybe this explains how authors like Porter and Kramer on the one hand and Crane et al. on the other can have such contrasting views about the same concept. Further, this might also explain why business has, so far, not been able to change its ways of operating in a more sustainable direction. Doing so requires much more than simply changing processes or designing new products and services. It actually requires a new ideology regarding the foundation upon which business in modern society operates. In other words, it requires developing a new belief system, new reference points for the way you do business, and new business models to support doing so that move beyond the way CSR has been addressed so far. Marques and Mintzberg represent authors that have pointed this out in a way that leaves nothing to the imagination and little room for doubt: 'economists keep telling us to trust the marketplace' (2015: 9) but 'it's naïve to think that corporate social responsibility [programmes] can turn the corporate landscape into a win–win wonderland' (2015: 7). They elaborate on their argument by clearly stating that moving beyond the current stagnation point with regard to sustainability thinking is something that cannot be left to governments. Somehow, it will be up to business to take the lead in this process, possibly in cooperation with governments but also with (activist) non-governmental organisations, social movements and social initiatives.

9.1.4 Ethical leadership

Regardless of whether companies will join or take the lead in such grass-roots movements, being a part of them requires new business models and decision-making (models and processes) that move beyond focusing on financial performance and self-interest. Taking this new route requires managers/owners with vision and leadership: ethical leadership. As indicated by Ciulla (2005), in her article on ethical leadership, there are two questions that play a central role with respect to evaluating the ethics of a leader: (1) Does he or she tend to do the right thing, in the right way and for the right reasons? and (2) What standards do we use to determine what is right? Given that this chapter reviews the relationship between business and sustainable development, the answer to the second question, when it comes to business leaders(hip), would be those actions and decisions that contribute to the collective challenge of realising sustainable development. This means that the role of business in society would automatically change from being focussed on financial performance and self-interest to a focus on the economic *and* the environmental and social consequences of its actions. In other words, whereas in 'traditional' business models and decision-making the emphasis would be on generating economic returns and creating owner/shareholder value, in 'ethical' business models and decision-making the overall reference point would include issues such as equality, inclusiveness, justice and liberty. More specifically, decisions would be based on ensuring that a company's actions contribute to 'development that meets the needs of the present without compromising the ability of future generations to meet their own needs' (WCED (United Nations' World Commission on Environment and Development), 1987). Doing so means sticking to two crucial reference points: (1) acknowledging that the needs of generations refer to the needs of all people, not just those fortunate enough to enjoy living in privileged circumstances, and (2) acknowledging that the needs of future generations require current generations to account for the fact that actions performed today have consequences for the state of our planet tomorrow and its ability to provide enough resources and satisfactory living conditions to meet the needs of people living at that time. Doing so is also not easy. That is why Ciulla concludes her review of the state of ethical leadership by stating: 'to assess the ethics of leaders and leadership, you have to start with the obvious proposition that a good leader is ethical and effective' and 'the relationship between ethics and effectiveness (or technical and moral excellence) is at the core of leadership ethics and, for that matter, all areas of professional ethics' (2005: 333).

9.1.5 In conclusion

It has been argued above that business is one of the causes of the unsustainable course of our societies. It has also become clear that the answer to the question of how to turn this around is contested. A typical example is the shared value concept, which is promoted as a means to create economic value through creating societal value, but criticised for not actually addressing the almost omnipresent tensions between social and economic goals. One might argue that, for businesses to truly contribute to sustainable development, they do not need improved business models and concepts, but a new ideology on which business is founded and also a change in ethics of those who are in charge. This 'new' ethics should include reference points directly linked to the concept of sustainable development, such as equality and inclusiveness, also acknowledging that current generations need to account for the needs of future generations in the way they act.

These theoretical backgrounds and reference points with regard to sustainable business create the context for three discussions presented in the rest of this chapter, together with the dilemmas that they (re)present. First, Melissen argues that 'traditional' business models have lost their relevance, given the challenges the world currently faces. 'New' business models should rest upon sustainable thinking. He illustrates his position with a case which conveys the main principles for a 'new' business model in the context of hospitality. Secondly, Koens reflects on the interrelationships between sustainability, tourism and governance and conveys a case which reflects the ethical dilemmas that are in play for different stakeholders, who share different interests and opinions with regard to implementation plans for ensuring sustainable tourism in a big metropolis. Thirdly, Peeters and Nawijn, staying within the realm of tourism, draw attention to the impact of tourism's carbon footprint on climate change and human well-being, and also to the ethical dilemmas surrounding them. Their case identifies the factors which should be dealt with when working towards climatic sustainability and the eradication of poverty.

9.2 Sustainable business models

Frans Melissen

9.2.1 Introduction to sustainable business models

Our current economic system is based on capitalism, which amounts to free markets acting as the main coordination mechanism and a focus on private property, autonomy and economic growth. There is no doubt that this system has helped many people to acquire the (material and financial) means to live comfortable lives. Simultaneously, however, as indicated in the previous section, this system has also resulted and continues to result in a number of environmental, social and economic problems. What is more, these problems actually threaten the lives of more and more people, especially in years to come. Not only is wealth created by this economic system distributed unequally, the way this system interacts with the planet – the (environmental) system that needs to provide the resources for the functioning of our economic and social systems – is not sustainable.

9.2.1.1 The role of business in pursuing sustainable development

Business represents a key player in the current socio-economic system and has a crucial role to play in turning this challenging situation around and striving for sustainable development. Not only do businesses represent an influential force in policymaking: for most people they are an integral part of their lives. For example, people buy their products and services, they provide them with income. If society is to be put on a more sustainable course, business will need to support this course adjustment and possibly even lead the way (Marques and Mintzberg, 2015).

There are many ways in which business can make such a contribution. As indicated by Baumgartner and Ebner (2010), business can contribute to all three pillars of sustainable development: the economic dimension, the environmental dimension and the social dimension. For each of these dimensions, they describe a number of aspects that companies could focus on. Within the context of the economic dimension, a business could address aspects such as innovation and technology, collaboration, production processes, purchasing and sustainability reporting. All of these aspects relate to business activities that could strengthen the financial performance of the firm through addressing sustainability. With respect to the environmental dimension, a business could try to make a direct contribution to sustainable development through reducing resource use, emissions into air, into water or into ground, and (hazardous) waste, not only related to its own production processes and products and services, but also those of its suppliers and buyers. Finally, the way the social dimension could be addressed by a business includes internal aspects such as health and safety and human capital development, as well as external aspects such as corporate citizenship – the latter representing (voluntary) actions by the company that contribute to the well-being of the environment and people, also those not directly involved in its operations. Overall, one could claim that the more advanced and comprehensive the efforts of a company in relation to all of these aspects, the bigger its contribution to sustainable development and the more sustainable its business model.

Unfortunately, though, truly realising sustainable development probably requires more fundamental changes to the role of business in society than are included in this overview (also see Crane et al., 2014). The best way to explain this is to focus on which products and services are offered, the way in which they are delivered, and the way in which costs and revenues are dealt with. Together, these three elements constitute the so-called business model of a company (see e.g. Bocken et al., 2014).

9.2.1.2 The curse of treating sustainability as an add-on

Over the years, many companies have focussed their sustainability efforts on the environmental dimension of sustainable development, for instance through redesigning their products and services, recycling, and adjusting production processes to control and avoid pollution. Many of them have also managed to reduce the materials and energy needed to create their products and services, and some of them have successfully switched to using renewable energy as their main source of energy.

Other companies have already moved beyond a sole focus on the environmental dimension and explicitly account for all three dimensions of sustainable development in the way they do business – the well-known principle of triple-bottom-line reporting (Elkington, 1997). Some of these companies combine their efforts to reduce the negative impacts of their production processes with corporate citizenship initiatives and community development projects, whereas others mainly focus on the well-being of their own employees.

However, whichever focus is chosen by these companies, most of them have not made any fundamental changes to the third element of their business model: the way they deal with costs and revenues. Ultimately, most of them are still 'in business' to make money. Doing so still requires them to try and gain a bigger market share and to minimise their costs, if only to please their investors and shareholders. Within this context, sustainability efforts are automatically treated as an add-on – as the so-called icing on the cake (Marques and Mintzberg, 2015) – not as the reason for doing business. Consequently, when economic circumstances decline or the profit and loss statement is not up to expectations, or simply when customers are not willing to pay extra for costs involved with making products and services more sustainable, these efforts are the first to suffer or even abandoned altogether.

Unfortunately, this usually also applies even to those companies that claim to base their operations on the shared value concept (Porter and Kramer, 2011) or apply another form of so-called social or societal business models. Even though some of these businesses explicitly claim to consider profitability as the means to an end, not an end in itself (Wilson and Post, 2013), survival in the free market still requires them to realise a profit. Doing so within the context of the regulatory and tax systems of our current socio-economic system, and a market consisting of consumers that often prefer short-term personal benefits associated with non-sustainable products and services over long-term collective benefits associated with sustainable products and services, can prove to be quite a challenge (also see Doane, 2005; Crane et al., 2014; Laukkanen and Patala, 2014)! This is why many of these businesses have not survived or have never moved beyond being a niche player in a niche market, or have had to give up on some elements of their original mission – usually amounting to having to make concessions with respect to the societal value they set out to create.

Visser (2011) refers to these problems as the curse of CSR. Within the boundaries set by the current socio-economic system and within the context of operating in today's neo-liberal free markets, it is almost impossible to move beyond creating economic value at the expense of environmental and social value.

9.2.1.3 Escaping the lock-in

Escaping this lock-in can only be realised by developing and applying new, truly sustainable business models – which are based on a new and improved role of business in society (Crane et al., 2014), behaviour and virtues that support equality and inclusiveness, and ethical leadership (Ciulla, 2005). What is more, in order to be successful, these business models need to include mechanisms which ensure the support of consumers. As indicated by Melissen (2016) and Melissen and Moratis (2016), these mechanisms need to be based on tapping into the evolutionary processes that shaped us (Griskevicius, Cantú and van Vugt, 2012). Only through making smart use of people's desire for status, tendency to copy behaviour and the positive effects of social mechanisms such as reciprocal altruism and social obligation, can one expect to have a significant positive impact on society. Doing so requires business models that are based on a holistic approach, which entails that advanced physical technologies are combined with new social technologies (Laukkanen and Patala, 2014); new ways of organising society, including the role of businesses, which may very well involve redefining human needs in relation to what the resources available on the planet can (continue to) provide for, and experimenting with alternatives to capitalism and neo-liberalism as the reference points for our socio-economic system. Individual businesses cannot do so in isolation. The innovations that are needed and the circumstances in which they need to be applied are too complex and clearly reach beyond the boundaries of an individual business (see Melissen, 2016; Melissen and Moratis, 2016).

Therefore, these (sustainable) business models are based on setting up collaborations with other businesses, policy makers and public authorities, non-governmental organisations, action groups and all other people that are in some way involved or have an interest in the production and consumption of the (redefined and/or redesigned) products and services that a business delivers. The logical starting points for setting up these collaborations are (local or virtual) communities and social networks. The ultimate challenge incorporated in these business models is for businesses to join up with other actors within these communities and networks to jointly experiment with alternatives to the current socio-economic system and shape the contours of a system that is truly based on equality, inclusiveness and a sustainable way of using the natural environment as a resource to fulfil the needs of all people (Loorbach, 2014). Placing those needs at the centre, and not the profitability of business, requires courage and the willingness to give up some of the autonomy businesses have. Therefore, business leaders will need to ask the right questions at the right time and do the right things for the right reasons to be accepted as an integral part of these communities and networks based on long-term commitment and reciprocity instead of principles of the free market with its short-term (financial) gains and winner takes all mentality (Doane, 2005), thus displaying the kind of ethical leadership discussed earlier (Ciulla, 2005).

To illustrate what applying these truly sustainable business models could look like in practice, the following case portrays the implications for individual hotels and restaurants within the context of a specific local community.

Case 9.2.2: Hospitality 2.0

Introduction: debating hospitality and sustainability

A few months ago, an international conference was organised in a big European city. The main theme of the conference was 'Hospitality and sustainability: Towards a new narrative for business'. One of the panel discussions specifically addressed the question of how to create a sustainable future for the hospitality branch given the many challenges business and society, and more specifically, local communities, currently face. What follows is an excerpt from the dialogue between the two keynote speakers in that session, Dr Laura Bradley and Dr Jonathan Seeger, the moderator of the session, Mrs Brown, and someone from the audience – a student called Paul.

Dr Bradley: 'Let us take a closer look at the hospitality industry and how principles and mechanisms such as tapping into evolutionary process, collaboration, distributed control, and ethical leadership can be applied in order to ensure a sustainable future for the hospitality branch. Melissen, for example, argues that hotels and restaurants have a crucial role to play in our collective challenge to realise sustainable development. Not only because of their significant current impact on the environmental, social and economic dimensions of sustainability, but also given their huge potential to act as catalysts for sustainable practices and inclusiveness (see his 2013 paper on sustainable hospitality). A way to fulfil this potential would be for hotels and restaurants to apply some of these principles and mechanisms identified as crucial elements of truly sustainable business models. Through applying some of these principles and mechanisms, hotels and restaurants could play a vital role not only in making local communities better places to live in, but also in making them attractive destinations for visitors and shaping those visits in such a way that they benefit the local community while protecting our natural environment... If (...).'

Dr Seeger: 'I would like to jump in here and point out that hotels and restaurants are experts in creating experiences. They could take the lead in collectively creating surroundings that unleash the positive effects of the phenomenon called human biophilia. This concept is well explicated in a paper written by Griskevicius and colleagues in 2012. Biophilia, literally means "love of life". It relates to the appreciation of the natural world that we humans have inherited from our ancestors, to the positive effect that exposure to surroundings that incorporate natural elements has on our stress levels, and to our desire to make a positive contribution to the world around us. Seemingly human beings inherited a "meme" for wanting a good and safe world. It is there. We just have to reactivate that.'

Dr Bradley: 'I agree, but I would like to go back to the principles and mechanisms I have mentioned before, and the impact they have on local communities. Applying them would imply that hotels and restaurants would also not try to fight new developments such as the sharing economy – with Airbnb and various meal-sharing initiatives obviously representing some particularly noteworthy developments for these businesses. In fact, they would focus on trying to find ways to collaborate with local representatives of this movement. Based on their expertise and through opening up their network of suppliers and distributors, hotels and restaurants could assist many of these micro-businesses in developing more sustainable practices and making use of more sustainable products and technologies. Together with local suppliers and specialised companies they could make a collective effort to optimise the local food and energy production and consumption systems.'

Dr Seeger: 'Yes, and what is more, these hotels and restaurants could not only serve as inspirational employers for local residents, they could also serve as the hosts for groups of engaged citizens getting together to discuss new sustainability initiatives and then join them in putting those initiatives to practice – thereby increasing their chances of success. They could also join forces with individuals and organisations aiming to ensure that these developments and resulting benefits reach all inhabitants of the local community, not just those eager and confident enough to step in at the early stages. Finally, using their influence to lobby for the support of policymakers and public authorities could prove to be an indispensable element in making all this work.'

Can hospitality 2.0 be implemented?

The moderator of the session, Mrs Brown, commented on this dialogue as follows: 'You clearly are not at loggerheads with regard to this issue, and apparently fully agree on the necessity to take the next steps on the road to a sustainable future for the hospitality branch. Obviously, this specific example of the hospitality industry has only highlighted a small selection of the types of actions that businesses could take based on applying the mechanisms and principles discussed by Dr Bradley. But ultimately, these actions could allow these businesses to make a truly significant contribution to sustainable

(continued)

Case 9.2.2: Hospitality 2.0 (*continued*)

development, based on experimenting with alternatives to the social technologies usually applied in our current socio-economic system. In this specific example, at the centre of the network of collaborating players we neither find a specific business nor a focus on profitability or ownership, but sustainable and inclusive hospitality as a crucial concept and building block for tomorrow's society. It reflects the essence of hospitality 2.0. That is what I call "visionary"!'

A student from the audience, Paul, put up his hand and said: 'It sounds a bit too easy to me. As if all will be well if we just apply some principles and mechanisms. I have just done my fieldwork at a well-known hotel in this city and I can assure you that hotels and restaurants cannot survive if they don't make money. It is as simple as that. It is not that easy to turn everything around in one minute. Which incentives do hotels and restaurants have to change and become convinced by what Dr Bradley, for instance, proposes?'

Dr Bradley: 'I really do believe that it can work. There is more to say about this other than only describing some of the actors involved in the community in which businesses such as hotels and restaurants operate. My proposal also highlights some of the adjustments that have to be made to "business as usual". Hotels and restaurants should take on their new role as members of a community focusing on fulfilling the needs of all stakeholders … I repeat … *all* stakeholders should be involved in a sustainable way. This is the way we should go.'

Paul: 'It sounds good, but how?'

Questions for discussion

- If you were the owner/manager of a hotel or restaurant in this community, would you (a) be willing to work together with local Airbnbs, even if this, in case of accommodation, means that some of the guests that would have booked your hotel will now be staying in those Airbnbs and (b) be willing to allow other stakeholders such as local inhabitants, other restaurants and local farmers to have a say in what dishes will be on your menu? Please give moral reasons for your answer.
- Do you feel that as a hotel or restaurant owner/manager you share responsibility in ensuring that all people living in the community in which you are located can fulfil their needs and live comfortable lives? If yes, to what degree? If no, why not?
- Would you feel okay with living in a community in which you earn (a lot) less money and having your local community, including local restaurants and hotels, providing you with food and drink for free?
- How does the business model that Dr Bradley proposes differ from 'business-as-usual-models'? Could you tease out the ethical principles upon which both categories of models rest? Is Dr Bradley's model feasible?
- Paul sounds a bit sceptical about the view of Dr Bradley. Which arguments could she use to persuade him?

9.3 Balancing interests in urban tourism governance

Ko Koens

9.3.1 Introduction

Within the framework of the creative, cultural and service industries, the tourism, events and hospitality sector depend strongly on resources from their natural and social environment for the long-term viability of their products. This would suggest that the industry puts a strong emphasis on ensuring the viability of their natural and social environment by operating as sustainably as possible. However, this is not necessarily the case. Take for instance tourism: historically, it was deemed to have a relatively limited impact on people, communities and the environment. However, that is currently challenged. McKercher and Prideaux, for example, argue that it is quite difficult to compare the economic, social and environmental impact, which makes it very difficult to determine the extent to which tourism is actually sustainable (2014). This is particularly the case for tourism in an urban setting, and since most work that has been done on the impacts of tourism up to now has especially focussed on rural areas (Miller, Merrilees and Coghlan, 2015), this section will shine the limelight on the sustainability of tourism in a city environment.

9.3.1.1 Sustainable city tourism

It is quite important to study the impacts of tourism on the sustainable well-being of cities and their inhabitants, because about 50 per cent of the population of the world reside in cities and this number is set to increase further. More specifically, it is important to be knowledgeable about the various tensions between the environmental, social and economic elements of sustainable tourism and also about the way in which different interpretations of these issues by various stakeholders (both in practice and academia) hinder progress. These diverse (scholarly) positions explicated in the following, very brief, literature review are illustrative of the issue at hand.

It is interesting to note that the negative aspects surrounding the sustainability of city tourism that attract most attention, at least in popular media, tend to be social in nature. For example, visitor pressure is now common in several large cities and no longer confined to specific smaller heritage tourism hotspots like Venice (Borg and Russo, 2001). In other parts of the world, the ethics of trips undertaken by rich tourists to economically impoverished areas, and the way in which these areas are represented are questioned (Frenzel et al., 2015). While the negative aspects of tourism are indeed addressed by city governments in certain places (see e.g. Füller and Michel, 2014; Garay, Cànoves and Prat, 2014), in most destinations the main emphasis lies on environmental factors (Timur and Getz, 2009). This is not to say that city governments deny the importance of sociocultural and economic aspects in achieving sustainable urban tourism, but that, generally speaking, environmental goals are prioritised. Maxim's findings about the way policymakers in

London deal with the negative issues underline this. Nine out of the twelve most important sustainable tourism principles relate to social issues (i.e. enhancing the sense of place, differentiate from other destinations, add value to the area), yet the only two environmental tourism principles are both placed in the top four when it comes to having been included in policy documents. This is striking, since it can be argued that the importance of *socially* sustainable tourism in urban areas is far greater than in rural areas, given that the urban environment is largely man-made and that, due to the higher population density, social issues will affect a greater number of people (2016: 12).

In academic work similar trends can be observed. Here too sustainable urban tourism is often conflated with environmentally sustainable tourism (Miller et al., 2015). The literature on urban planning is more developed with regard to sustainable urban development and also addresses issues like conflicts of interest, disturbance, safety and security at least as prominently as environmental issues (e.g. Flint and Raco, 2012; Joss, 2015; Newman and Jennings, 2008; and Healey, 1998). One field of research where social issues are discussed more commonly is slum tourism. Slum tourism entails tourists visiting economically impoverished areas where residents' daily lives are part of the attraction. The literature in this regard concords with the wider city planning literature in the sense that it highlights both ethical tensions between the social and economic gains of this kind of tourism and also accentuates the need for clear perspectives on representation, power relations and safety (Frenzel et al., 2015). This finding leads to a fuller understanding of the social issues involved in urban tourism which make it very difficult to achieve sustainable urban tourism governance.

The body of work done on this theme is quite small, though, and, ironically, ignores the environmental aspects of sustainable development. This stresses the need for academia to work towards a more comprehensive framework of what constitutes sustainable urban tourism for city governments, which could be used as points of reference (Maxim, 2016). This requires researchers to be willing and able to get involved and engaged with both policymakers and the industry in order to learn about the issues that exist in everyday practice (Melissen and Koens, 2016).

However, even when cities do have clear policy goals for a sustainable development of tourism, it is not evident that it will lead to positive action and successful implementation by all stakeholders. Savage, Huang and Chang relate the difficulties of urban tourism governance to the fact that a far greater variety of groups and stakeholders are active in cities within a relatively small area, compared to semi-urban or rural tourism. They need to be brought together in order to align efficiently (2004: 224). In this setting, it is more likely that dealing with only one specific problem or group of stakeholders (e.g. visitors coming by car who cause problems with traffic), will harm the interests of other stakeholders (e.g. influencing the mobility of residents). Koens and Thomas focus in their 2016 publication on the difficulty city governments have in appreciating the local context and power relations among tourism stakeholders. They found that, in Cape Town, for example, government lacked an understanding of the intense competition among small businesses when trying to develop socially sustainable policy measures. Rather than providing regulation and trying to improve the social cohesion among stakeholders, the emphasis was placed on the economic growth of new (and existing) businesses.

Sustainability and business

While well intentioned, these policy solutions did little to solve the dilemma. They might even have complicated it.

Another key issue with regard to sustainable city tourism is the lack of communication between different tourism departments and other policy officials, for example those involved in planning, logistics or sustainable development (Ashworth and Page, 2011; Maxim, 2016). To be able to develop city tourism in a sustainable way, a coordinated policy effort is required that brings all those players together with the purpose of alignment. This will prevent effective solutions from getting lost in the wider agenda – especially as far as implementation is concerned (Maxim, 2016). To create synergy between different governmental departments will be time-consuming with the result that in cities which are highly dynamic and in constant change, it may be difficult to implement lasting solutions effectively (Savage et al., 2004). Smart governance tools certainly have potential for dealing with these issues in the future, but for the moment a successful implementation of such tools is quite limited (Anttiroiko, Valkama and Bailey, 2013). The effect of this will be demonstrated in the case below – which for its part challenges readers to try to balance different aspects of sustainable development and appreciate differences of interest in practice.

Case 9.3.2: Balancing sustainable tourism and liveability in an urban context

Introduction: Making cities greener tourist destinations

A large European metropolis has tourism relatively high on the agenda since it is an important source of revenue. Policymakers in departments with direct links to the industry (e.g. Economic Affairs) pay a lot of attention to the opportunities and developments in this sector, while, in contrast, tourism is not a priority in other departments, even though it has a strong impact on the development of the infrastructure of the city and the environment, for example. This could have implications for the sustainable development of tourism, particularly since, in terms of budget, Economic Affairs is only a relatively small player. Not only is the support of other larger departments required to make sustainable structural changes to the wider city infrastructure, but the effects of proposed solutions for working on sustainable tourism are also insufficiently taken into account.

In recent years visitor numbers have been rising up to 4 per cent annually in the city. While this has been economically beneficial, the increase of air traffic and local air pollution due to the traffic has come under scrutiny from local environmental groups, particularly because the number of people living in and commuting into the city has also grown by more than 7 per cent. The Department of Infrastructure and Environment has worked very hard to deal with air pollution by setting up an ambitious programme to green up the city. Tourism policymakers noted that the programme could negatively impact the

(continued)

Case 9.3.2: Balancing sustainable tourism and liveability in an urban context (*continued*)

mobility of visitors, with the result of potentially harming the industry economically. However, since these policymakers had too little impact to make significant changes, they have tried to use the programme to put tourism higher on the policy agenda and stimulate its sustainable development. They started a campaign to get the city better known as a smart and green destination, with one of the key focal points a mobile phone app that educates users on how to prevent polluting the city.

Last year, on a warm spring day in May, a significant event took place. As a result of the steady increase of residents, commuters and visitors, the streets became overcrowded during the annual spring festival, which took place in the city centre. The organisers of the festival were not prepared for the large number of visitors, which created a great nuisance for the residents in the surrounding neighbourhoods. Many residents complained about it to the local newspaper and there has been a general sense of unrest ever since. The municipality has decided to address this issue, but progress is slow and the results are not visible yet.

Sustainability between the devil and the deep blue sea

Jorrit was recently hired as the coordinator of sustainable tourism development at the Department of Economic Affairs. Coming from an environmentalist background, he is excited about his new job, particularly because of the ambitious plan to change the city into a green city destination. Based on his reading of several academic papers, Jorrit is confident that no one could be against the plans to make the city more environmentally sustainable, particularly since they also offer specific growth opportunities for new green-minded businesses. He was invited to introduce and explain the new sustainable tourism policy at a public platform where residents and the tourism industry meet in order to discuss the future development of the city.

During the meeting, the debate rages and emotions run high. At one point, the spokesperson of the local resident's association, Sally, argues that the municipality focusses too much on the environmental aspects of sustainable tourism to the detriment of social issues, which are much more pressing for the immediate liveability of the city. Sally is particularly upset about the fact that no measures are taken to curtail the disturbance caused by visitors walking and cycling through the city centre. This kind of mobility is actually stimulated by the municipality in its bid to reduce carbon emissions. It is key to the new green strategy of the city. Jorrit has been told that Sally has good contacts at the local newspaper and starts to fear negative publicity.

While he is contemplating his response cautiously, a well-known and respected restaurant owner storms forward, grabs the microphone and shouts that his business is suffering because 'the government' listens too much to environmental groups and residents who do not understand the economic importance of tourism. He argues that the smart green city destination programme is not desirable for local business at all, since it only emphasises the negative environmental impacts of the tourism, hospitality and events industry. In addition the current measures planned to limit social disturbance give the city a bad reputation among potential visitors. Rather than pestering businesses with environmental and social measures, the municipality should focus on ensuring that visitor numbers remain high. Not doing so will mean that shops, cafes and restaurants in the city centre will have to close down, as they rely for their income on the money spent by tourists. Should this happen, the liveability of this part of the city will undoubtedly suffer.

Jorrit is somewhat annoyed that most people in the room fail to acknowledge the complexity of the issue. He feels that it will be impossible to please everyone on this matter and in trying to calm down the situation, he emphasises that the Department of Economic Affairs will never be able to make tourism more sustainable on its own. It requires the cooperation of multiple layers of government, as well as all parties involved at the meeting.

The next day, at work, Jorrit is called in by the chief manager of the department who is quite annoyed. He confronts Jorrit with a scathing article that has been published in the local newspaper, stating that the local government is shying away from its responsibility and refusing to show leadership. He blames Jorrit for not being steadfast enough under the pressure of the moment and urges him to come up with a plan to turn the tide and restore public trust. Jorrit is taken aback and wonders how on earth he can deal with this dilemma in a satisfactory way.

Questions for discussion

- In this case, which of the following should take preference: environmental, economic or social sustainability? Use ethical principles to support your answer.
- What options does Jorrit have to engage the different stakeholders (residents, industry and environmental NGOs)?
- Who is responsible for ensuring that a city develops its tourism, events and hospitality offering in a sustainable way? Which ethical arguments could those responsible use to make a case for sustainable tourism in cities?
- To what extent should policymakers follow or ignore public opinion or business lobbies when it comes to the highly complex topic of sustainable development? Give moral reasons for your position.
- What are the main differences between sustainability in urban areas and in rural areas? Are the ethical arguments for advocating one or the other the same?

9.4 Carbon footprint and human well-being

Paul Peeters and Jeroen Nawijn

9.4.1 Introduction

The tourism industry is driven by enthusiastic and dedicated men and women, who love their trade, live to travel, are curious to what is beyond the horizon, are eager to learn about other cultures, gaze at spectacular landscapes, and explore the globe. As a service industry, most employees involved go out of their way to make their customers feel welcome, happy, relaxed and revitalised for the upcoming period of labour, care and other day-to-day worries. In short: tourism is a very positive industry, which also pursues aims such as tourism growth, environmental protection and social well-being – issues that fit the three main elements of sustainable development quite well (UNEP and UNWTO, 2012: 127). In addition, tourism is considered to help alleviate poverty, harness biodiversity, take into account landscape and cultural heritage, and support the development of infrastructure like roads, water supply and energy in poor countries (UNEP and UNWTO, 2012: 38). Tourism seems to be geared towards enhancing human well-being. Although this sounds quite positive and even noble to some extent, there are unfortunately several ethical dilemmas the tourism industry is confronted with.

9.4.1.1 Climate change, tourists' well-being and the common good

Travel and tourism have many negative impacts such as distributing diseases as in the case of the 2002–2003 SARS pandemic (Gerencher, 2010) and child sex tourism (Panko and George, 2012). Tourism also has negative impacts on coastal ecosystems and – as widely assumed – on climate change (Davenport and Davenport, 2006).

Let us focus on the impact of tourism on climate change (Gössling et al., 2010) and contrast it with the general 'good' goal of the industry, namely to create 'well-being'. Tourists generally enjoy their holiday trips, although the effects of the enjoyment are temporary (Nawijn, 2011). Motivations for having a holiday trip differ from person to person, but they can be reduced mainly to motivations such as learning, novelty, pleasure, relaxation, image affirmation and image building (Pearce, 1993). There is currently no evidence to suggest that tourists enjoy long-haul holiday trips more than other types of trips. In other words, it seems that increasing greenhouse gas emissions by flying longer distances does not necessarily enhance the tourism experience of well-being in general. This justifies the question whether tourists and the tourism sector pose a problem for the climate.

Gardiner (2011) observed that climate change can only be defined as a 'problem' when we are not open to making moral assessments of *all* interests – not only of the (often personal) hedonistic ones. One should also consider the interests of people living in the destination area, the hosts who serve the visitors, and certainly also of future generations. Gardiner calls it a 'perfect moral storm', because selective moral awareness makes humanity vulnerable to moral corruption in three ways (2011). First, the dispersion of causes and effects. Second, the fragmentation of agency, and third, institutional inadequacy could influence people's moral perceptions and decision-making.

So, when it comes to evaluating climate change and the effects of greenhouse gas emissions specifically due to travel and tourism, it is important to consider the whole picture. With reference to causes and effects: where the emissions are highly concentrated and the number of stakeholders limited, the effects are immediately and unavoidably global. Combined with the fragmentation of agencies, it makes climate change an extreme form of the 'tragedy of the commons' (Hardin, 1968). The institutional problem is especially caused by the basic governance principle, which is mainly based on the nation state, while the tragedy of the commons can only be solved by making the common interest equal to the individual (nation) interest.

9.4.1.2 Solutions for the impact of tourism on climate change

It is important to look at tourism's role in climate change more closely. The 2015 Paris climate agreement calls for very strong CO_2 emission reductions to avoid a global temperature rise of 2°C, or even 1.5°C (UNFCCC, 2015). Tourism's CO_2 emissions double every 25 years. It has been estimated that – if nothing changes – the emissions will be more than eight times higher by the end of the 21st century, compared to 2015 (Gössling and Peeters, 2015). In addition, tourism's emissions alone might become larger than the global carbon budget available in a 2°C maximum temperature anomaly scenario by 2060 (Gössling et al., 2010).

The main cause of the growth of the emissions is the large increase in long-distance travel, which is associated with a shift from surface modes to air transport. This shift is explained by the preference for the much higher speed of air transport compared to the main transport mode in tourism, the personal car. This tendency aggravates the 'perfect moral storm' for tourism, since air transport is too internationally embedded to be regulated by individual states.

What solutions are available to reduce tourism's emissions by 2050 by a factor of five instead of letting it increase by a factor of five? There is a global tourism emission gap of a factor of 25. In other words, tourism's CO_2 emissions per 'unit' (i.e. the emissions per trip) needs to be reduced by 96 per cent. Currently, 75 per cent of the emissions are caused by transport and the remainder primarily by accommodations. As stated before, the core cause of the increase of emissions is the growth of aviation transport. The traditional response of the aviation industry to this problem is: more efficient aircraft, more efficient operations, biofuels and offsets. However, Peeters et al. (2016) uncovered a lot of myths about the opportunities for technological progress in aviation. In contrast to, for instance, road transport, aviation is already very efficient and the potential for further improvements is less than 50 per cent of the current efficiency. The pace of the improvements will be very slow: approximately 1 per cent per year. Operations are already quite efficient (90–95 per cent), which means that there is a maximum one-time opportunity to save 5–10 per cent emissions, which in turn, represents less than five years of emission growth. The scales required to cover the whole of the aviation industry's fuel demand with biofuels are larger than the earth can provide, assuming that the biofuel production will not be at the expense of nature and agriculture. Offsetting, leaving it to the industries to solve the problem, is a possible option, but it has its limitations as well – both with regard to ethics and the law, and also 'additionality' of the projects funded by offsetting revenues (Cames et al., 2016). So, what else could be done?

A long-term scenario study provides two solutions to mitigate tourism's impact on the climate (Peeters and Dubois, 2010). The first solution entails that globally a massive shift from trips by car to public transport, coaches and (high-speed) rail is instigated. That will bring the volume of air transport (passenger-km) back to the level of the early 2010s. The second solution entails leaving the modal split between car and other surface-based transport (rail, etc.) as it is right now. The only way to reduce the emissions according to the Paris agreement will be to bring the volume of air transport (again passenger-km) back to the level of the 1970s. Although that might sound like quite a drastic step backwards, it is not the case. A mere 20 per cent of current tourism trips take place through the air. Many of these flights are very short, so the share of this score – that has no other (surface-bound) alternative – is even less than 20 per cent. That means that the majority of tourism trips will not be affected by an effective climate policy, though most of the long-haul trips will definitely be affected by much higher costs or legal limitations.

9.4.1.3 Ethical dilemmas in mitigating tourism's impact on the climate

For the tourism sector, such large modal and destination shifts as described above cause other ethical dilemmas at different levels. Consider the following three levels. First, there is the personal level. Unpublished research in the Netherlands pointed out that people voting for the Green Party flew the most frequently, which demonstrates that even people who are well aware of environmental problems caused by flying, who actively reduce their own footprints by investing in solar panels, who drive electric or hybrid cars, or even cycle to work, are often unable to avoid flying. The sad conclusion of this assessment is that, while all sectors are starting to save massively on CO_2 emissions by investing large amounts of money and taking many mitigation measures, the positive environmental effect is at the same time destroyed by a minority of the global population which continues to fly. Not surprisingly, the difficulties in avoiding flying even for people who acknowledge the negative impacts thereof, are partly explained by the low prices and larger networks, which currently are characteristic of this sector. Cohen et al. (2011) even note that this situation works like an addiction for many.

On a second level, that of the tourism company, other ethical dilemmas emerge as well. For example, CARMATOP (Carbon management for tour operators), a multi-award-winning project undertaken by a number of small and medium-sized tour operators and supported by the Dutch tourism trade organisation (ANVR) developed an innovative carbon calculator called Carmacal. Carmacal (2016) not only calculates emissions detailed at the level of airline/aircraft combination per all real flown direct flights, combining in the case of connections, but it also estimates the CO_2 emissions per guest-night for 800,000 accommodations, more than 20 non-air transportation modes, and a range of high-carbon tourist activities.

This enables tour operators to assess the carbon footprint of all their products in such a detailed way that they can modify their products to reduce the footprints: for instance, by choosing alternative accommodations, changing itineraries, other routes to the destination, other airlines or even other days of travel in which the airline uses a more efficient aeroplane. This tool also helps tour operators to provide their customers with detailed carbon footprint information about their products, allowing them to let their choices be partly guided by their concerns about climate change.

However, the idea that the carbon footprint of travel products could inform management while developing the product portfolio was not considered a viable option by most tour operators. They believed that their products perfectly fitted the demand and changing them would not be worth the risk of loss of demand. Creating a label, including a value judgement about the climate impact, was considered to be threatening, because some of the products might be labelled as 'red' due to their high carbon footprints. Interestingly enough, some of the companies involved actually believed that they were just satisfying the demands and needs of their customers and that implementing a clear carbon label to their products might cause their customers to change to lower carbon products – which they assume would be bad for business. However, this is most likely not the case, because the market prices between short-haul and long-haul holiday products (packages as offered by tour operators) do not vary much. In addition, the costs of rail and car transport are generally much higher than for short-haul air transport. Gardiner observed that such behaviour means that current interests (however trivial) have 'absolute priority over the interest of the future' (however serious) (2011: 456). This mechanism is clearly at work in the Dutch tour operator sector.

Watson (2014) holds that, if one really cares about climate change, one should not fly at all. But is it possible to fly less or not fly at all? Take for instance – and that is the third level to be discussed – the work done on this phenomenon by academics and scientists. Even they, in studying climate change, fly quite frequently (Hopkins et al., 2016). Is it possible that academics and environmental scientists could still perform their duties well while flying much less? There are signs within the academic world that the ever-increasing travel obligations are gradually becoming more controversial. An initiative has recently been launched by about 750 scientists who called upon their institutions to reduce travel and specifically flights (Wilde, 2016). Would an ethical stance on this dilemma demand that academics and researchers fly substantially less or in some cases even stop flying at all, when the work done by them shows that global aviation should not grow any more and even needs to decline later on in this century? At the same time, can scientists ever be effective when, working in international settings, they have to partly miss face-to-face deliberations in working groups and also the meetings where the decision-making takes place? It is the strong belief of the authors of this chapter that flying infrequently can be perfectly combined with doing 'good science'. Interestingly, this discussion is not entirely new. For instance, Kehlmann (2005) points to the enormous difference in travel behaviour of the naturalist von Humboldt, who travelled all over the world (without flying by the way) and the mathematician Gauss, who almost never left his own village. Both had a distinct impact on science in their respective disciplines.

Case 9.4.2: Climatic sustainability, tourism and the eradication of poverty

Introduction: Discussing the interconnections between tourism and poverty

Three journalists working for a national newspaper in the Netherlands have been assigned to write a comprehensive article for the following weekend edition of the paper, exploring the question of how tourism could be climatically sustainable on the one hand, and supporting the eradication of poverty in countries it is active in, on the other. Sally, John and Peter have done some research the week before and agree to meet on Thursday night at the 'opinion desk' of the newspaper to discuss the topic and try to align and write a joint article that is informative to the readers, but which also evokes critical and ethical discussion.

Sally opens the discussion and says: 'As we all know, there is some discussion going on out there about the impacts tourism has on climate change. I've talked to a professor of Environmental Studies at Border University and she told me that there is international concern about the contribution transportation and mobility by air make to CO_2 emissions and climate change. Tourism, especially, contributes to that. But, interestingly, while tourism seems to be fully aware of the impacts of its trade on climate change, its international organisations, like the UNWTO and WTTC, promote tourism as a way to alleviate poverty, even starting the ST-EP project, which means "sustainable tourism to eradicate poverty". The main idea of ST-EP and related UN programmes is to fly rich people from the West to the poor South, always involving long-haul flights and tons of CO_2 per tourist, where an average tourist would emit something like 200 kg. The professor said that, at the global level, the tourism sector suggests strongly that reducing aviation would cause poor countries to suffer a great deal. She based her statement on a UNWTO and ICAO report on aviation from 2007. It would, according to this report, be "unethical" to stop doing business over there or even reduce business activities. For many poor countries, international long-haul aviation-driven tourism is considered the main source export industry.'

Peter intervenes: 'Let me get this straight. If we apply the professor's argument to another example, we get the following: if a Dutch family, for example, decides to book a green camping holiday by train to the German Alps, they are actually considered to increase the growth of poverty elsewhere in the world by *not* having decided to fly to a poor country in Africa. They may even be accused of being "unethical" even though the climatic impact of such a trip would be probably less than 100 kg per person, while a pro-poor trip to the south of Africa would emit 2000–4000 kg per person. This sounds ridiculous to me!'

John: 'I agree. This is a "false" ethical problem and therefore actually an ethical issue in itself. Poverty does not exist because of a lack of long-haul tourism, but because of failing institutions, corruption, war, unequal income distribution, and misaligned geopolitical interests, to name a few causes. I got my information from a friend who works as a researcher on geopolitics in sub-Saharan Africa at the African Institute for Local Economic Development. To hold that tourism is the only factor in the aggravation of poverty is going way too far!'

Getting the dilemmas clear ...

Sally: 'We must try to wrap up and start to establish a plot for our article. We have now two perspectives on this issue. Peter argues that it is untenable to hold that travelling per se is causing the poverty of people and communities at long-haul destinations. This is in line with the notion of the industry that flying to long-haul destinations actually contributes to the welfare and well-being of the local people. If the industry were to stop organising holiday trips to poor countries, it would be disastrous for the local economy and thus also for the people. And John suggests that we look at the real causes of poverty. Tourism is not the culprit. There is a vast array of factors – corruption, war and the like – which are to blame. So, John's argument is also pro-tourism. Okay, but I feel that we should address at least two more ethical issues related to these pro-poor-tourism arguments, which are fundamentally supporting the unsustainable growth of aviation. First, an increase in aviation activities to poor countries would make their tourism industries even more dependent on high-carbon emissions than they currently are. In the long term, this cannot be sustained. It doesn't seem a fair way to help a country that is in despair and crisis and, in addition, it doesn't help the tourism sector to become more sustainable and environmentally friendly. The second ethical point to be considered is that the poverty argument is certainly not the driver for developing exotic travel products such as pro-poor packages. Tourists enjoy their holiday trips and want to have memorable experiences. Anything that is out of the ordinary is remembered better. Long-haul holiday trips are therefore perceived to be remembered better than other types of holiday trips. As a consequence, tourists may value these long-haul exotic trips more than other trips, which, in turn, increases the demand for such exotic trips. The professor I spoke to cited Nawijn and Peeters's publication from 2014 on this issue.'

John: 'I see where you are going. Tourism supply will gladly match this potential demand. Poor people are thus more or less taken hostage by an economic mechanism that is very much dominated by and beneficial to rich people. How ethical is this kind of industry behaviour? Is the argument "it is good for our hosts" ethical? It may be in some cases, but we often feel that the statement is not genuine, because the major and sole reason to develop the travel product to those poor places is to fulfil the hedonistic desires for well-being, comfort, the novel and the exotic. And also the desire to make money. The result of this perceived luxury will be an overheated planet leading to millions of climate refugees and a significant increase in poverty.'

Peter: 'We have to address both pro and contra arguments in our article in order to enable the readers to decide for themselves ...'

(continued)

> ## Case 9.4.2: Climatic sustainability, tourism and the eradication of poverty (*continued*)
>
> ### Questions for discussion
> - Which ethical principles could be used to make a case for or against continuing to organise long-haul trips to exotic, but poor countries?
> - Can you build a case for 'forcing' tour operators to resort to climatically sustainable business – even if it would lead them to go bankrupt?
> - Which is more important: the environment, or the welfare and well-being of the local people and communities at tourism destinations? Give reasons for your position.
> - It has been stated that selective moral awareness will cause a 'perfect moral storm', which suggests that people will become vulnerable to being morally corrupt in the face of the dispersion of causes and effects, fragmentation of agency, and institutional inadequacy. In order to prevent a 'moral storm', which of these three characteristics would, to your mind, convey the best solution for mitigating the impact of CO_2 emissions on the climate? Which stakeholder group (tourists, NGOs, the industry, governments, local communities, etc.) should take what action?
> - Do you think that the economy plays an important role in preventing tour operators from going 'green'? If so, how? And what could be done to change that?

9.5 Concluding thoughts

Sustainability literally means to 'endure' or 'support', implying that something could 'continue' or 'last' for quite some time. The term was initially used to raise awareness and undertake action towards the use and conservation of natural resources, such that a future is secured for forthcoming generations. Sustainability can have different meanings in different cultures. For example, in business, the term is in the USA especially associated with the environment, while in Europe it has been broadened to indicate economic concerns as well.

Generally speaking, sustainability in business is usually associated with the so-called triple bottom line, indicating that business activities should strive to minimise the negative economic, social and environmental impacts thereof. Some scholars/practitioners add a fourth pillar to the bottom line, namely culture. Others would like to see 'purpose' added to the list. Sustainability in business therefore means pursuing value among, or the well-being of individuals, organisations (i.e. the business itself), societies, cultures and the environment, based on business strategies that focus on the longer term.

In practice, this presupposes ethical and responsible leaders and ethical business organisations (see also Chapter 8) who follow a sustainability agenda and policies that are value-driven and take care that all activities, processes, products and services – throughout the entire supply chain – live up to the ideal of treating people and the planet with respect and fairness, while growing economically at the same time.

Further reading

Brown, D.A. (2013). *Climate Change Ethics: Navigating the Perfect Moral Storm*. London/New York: Routledge.

Weidinger, C., Fischler, F. and Schmidpeter, R. (Eds.) (2014). *Sustainable Entrepreneurship: Business Success through Sustainability*. New York/London: Springer.

Wells, G. (Ed.) (2013). *Sustainable Business: Theory and Practice of Business under Sustainability*. Cheltenham/Northampton, UK: Edward Elgar.

Wells, P.E. (2013). *Business Models for Sustainability*. Cheltenham/Northampton, UK: Edward Elgar.

Zubir, S.S. and Brebbia, C.A. (Eds.) (2014). *The Sustainable City*. Southampton, UK: WIT Press.

References

Anttiroiko, A-V., Valkama, P. and Bailey, S. J. (2013). Smart Cities in the New Service Economy: Building Platforms for Smart Services. *AI & Society*, 29(3): 323–334.

Ashworth, G. and Page, S.J. (2011). Urban Tourism Research: Recent Progress and Current Paradoxes. *Tourism Management*, 32(1): 1–15.

Baumgartner, R. and Ebner, D. (2010) Corporate Sustainability Strategies: Sustainability Profiles and Maturity Levels. *Sustainable Development*, 18: 76–89.

Bocken, N., Short, S., Rana, P., Evans, S. (2014). A Literature and Practice Review to Develop Sustainable Business Model Archetypes. *Journal of Cleaner Production*, 65: 42–56.

Borg, J. van den, and Russo, A. P. (2001). Towards Sustainable Tourism in Venice. In Muzo, I. (Ed.) *Sustainable Venice: Suggestions for the Future* (pp. 159–193). New York: Springer.

Cames, M., Harthan, R.O., Füssler, J.R., Lazarus, M., Lee, C. M., Erickson, P. and Spalding-Fecher, R. (2016). *How Additional is the Clean Development Mechanism? Analysis of the Application of Current Tools and Proposed Alternatives* (CLIMA.B.3/SER-l2013/0026r). Berlin.

Carmacal. (2016). CARMACAL – Carbon Management Tool for Tour Operators (2016). Centre of Sustainability, Tourism and Transport. Retrieved 20 April 2016 from http://www.cstt.nl/carmacal.

Ciulla, J.B. (2005). The State of Leadership Ethics and the Work That Lies Before Us. *Business Ethics: A European Review*, 14(4): 323–335.

Cohen, Scott A., Higham, James E. S. and Cavaliere, C.T. (2011). Binge Flying: Behavioural Addiction and Climate Change. *Annals of Tourism Research*, 38(3): 1070–1089.

Crane, A., Palazzo, G., Spence, L.J. and Matten, D. (2014). Contesting the Value of 'Creating Shared Value'. *California Management Review*, 56(2): 130–153.

Davenport, J. and Davenport, J. L. (2006). The Impact of Tourism and Personal Leisure Transport on Coastal Environments: A Review. *Estuarine, Coastal and Shelf Science*, 67(1–2): 280–292.

Doane, D. (2005). Beyond Corporate Social Responsibility: Minnows, Mammoths and Markets. *Futures*, 37: 215–229.

Elkington, J. (1997). *Cannibals with Forks: The Triple Bottom Line of 21st Century Business*. Oxford: Capstone.

Flint, J. and Raco, M. (2012). *The Future of Sustainable Cities: Critical Reflections*. Bristol: Policy Press.

Frenzel, F., Koens, K., Steinbrink, M. and Rogerson, C. M. (2015). Slum Tourism: State of the Art. *Tourism Review International*, 18(4): 237–252.

Füller, H. and Michel, B. (2014). 'Stop Being a Tourist!' New Dynamics of Urban Tourism in Berlin-Kreuzberg. *International Journal of Urban and Regional Research*, 38(4): 1304–1318.

Garay, L. A., Cànoves, G. and Prat, J. M. (2014). Barcelona, a Leader Destination in Cruise-Passenger Tourism: Keys, Impacts and Facts. *International Journal of Tourism Sciences*, 14(1): 23–49.

Gardiner, S. (2011). *Reflecting on a Perfect Moral Storm*. New York: Oxford University Press.

Gerencher, C. L. (2010). TRB Conference Proceedings: Research on the Transmission of Disease in Airports and on Aircraft: Summary of a Symposium. Washington, DC.

Gössling, S., Hall, C. M., Peeters, P. M. and Scott, D. (2010). The Future of Tourism: Can Tourism Growth and Climate Policy be Reconciled? A Climate Change Mitigation Perspective. *Tourism Recreation Research*, 35(2): 119–130.

Gössling, S. and Peeters, P. M. (2015). Assessing Tourism's Global Environmental Impact 1900–2050. *Journal of Sustainable Tourism*, 23(5): 639–659.

Graafland, J.J. (2009). Do Markets Crowd Out Virtues? An Aristotelian Framework. *Journal of Business Ethics*, 91(1): 1–19.

Griskevicius, V., Cantú, S. and Vugt, M. van (2012). The Evolutionary Bases for Sustainable Behavior: Implications for Marketing, Policy, and Social Entrepreneurship. *Journal of Public Policy & Marketing*, 31: 115–128.

Hardin, G. (1968). The Tragedy of the Commons. *Science*, 162(3859): 1243–1248.

Healey, P. (1998). Building Institutional Capacity through Collaborative Approaches to Urban Planning. *Environment and Planning A*, 30(9): 1531–1546.

Hirschman, A.O. (1982). Rival Interpretations of Market Society: Civilizing, Destructive or Feeble? *Journal of Economic Literature*, XX: 1463–1484.

Hopkins, D., Higham, J., Tapp, S. and Duncan, T. (2016). Academic Mobility in the Anthropocene Era: A Comparative Study of University Policy at Three New Zealand Institutions. *Journal of Sustainable Tourism*, 24(3): 376–397.

Joss, S. (2015). *Sustainable Cities: Governing for Urban Innovation*. New York, NY: Palgrave Macmillan.

Kehlmann, D. (2005). *Die Vermessung der Welt*. Reinbek: Rowohlt Verlag.

Koens, K. and Thomas, R. (2016). 'You Know That's a Rip-Off': Policies and Practices Surrounding Micro-Enterprises and Poverty Alleviation in South African Township Tourism. *Journal of Sustainable Tourism*, 24(12): 1641–1654.

Laukkanen, M. and Patala, S. (2014). Analysing Barriers to Sustainable Business Model Innovations: Innovation Systems Approach. *International Journal of Innovation Management*, 18(6). Retrieved 15 March 2019 from https://doi.org/10.1142/S1363919614400106.

Loorbach, D. (2014). To Transition! Governance Panarchy in the New Transformation – Inaugural Speech. Rotterdam: Erasmus University Rotterdam.

Marques, J.C. and Mintzberg, H. (2015). Why Corporate Social Responsibility Isn't a Piece of Cake. *MIT Sloan Management Review*, 56(4). Retrieved 15 March 2019 from http://ilp.mit.edu/media/news_articles/smr/2015/56413.pdf.

Maxim, C. (2016). Sustainable Tourism Implementation in Urban Areas: A Case Study of London. *Journal of Sustainable Tourism*, 24(7): 971–989.

McKercher, B. and Prideaux, B. (2014). Academic Myths of Tourism. *Annals of Tourism Research*, 46: 16–28.

Melissen, F. (2013). Sustainable Hospitality: A Meaningful Notion? *Journal of Sustainable Tourism*, 21(6): 810–824.

Melissen, F. (2016). *4th Generation Sustainable Business Models – Inaugural Speech*. Breda: NHTV Breda University of Applied Sciences.

Melissen, F. and Koens, K. (2016). Adding Researchers' Behaviour to the Research Agenda: Bridging the Science–Policy Gap in Sustainable Tourism Mobility. *Journal of Sustainable Tourism*, 24(3): 335–349.

Melissen, F. and Moratis, L. (2016). Turning Point: A Call for Fourth Generation Sustainable Business Models. *Journal of Corporate Citizenship*, 63: 8–16.

Porter, M.E. and Kramer, M.R. (2011). Creating Shared Value. *Harvard Business Review*, 89: 62–77.

Miller, D., Merrilees, B. and Coghlan, A. (2015). Sustainable Urban Tourism: Understanding and Developing Visitor Pro-Environmental Behaviours. Journal of Sustainable Tourism, 23(1): 26–46.

Nawijn, J. (2011). Happiness through Vacationing: Just a Temporary Boost or Long-Term Benefits? *Journal of Happiness Studies*, 12(4): 651–665.

Nawijn, J. and Peeters, P. M. (2014). Rose Tinted Memories as a Cause of Unsustainable Leisure Travel. In Garling, T., Ettema, D.F. and Friman, M. (Eds.), *Handbook of Sustainable Travel* (pp. 185–197). Dordrecht: Springer Science & Business Media.

Newman, P. and Jennings, I. (2008). *Cities as Sustainable Ecosystems: Principles and Practices*. Washington/London: Island Press.

Panko, T. R. and George, B. P. (2012). Child Sex Tourism: Exploring the Issues. *Criminal Justice Studies*, 25(1): 67–81.

Pearce, P. L. (1993). Fundamentals of Tourist Motivation. In Pearce, D.G. and Butler, R.W. (Eds.), *Tourism Research: Critiques and Challenges* (pp. 113–134). London/New York: Routledge.

Peeters, P., Higham, J., Kutzner, D., Cohen, Scott A. and Gössling, S. (2016). Are Technology Myths Stalling Aviation Climate Policy? *Transportation Research Part D*, 44: 30–42.

Peeters, P. M. and Dubois, G. (2010). Tourism Travel under Climate Change Mitigation Constraints. *Journal of Transport Geography*, 18: 447–457.

Savage, V. R., Huang, S. and Chang, T. C. (2004). The Singapore River Thematic Zone: Sustainable Tourism in an Urban Context. *The Geographical Journal*, 170(3): 212–225.

Timur, S. and Getz, D. (2009). Sustainable Tourism Development: How Do Destination Stakeholders Perceive Sustainable Urban Tourism? *Sustainable Development*, 17(4): 220–232.

UNEP and UNWTO (2012). Tourism in the Green Economy – Background Report. Madrid: UNWTO.

UNFCCC (2015). *Adoption of the Paris Agreement: Proposal by the President. Draft Decision -/CP.21*. Paris: Framework Convention on Climate Change.

UNWTO and ICAO. (2007). *Tourism, Aviation and the Environment*. Madrid: UNWTO.

Visser, W. (2011). *The Age of Responsibility: CSR 2.0 and the New DNA of Business*. London: Wiley.

Watson, C. (2014). *Beyond Flying: Rethinking Air Travel in a Globally Connected World*. Cambridge (UK): UIT Cambridge Limited.

WCED. (1987). *Our Common Future*. United Nations World Commission on Environment and Development (Brundtland Commission). Oxford: Oxford University Press.

Wilde, P. (2016). Call on Universities and Professional Associations to Greatly Reduce Flying. *Change.org*. Retrieved 21 April 2016 from http://www.change.org/p/universities-and-professional-associations-call-on-universities-and-professional-associations-to-greatly-reduce-flying.

Wilson, F. and Post, J. (2013). Business Model for People, Planet (& Profits): Exploring the Phenomena of Social Business, a Market-based Approach to Social Value Creation. *Small Business Economics*, 40: 715–737.

Chapter 10

Human rights and business
Rami Isaac, Mata Haggis and Esther Peperkamp

10.1 Introduction to human rights and business
Rami Isaac

The Universal Declaration of Human Rights was adopted by the United Nations Assembly in 1948 without a single dissenting vote (Glendon, 1988). The Declaration itself was a collective and global response to human abuses that preceded and accompanied the Second World War – a global war that created a global moral crisis. The Declaration starts as follows:

> Whereas recognition of the inherent dignity and of the equal and inalienable rights of all members of the human family is the foundation of freedom, justice and peace in the world, and whereas disregard and contempt for human rights have resulted in barbarous acts which have outraged the conscience of mankind, and the advent of a world in which human beings shall enjoy freedom of speech and belief, and freedom from fear and wants has been proclaimed as the highest of the common people (…) (cited in Cragg, 2000: 1–2).

In addition, the General Assembly:

> Proclaims this Universal Declaration of Human Rights as a common standard of achievement of all peoples and all nations, to the end that every individual and every organ of society … shall strive to … secure their universal and effective recognition and observance (Cragg, 2000: 1–2).

The Declaration also specifies in article 25 that 'everyone has the right to a standard of living adequate for the health and well-being of himself and his family, including food, clothing, housing and necessary medical care and necessary social services and the right to security in the event of unemployment'. It also recognises the right to work, to just and favourable remuneration and working conditions, to rest and reasonable limits on working hours, to social security and to education (Cassel, 2001: 262).

Even before the Declaration was adopted, certain human rights, particularly labour rights, had been recognised by the charter of the League of Nations in 1919, which led to the establishment of the International Labour Organisation (ILO). The ILO still exists as an agency of the UN (Cassel, 2001). It is organised on a three-way basis with representation from governments, business and labour. The ILO adopts international standards on human rights issues, including child labour, forced labour, gender equality, rights for workers to organise, collective bargaining and maximum working hours. Its standards are expected to be enforced by the legal machinery of those governments that adopt them. The ILO provides technical support to those governments, for example, through establishing procedures that allow workers and unions to ventilate their criticisms directly to the ILO (Cassel, 2001).

The above points out that social and economic human rights are well and long established – at least in the 'words' of international law. Experience teaches that rights like those proclaimed by the Universal Declaration of Human Rights and the ILO cannot be guaranteed by governments alone (Cassel, 2001). However, one consequence of the assumption that protecting and enhancing human rights was a government responsibility, was that it de facto led to a division in responsibilities between governments and the private sector (Cragg, 2000). The private sector primarily assumed responsibility for generating wealth while the public sector accepted responsibility for ensuring respect for human rights. Cragg argues in this regard that nowadays many in the corporate world tend to pay little attention to human rights issues as a corporate responsibility (2000: 3). The evidence supporting the existence of a hidden understanding of the social responsibilities of the private sector is extensive and multidimensional. As Milton Friedman's infamous 1970 article in the *New York Magazine* put it quite clearly: the social responsibility of the modern corporation is simply to maximise profits. To go beyond this objective, he argues, is a misuse of power that is doomed to fail and, in the process, obstruct civil authorities in exercising their own proper responsibilities.

It is expected that companies which see profit maximisation as their primary obligation will define their social and ethical responsibilities narrowly. They would regard themselves as having a limited number of informal obligations defined by local conventions and culture, which would include both the obligations companies have towards their employees and the reciprocal obligations employees have towards their employer (Cragg, 2000). Evidence that this is happening comes from the private sector itself. A good example is the statement made by F. Vincke, secretary general of PetroFina, saying in a discussion of the International Chamber of Commerce's campaign against bribery that 'until recently (…) corporate responsibility was dictated by the law, or to put it even simpler terms: the ethical code of a company was the criminal code' (Vincke et al., 1999: 15). Perhaps more convincing is a report that a business sector advisory group submitted to the Organisation for Economic Cooperation and Development (OECD), stating categorically that 'most industrialized societies recognize that generating long-term economic profits is the corporation's primary objective' (Millstein, 1998: 25). The authors of the report acknowledged that ethics and ethical codes have a clear place in corporate governance, but to their minds, they should not jeopardise the primary goal – which is profit maximisation. Commitment to respecting human rights in international commerce – even where it is not required by law – implies a willingness to diverge from the goal of maximising long-term economic profitability (Millstein, 1998). This is, however, not commonplace in (international) business yet. Profit maximisation as the primary goal for business has become the dominant view since the Second

Human rights and business

World War. As far as the protection of human rights in business is concerned, the international community is still in the early stages of adopting those rights regime and providing more effective protection to individuals and communities against corporate-related human rights harm. A report, authored by Ruggie, and presented at the United Nations in 2008, presents a principle-based conceptual and policy framework intended to help achieve this aim.

10.1.1 Business, the market and human rights

Ruggie asserts:

> Business is the major source of investment and job creation, and markets can be highly efficient means for allocating scarce resources. They create powerful forces capable of generating economic growth, reducing poverty and increasing demand for the rule of law, thereby contributing to the realization of a broad spectrum of human rights (2008: 1).

Nonetheless, markets work optimally only if they are rooted within rules, customs and institutions. Markets themselves need these to survive and thrive, while society needs them to manage the opposing effects of market dynamics and produce public goods that market undersupply. Ruggie (2008) states that history teaches us that markets pose the greatest risk to society and business itself, when their scope and power far exceed the reach of the institutional keystones that allow them to function easily and ensure their political sustainability. This is such a time and escalating charges of corporate-related human rights abuses are the canary in the coal mine, signalling that all is not well.

The root cause of the business and human rights quandary today lies in the governance gaps created by globalisation, between the scope and impact of economic factors, forces and actors, and the capacity of societies to manage their adverse consequences (Ruggie, 2008: 1). These governance gaps provide the liberal environment for companies performing wrongful acts of all kinds without adequate sanctioning (Ruggie, 2008: 1). Ruggie states that 'how to narrow and ultimately to bridge the gaps in relation to human rights is our fundamental challenge' (2008: 1).

10.1.2 The human rights responsibilities of transnational corporations

The economic power of transnational corporations (TNCs) is definite. They are the driving agents of the global economy, exercising dominant control over global trade, investment and technology transfer. Flowing directly from such positions of economic influence, TNCs also manage to exercise considerable political leverage in both domestic and international spheres (Kinley and Tadaki, 2004: 933).

It must be recognised at the outset that foreign direct investment, introduced by TNCs into developed, as well as developing destinations, can and does bring jobs, capital and technology. In doing so, they safeguard and promote the rights to work and acceptable living standards, but also derivative rights such as health, education, housing and even political freedoms (Kamminga, 1999). That said, it is equally certain that human rights abuses by TNCs do happen, and do so frequently in the sphere of economic, social and cultural rights. Many TNCs, including Nike and The Gap, have been suspected of violating their workers' rights to just and satisfying conditions of work by paying unfair and insufficient wages, demanding unreasonable overtime, and providing unsafe working conditions (Kinley and Tadaki, 2004; see more in Baez et al., 1999).

Furthermore, there is also evidence that TNCs are involved in suppressing trade unions and thereby denying workers the right to organise (Kinley and Tadaki, 2004: 933–934). It has been suspected, for instance, that Coca-Cola in Colombia and Phillips-Van Heusen in Guatemala have been associated with, or are directly responsible for, the systematic intimidation, torture, kidnapping, unlawful detention and murder of trade-unionist employees by paramilitaries, who operated as agents for both of these corporations (see Kinley and Tadaki, 2004: 934; Human Rights Watch, 1997). TNCs in the extractive industries have caused environmental disasters, threatening the right to adequate food and the right to an adequate standard of living. Royal Dutch Shell's oil production in Nigeria, and BHP Billiton's copper mining in Papua New Guinea, for instance, truly damaged the environment and the living of indigenous people in local communities (Cassel, 1963, cited in Kinley and Tadaki, 2004: 934). Such examples of corporate responsibility for, or involvement in, human rights exploitations are gradually being widely publicised (see for example Kamminga, 1999), especially by non-governmental organisations (NGOs) using closeness of global communications (Kinley and Tadaki, 2004: 934). Mounting activism by NGOs, workers and consumers in developed countries in the form of protests, demonstrations, product boycotts – such as of Israeli products coming from illegal settlements in the West Bank, Palestine – and selective purchasing have forced many TNCs to accept some level of human rights responsibility by adopting internal codes of conduct.

Nevertheless, the fact that the explosion of corporate codes of conduct and other initiatives might lead to the reinforcement of international legal human rights standards for TNCs, should not lead to ignoring two important questions, namely how does TNC obligation arise and what are their fundamental duties? This is important because some TNCs are considered to be more powerful than many states (Baez et al., 1999), and some provide many of the jobs usually expected from governments. It cannot be expected from TNCs that they have the same human rights tasks as states (Baez et al., 1999). As mentioned previously, private entities, such as TNCs and other businesses, are designed to serve the primary economic purpose of profit maximisation, not to assume broad-based welfare functions (Kelly, 2001). To stress the duties of states with respect to human rights more than those of business enterprises, is to ignore the differences between the nature and the function of states and corporations.

Of particular significance in this respect is the question of jurisdiction. Under international human rights law, a state is considered to have responsibility for the human rights impacting the actions of all stakeholders within its jurisdiction. This also applies to private sector stakeholders, because the government has, at least in theory, the constitutional authority to legislate and regulate their actions in order to ensure compliance with its international obligations and duties. But how far, it may be asked, can any equivalent jurisdictional claim be made with respect to corporations? To what extent might corporations be held legally responsible for the human rights abuses of their subsidiaries, agents, suppliers and buyers (Kinley and

Tadaki, 2004: 961)? There are no easy answers to these questions. The UN Human Rights Norms for Corporations call upon corporations to feel obliged to promote and protect the norms within their spheres of influence, but whether that means that corporations might be held responsible in situations where, short of promised obligation, they nonetheless de facto exercise some power, is a debatable point. Fundamentally, this observation rests upon the basic axiom that where there is power, there must be responsibility (Weeramantry, 1999). And there is legitimate concern that the selectivity of the liberalised global market has undercut this fundamental principle in favour of TNCs. Consequently, TNCs have escaped the reach of international human rights law, regardless of TNCs' massive power over countries, which often threatens the enjoyment of human rights.

Therefore, there is a need to reconstruct the current form of international human rights law so that TNCs can be assigned tasks and obligations which fit their nature and activities in a balanced way (Kinley and Tadaki, 2004: 962). Mechanisms for controlling powerful and influential non-government stakeholders like TNCs, which are, by definition, not restrained by notions of territorial sovereignty, are not sufficient any longer (Kinley and Tadaki, 2004: 963).

10.1.3 In conclusion

This chapter began with analysing the relationship between human rights and business, followed by a specific discussion of the human rights responsibilities of TNCs. It has been observed that, despite the powerful symbolic significance the Universal Declaration of Human Rights and the ILO have, states and governments do not have the power to ensure full compliance by (international) business corporations. The classic Friedmanian view, stating that the only purpose businesses have is to maximise their profits, still prevails under the pressure of the liberalised global market. Businesses have a lot of power, which is badly controlled. Therefore, it is argued, international human rights law should be reconstructed in order to guarantee that TNCs live up to their responsibilities of having respect for and protecting human rights in business.

In the second part of this chapter, the way in which human dignity and human rights feature in practice are explicated in three discussions, followed by three cases respectively. The first discussion reflects on how the human dignity of minorities and women is often portrayed in video games. The author, Haggis, points out that people of colour, for example, are quite negatively portrayed in games. The negative and positive reflections different target groups have on a fictitious case in which a black woman is the protagonist, are demonstrative of that. Isaac introduces the second discussion, which is about the interactions between tourism, human rights and ethics as reflected in the case of Palestine within the setting of an illegal Israeli occupation. It becomes clear that Palestine, to this day, has been unable to fully explore its tourism potential, a situation which calls for broad international reflection on, and action at, different levels of aggregation. The third and last discussion deals with the theme of the 'working poor'. Peperkamp offers insight into the values people have with regard to paid work and the importance thereof to human identity. The case she includes points out that there are – especially in the amusement park sector – many examples of people being exploited despite the existence of, in the case of Germany, a national minimum wage regulation.

10.2 Human dignity and the presentation of minorities and women in video games

Mata Haggis[1]

10.2.1 Introduction to human dignity in video games

Video games are used for a multitude of practical applications in modern life, ranging from increasing empathy for the experiences of dementia patients (Botek, 2014) through to stimulating the creative sector in exhibits at MoMA New York (Antonelli, 2012). These uses of games technology are subject to the ethics of their own domains, such as medicine or the art world.

The entertainment sector of the games industry has less direct practical consequences, but its social significance is substantial. It is financially the largest entertainment medium in the world, with an estimated revenue of US$111bn in 2015 (Fuchs, 2015). Titles such as *Assassin's Creed*, *Call of Duty*, *Grand Theft Auto* (also known as *GTA*), *Candy Crush* and *Minecraft* command audiences in the millions for their updates and instalments, and as such represent significant artefacts for the interpretation of contemporary social and cultural narratives. Equally, these games are part of a dialogue with society that functions through explicit mediums such as conferences, YouTube reviews, magazines and newspapers, and online forums, and through the implicit audience engagement of purchasing/download patterns. As support for the significance of entertainment games, the most popular YouTube channel is not from a mainstream media producer such the BBC or Fox, but the Swedish games player Felix Kjellberg, known as 'PewDiePie' (Sydell, 2013).

Therefore, this section will focus on the content of entertainment-focused video games and more specifically, on the representation of minority groups and gender.

10.2.1.1 Minorities and gender in video games

As with many other forms of media, the 21st century has brought increasingly negative criticism of the representation of minorities and gender in video games. The most prominent example of this is Anita Sarkeesian's 'Tropes Versus Women' series, where Sarkeesian collects and analyses negative and problematic representations of women in games (Feminist Frequency, 2013). This series has proven controversial amongst video-game players, with wide-ranging discussions about the validity of the criticism, some supporting Sarkeesian's research and approach and others arguing against it. There have been very strong reactions by some groups who perceive Sarkeesian's criticism, and the work of similar cultural analysts, as an attack on the medium that they enjoy, rather than a discussion intended to strengthen the medium.

A study led by Dmitri Williams in 2009 examined the range of characters that played leading roles in video games, and found that outside of sports games the representation of African American men drops precipitously, with many of those remaining featured as gangsters and street people in games such as *Grand Theft Auto* and *50 Cent Bulletproof*. His research also showed a systematic over-representation of males, white and adults and a systematic under-representation of females, Hispanics, Native Americans, children and the elderly. Overall, the results are similar to those found in television research (Williams et al., 2009).

Another study demonstrates that there is a difference in the effect of violent representations of the people who are black compared to white. Although it is difficult to empirically prove, it is suggested that the pre-existing social discourses of violence in relation to people who are black are being amplified and reinforced by the content of video games, producing this result. Video games are immersed in, and contributing to, a wider social trend towards negative representations of people who are black (Yang et al., 2014).

Gender in video games is also a widely debated and studied topic. Like the topic of race, this is split into two main discussions, one of presence, and another of role. In terms of presence, a 2014 study of video-game consumers found that there was a 52 : 48 split in men : women playing games (Entertainment Software Association, 2014), but Williams et al. found that only 13.9 per cent of characters in games are identifiably female (Williams et al., 2009). Within this minority presence, and as with other creative industries, there is often criticism of the roles allotted to women in games, and a near-total absence of transgender characters in game worlds. This has been explored by Sarkeesian and other feminist critics, and although the roles of women in games are the central point of discussion, there is also some discussion of the often stereotypical roles for men in games. Like in cinema, there is a preponderance of hyper-masculine characters in video games: the lead characters are physically strong, good fighters, have a high degree of physical symmetricality, and charismatic personalities. One example of such a hero is Jason Brody from the game *Far Cry 3*; however, Jeffery Yohalem, the lead writer of the game, states that he intended Brody to be a satire of masculinity in games. This satire was not noticed by any reviewers of the game. In an article for the online journal *Gamasutra*, Haggis concluded that the reason this was not noticed was not the writing, but the commonality of hyper-masculine narratives in video games (2013).

Beyond gender, sexuality has to be mentioned here as well. It is rarely featured in games, with sexual behaviour largely missing from game worlds, or a disproportionately heavy weighting towards heterosexual preferences where sexuality is addressed. Sexuality is a feature in game series such as *Mass Effect*, *Dragon Age* and *Fable*, but it is rarely explored in great depth as a core thematic structure of the narrative. There have been some efforts to explore sexuality in a deeper way, such as *The Path*, or *Hurt Me Plenty*. Such games have been emerging with greater frequency in recent years, but these are largely coming from the 'indie' development community, named for its lack of, or very inconsistent, support from major publishers and the resulting lower market penetration. Wider issues of gender identity such as those encountered by people who are transgender or self-identify as queer, are almost never addressed in mainstream games and, as in wider society, some people argue that games should never address these topics.

10.2.1.2 Diversity and the future of game development

Although many game developers are reasonably liberal in their mindset, the games industry has many of the same conflicts that general society also faces. In addition, although it cannot be easily proven that the social and cultural status of game developers creates the biases in the content of their games, it is likely that the lack of diversity in the development teams contributes significantly to the limited range of content in the majority of games released: creators are likely to produce works that they find compelling and relevant to their own social and cultural environments. The current situation is challenging, but the opportunities for entering game development have become significantly broader than they were at the beginning of the 21st century. Since 2015, several major developers have released very affordable or free versions of their software for creating games, and other tools are allowing people from many backgrounds to enter game development professionally. Groups such as the Code Liberation Foundation (founded 2015) are specifically targeting and supporting 'women, non-binary, femme, and girl-identifying people to diversify STEAM fields [including the game industry]' (Code Liberation Foundation, 2017) if they have the wish to do so. Although the outcome of this increased accessibility is unpredictable, the rapid growth of the indie development community does suggest increasing diversity and in turn the range of characters and situations in games are also reflecting experiences outside of the current common milieu. Whether the non-indie industry will choose to embrace this shift is currently uncertain, but it is likely that the larger businesses will absorb some influences from these smaller groups and that their content will adapt too.

For now, the low incidence of people of colour, and the negative portrayal of them in games, are a growing point of discussion in game development, and likely to continue being debated and studied for the foreseeable future. The case presented below is *purely fictional*, but based on a combination of real examples and can serve as a point of discussion for these topics.

Case 10.2.2: *New York Dawn*'s race, gender and social dialogues

Introduction: Miny Games, *New York Dawn* and Dana

'Miny Games', a large video-game development studio, is working on a new action game called *New York Dawn*. The lead character is Dana, a woman who is also a black American, and the casting of a woman who is black as the lead in a high-budget game is highly unusual. The plot is that Dana is involved with the New York disco scene in the late 1970s. At the end of a club night, a fight breaks out and her fiancé is accidentally killed. When Dana reports this to the police, she discovers that the killer was part of the Italian mafia and the police are controlled by the same organisation. Rather than supporting her, she becomes a target for officers on the mob's payroll. She escapes the station and decides that the only way to save her life and to find justice for her fiancé's death is to take matters into her own hands: she must destroy the mob herself.

The script of the game treats the events seriously and without hint of satire or parody. The game is not presented in a retro 1970s 'blaxploitation' (Buchanan, 2010) manner, reminiscent of films such as *Shaft* (Parks, 1971) or more recently Quentin Tarantino's work; instead, it is treated as the story of a person forced to resort to extreme measures after being let down by authority figures. Although Dana's styling initially begins as consistent with stereotypes of a woman who is black in the disco scene of the era, her presentation in the game quickly becomes more practical and in alignment with her goals.

After two years of production, the announcement trailer (giving the first public information about the game) is created. It begins with shots of Dana and her friends in the club, wearing bright colours and natural hairstyles, accompanied by disco music, but quickly transitions to: combat action sequences (fighting and shooting), Dana dressed in practical black clothing while stealthily moving through dark locations, and dramatic confrontations of strong personalities, including male, white police officers that are threatening Dana. The music for these sections of the trailer is a modern orchestral soundtrack.

When the game is announced, there is very varied reception from the games press, potential players and cultural critics: Firstly, some of the video-game press welcome the announcement. This group particularly praise the use of a woman who is black as the lead character, and the clear attempt to both reflect a period and cultural scene that prominently featured people of colour, while at the same time showing that the visual style is not the only point of interest for the people involved, i.e. that people of colour have personal lives beyond the stylistic surface of tropes such as 'disco diva'. Some reviewers mention that they felt discomfort when seeing the police officer in the trailer threatening Dana, and that this was something that they did not want to draw a judgement on until seeing it in the context of the full game. They say that it is admirable, but risky, to include such an important current social issue (tension between black Americans and the police) in an action game, but many do not mention this section of the trailer at all. Others from the video-game press are less complimentary. It is either hinted or openly stated by some of the press that they feel the protagonist might be a woman who is black as a marketing ploy rather than as a narrative necessity, and question why a woman, and in particular a woman who is black, was chosen for the lead role and what this is expected to add to the game. The final tone of the coverage is somewhat sceptical about the believability of the lead character's place in the story. Some of the press argue that the addition of racial issues into a mob story devalues the importance of serious discussions regarding race in America, both historically and in the present day, and so is inappropriate material for a video game.

Secondly, potential players react in varying ways too. Some wholeheartedly greet the protagonist and use her as an example of game developers finding inspiration from outside of the stereotypical milieu of lead characters, both in the choice of her race and particularly the culture around her. Many potential players openly state that they find Dana sexy. These threads of discussion quickly progress towards heated debates about how appropriate it is to say this about a character who: is fictional; has not consented to being viewed as a sexual object; is part of a post-segregation society where people of colour, and particularly women who are black, are still combating stereotypes of sexual

(continued)

Case 10.2.2: *New York Dawn*'s race, gender and social dialogues (*continued*)

objectification; is living in a world where sexual appeal is often seen as the primary factor of a woman's value; is in mourning; is in danger or fighting for her life. Some argue that although Dana is a woman who is black, and that this is positive for games, she still conforms to many conventional aspects of objectified women's sexuality: she is tall, slim, in her early twenties, with clear skin, is able-bodied, and was in a heterosexual relationship. Yet others argue that if elements such as race and gender are going to be included in a video game, particularly in light of the historical period of cultural progress in which *New York Dawn* is set, then the cultural context should be addressed. The full game may indeed do this, but again there is disagreement about whether this would be desirable, pointing out that discussions of Caucasian masculinity would not be considered essential in a game with a man who is white as the protagonist.

Thirdly, some commenters complain very vocally that the use of a woman in the lead role undermines the game: they argue that a woman would not be capable of the physical combat shown in the trailer, and that she would also be unlikely to possess such a high level of skill with firearms. They argue that a man who is black would be a much more believable lead protagonist. In contrast, a minority of commenters make the point that Dana should not be black, because it reinforces a narrative of black people being associated with violence. Cultural critics from outside the market of video-game journalists or players, argue for and against her representation in the trailer. Those in favour generally argue for any positive visibility of both women and people of colour in games is a good thing, and those against do accept this argument but prefer to add nuance by questioning whether New York and the 1970s disco scene are truly the ideal starting point for any discussion of race that is going to step beyond the boundaries of stereotypes. Although these small disagreements exist within the discussion, outside of the mainstream gaming press and culture, Dana's character and the game's setting are generally greeted as a positive addition to the medium, but many articles also mention that the game play appears to revolve around extreme violence, and as such does not have mechanics to match the somewhat innovative storytelling ambitions.

Character representation and social impact of *New York Dawn*

Two weeks after the announcement trailer is released, a male teenager who is black is shot and killed with very minimal provocation by a police officer who is white. A cultural critic discussing media representation of people who are black highlights the scene in the *New York Dawn* trailer where Dana is threatened by a male police officer who is white. Although the mention of *New York Dawn* is very brief, it triggers a few other articles reflecting on the representation of the police in video games. While many of these representations

Human rights and business

are cartoonish, *New York Dawn* is highlighted because of the realism of the graphics and performances. This leads to discussion of whether video games are currently in a stage of sophistication where they can respectfully address topics of such social importance as racism. While the initial articles about the game's trailers are positive, centring on the refreshing placement of a woman who is black in the lead role, these later articles are more ambivalent, and many end with anxious questions about whether *New York Dawn* will be able to tread the thin line of creating a character that feels believable alongside interesting game-play scenarios.

Miny Games is making *New York Dawn* at a studio based in the United Kingdom, but the head office of Miny Games is in Seattle. Three weeks after the game's trailer is released, an internal email is sent from the head office requesting information on the diversity reflected in the 110 staff in the UK studio: how many women are on the staff and what percentage of the staff is this in total? What racial groups are represented amongst the staff and in what numbers? In particular, are there any women who are black Americans amongst the writers? When it is revealed that there are no women who are black on the entire team, Miny Games begins to consider hiring a consultant writer who is specifically a woman and a black American.

In response to the announcement coverage, the publisher asks the studio to consider whether they would like to make any changes to the lead protagonist or the story.

Questions for discussion

- Why do you think Miny Games wants to hire a woman who is a black American for consulting on the game's writing at this point in development? Can you think of any moral or ethical reasons why this might not be a good idea? Which argument is stronger?
- If you were a game developer looking at the response to *New York Dawn*, would you be interested in making a game with a woman of colour as the lead character? What factors would you weigh up in making your decision? How do those factors change for a lead white character and/or a man?
- In light of research that suggests diversity is of financial benefit to decision-making processes, if you were leading a game company, how comfortable would you be in enforcing diversity in your hiring policy regarding game developers? Is affirmative action a morally sound principle in business?
- Which moral values and principles should be applied in assessing whether the dignity or rights of characters representing sociocultural minorities in a game are violated?
- Should games be considered to have similar protections and rights to free speech as other artistic mediums, even if the content is offensive to certain groups in society, or does the interactive nature of them bring additional responsibilities to society? Argue your position.

10.3 Tourism, human rights and ethics

Rami Isaac

10.3.1 Introduction to human rights, tourism and ethics

In the era in the aftermath of the world wars, countries built economies in which leisure and consumerism could thrive. The result was that middle classes developed, countries gained independence and global interconnectedness grew through globalisation. Tourism, amongst other sectors, played an essential instrumental role in the realisation of those ideals. Tourism is regarded as a transitory movement of people across the varied range of geographic areas and cultural products. It has the purpose of creating a direct experience of these products and realising mental transformations in those who travel (Alder, 1989). In the optimism of this era, the psychological, social, economic and environmental benefits of tourism were deemed so powerful that the right to travel was incorporated in key international documents, including the Universal Declaration of Human Rights of 1948, the International Covenant on Economic, Social and Cultural Rights of 1966, the World Tourism Organization's Tourism Bill of Rights and Tourist Code of 1985 and the Global Code of Ethics for Tourism of 1999.

Especially the Universal Declaration of Human Rights underpins the right to travel with two passages in articles 13 and 24. Article 13 (1) states: 'everyone has the right to freedom of movement and residence within the borders of each state' and article 13(2) puts forward that 'everyone has the right to leave any country, including his own, and to return to his country' (United Nations, 1948). O'Byrne holds this article to be the underpinning of the human right to travel (2001: 411–413). Article 24, which holds 'everyone has the right to rest and leisure, including reasonable limitation of working hours and periodic holidays with pay' (United Nations, 1948). These articles included in this fundamental document of international law situate travel and tourism within the domain of the humane, which is quite important to note. The vision behind the assertion that travel and tourism are worthy of inclusion in this document, together with basic rights such as the right to life, liberty and security, resonates with the texts of the UN World Tourism Organization (UNWTO). The UNWTO declares tourism's potential value as 'contributing to economic development, international understanding, peace, prosperity and universal respect for, and observance of, human rights and fundamental freedoms for all' (UNWTO, 1999). It is for these noble and important reasons that the idea of making travel and tourism as widely available as possible through an articulation of human rights was embraced (Higgins-Desbiolles, 2016).

However, this right to travel has a flip side. The optimism that tourism could be the '"smokeless" industry that could benefit communities around the world, contributing to social and economic well-being', has been subdued by the knowledge that tourism also has a 'dark' side, because of the adverse impacts it has on different levels of society – including the environment (Lovelock and Lovelock, 2013: 2–3). In particular, the environmental impacts of tourism have dictated the discussion in the sector since the late 1980s. Sustainable tourism became the lead principle in the years that followed, but critics have, relatively recently, started to declare this notion problematic, because it is apparently still 'predicated upon economic growth' (Lovelock and Lovelock, 2013: 3). It will therefore not be able to create

Human rights and business

the envisaged outcomes that sustainable thinking caters for. Weeden advocates a broader ethical approach which embraces 'responsible tourism', which, in turn, caters for more than only the three 'classical pillars' of sustainable tourism (economic, social and environmental value) (2002). It was effectively a call for ethical tourism, which, though relatively recent in origin, has become universal.

Calls for ethical tourism are reflected in academic literature, industry marketing, media accounts and even in NGO campaigns (Butcher and Svensson, 2015). As far as literature is concerned, take for example Krippendorf's *The Holiday Makers* which mentions the 'ethical tourist' (1987), Croall's *Preserve or Destroy: Tourism and the Environment*, which narrates how cultures and landscapes have been destroyed by tourism (1995) and MacLaren's *The Paving of Paradise and What You Can Do to Stop It,* which calls for rethinking tourism and eco-travel (1998). All these titles are characteristic of a negative perspective on the development of mass tourism and travel. More recent authors such as Fennell (2006) and Smith and Duffy (2003) have sought to develop a more extensive understanding of ethical tourism. Furthermore, MacCannell's *Ethics of Sight-Seeing* (2011) is a notable addition to the ethical tourism literature, as he focusses on the construction of tourism as a moral field. Lovelock and Lovelock (2013) have also provided a recent book on the influence of growing ethical concerns in relation to a range of social and political issues. They touch upon ethical dilemmas such as tourism in relation to medical care, sex, disability, indigenous people, animals and climate change, but also address the question of human rights. Human rights are those basic standards without which people cannot live in dignity (Donnelly, 2003). These are the rights one has, for the basic reason that one is a human being (George and Varghese, 2007). And those rights are often structurally violated in host countries, or worse, through tourism activities themselves.

This implies that a tour operator should not only be aware of the moral issues that come up in daily business, in the communication with clients or in business relations, but also of the (ethical) impact his products and services have on people and communities at the destinations in which they operate. Tour operators have a responsibility to protect and respect (Rendtorff, 2017: vi–vii). This responsibility also applies to human rights related to supply chains, labour rights, security, information technology, freedom of expression, forced and child labour, and also to investment issues (Posner, 2016: 705). However, in the following case the focus will be on the way in which the human rights discourse has been dealt with in regard to tourism in the occupied territories of Palestine where the Palestinian people live.

Case 10.3.2: Palestine, tourism and human rights

Introduction: mobility in an occupied territory

Mobility, being able to move freely, is one of the fundamental human needs. People through all centuries were fascinated by what lies over the horizon. Sometimes our ancestors were forced to move home to another place in search for better living conditions, but people also have the need to satisfy

(continued)

Case 10.3.2: Palestine, tourism and human rights (*continued*)

their sense of wonder and explore and understand the world they are living in. Thus, mobility, travel, is a phenomenon that is not restricted to movement from one geographical place to another. Mobility is also an existential exercise through which people meet and interact with other people and cultures. It is to some extent a search for self, for personal enrichment, for meaning.

Today, as Sheller and Urry state, 'all the world seems to be on the move' (2006: 207). But while the entire world might seem to be on the move, the nature of these movements could differ a great deal depending on the subjects and places under examination (Harker, 2009). Let us look at Palestine.

Since the beginning of the 20th century Palestine has seen complicated changes in its political circumstances. These have included the creation of Israel in 1948, and the 1967 war. As a consequence of the latter, Israel occupied the West Bank including East Jerusalem and the Gaza Strip. These events have created catastrophic political, economic, psychic and social consequences which have deeply affected the life of the Palestinian people, many of whom became refugees relocated to neighbouring countries and indeed the whole world as a Palestinian diaspora. In many ways, Palestine itself was simply wiped off the map (Isaac, 2010a, 2010b). Historic Palestine came to be known as Israel. In this context tourism became a political tool in the supremacy and control of the Israel establishment over land and people, and an instrument for preventing the Palestinians from enjoying the economic benefits of the fruits of the cultural and human interaction on which tourism thrives.

Israel's military used the issuance of permits to travel into Israel ostensibly as a means to prevent terrorism. As Bronner noted, in 2011 about 60,000 permits were issued; a token amount for a population of 2.5 million people (Bronner, 2011). It is particularly the threat of suicide bombers that saw the current era of restrictions imposed, but as Hage has pointed out, lying behind that was a struggle by Israel 'to consolidate a "normal peaceful life" inside a colonial settler state …' (2003: 68), predicated on the permanent dispossession of Palestinian people.

For example, in the West Bank, closure is implemented through an agglomeration of policies, practices and physical impediments that have disjointed the territory into ever smaller and more disconnected cantons (World Bank, 2007). While physical barriers are the visible manifestations of closure, the means of curtailing Palestinian movement and access are actually far more complex and are based on a set of administrative practices and permit policies that limit the freedom of Palestinians to move home, obtain work, invest in business, expand or/and construct properties, and move about outside of their municipal control. These administrative restrictions, rooted in military order associated with the Israeli occupation of the West Bank, are used to restrict and limit Palestinian access to large segments of the West Bank including all spaces within the municipal boundaries of settlements, the 'seam zone', the Jordan Valley, East Jerusalem, restricted roads and other 'closed' areas. Estimates of the total restricted areas are difficult to come by, but it appears to be in excess of 50 per cent of the land of the West Bank (World Bank, 2007). Since 1995 the Palestinians have been locked into 70 tiny enclaves comprising only 42 per cent of the West Bank. They are encircled by more than 500 checkpoints and other obstacles to movement, and isolated from one another by the settlements, Israeli-only highways, and now also by the Separation Wall (Amnesty International, 2004; B'tselem, 2002; Coon, 1999; Halper, 2005). Halper uses the term 'Matrix of Control' to describe this state of affairs:

> This strategy was strikingly similar in concept to the East Asian game of 'Go'. Unlike chess, where two opponents try to 'defeat' each other by eliminating one another's pieces, the aim of 'Go' is not actually to defeat but rather to immobilize your opponent by taking control of key points on the game board, which is, indeed, a matrix. It was a strategy used effectively in Vietnam, where small forces of Viet Cong were able to pin down and virtually paralyze half a million American soldiers possessing overwhelming firepower. Israel's Matrix of Control accomplishes the same with the Palestinians (2008: 152).

The impact on tourism and freedom of movement

Right now, the primary obstacle facing the Palestinian tourism industry is lack of accessibility. Isaac states that 'currently freedom of movement and access to Palestinians within the West Bank is the exception rather than the norm, contrary to the commitments undertaken in a number of agreements between Israel and Palestine' (2010b: 581). All Palestinians living in Palestine (West Bank, including East Jerusalem and the Gaza Strip), face serious challenges to their relative mobility when they travel through the West Bank or even abroad (Barghouti, 2000; Harker, 2009; Weizman, 2007). The lack of control over borders, the vulnerability to regular incursion and consequent physical damage to the tourism infrastructure, the lack of freedom of movement for Palestinians and tourists, the regular closures of Palestinian areas, and the Segregation Wall (Isaac, 2009), which cuts deep into Palestinian areas, are only some of the problems resulting directly from the Israeli occupation. In addition to, or as a consequence of, this occupation, Palestinians have been unable to fully develop their tourism potential and, more importantly, have been unable to plan for future development without a clear indication of when the conflicts will end and how Palestine will look once a final status agreement is reached.

Murphy (2004) stated that religious tourism and freedom of movement are denied in isolated Bethlehem in Palestine. She wrote about a group of Brazilian tourists who were staying at one of the hotels in Bethlehem in 2002. A day trip to Jerusalem (which is about 9 km away from Bethlehem) was part of their itinerary. After the visit to Jerusalem, when they attempted to pass through the Gilo checkpoint (controlled by the Israeli military police), which prevents free movement between Jerusalem and Bethlehem, they were initially denied access. When they explained to the Israeli soldiers that their documents and possessions

(continued)

Case 10.3.2: Palestine, tourism and human rights (*continued*)

were in the hotel in Bethlehem, the soldiers confiscated their passports and gave them only one hour to retrieve their belongings from the hotel and return to the checkpoint. They were not allowed to tour Palestine any longer.

This calls for ethical reflection on the relationship between tourism, human rights and destinations – both in academia and professional practice. Within the academic tourism discourse, ethics has known a relatively longer history but the concept, exploration and application of human rights, as an essential part of ethical reflection, have not yet been structurally incorporated into the discourse. The case on tourism and human rights in the Palestinian–Israeli conflict explicated above stresses the importance of giving special attention to human rights in the context of tourism, development and mobility.

Questions for discussion

- Which ethical values complement the discussion about respecting human rights in business, and more specifically, in tourism?
- With regard to the case described above: do you think that business is able to, or should, play a role in forcing a breakthrough in the Palestinian–Israeli conflict?
- Make an ethical argument for and against each of the following two statements: (a) The cancelling of all holiday excursions to Palestine and Israel will contribute to respecting human rights; (b) Palestinian business should not cease cooperation with Israeli business.
- Is it morally right for business to make profits from people living under circumstances like those of the Palestinians?
- What is the individual and sociocultural impact of the violation of human rights in the context of tourism?

10.4 The working poor

Esther Peperkamp

10.4.1 Introduction to the 'working poor'

For centuries, people have turned to wage labour in order to make a living and provide for their families. As workers, they sell their labour to an employer. From the introduction of wage labour, there have always been areas in which wage labour has been poorly remunerated, such as in the factories at the onset of the Industrial Revolution. However, lately the percentage of people who are poor despite having a paid job is on the rise, and the gap between the rich and the poor is increasing. In more liberal countries like the United States (USA), Britain and Australia, labour market polarisation is more severe than in egalitarian labour markets. While employment reduces the poverty risk considerably, in the area of the OECD on average 7 per cent of individuals living in households with at least one worker are still poor (according to the OECD, people are poor when they earn less than half their country's median income). Consequently, the working poor account for more than 60 per cent of all the poor of working age (OECD, 2009). Poverty also occurs in the service sector, specifically the sector of hotels and restaurants. For example, fast-food workers, waitresses and retail workers are especially at risk. In the USA for example, 14.1 per cent of the service workers found themselves below the poverty line in 2013. The service sector accounted for 3.6 million working poor, which is almost 40 per cent of the total number of working poor ('A Profile of the Working Poor', 2015). Poverty is caused by low wages, often in combination with part-time, flexible jobs, and especially when a household is dependent on this income. These jobs are often carried out by women, migrants, minorities and young people, who therefore are especially at risk.

Whether low-paid work results in poverty also depends on national politics. Governments can adopt tools to alleviate in-work poverty such as setting a statutory minimum wage (provided that people work full-time) and provision of social benefits. Welfare policies help to mitigate the negative effects of low-paid jobs. Welfare policies include unemployment insurance, social security, family assistance, and subsidies for childcare, healthcare, housing, transportation and food.

Liberal societies like the USA tend to have less developed welfare systems. Welfare politics in the USA became even stricter after former president Bill Clinton signed the welfare reform law in 1996. The law was intended to increase labour market participation. Under the new regulations, welfare recipients were expected to work in order to receive benefits, which would end what is commonly called the 'cycle of dependency'. The idea was that people on welfare were discouraged from trying to find a job, because they would lose access to benefits and have higher costs because of childcare and transportation, while not being certain that a job would provide them with the means to cover these expenses, as well as their health insurance. The results of the reform are controversial. A major concern of critics is that many people moved from welfare to low-paid jobs which have kept them in poverty, or even exacerbated their situation, especially in the case of single mothers (Hays, 2003; Shipler, 2008).

Welfare policies are more common and generous in social democratic countries in Europe than in the USA. Nevertheless, also in Europe there are tendencies towards liberalisation of the labour market and cutting welfare, often in the name of stimulating people to "participate" instead of standing passively on the sidelines (Andreß and Lohmann, 2008). The idea behind this is that it should pay off to have a job. In other words, having a job should be more profitable than living on welfare. In addition, having people enter the labour market reduces unemployment rates. In Germany for example, unemployment has decreased since the deregulation of the labour market and the introduction of mini-jobs. Flexible working practices and government-subsidised reduced working hours have enabled employers to adjust to the economic cycle without hiring and firing. However, as a consequence, low-wage employment now accounts for 20 per cent of full-time jobs in Germany according to an OECD report, which states that one out of five jobs is a now a 'mini-job', which delivers workers maximum earnings of €400–450 a month tax-free. For around 5 million people, this 'mini-job' is their main job. In order to make ends meet, people rely on subsidies and welfare. A statutory minimum wage was only introduced in 2015. In 2014, one in five workers in East Germany were paid less than the new minimum wage, and in the hotels and restaurants sector up to two-thirds were paid less than that (OECD, 2014).

Employers who get away with paying low wages, and governments who try to remove people from welfare, are thinking in terms of costs and benefits. From an ethical perspective, they are taking a utilitarian position: decisions are morally justified when benefits outweigh the costs. From a political perspective, removing people from welfare seems justified, since it supposedly saves public money. From an economic perspective, low wages and short-term contracts are justified. Wages are largely set on the basis of supply and demand: if many people can do the job, wages in general will be lower than in cases in which a highly skilled worker is needed. Furthermore, flexibility is especially important in the service sector, where demand can vary quite substantially throughout the year. From the employers' perspective, it is therefore understandable why they should hire temporary workers at low cost. However, if thinking in costs and benefits leads people to not being able to get by on their salary, this raises the question of morality from a deontological perspective: is it just to pay people low wages? What about rights and duties?

10.4.1.1 Work, poverty and morality

The phenomenon of the working poor is not only an economic and political issue, but also an ethical one. Three ethical positions can be distinguished. First, there is a prevailing opinion that people are morally obliged to work. They are seen as having the moral duty to be useful to society. Secondly, there is the opinion that people have a right to work because work is important to people's identity and sense of self-worth. Thirdly, it is considered a human right to lead a life of dignity, which is also associated with decent pay. While the first two positions are public opinions that can vary between countries, the third – human rights – is considered to be universal.

Paid work provides people with a moral identity in a sociopolitical sense. The opinion that people have an obligation to work prevails in many societies. The flip side of this opinion is that people who depend on welfare do not fulfil this obligation and are blamed for that. They are the so-called undeserving poor. However, there are some differences when it comes to the image welfare recipients have in different countries. These differences are related to the political system. A comparison between the UK, Denmark and Sweden, for example, shows that the poor and welfare recipients are depicted negatively in the UK, a country with a liberal welfare regime. In Sweden and Denmark, social democratic welfare regimes, they are depicted positively (Larsen and Dejgaard, 2013). Also in the USA, a liberal country, welfare recipients are often depicted negatively. Working people are considered to be better citizens than non-working people. As Munger puts it: 'we measure the worthiness of all our citizens by their level of commitment to the labour market' (2002: 3). An important factor here is the degree of control individuals are thought to have over their lives. It is a universal given that people who have little control over their situation (elderly, disabled) are judged to be more 'deserving' than people who are seen to have more control, like the unemployed (Coughlin, 1980). However, the extent to which individuals, including the unemployed, are seen as in control of their lives varies between countries. The American dream tells people that through hard work, one can achieve anything. This implies that somebody who has not achieved a lot has not worked hard enough. Poverty is morally condemned and blamed on the individual. In the USA, this opinion is in addition informed by stereotypes of African

Human rights and business

Americans (Gilens, 2009). Welfare should be available only to the 'deserving poor', not to people who are capable of working and providing for their living themselves.

The thought that people have a duty to work and contribute to society is often accompanied by the idea that having a job positively affects people's sense of self-worth in relation to society, their family and themselves as a person. In contexts in which work is highly emphasised, people feel useful to society when they have a job. It also increases their sense of self-respect when being able to provide for one's family, and last but not least: a job can provide people with self-esteem, because their effort and strengths are recognised by society (Velasquez, 2014). A paid job therefore adds to leading a meaningful life in various respects. This idea justifies sober welfare policies, not only for the benefit of society, but also for the benefit of the individual concerned. One could question, however, whether this is an intrinsic feature of paid work, and to what extent these positive individual benefits have to do with social recognition. It seems likely that a paid job is more meaningful to people in societies in which paid work is seen as a moral obligation, and failure to provide for one's living seen as a weakness.

Ideas about rights and duties, when it comes to paid work, thus vary between countries. Belief systems of individual workers and employers regarding their mutual obligations show considerable cultural diversity (Rousseau and Schalk, 2000). On the other hand, article 23 of the Declaration of Human Rights states: 'Everyone who works has the right to just and favourable remuneration ensuring for himself and his family an existence worthy of human dignity, and supplemented, if necessary, by other means of social protection' (United Nations, 1948, art. 23). The Declaration of Human Rights therefore suggests that there is a universal standard to be followed.

How work, payment and poverty interact will be demonstrated by the following case, in which two mini-cases from the world of entertainment are described to illustrate the phenomenon of getting paid, but still being poor.

Case 10.4.2: Amusement parks, wages and poverty

Introduction: Stukenbrock, Disney and working conditions

Amusement parks are supposed to be fun places. Visitors expect to enjoy themselves and experience relaxation. Therefore it does not come as a surprise that many people also dream of working in an amusement park. However, amusement parks suffer from similar problems and dilemmas to the service industry – of which they are part. As indicated above, in the service sector many low-wage jobs are to be found. Amusement parks are no exception, as the following two mini-cases illustrate.

The first mini-case regards an article published by Reuters in 2012, which led to follow-up investigations about wages and working conditions in amusement parks in the years that followed. The article reports on Germany's 'job miracle'. It quotes Anja, who had been scrubbing floors and washing dishes for €2 an hour over the past six years in the attractive seaside town of Stralsund. The head of

(continued)

Case 10.4.2: Amusement parks, wages and povertys (*continued*)

the job agency reports that some people earn as little as 55 c per hour. Employers explain the necessity of employing people for low wages on minimal contracts. It allows them to be flexible. Besides, they argue, such small jobs are perfect for students and housewives who like to earn some extra money. In the meantime, these jobs are not only performed by housewives and students, but by people for whom it is their main source of income. Some companies go even further, as a 33-year-old unemployed man in Stralsund reports to Reuters: 'A lot of my friends work as carpenters, but companies describe them as janitors in their contracts to avoid paying the salary negotiated in the collective wage agreement. By carefully designing job descriptions, employers manage to apply less restrictive legislation' (Reuters, 2012).

Two years later the illustrious German journalist Gunter Wallraff dives into the world of theme parks and zoos. He finds out that theme parks save on human resource expenditure, and zoos, in addition, save on living conditions of animals. In a few instances, lack of training has resulted in dangerous, even lethal situations.

As part of the journalistic inquiry, a female journalist, pretending to be a student, applies for work at Safaripark Stukenbrock in the region known as Ostwestfahlen. Many seasonal employees, mainly from Eastern Europe, are employed at the park. The journalist receives an hourly wage of €4. Employees with permanent contracts earn €1100 gross per month. Taking into account the six-day workweek, their hourly wage amounts to €5.70 gross. In addition, they need to pay €70 per month to stay in tiny apartments in the park.

The journalist returned to the park one year later. In 2015, a national minimum wage of €8.50 had been introduced, which allegedly was paid to the employees. However, the situation was that the employees regularly worked more hours, and they had to pay €150 to live on the site of the park – double the amount of the previous year.

In order to make a comparison between two different countries on two different continents, let us have a look at the second mini-case, namely that of Disney, in the USA, a country with a large number of 'working poor'.

Disney claims to 'make the world a better place' and to pay a lot of attention to sustainability. Indeed, initiatives have been taken to reduce waste, the company invests in reforestation and conservation projects, and provides financial support to children's hospitals, emergency relief funds, and many more. According to Disney, cast members and their families performed more than 569,000 hours of community service through Disney in 2009. Disneycareers.com states: 'If you join The Walt Disney Company, you can help us maintain high ethical standards in the creation, production and marketing of our products, services and experiences. And together, we'll strive for an even brighter future that allows our people to tell extraordinary stories for years to come' (Disneycareers.com, n.d.).

But also at Disney, all that glitters is not gold. In 2010, Disney employees disclosed a union-produced documentary that showed their poor working conditions. Although a 3 per cent wage increase had been proposed, union members were of the opinion that the increase was too small when taking into account their long working hours with small benefits. In the released video, David, a Disney employee, complains that he has worked there for three years and is still making less than $8 an hour. The case was discussed in the media. Themeparkinsider.com devoted an article to it, which evoked interesting reactions. One Internet user for example commented:

> This is the entire reason that I worked part time when I worked there. I know that most of the full timers worked long and bizarre hours to make ends meet. As a first job, it's fine. As a retiree job, supported by pension, it's fine. As a part time job, again, I can't say enough about it. Working for $8.00 an hour as a full time job, working 50–60 hours a week… that has to take it's [sic] toll on people, and I saw it time and time again. People get burnt out doing this, and you can see the wear it places on them and their families. But they do it, because they love it, and there are few other places to work in the area.

However, another person, supporting the idea of the American dream, commented:

> Again, if you don't like it, don't work there. It's still America. You still have choices (albeit more limited right now).

And a third person – a former employee – wrote:

> I no longer work for them. Ive moved on not because I didnt enjoy it far from it. I couldnt afford to live on it. ANd thats a shame'. [language mistakes in original] (PyraDanny V., 2010)

Who is responsible for the fate of the working poor?

The two mini-cases from the world of amusement parks as explicated above raise questions about rights and duties, and whose responsibility it is to safeguard these rights and duties.

The Germany mini-case calls for reflection on the moral attitude and behaviour of employers. Why did they choose to raise the costs for the accommodation of the employees and push them towards working longer hours after the national minimum wage was introduced? Does it relate to personal greed or are there other possible explanations? For example, that such business behaviour towards often vulnerable and dependent people is inherently based on the economic or political system? Why is compliance with the rules not enforced by the government? Is the government or the employer responsible for the 'silent poverty' that often is characteristic of so many people working in this sector?

The Disney mini-case raises other perspectives and questions. The second person quoted above conveys the idea that people fundamentally have a choice, which, in turn, implies that it is also their own choice to remain in a poorly paid job. The employee is in control of his/her own destiny. As a consequence, it is easy to blame people for living in poverty. The former Disney employee actually agrees with the first person quoted, who holds that it is a

(continued)

Case 10.4.2: Amusement parks, wages and povertys (*continued*)

shame that one cannot make a living from the salary paid by Disney, but at the same time he emphasises that he had the choice to take another job. Although he feels it is a shame, he does not blame his employer or the political system: it seems to be his individual problem, which he dealt with individually. Can this remarkable attitude be ascribed to culture, or is there more to it?

To conclude: indeed, many people dream of working in an amusement or theme park. But it should be noted that the discussion about working conditions and remuneration takes on an extra dimension in the leisure sector, since workers in the leisure sector often are quite satisfied with the tasks that go with their job. They experience high levels of job satisfaction, but one could ask oneself whether job satisfaction justifies poor working conditions and low salaries, and whether working for a theme park is still fun when one cannot make a living from it.

Questions for discussion

- Do people have a human right not to be poor? Convey moral arguments for your position.
- Does business have a moral responsibility to society and more specifically, to the eradication of poverty? Explain your answer.
- Decisions about the level of remuneration can be made by applying either a utilitarian (such as the well-being of all parties involved) or deontological principle (such as rights and duties). Which principle do you deem most important? Do you see a possibility to reconcile these two positions?
- Try to trace the moral positions of both the employers and employees in the two mini-cases explicated above (Germany and the USA) with regard to underpayment. Consider the notions of law, power, responsibility, care and choice.
- Reflect on the following three questions and give reasons for your answers. (a) Do you think that countries (and societies), which hold different (cultural) opinions about the value and meaning of work, have different ethical standards as well? (b) Do you think that people are more entitled to work and fair pay in societies in which being dependent on welfare is seen more negatively? (c) Do you believe that universal ethical standards can be implemented to regulate fair allocation of work and payment? If yes, what would those universal ethical standards be?

10.5 Concluding thoughts

Human rights are those rights every human being fundamentally has due to his/her very existence. They are based on treating all people as equals and with dignity, respect and fairness, and are steered by the ethical principle of inflicting 'no harm'.

In business contexts this means, for example, that no child labour or any form of forced labour is tolerated, no employee is ever exposed to unsafe working conditions, people's privacy is respected and their data protected against misuse (see also Chapter 12). In addition, 'inflicting no harm' also implies that businesses have a responsibility to prevent and remove negative impacts of their activities – also those of *partners* they have relations with.

Respecting human rights therefore challenges businesses to (re)consider the economic benefits they have from measures and unethical laws that oppressive regimes have passed on their people, and de facto also on the labour force. Think about harsh labour conditions, underpayment, slack environmental regulations, corruption, bribery, fraud, tax avoidance, discrimination with regard to race and gender, and denying citizens' rights to freedom of movement, speech and association.

Note

1 With additional editing and content review by Tanya DePass, Director of I Need Diverse Games.

Further reading

Bernaz, N. (2016). *Business and Human Rights: History, Law and Policy – Bridging the Accountability Gap*. London/New York: Routledge.
Cernic, T.L. and Ho, T. van (2015). *Human Rights and Business: Direct Corporate Accountability for Human Rights*. Oisterwijk: Wolf Legal Publishers.
Cragg, W. (2012). *Business and Human Rights*. Cheltenham/Northampton, UK: Edward Elgar.
Guiding Principles on Business and Human Rights (2011). *Implementing the United Nations 'Protect, Respect and Remedy' Framework*. New York/Geneva: United Nations.
Mares, R. (Ed.) (2012). *The UN Guiding Principles of Business and Human Rights: Foundations and Implementation*. Leiden/Boston, MA: Martinus Nijhoff Publishers.
Rendtorff, J.D. (Ed.) (2017). *Perspectives on the Philosophy of Management and Business Ethics: Including a Special Section on Business and Human Rights*. New York/London: Springer.

References

Alder, J. (1989). Travel as Performed Art. *American Journal of Sociology*, 94(6): 1366–1391.
Amnesty International. (2004, 17 May). *Israel and the Occupied Territories: Under the Rubble; House Demolition and Destruction of Land and Property*. In Amnesty International. Retrieved 8 July 2015 from https://www.amnesty.org/en/documents/MDE15/033/2004/en/.
Andreß, H. J., and Lohmann, H. (2008). *The Working Poor in Europe*. Cheltenham, UK: Edward Elgar.
Antonelli, P. (2012). Video Games: 14 in the Collection, for Starters. In *MoMA – Museum of Modern Art*. Retrieved 8 July 2015 from http://www.moma.org/explore/inside_out/2012/11/29/video-games-14-in-the-collection-for-starters.
A Profile of the Working Poor. (2015). *BLS Reports*. US Department of Labour Statistics. Retrieved 30 May 2016 from http://www.bls.gov/opub/reports/working-poor/archive/a-profile-of-the-working-poor-2013.pdf.
Baez, C., Dearing, M., Delatour, M. and Dixon, C. (1999). Multinational Enterprises and Human Rights. *University of Miami International and Corporate Law Review*, 8: 1999–2000.

Barghouti, M. (2000). *I Saw Ramallah*. New York: Anchor Books.
Botek, A.-M. (2014). Will it Work? Video Game Empowers People Living with Dementia. *Aging Care*. Retrieved 8 July 2015 from http://www.agingcare.com/Articles/video-game-empowers-people-with-dementia-166863.htm.
Bronner, E. (2011). Where Politics are Complex, Simple Joys at the Beach. *New York Times*. Retrieved 3 March 2013 from http://www.nytimes.com/2011/07/27/world/middleeast/27swim.html?_r=0.
B'tselem. (2002, May). *Land Grab: Israel's Settlements Policy in the West Bank*. Jerusalem: B'tselem.
Buchanan, I. (2010). Blaxploitation. In *A Dictionary of Critical Theory*. Oxford: Oxford University Press. Retrieved 15 April 2016 from http://www.oxfordreference.com/view/10.1093/acref/9780199532919.001.0001/acref-9780199532919-e-89.
Butcher, C. and Svensson, I. (2015). Manufacturing Dissent: Modernization and the Onset of Major Nonviolent Resistance Campaigns. *Journal of Conflict Resolution*, 60(2): 311–339.
Cassel, D. (2001). Human Rights and Business Responsibilities in the Global Marketplace. *Business Ethics Quarterly*, 11(2): 261–274.
Code Liberation Foundation (2017). Retrieved 2 May 2017 from http://codeliberation.org/.
Coon, A. (1999, 8 December). *Demolition and Dispossession: The Destruction of Palestinian Homes*. In *Amnesty International*. Retrieved 8 July 2015 from https://www.amnesty.org/en/documents/MDE15/059/1999/en/.
Coughlin, R. M. (1980). *Ideology, Public Opinion and Welfare Policy: Attitudes Towards Taxes and Spending in Industrial Societies*. Institute of international Studies. Research Series No. 42. Berkeley, CA: University of California.
Cragg, W. (2000). Human Rights and Business Ethics: Fashioning a New Social Contract. *Journal of Business Ethics*, 27: 205–214.
Croall, J. (1995). *Preserve or Destroy? Tourism and the Environment*. London: Calouste Gulbenkian Foundation.
Disneycareers.com. (n.d.). Retrieved 30 May 2016 from http://disneycareers.com/en/about-disney/corporate-citizenship/.
Donnelly, J. (2003). *Universal Human Rights in Theory and Practice*. Ithaca, NY: Cornell University Press.
Ehrenreich, B. (2001). *Nickle and Dimed*. New York: Henry Holt and Company.
Entertainment Software Association. (2014). Essential Facts about the Computer and Video Game Industry. In *The ESA*. Retrieved 8 July 2015 from http://www.theesa.com/wp-content/uploads/2014/10/ESA_EF_2014.pdf.
Feminist Frequency. (2013). Damsel in Distress: Part 1 – Tropes vs Women in Video Games. *YouTube*. Retrieved 8 July 2015 from https://www.youtube.com/watch?v=X6p5AZp7r_Q.
Fennell, D. (2006). *Tourism Ethics*. Bristol: Channel View Publications.
Friedman, M. (1970). The Social Responsibility of Business is to Increase Profits. *New York Magazine*, September, 13: 32–33.
Fuchs, K. (2015, March 16). *Presentation on Marketing for Nintendo of Europe*. Breda, Netherlands: Nintendo of Europe.
George, B.P. and Varghese, V. (2007). Human Rights in Tourism: Conceptualisations and Stakeholder Perspectives. *Electronic Journal of Business Ethics and Organisation Studies*, 12(2): 40–48.
Gilens, M. (2009). *Why Americans Hate Welfare: Race, Media, and the Politics of Antipoverty Policy*. Chicago: University of Chicago Press.
Glendon, M. (1988). Propter Honoris Respectrum: Knowing the Universal Declaration of Human Rights. *Notre Dame Law*, 73: 1153.
Hage, G. (2003). Comes a Time We Are All Enthusiasm: Understanding Palestinian Suicide Bombers in Times of Exighophobia. *Public Culture*, 15(1): 56–89.
Haggis, M. (2013). 'Straight-Faced Satire' and Gender in Video Games: Hyper-Masculinity in Far Cry 3 and the Wider Games Industry. *Gamasutra*, Retrieved 8 July 2015 from

http://gamasutra.com/blogs/MataHaggis/20131213/207011/Straightfaced_satire_and_gender_in_video_games_hypermasculinity_in_Far_Cry_3_and_the_wider_games_industry.php

Halper, J. (2005). Israel in a Middle East Union: A Two Stage Approach to the Conflict. *Tikkun,* 2(1): 17–21.

Halper, J. (2008). *An Israeli in Palestine: Resisting Dispossession, Redeeming Israel.* London: Pluto.

Harker, C. (2009). Student Im/Mobility in Birzeit, Palestine. *Mobilities,* 4(1): 11–35.

Hays, S. (2003). *Flat Broke with Children: Women in the Age of Welfare Reform.* Oxford: Oxford University Press.

Higgins-Desbiolles, F. (2016). Walled Off From the World: Palestine, Tourism and Resisting Occupation. In Isaac, R. Hall, C.M. and Higgins-Desbiolles, F. (Eds.), *The Politics and Power of Tourism in Palestine* (pp. 178–194). London: Routledge.

Human Rights Watch. (1997). *Freedom of Association in a Maquila in Guatemala Report.* In *Human Rights Watch.* Retrieved 30 September 2015 from http://www.hrw.org/reports/1997/guat2/.

Isaac, R. (2009). Alternative Tourism. Can the Segregation Wall in Bethlehem Be a Tourist Attraction? Tourism and Hospitality Planning & Development, 6(3): 221–228.

Isaac, R. K. (2010a). Alternative Tourism: New Forms of Tourism in Bethlehem for the Palestinian Tourism Industry. *Current Issues in Tourism,* 13(1): 21–36.

Isaac, R. K. (2010b). Moving from Pilgrimage to Responsible Tourism: The Case of Palestine. *Current Issues in Tourism,* 13(6): 579–590.

Kamminga, M.T. (1999). *Holding Multinational Corporations Accountable for Human Rights Abuses: A Challenge for the EC, in the EU and Human Rights.* Oxford: Oxford University Press.

Kelly, G. (2001). Multilateral Investment Treaties: A Balanced Approach to Multinational Corporations. *Columbia Journal of Transnational Law,* 39.

Kinley, D. and Tadaki, J. (2004). From Talk to Walk: The Emergence of Human Rights Responsibilities for Corporations at International Law. *Virginia Journal of International Law,* 44(4): 932–1023.

Krippendorf, J. (1987). *The Holiday Makers: Understanding the Impact of Leisure and Travel.* London: Butterworth-Heinemann.

Larsen, C. A., and Dejgaard, T. E. (2013). The Institutional Logic of Images of the Poor and Welfare Recipients: A Comparative Study of British, Swedish and Danish Newspapers. *Journal of European Social Policy,* 23(3): 287–299.

Lovelock, B. and Lovelock, K. (2013). *The Ethics of Tourism.* London: Routledge.

MacLaren, D. (1998). *Rethinking Tourism and Eco-Travel: The Paving of Paradise and What You Can Do to Stop It.* Connecticut: Kumarian Press.

MacCannell, D. (2011). *The Ethics of Sight-Seeing.* California: University of California Press.

Millstein, I.M. (1998). *Corporate Governance: Improving Competitiveness and Access to Capital in Global Markets.* Report to the OECD by the Business Advisory Group. Paris: OECD.

Munger, F. (Ed.). (2002). *Laboring Below the Line: The New Ethnography of Poverty, Low-Wage Work, and Survival in the Global Economy.* New York: Russell Sage Foundation.

Murphy, C.M. (2004). Religious Tourism and Freedom of Movement Denied in Isolated Bethlehem. *Electronic Intifada.* Retrieved 10 January 2015 from https://electronicintifada.net/content/religious-tourism-and-freedom-movement-denied-isolated-bethlehem/5382.

O'Byrne, D. (2001). On Passports and Border Controls. *Annals of Tourism Research,* 28(2): 399–416.

OECD. (2009). Is Work the Best Antidote to Poverty? In *Employment Outlook 2009 – Tackling the Jobs Crisis.* Retrieved 30 May 2016 from https://www.oecd.org/els/emp/45219514.pdf.

OECD. (2015). *Employment Outlook 2015 – How Does Germany Compare?* In *OECD.org*. Retrieved 30 May 2016 from https://www.oecd.org/germany/Employment-Outlook-Germany-EN.pdf.

Parks, G. (Director). (1971). *Shaft* [Motion picture]. Produced by J. Freeman. Written by E. Tidyman and J D. F. Black. United States: Metro-Goldwyn-Mayer.

Posner, M. (2016). Business and Human Rights: A Commentary from the Inside. *Accounting, Auditing and Accountability Journal*, 29(4): 705–711.

Rendtorff, J. (Ed.) (2017). *Perspectives on Philosophy of Management and Business Ethics. Including a Special Section on Business and Human Rights*. New York/London: Springer.

Reuters. (2012). Insight: The Dark Side of Germany's Jobs Miracle. *Reuters*. Retrieved 30 May 2016 from http://www.reuters.com/article/us-germany-jobs-idUSTRE8170P120120208.

Rousseau, D. and Schalk, R. (Eds.) (2000). *Psychological Contracts in Employment: Cross-National Perspectives*. Thousand Oaks, CA: Sage Publications.

Ruggie, K. (2008). *Protect, Respect and Remedy: Report of the Special Representative of the United Nations Secretary-General on the Issue of Human Rights and Transnational Corporations and other Business Enterprises*. Geneva: United Nations.

Sheller, M., and Urry, J. (2006). The New Mobilities Paradigm. *Environment and Planning*, 38(2): 207–226.

Shipler, D. K. (2008). *The Working Poor: Invisible in America*. New York: Vintage.

Smith, M. and Duffy, R. (2003). *Ethics of Tourism Development*. London: Routledge.

Sydell, L. (2013). Hot On YouTube: Videos about Video Games, and Science, too. *NPR*. Retrieved 8 July 2015 from http://www.npr.org/sections/alltechconsidered/2013/12/30/257552199/hot-on-youtube-videos-about-video-games-and-science-too.

Pyra-Danny V. (2010, 30 November). Union documentary portrays poor working conditions at Walt Disney World. In *Theme Park Insider*. Retrieved 30 May 2016 from http://www.themeparkinsider.com/flume/201011/2212/.

United Nations (1948). *Universal Declaration of Human Rights*. United Nations. Retrieved 15 March 2015 from http://www.un.org/en/documents/udhr/.

United Nations World Tourism Organization (UNWTO) (1999). *Global Code of Ethics for Tourism*. United Nations. Retrieved 8 March 2000 from http://www.world-tourism.org/pressrel/CODEOFE.htm.

Velasquez, M. G. (2014). *Business Ethics: Concepts and Cases* (7th ed.). Harlow, UK: Pearson Education Limited.

Vincke, F., Heiman, F. and Katz, R. (1999). *Fighting Bribery: A Corporate Manual*. Paris: International Chamber of Commerce.

Weeden, C. (2002). Ethical Tourism: An Opportunity for Competitive Advantage? *Journal of Vacation Marketing*, 8(2): 141–153.

Weeramantry, C.G. (1999). Human Rights and the Global Marketplace. *Brooklyn Journal of International Law*, 28: 27.

Weizman, E. (2007). *Hollow Land: Israel's Architecture of Occupation*. London: Verso.

Williams, D., Martins, N., Consalvo, M. and Ivory, J. D. (2009). The Virtual Census: Representations of Gender, Race and Age in Video Games. *New Media and Society*, 11(5): 815–834.

World Bank. (2007). *Report on Movement and Access Restrictions in the West Bank: Uncertainty and Inefficiency in the Palestinian Economy*. Paris: World Bank Technical Team.

Yang, G. S., Gibson, B., Lueke, A. K., Huesmann, L. R. and Bushman, B. J. (2014). Effects of Avatar Race in Violent Video Games on Racial Attitudes and Aggression. *Social Psychological and Personality Science*, 5(6): 698–704.

Chapter 11

Responsible entrepreneurship and innovation

Marco van Leeuwen, Diana van Dijk and Greg Richards

11.1 Introduction to responsible entrepreneurship and innovation

Marco van Leeuwen

11.1.1 A brief exploration of the key concepts

The three concepts leading the discussions in this chapter are *entrepreneurship*, *innovation* and *responsibility*.

Entrepreneurship is a fuzzy concept and the literature shows a myriad of definitions and explications of its meaning. It originates from French and means 'to undertake' or to be 'adventurous', yet is currently used in many constructs of meaning. It is often used as a synonym for 'doing business', but fundamentally speaking, there is a conceptual difference between those two economic activities. Whereas 'doing business' is related to competition, entails the creation of economic value (making profit) and is driven by an existing business idea or concept, entrepreneurship is related to cooperation, entails the creation of (added) value to people or communities and is driven by a new or unique (business) idea or concept. Entrepreneurship rests on activities which are associated with recognising and exploiting emerging (business) opportunities, taking risks in realising them and using innovative methods and approaches to come up with new products, processes or services.

Innovation, in turn, is usually conceived as a process in which an idea is transformed into a (new or modified existing) product or service, such that value is created for people, communities, or society and specific needs and expectations are fulfilled. It is the lifeblood of entrepreneurship and the tool used to effectuate change and translate the underlying idea into application. Innovation is related to solving problems, not only in the field of business and the economy, but also in other industries, such as healthcare, education, fashion, travel and government. In a social setting, for example, innovation is more than developing new products and techniques; it is developing solutions to social problems that are context-dependent and ever-changing.

The third concept, *responsibility*, is introduced to designate the values of truthfulness, fairness and accountability, which arguably should accompany the innovation processes entrepreneurs pursue and set out to realise. Responsibility is a core concern in this chapter since it is an ethical category depicting good judgement in behaviour – especially with regard to issues of integrity and making decisions which are to the benefit of people, communities, society and the environment. This means that responsible entrepreneurs purposefully strive to minimise the harmful impacts of their innovative activities and enhance the positive impacts thereof on all stakeholders and contexts that might be affected in any way.

The discussion of the interrelationships between responsible entrepreneurship and innovation in this chapter will specifically revolve around services provided to the public in different (public, semi-public and social) settings – as opposed to entrepreneurship in a 'classical or traditional' business (private) setting.

11.1.2 The entrepreneurial transition

As indicated above, entrepreneurial thinking is not strictly limited to business contexts, but also cherished as useful for other domains of society. Moreover, it has, notwithstanding the adverse side of it, been hailed as the 'new and right way of thinking' in several industries and sectors of society. A real transition of its application has taken place in recent times which spilled over into the public sector as well. No longer is entrepreneurship confined to the realms of business or the private sector. And services provided to customers, or the general public, within the public sector are more and more subjected to entrepreneurial thinking and activity – as will be demonstrated later on in this chapter.

In large parts of (at least) the Western world, the division of different kinds of tasks in the public domain is changing. Hospitals, for example, are increasingly being run like businesses; public transport organisations and postal services are turning into for-profit companies, and many other tasks that in the past might have naturally resided with the government or government-run organisations are now being outsourced.

The intended benefits of this transition are that managers of for-profit organisations, through free-market competition, have evolved to provide the best products or services in the most efficient, cost-effective way. State-run monopolies (e.g. a national postal service, telephone company or rail transport provider) might not have strong incentives to work at optimum efficiency, but when the element of needing to compete for the favours of critical customers is introduced, product portfolios, operational efficiency and service levels will need to align with what customers want.

Here is an example of such a transition. As early as the 1990s, politicians in the Netherlands started talking about the need to transform the 'welfare state' into a 'participation society'. In the 2010s, this evolution started to speed up, with the Dutch government's 2013 policy plans making this transition an explicit goal (Rijksoverheid, 2013). This policy had particularly significant effects in the healthcare sector. The need for a policy change was great: due to increased life expectancy and improved diagnostic techniques, healthcare demand has been on the rise, and will continue to be, while simultaneously capacity at hospitals and care organisations is diminishing due to decreasing budgets, or the desire to at least limit cost growth. In the 2013 plan, the suggested solution was to put a bigger emphasis on the prevention of illness, and by shunting the responsibility for prevention to the personal (rather than the institutional or governmental) level, e.g. by educating and stimulating citizens to choose a healthy lifestyle. Also, if the need for healthcare intervention does arise, organising the required treatment should take place in small-scale, local networks. That is, elderly patients, people with physical or mental impairments and the chronically ill are, in all but the most serious cases, expected to solve problems themselves, primarily by organising health support in their own social support networks (family, friends, neighbours, etc.). This means that it is increasingly unlikely that elderly people end up in an expensive care home, and more likely that they will instead continue living in their own homes, although they are dependent on informal caregivers for everyday support. The care homes themselves were also privatised, and are now run like companies rather than government institutions.

There are many more examples of tasks and responsibilities that are being transferred from the public sector to the private sector. Municipal leisure and sports facilities such as swimming pools and indoor sports centres are becoming less common, and leisure entrepreneurs are filling the void. Another development that fits with this transition is a decrease of state subsidies for artists (painters, sculptors, musicians, actors) and cultural organisations (museums, theatre or dance companies, etc.), and a transition towards a more market-driven arts and culture sector (with artists who adopt a much more entrepreneurial attitude, depending mostly or wholly on paid assignments, ticket sales and crowdfunding initiatives for their income). In addition to these public-to-private transitions, there are also intermediate variants: public–private partnerships, or organisational structures from the public sector such as municipal governments acting like entrepreneurs.

Against this background, the following question arises: Who is responsible for the quality of life in a neighbourhood or city, or in society as a whole? The necessity of asking the question seems obvious, but it is quite difficult to find an answer that most would agree with. The reason for this difficulty is that the meaning of the question as well as the arguments that would support a specific answer, depend quite profoundly on one's fundamental ideas about what organisational principles should prevail in society. An important distinction here is between broadly socialist and broadly capitalist ideas of what the division of responsibilities between government and civil society needs to be: should the public sector (the government and government-run organisations) or the private sector (including large companies and private entrepreneurs) be responsible for the provision of services that lie at the core of the efficient, affordable and pleasant functioning of society – such as healthcare, water and power, safety and security, education and public transport? Is the government, with a (democratic) mandate for the ideologies underlying its policies and the financial and bureaucratic resources to execute those policies, the most logical institution to safeguard the content and quality of these services? Or can companies or entrepreneurs be trusted to provide (some of) those services more effectively?

In finding an answer to these questions one also has to consider the kind(s) of value a certain entrepreneurial activity generates.

11.1.3 Moral value in entrepreneurship

It has been stated that entrepreneurship is about creating value. Yet a tension could be detected between prioritising economic factors (such as cost-efficiency) or 'human' factors in services provided to the general public, such as healthcare and sports. Social entrepreneurship is an attempt to make a concerted choice for the latter and is therefore oriented towards creating *social* value.

Different sectors or practices will be addressed further on in this chapter, such as healthcare, sports, municipal government and social entrepreneurship. They all deal with the creation and management of value – for patients, athletes, citizens or other stakeholders. But then, of course, the question becomes: what *kind* of value is created (monetary value, social value, environmental value), and for *whom*?

Moral value is a core concern in these practices. After all, if the forces of 'the market' have non-trivial influence on the outcome of processes which are socially important (i.e. important to people's health, or their livelihood, or the quality of life in a neighbourhood), a leading question is *who* (which individual or organisational subdivision) feels *responsible* for the positive outcome of these processes? Not just 'who or what can be held accountable', but 'who actually feels morally compelled to do the right thing' – over and above the kinds of actions necessitated by the blunt goal of 'making money'?

Apart from the more specific moral dilemmas that will be raised in the respective discussions below, there are several more general questions that are to be addressed. The provision of important services (healthcare, education, energy and water and security, but also sports and leisure facilities) has changed, and is continuing to change, in different countries and in different ways. Also, in more specific sectors (e.g. leisure and sports, tourism and recreation, media, etc.), these developments can have their own dynamics, with different roles in the public and private sectors, and that of public–private partnerships. If, in the midst of all that variety and change, publicly important services are increasingly subject to market forces, how can those services be delivered in such a way that the quality of life of the public is ensured? What criteria should such services meet? Is it more or less difficult to define and meet such criteria if public services are privatised? Moreover, if such lines of questioning are shifted to the ethical domain, what role does *responsibility* (in a morally relevant sense, i.e. of feeling personally responsible for the positive outcome of a process) play in all of this?

If public services, for example, are marketed and sold in a free market, and citizens are treated as customers who can freely decide to purchase (or not to purchase), who is responsible if something goes wrong (for example, if the prices of necessary medical drugs spiral out of control)? Which stakeholders should feel such responsibility?

11.1.4 The responsible entrepreneur

At the fringes of all the developments mentioned above which favour entrepreneurial thinking, another kind of (responsible) entrepreneurship emerges to, ostensibly, 'pick up the slack'. That is the rise of social entrepreneurs who feel compelled to assume part of the role that, in the past, was perhaps most logically located at the governmental level, namely to 'take care' of society, to optimise social value – i.e. to provide those services and facilitate those safeguards that cannot be expected to emerge automatically from the entrepreneurial class, focussed as it is on optimising economic value. Instead, social entrepreneurs concentrate on creating another kind of value, namely *social* value – for individuals, groups and organisations which threaten to fall by the wayside in an economic system where both the private and public sector implement an entrepreneurial, cost-and-efficiency-focussed approach.

The connection between entrepreneurship and promoting social value is not particularly new, as the concept of corporate social responsibility (CSR) in business should already be quite familiar to most (see Chapter 8), but social entrepreneurship is something different. The distinction between implementing CSR strategies as an entrepreneur, and being a social entrepreneur, is one of priority: in the former case, running a healthy business is the primary goal, and success criteria in the execution of the business plan can include paying particular attention to issues like the well-being of employees, ecologically sustainable production methods and upholding certain standards in all links of the supply chain (with such standards aimed at taking responsibility for the effects – on society or the environment – of running the business). A social entrepreneur, on the other hand, does not necessarily understand running the business as her primary goal, but as a means to realise other, socially and/or environmentally defined improvement goals (e.g. supporting women in disadvantaged neighbourhoods in starting small businesses, or developing recycling strategies for a polluted tourist destination). It is also called social innovation. (For a more elaborated explication of social entrepreneurship and social innovation, see sections 11.4.1.1 and 11.4.1.2).

11.1.5 In conclusion

An entrepreneur is, generally speaking, someone who operates in the private sector on a for-profit basis (i.e. to use their company to generate monetary value), but in recent years, variations on that theme have emerged. Think about social entrepreneurs, who focus on realising social value rather than monetary value, but also entities that traditionally have pursued social value (such as governments, or public or semi-public organisations such as hospitals) adopting entrepreneurial techniques, practices and goals. This touches upon the 'ethically relevant consequences of entrepreneurial behaviour of organisations' and will be demonstrated in the remainder of this chapter in three discussions and cases, which all deal with shifting meaning of value in a society in transition. The first two discussions and cases explore the ethically relevant consequences of entrepreneurial behaviour by organisations from the public and semi-public sector – specifically, healthcare organisations needing to adapt to a sector that is ever more market-driven, and entrepreneurial cities as they compete for the right to host major sporting events. The third discussion and case flips this structure around, as it discusses social entrepreneurship, and investigates several ethical consequences of social awareness and activism from the entrepreneurial perspective.

More specifically, van Dijk discusses the interrelationships between healthcare, entrepreneurship and managing costs in the first discussion. She goes into more detail about the moral dilemmas that can emerge when healthcare institutes like hospitals are forced to start behaving like companies, and need to deal with the dynamics of the market, including factors such as economic efficiency, the need to transform from supply-driven to demand-driven organisations mergers, benchmarking and, for instance, the pressure on hospitals to specialise and compete with other hospitals. One of the main ethically relevant issues here is, as stated earlier, that these market forces, specifically the need to compete and cut costs in a very complex sector, create incentives for certain stakeholders to act in potentially immoral ways. The ways in which entrepreneurial thinking in the healthcare system can influence medical choices on a grass-roots level is compellingly demonstrated in her case. The second discussion is titled 'Cities, entrepreneurship and events'. The author, Richards, proposes that cities can act as entrepreneurs if they wish to market themselves as relevant locations for investors and tourists. One of the tools at their disposal is the attempt to organise a large-scale event (e.g. the FIFA World Cup, the Olympic Games) as an attention-grabbing strategy. The impacts this has on different stakeholders are colourfully demonstrated in the case he includes. The impacts are ethically interesting at least three levels: the extreme cost of organising such events and the weak track record of return on investments for the inhabitants of the host cities; the long history of corruption and bribery in the sports organisations that govern the selection procedures (e.g. the International Federation of Association Football, FIFA); and the many moral complexities in sports itself (for example, fair play and doping). In the third discussion, titled 'Social entrepreneurship and social innovation', van Leeuwen reflects on how some forms of business transform in such a way that they become focussed on increasing social value. This includes efforts by entrepreneurs to redesign or improve specific systems in accordance with a specific ideology. He discusses the difference between social entrepreneurship and social innovation, identifies the ethical basis underpinning the activities of social entrepreneurs and innovators, and looks into possible guidelines for ethical entrepreneurial behaviour. He closes his section with a case which explicates the potential (adverse) impacts of voluntourism in a social entrepreneurial context (volunteering at an afterschool programme for low-income students in San José, Costa Rica).

To conclude: an important moral value in all three cases appears to be 'fairness'. The reader is called upon to reflect on the meaning of 'fairness' and how it could be defined and operationalised (i.e. be made concrete and applicable in a specific practical situation) in the many different contexts that emerge, as suggested above. In the healthcare example fairness is related to a 'fair fighting chance' for different types of patients after contracting an illness, with equal access to treatments; in the sports example, to facilitating 'fair competition' on the sports field, and fair governance (including the democratic, defensible and non-wasteful distribution and use of resources) outside it; and in the social entrepreneurship example, to the efforts of social entrepreneurs to act as equalisers of fairness, intervening in social or environmental systems to right a perceived wrong.

11.2 Healthcare, entrepreneurship and managing costs

Diana van Dijk

11.2.1 Introduction to healthcare, entrepreneurship and managing costs

11.2.1.1 Healthcare as part of the service industry

The healthcare industry offers specialised services to patients via joint organisations and can therefore be seen as part of the service industry in society. The quality of these services can be determined by comparing the expected services (client/patient expectations) with the perceived received services (client/patient perceptions). The gap between expectation and perception should be as narrow as possible in order to ensure the optimum level of client/patient satisfaction (Parasuraman, Zeithaml and Berry, 1985: 44). For most patients the functional quality of a service, the caring side (interpersonal and environmental factors), is more important than the technical quality (excellent and competent staff).

Therefore hospitals, the main providers of care in the healthcare sector, need to transform from supply-driven organisations (push) into more demand-driven (pull) organisations, which put the patient at the centre of the care process, instead of professional staff or resources. In doing so, most hospitals in the Netherlands have successfully started to implement logistic and hospitality concepts and innovations that are traditionally utilised in the production, service and facility industries. This has induced a form of competition in healthcare provision: providers try to distinguish themselves from others in order to persuade patients to choose their 'products', for example, by offering the shortest waiting list or claiming the best operation results. It is important that competition in this sector functions properly and serves the best interests of the client. Entrepreneurship in healthcare can lead to morally undesirable practices. For example, situations in which clinics test new drugs on volunteers who are willing to pay for them without considering the negative side effects, or in which private clinics lure patients from hospitals, or specialists request unnecessary scans because of the revenues they gain from them.

11.2.1.2 Complexity of healthcare

Healthcare is not only a huge sector in terms of institutions, organisations and personnel, but also a complex one in terms of its numerous stakeholders, conflicting interests and financial structure. On top of that it is a dynamic environment for patients who have different needs of care. Four examples illustrate this complexity.

Firstly, healthcare in the cure sector (mainly hospitals) has a great variety of services, flows, movements and treatments and a high variability (Glöckner and Weijers, 2009: 48). The flow of incoming and outgoing patients and the use of resources do not show a regular or constant pattern. In winter, for example, more beds are occupied than in summer. This changing pattern can lead to either over- or understaffing of personnel and irregular use of examination rooms and technical equipment, resulting in higher costs, a higher or lower workload and dissatisfied patients. During peak periods the planning of consultations, examinations, and operations can be difficult and result in longer waiting times, double bookings, postponement of treatment and stressed-out staff. This is an undesirable and unsatisfactory situation for patients who are waiting for their test results or treatment.

Secondly, the vertical organisational structure and the dual management system of healthcare institutions, as well as the horizontal healthcare process with regard to the patient, make the system quite complex. This applies to both cure and care contexts. Healthcare professionals typically act autonomously. They are technical experts in their field and do their best to treat their patients to the best of their ability. Yet they do not always realise that a patient in need of care has to go through different stressful processes, varying from consultations with doctors, undergoing necessary blood tests, X-rays, scans, and waiting for results, to the necessary preparations for a complicated operation. During that process a patient is confronted with healthcare professionals who in many cases work independently of one another, which sometimes results in miscommunication, overtreatment and wrong or even no information being passed on about their illness.

Thirdly, the financial structure of the healthcare sector is complex and lacks transparency due to the need for more regulation and registration of the demand for care. Healthcare professionals are forced to use a complex registration system (DBCs: diagnosis treatment combination) for all diagnosed activities (see Werken mit dbc's, n.d.). Therefore healthcare professionals have to spend more and more time behind their computer screen, filling in activity codes related to specific healthcare products. These activities have no direct value for the patient, who expects full attention and empathy from his doctor, especially when important decisions have to be taken.

Fourthly, one of the fundamental tasks of the healthcare institutions is to manage the costs of care in order to give all patients/clients the care they are entitled to.

11.2.1.3 Managing costs in the healthcare sector

There is increasing pressure on the healthcare sector from national and international governments and insurance companies to cut costs and optimise processes. These measures are necessary in order to keep healthcare affordable for everyone. A vast percentage, for example, of the Dutch national budget (11 per cent of gross domestic product) is spent on healthcare. In 2015 the expenditure on healthcare in the Netherlands was €95 billion ('Zorguitgaven stijgen langzamer', 2016). Hospital costs, long-term care, and mental healthcare account for the largest share of these expenditures. The average care costs in the Netherlands amount to €5628 a year per person. This can be illustrated by the following situation: A single day in a hospital costs €1200 on average, almost as much as the healthcare premium per person per annum. The main reasons for the increase in costs are related to the ageing population's increasing need of care and medication; an increased in the number of cases of chronic diseases like COPD (a chronic lung disease), diabetes, dementia and obesity; the need to carry out more research; the cost of cancer treatments; overtreatment through unnecessary tests; and the cost of X-rays, second opinions, and innovations in the field of advanced medical technologies such as robots, scans, and 3D printing ('Trends in de zorg', n.d.).

It is quite a challenge for policymakers and healthcare providers to manage these costs on the one hand, while offering high-quality care on the other. One of the actions taken to manage the costs in the Netherlands has been the so-called 'transition of healthcare'. In 2015 the responsibilities and tasks of the provinces with regard to healthcare were transferred to local authorities (municipalities). This process meant budget cuts and the expectation that care consumers should take the lead in planning and organising their own healthcare from their home setting. *Participation* and *self-reliance* are the steering principles of this move. This has led to an increase in care intensity requirements, which, in turn, has caused greater difficulty for people who need intensive care and need to be admitted to a care institution. The transition of healthcare in the Netherlands has also affected the role of the (care) consumer/client. Individuals increasingly take a more active role in their own medical treatment, which results in a high demand for homecare technology (home automation) and for informal care. It also enables people to retain their freedom of movement and their independence, as opposed to being nursed in care homes. But there is a downside to this transition in healthcare. The upcoming sophisticated domestic-care technologies like e-health, distance health and robotics can also lead to ethical problems with regard to limited accessibility, unequal availability, freedom of choice, quality of care and privacy issues. Furthermore, it is no longer self-evident that patients should go to the nearest hospital for treatment or follow the advice of their general practitioner. They obtain specific information from the Internet concerning their health and also compare service performance indicators, like waiting lists, safety and quality of hospitals with one another. This could mean that those who are more highly qualified or skilled have important healthcare information at their disposal that is not accessible to others.

Last but not least, assuming responsibility for the well-being of all your customers, and at the same time managing the costs, is a tall order. It almost certainly leads to ethical dilemmas that are not at stake in a more 'communitarian' practice.

11.2.1.4 New ethical dilemmas in healthcare and the market

Healthcare professionals have always been challenged by all kind of choices, both of a technical and moral nature. They vary from issues like performing or withholding surgery, euthanasia, abortion, treatment, necessary organ transplantation and genetic manipulation to testing new medicine on subjects. As Loewy puts it: 'For healthcare professionals to act ethically they must, first of all, be technically competent in their field of practice and must have informed themselves about the particulars of the case' and 'physicians need to know not only what they do know but also what they do not know, and they need to be ready to call in "experts" or to ask for a consultation when there is doubt' (1996: 80).

But on another level, market forces, and the necessary cuts in healthcare, have created new ethical dilemmas. That entails, amongst other, the relationship between doctors, researchers, and the pharmaceutical industry. One of the main drivers of these relatively new ethical dilemmas is the fact that the pharmaceutical industry pays doctors, researchers and care-providers sponsor money in exchange for information about patients and rare diseases. A rare disease is a lifelong source of income for the pharmaceutical industry. More and more so-called orphan drugs, expensive medicines for small groups of patients, are put on the market. Ehni states that 'providing access to drugs for orphan diseases has been considered an important ethical problem and was addressed by the European Union in 2000' (2014: 328). Hospitals negotiate 'secret' discounts for these type of drugs. In return pharmacists invest in research in hospitals so that doctors will prescribe a certain brand of drug

('Farmaceuten Gebruiken Ziekenhuis als Reclamespotje', 2016: 27). This necessitates closer reflection on those activities of the healthcare industry that are especially related to entrepreneurship and innovation.

11.2.1.5 The entrepreneurial side of the healthcare industry

As indicated earlier, healthcare is one of the service industries in society. In order to cut costs and keep healthcare affordable, the need for new solutions and perspectives has increased. Managers and policymakers have started to explore whether the market could bring relief. This means analysing the issues that are at stake due to market forces (for example: mergers, benchmarking or specialisation of hospitals). Two factors are relevant here: on the one hand, the development of entrepreneurship, innovation and new technologies are driven by the need to compete. On the other hand, insurance companies, by government order, enforce a complex registration system for all diagnosed activities and related costs that take place in the healthcare environment, by which they hope that transparency and lower costs could be realised. Healthcare insurance companies are very powerful stakeholders and negotiate with hospitals about budgets, the cost price of treatments and the number of operations that can be performed, or financed in a given year. It is obvious that different interests can cause friction and sometimes create the wrong incentives for action. There exists an area of tension between the need for entrepreneurship and innovation and the need for regulation in the form of an extensive registration system.

Furthermore, healthcare insurance companies with their so-called preference policy (indicating payment for the cheapest drug of those available) compete on price and thereby force pharmacists to sell the cheaper alternative to their patients. In that way the patient receives the same quality for a lower price. Preference policy is introduced to stop the payment of high bonuses by manufacturers (which is a bad incentive to doctors, for instance) and to control the price of drugs.

Another issue which caused debate in the public and political arena in the last decade was that health insurance companies were putting pressure on doctors to prescribe less expensive drugs. One of the reasons for that was that the costs for cancer therapies had rocketed skywards. They increased from €376 million in 2011 to €675 million in 2014. In 2016 a further increase to almost €1 billion euro was expected ('Volksgezondheidenzorg', n.d.).

The budget for hospitals allocated by health insurance companies is not sufficient for some expensive (e.g. oncological) drugs and treatments that are not on the list of 'regulation expensive drugs', the so-called add-on drugs. And even if expensive drugs fall within the regulation, hospitals have to pay a share of the costs. This means that not all patients receive the standard treatment for an ailment based on the 'standard' drug that goes with it. Patients are not always aware of this fact. Research shows that, for example, half of oncological drugs against bowel cancer, like Avastin, are not administered to patients (Berkhout, 2015). This problem will become more serious in the future due to the development of new biotechnical drugs for specific types of cancer, the increase of the number of cancer patients whose life expectancy will be higher than before, and the fact that producers of drug manufacturers want to earn back their production costs. Therefore small-scale hospitals send some of their patients to academic hospitals, hoping that they will receive the right treatment. Academic hospitals, however, focus on complex care.

Their budget is not sufficient for every type of patient. This could lead to hospitals having to choose, for example, between spending money on a cancer treatment or, rather, recruiting new personnel.

The inequality of cancer care has sparked off a social debate on the basic right of every citizen to receive the care that he or she deserves. Even if all citizens were willing to pay a higher healthcare premium, there would still be insufficient care for everyone as the demand for effective healthcare exceeds the supply. This means that there will still be some patients who receive expensive care and others who do not. This raises the question of whether new or expensive drugs should by definition be available to all patients. This question is at stake in the case presented in the next section.

Case 11.2.2: Fairness in administering scarce and expensive medicine

Introduction

Dr Jan de Vries, oncologist, 45 years old and married, is a specialist in colon cancer. He is an expert in his field and head of oncology at the Riverside Hospital in Rotterdam. Patients from all over the Netherlands come to his hospital for treatment. Not long ago, he gave an excellent presentation on the effectiveness of the drug Avastin for the treatment of colon cancer at an oncology conference in Washington (United States). His presentation was covered by all kinds of media, including newspapers and online resources.

Paula, 75 years old, widow and mother of two grown-up children, has been a patient of Dr de Vries for the last five years. She had surgery for colon cancer in 2011. After her operation she received intensive chemotherapy for quite some time. During one of her regular check-ups in 2016 a scan showed that she had metastasis in her liver. Paula does not own a computer, which means that she is not able to search the Internet for information on, for example, the treatment of colon cancer. However, she has established a very good relationship with Dr de Vries and fully relies on his professional advice.

Karin, 32 years old, well educated, married, and mother of three small children, was recently diagnosed with advanced colon cancer. Together with her husband – a researcher at the Eindhoven Technical University in the Netherlands – she searched the Internet and discovered information on Dr de Vries' work. The presentation he gave on Avastin led them to conclude that the Riverside Hospital would be the best option for the treatment of her colon cancer. She checked whether her insurance company financed treatment at the Riverside Hospital and made an appointment with Dr de Vries for consultation and further treatment. Her husband accompanied her.

Who deserves which drug?

Both Paula and Karin have an appointment with Dr de Vries on the treatment of their disease in the same week. Paula meets with him first. Dr de Vries discusses

(continued)

Case 11.2.2: Fairness in administering scarce and expensive medicine (*continued*)

the results of the last scan with her and the possible actions that could be taken. He has several patients with colon cancer and would like to prescribe the expensive, but effective, drug Avastin to her. However, it would mean that there would only be a small portion of the budget left to treat other patients with the same drug. There are other, cheaper, drugs available, and choosing one of these would mean that more patients with colon cancer could be treated. The downside is that these drugs are not as effective as Avastin. Dr de Vries could prescribe one of these drugs to Paula, but needs to take a calculated decision as soon as possible.

A few days later, Karin and her husband meet with Dr de Vries. He discusses her case with them and tells them that she will first have to undergo surgery. He also discusses the possibilities of further treatment after the operation was done. Jan, Karin's husband, who has done some research on the Internet, brings up Dr de Vries' academic articles on the treatment of colon cancer, which report on the effectiveness of the drug Avastin. They ask him whether Karin could get this drug administered. This puts Dr de Vries in a difficult situation. What should he do?

Questions for discussion

- What are the ethical problems Dr de Vries is facing? Apply ethical principles in helping him to solve these problems.
- To which extent are these problems related to the 'entrepreneurial road' healthcare institutions are expected to follow? How do you evaluate that ethically?
- What kinds of innovations could help healthcare institutions to solve the seemingly eternal dilemma of, on the one hand, giving individual patients and clients the care they are rightfully entitled to, and, on the other hand, fulfilling their obligation to society in keeping the costs of care within reasonable and fair boundaries?
- The pharmaceutical industry is regulated not only by the law, but also by codes and ethical principles, such as caring for the health and safety of human beings and protecting large investments and their stakeholders. Does balancing these responsibilities legitimate the administering of the most effective medicine to a select group of severely ill patients on a first-come-first-served basis, while others receive a less effective medicine when the budget has reached its limits? Give ethical reasons for your answer.
- Healthcare is part of the service industry. It is said that most of the 'clients' value the functional quality of the service (interpersonal and environmental factors) more than the technical quality (excellent and competent staff). Could you identify the values that underpin the expectations of the 'clients' of healthcare institutions? Does this apply to other sectors within the service industry as well?

11.3 Cities, entrepreneurship and events
Greg Richards

11.3.1 Introduction to cities, entrepreneurship and events
11.3.1.1 The rise of the entrepreneurial city

Globalisation and the hypermobility of capital has stimulated significant changes in the external environment of cities (Cox, 1993), producing a more competitive urban landscape in which those cities have to be creative and entrepreneurial in order to survive. Declining central government funding means that cities increasingly have to raise revenue themselves if they want to grow.

The growth regimes that emerged in the late 20th century in many cities in Europe and North America were characterised by neo-liberal politics and a focus on local economic development. Hall and Hubbard (1998) saw the rise of 'entrepreneurial cities' as part of the 'new urban politics', which increasingly brought cities into competition with each other.

Large-scale development projects were an obvious way of stimulating local development and attracting attention and investment for the entrepreneurial city. New iconic buildings became a fashionable development strategy, leading to the global spread of consumption-related architectural projects (Ponzini, Fotev and Mavaraccio, 2016). Iconic structures such as the Bilbao Guggenheim became a means of distinguishing places and attracting investment and tourism (Richards and Wilson, 2006). Very often, however, these development-led strategies ended up producing very similar icons designed by the same group of 'starchitects' selling their designs to competing cities (Ponzini et al., 2016) and therefore lost their distinctive qualities.

Large-scale events provided an alternative attention-grabbing development strategy (Richards, 2013). Events arguably had the advantage of being more flexible and attracting more media attention than buildings (Richards and Palmer, 2010). The global audience for the Olympic Games grew to over 3 billion people for the Summer Olympics in Beijing (2008) and London (2012), for example. The International Olympic Committee (IOC) therefore touts the Games as 'one of the most effective international marketing platforms in the world'. Not surprisingly, cities began to be 'staged' for mega-events designed to attract global attention (Greene, 2003). This practice began with cities such as Tokyo, Montreal and Barcelona, but spread during the latter part of the 20th century to emerging cities such as Johannesburg and Rio.

Cities compete fiercely to stage these major events, spending large sums of money just on bidding. Some cities are also serial Olympic bidders. For example Los Angeles has bid ten times for the Summer Olympic Games (1924, 1928, 1932, 1948, 1952, 1956, 1976, 1980, 1984, 2024), and staged the Games twice. But the value of bidding for or staging such major events is increasingly being called into question.

Doubts first began to emerge in the 1970s, after the Montreal 1976 Games. It took 30 years for the Canadian city to pay off the debt incurred by the 720 per cent cost overrun. But problems have grown as the cost of staging the Games has escalated, and as cost overruns become an occupational hazard for host cities. The average cost overrun is around 160 per cent. In recent years these events have been staged in cities which are even less prepared to bear the costs. Haferburg and Steinbrink (2017) illustrate how cities in emerging economies have struggled to extract significant benefits from these global events, in spite of their vast budgets. After the 2016 Olympic Games, taxpayers in Rio were left with a bill for US$11.6 billion, but with little to show for this investment.

Problems like these lead to growing scepticism about the benefits of mega-events to the host cities. In the competition to stage the 2022 Winter Olympics, for example, Oslo, Stockholm, Lviv and Krakow all pulled out. Seventy per cent of Krakow residents voted against staging the Games in a referendum (Ramaswamy, 2015).

In addition, recent scandals surrounding doping in Olympic sports are casting a shadow over the bidding process.

> Bidding is now being carried out against the backdrop of a crisis in perceptions of the integrity of sport. It's an issue for the cities, the IOC and other stakeholders, and the IOC knows that the bidding process has to be absolutely transparent, particularly at a time when, after the issues at FIFA and the IAAF, there is such a focus on good governance in sport. (Sport Business, 2016)

These problems have begun to raise important ethical issues about the staging of major sports events such as the Olympic Games or the FIFA World Cup. These issues become even more pressing when the cities hosting these events are located in emerging countries where the economy is weak and inequality between rich and poor is great. This section examines the ethical issues surrounding such major sports events.

11.3.1.2 Sports, events and ethics

The global sports industry was estimated to be worth US$145.3 billion in 2015 (PricewaterhouseCoopers, 2011), of which entry fees to sports events alone were estimated to generate US$44 billion. Not surprisingly, therefore, nations and cities compete fiercely for the honour of hosting major sports events, hoping to use them to put themselves on the global map and become 'eventful cities' (Richards and Palmer, 2010). In this competitive environment, sports events are increasingly raising ethical issues for those competing in, organising and watching them.

The growth of ethical concerns surrounding sport has not gone unnoticed in the academic community, where a raft of publications on sports ethics has emerged in the last 20 years (McNamee, 2007). Sport is an interesting field for ethical investigation, because the rules for acceptable and unacceptable behaviour are widely known, and there is a generalised sense of what is 'fair' in the game. In ethics, the concept of fairness involves treating everyone equally and impartially. 'Fair play' is usually understood to mean using only tactics that are in accord with the spirit of the sport. Fair play is therefore something that the organising bodies for sport try and promote, for example with the FIFA Fair Play programme.

The idea of fair play and having a 'level playing field' that creates equal chances for all is therefore deeply embedded in sport. However, the sense of what is fair is contextual, and subject to change. For example, in the late 19th and early 20th centuries Corinthian Football Club refused to take penalties when they were introduced into the game, in line with the 'Corinthian spirit':

> So principled, in fact, was Corinthians' ethos that some of the club's practices now seem comical, and belonging to a bygone age. If, for example, their opponents lost a player to injury or dismissal, they would immediately and voluntarily

remove one of their own men from the fray to retain a fair and level playing field. Even more amazing was their steadfast refusal to score from penalty kicks, which they would tap back to the opposition goalkeeper, content in the belief that no-one would ever attempt to gain an unfair advantage by deliberately fouling an opponent. Penalties, in Corinthians' view, were 'ungentlemanly'. FIFA (2012)

Of course the promotion of fair play by FIFA takes on a whole new meaning in the light of corruption allegations against some of its leading officials.

In 2010 the Football Association of Ireland refused the offer of a Fair Play award following the France vs Republic of Ireland 2010 World Cup play-off handball controversy. The CEO of the Football Association called Sepp Blatter 'an embarrassment to himself and an embarrassment to FIFA' for his handling of, and comments following, the controversy.

The areas in which ethical questions can arise around sports events are therefore many, and include:

- The use of banned substances.
- Bribery to officials (organisers, referees) and competitors.
- Trying to influence the result of a game.
- Gamesmanship – diving, time-wasting, feigning injury, etc.

Much of the effort of sports governing bodies therefore goes into the prevention of such practices, for example by the establishment of doping testing programmes.

But in the sphere of major sports events the ethical questions extend far beyond the events themselves and into the places where they are held. Cities now compete with one another to host sports events such as the Olympic Games and the FIFA World Cup. This has created a veritable industry in bidding for sports events, and the announcement of the 'winning' city has now become a global media event in itself.

Case 11.3.2: The FIFA World Cup and Olympic Games

Introduction

The growing competition between cities to host major sporting events has led to larger sums of money being spent on the bidding process. For example, a report by the National Olympic Committees (NOC) of Austria, Germany, Sweden and Switzerland (2014) found that:

> Monitoring the development of bid budgets of the last three bid processes reveals a remarkable trend: the official bid budgets have more than quadrupled in the last three processes. A city bidding for the Games 2010 spent an average budget of USD 9.5 million for the two-year-period preceding the IOC's host city election, whereas a city bidding for the Games 2018 invested an average of USD 34 million. (See NOC reports; NOCs of Austria, Germany, Sweden and Switzerland, 2014).

(continued)

Case 11.3.2: The FIFA World Cup and Olympic Games (*continued*)

With these escalating costs, it becomes increasingly important to ensure the bid is won – otherwise there is a risk of considerable political fallout from the money 'wasted' on the bid. Of course there are a lot of techniques available to try and ensure success, from increased marketing spend to political lobbying to bribery and corruption. These practices in turn raise the costs of bidding, and therefore the importance of winning the bid, leading to greater temptation to 'bend the rules'.

Bribes, doping, mismanagement, self-enrichment and fraud

For example, the IOC's Executive Board investigated IOC members for their part in taking bribes, gifts and scholarships worth an estimated $600,000 from the organisers of the 2002 Winter Games in Salt Lake City, Utah. More recently the German TV channel ARD broadcast a programme called 'Top-Secret Doping: How Russia Makes its Winners.' This indicated that senior officials at the International Association of Athletics Federations (IAAF), the world governing body for athletics, had tried to cover up positive drugs tests by Russian athletes. Shortly after the programme was broadcast in 2014 a number of IAAF officials resigned. In 2015, former Olympic champion athlete Sebastian Coe took over as IAAF president from Lamine Diack, who was subsequently arrested on suspicion of taking bribes to cover up the positive drugs tests of the Russian athletes. A report by the World Anti-Doping Agency (WADA) indicated that corruption was 'embedded' in the world athletics body IAAF and its leaders must have been aware of doping scandals in Russia and other countries. The WADA report concluded that Lamine Diack 'sanctioned and appeared to have had personal knowledge of the fraud and the extortion of athletes carried out by the actions of the illegitimate governance structure he put in place' (quoted in Meagher, 2016).

Russia was suspended from all international athletics competitions by the IAAF, and remained suspended at the time of writing, over a year later. There was much discussion about whether Russian athletes should be allowed to compete in the 2016 Rio Olympic Games. Blood-test data indicated that around a third of the medals in endurance events at the Olympics and all world championship events [between 2001 and 2012] were won by athletes with suspicious tests ('IAAF at the centre of new doping controversy', 2015). Pressure has been rising on the governing bodies to take away the medals awarded to these athletes. Sebastian Coe has taken responsibility for cleaning up world athletics, and yet he was the vice president of the IAAF during the presidency of Lamine Diack.

Recent accusations against top FIFA officials by the FBI and the eventual resignation of Sepp Blatter have also revealed the culture of bribery and corruption in world football. Interestingly, when allegations of corruption first began to surface, FIFA set up its own ethics committee to investigate the claims. Michael Garcia, the American lawyer who led the investigation into the 2018 and 2022 World Cup bid process, resigned from the FIFA ethics committee over concerns about the independence of the process. He was himself accused of unethical conduct by the FIFA Executive Committee led by Blatter.

American investigators have alleged that $10 million went to former Caribbean football chief Jack Warner, who is currently under arrest, as payback for him and two other senior FIFA executives for voting for South Africa to host the 2010 World Cup. The US Justice Department alleges that 14 officials accepted bribes and kickbacks estimated at more than $150m over a 24-year period.

Blatter is also suspected by Swiss investigators of criminal mismanagement and misappropriation of FIFA money linked to a $2 million payment to Michel Platini, former head of the European federation UEFA, and of selling undervalued TV rights for the 2010 and 2014 World Cup's to then-FIFA vice president Jack Warner. As a result of proceedings against Blatter the FIFA ethics committee (which Blatter himself set up) decided to ban Blatter and Platini for six years each. Both deny the charges and have appealed against their bans.

Jérôme Valcke, the former secretary general of FIFA and Sepp Blatter's right-hand man, was also sacked in January 2016 over a series of allegations including the sale of World Cup tickets. However, this was the second time that Valcke had been sacked by FIFA. In 2006 Valcke was dismissed as marketing director after a sponsorship row with credit card firms resulted in FIFA being forced to repay more than £60m to MasterCard. However, Valcke was reinstated by Blatter just eight months later. FIFA now alleges that Sepp Blatter, Jérôme Valcke and Markus Kattner awarded themselves pay raises and bonuses worth $80m over five years. According to FIFA the trio made a coordinated effort to extract money from the organisation between 2011 and 2015.

In February 2016 FIFA held the first election in many years that did not include Blatter on the ballot paper. It was hoped that fresh leadership would solve the problems that had been plaguing the organisation. However, the elections failed to stem criticism. New FIFA president Gianni Infantino has denied that promises to the United States over who will host the 2026 World Cup secured his election win, even though the US Soccer Federation head Sunil Gulati switched his vote to Infantino in the second round of the voting. Gianni Infantino promised that the overhaul of the structure and running of FIFA following the crisis would be 'implemented from day one, immediately' (Gibson, 2016).

But according to the UK *Daily Mail* newspaper, there is already evidence that calls Infantino's ability to turn FIFA round into question. The claims about Infantino's behaviour include:

- Plotting at a recent meeting of FIFA's Council to get rid of Domenico Scala, the official who had set his salary at $2m, reportedly described by Infantino as an 'insult'.
- Banning acting general secretary Marcus Kattner from attending that meeting in a clear attempt to control the wording of the minutes, which is against FIFA rules.

(continued)

Case 11.3.2: The FIFA World Cup and Olympic Games (*continued*)

- Insisting on making trips by private jet even though he boasted about taking Easyjet to the International FA Board meeting in Cardiff.
- Appointing his new general secretary unilaterally and without due process.
- And, in what could be construed as nepotism, bringing in a previously little-known friend and neighbour from his local village of Trelex, Luca Piazza, to work in the president's office, an appointment confirmed by FIFA to Sportsmail (Warshaw, 2016).

These developments underline the difficult ethical questions facing cities and nations hoping to host major sports events. Interestingly, to date relatively little attention has been paid to the tactics employed by the cities bidding for events, but this is likely just a matter of time.

Questions for discussion

- Given the necessity of innovation, which is essential to entrepreneurship, should cities: (a) invest large sums of public money in staging sporting events, (b) pay bribes to sports officials in order to secure a nomination? Give moral arguments for your position.
- Which ethical principles apply when evaluating the moral responsibility (entrepreneurial) cities have in organising events?
- Should sports governing bodies: (a) ban an entire country that could also include clean athletes in its team from participating in the Olympic Games because of doping cases, (b) 'reset' world records when there is evidence of doping, (c) remain independent and monitor their own ethics? Explain your answers.
- Can you build a case for good governance in sports?
- Upon which moral principles does sports integrity rest? When could sport be considered a 'clean' and culturally uplifting activity?

11.4 Social entrepreneurship and social innovation

Marco van Leeuwen

11.4.1 Introduction to social entrepreneurship and social innovation

This section discusses the difference between social entrepreneurship and social innovation. It also reflects on the ethical basis underpinning the activities of social entrepreneurs and innovators, and looks into possible guidelines for ethical entrepreneurial behaviour. The section closes with a case which explicates the possible (adverse) impacts of voluntourism in a social entrepreneurial context.

11.4.1.1 Social entrepreneurship

Entrepreneurs, in whatever field, will usually count 'making a profit' amongst their most important success criteria. The very existence of most businesses depends on their being financially sustainable, i.e. generating sufficient cash flow to make it possible for the business to continue to exist – for example, to pay the wages of employees or to enable new investments. However, the underlying reason for some entrepreneurs to start and maintain their business might be very different from 'making money'. Ideally, an entrepreneur has chosen a field for which she can muster a sufficient level of enthusiasm, with which she feels 'connected'. This, obviously, will help the entrepreneur to dedicate the time and energy needed to make the business into a success. Some entrepreneurs, however, take this idea one step further: they go into business because they want to express and implement specific values in their business ventures. To put it somewhat bombastically, they go into business because they want to make the world a better place. This, in a broad sense, is social entrepreneurship. It entails developing and implementing techniques and interventions, through business ventures, in order to find solutions to sociocultural or environmental problems. Abu-Saifan provides the following definition: 'The social entrepreneur is a mission-driven individual who uses a set of entrepreneurial behaviours to deliver a social value to the less privileged, all through an entrepreneurially oriented entity that is financially independent, self-sufficient, or sustainable' (2012: 25).

This way of doing business is often not (or at least not primarily) focussed on making profit, but rather on achieving a particular kind of societal impact that is in accordance with specific values. These values can be related to implementing and or safeguarding specific ideals for a specific society, such as fighting for social equality, the eradication of poverty and hunger, stimulating democracy and the rule of law, guarding the fundamental rights of disadvantaged groups, or in a broader context, ideals related to animal rights, environmental pollution and conserving cultural heritage. Along these lines, one can state that 'regular' entrepreneurship operates primarily to optimise 'the bottom line' – that is, to make money; to increase monetary profit. But although social entrepreneurship also needs to make financial sense, it generally intends to add a second (serving a social good) or even third (serving an environmental good) bottom line to the estimation of its success.

Abu-Saifan notes that it is important to avoid muddling the issue, by distinguishing between actual social entrepreneurship, and other activities with a social focus: 'philanthropists, activists, companies with foundations, or organisations that are simply socially responsible' are not social entrepreneurs (2012: 26). He goes on to distinguish between two main business strategies that social entrepreneurs might implement: on the one hand, non-profit with earned income strategies – which is to say a hybrid social and commercial organisation, which re-invests any profit to optimise the realisation of the entrepreneur's social objectives – and, on the other hand, for-profit with mission-driven strategies – which is also a hybrid social/commercial organisation, but with the explicit objective of realising financial sustainability and (personal) profit for owners and investors, in addition to the realisation of social goals (2012: 26).

Whatever strategy is implemented in their company, social entrepreneurs are usually highly driven individuals. Robert Stebbins, for example, notes that in establishing the motives for people to pursue this kind of activity, profit can at best be secondary, for there are far less risky business ventures that tend to have a more advantageous return on investment. Rather, social entrepreneurs should, claims Stebbins, be understood as practitioners of serious leisure, similar to career volunteers, who choose to devote large amounts of time and effort to their activity of choice, and strive for structural improvement – of themselves as skilled practitioners of their craft, and of the (social) context they choose to operate in (2010).

11.4.1.2 Social innovation

A concept related to social entrepreneurship is that of social innovation. Social innovation is a catch-all term for attempts to find new concepts and strategies to solve societal problems by employing the creative and/or innovative capacities of a social system. One could understand it as crowdsourcing solutions. The potential uses of such an approach can include innovation in business contexts via collective problem-solving – i.e. the co-creation of desired end-states, or, more broadly, socio-economic problem-solving.

Social innovation, thus, is an innovation-driven process, specifically one with implementations in society. In a broad sense, the term social innovation can refer to the development of new products, ideas and services which address problems in the social sphere more effectively than existing approaches. This development often includes new modes of collaboration in civil society, for instance through the mobilisation of social forces in novel ways (e.g. collective creativity in business and society, or open-source-based methods) which can result in strengthened social relationships and organisational structures. Osburg states that adding the 'social' component to 'innovation' means to realise innovations that '(…) are both social in their ends and in their means; simultaneously meet social needs and create new social relationships; (are) new solutions that address societal challenges; (and result in) new business models and market-based mechanisms that deliver sustainable prosperity' (2013: 18).

Social entrepreneurial endeavours, by comparison, often look for new solutions in a specific context, which need not be innovative in the sense of exploring new solutions for the sake of newness, but do tend to look for new solutions for the sake of solving the extant problem. In practice, social entrepreneurship does tend to emerge in contexts where old or traditional ways of working have failed to produce the desired result, and something different is required to break the status quo. Social entrepreneurship is a social-value-creating form of entrepreneurship, and it might – but does not need to – involve social innovation as an approach in order to reach its value-based societal goals.

11.4.1.3 The relevance of ethics for social entrepreneurs and social innovators

In order to reach a well-rounded understanding of social entrepreneurship and social innovation, it is important to consider the ways in which ethics is of importance to them. After all, both phenomena have value-based societal goals. Several such ways can be identified.

Two of these ways have to do with the character of social entrepreneurship as such. As has been stated before, social entrepreneurship, in general, means to intervene in social environments with the intent of stimulating the development of a specific aspect of that environment. So, first, social entrepreneurship is focussed on the improvement of some situation, which means that its associated activities are based upon value judgements like: 'this situation is not good enough, and it needs to change like *this*'. Some of the possible values to act upon might not be able to coexist. And, second, in many cases a social entrepreneur chooses to influence the ways in which a social system (e.g. a neighbourhood) operates. For instance, Sharma (2016), a social entrepreneur, describes herself as a 'social change-maker'. Wanting to change society means constraining the actions and choices of others, which immediately raises ethical questions.

An example can highlight both these moral issues: suppose that a regional development council decides to redevelop an area by creating a national park. This redevelopment will restore the landscape to its natural state, reintroduce several endangered animal species to the area and thus create an attractive environment to support nature preservation. As an added bonus, this will also stimulate (ecologically friendly, sustainable) tourism to the region. However, suppose further that executing this project also means that the current inhabitants of the area, who have been working farms there for several generations (with a type of farming that is incompatible with the nature- and tourism-related goals of the project), will need to be displaced. It seems obvious that this project is likely to involve conflicting values, correlated with different stakeholders: the value that is created in the eyes of nature preservationists, local tourism entrepreneurs and tourists, is to the detriment of the inhabitants. And, due to the nature of this project as a social entrepreneurial endeavour, the situation will develop in a specific direction, enforcing change that will not be universally welcomed.

A third ethical issue is one that underlies social entrepreneurship in a broader sense. Social entrepreneurship is, to an important extent, moral, value-based entrepreneurship, as has been indicated above. However, for a particular social entrepreneur, what are those values based on? Most of the values and moral attitudes that people hold emerge over time, influenced by personality, individual experiences and other contingencies, instead of an objective assessment of all pros and cons that pertain to a specific situation. Especially because social entrepreneurs are often highly motivated, driven individuals, can one be certain that every social enterprise is based on a fair, balanced decision-making process in which values and ideals are strived for? Is there a mechanism in place to assess the quality of those convictions, to save social entrepreneurs from being blinded by their enthusiasm? Before someone decides to become a social entrepreneur, the underlying, motivation-providing value system is already in place. Where did that value system come from?

Obviously, everyone is entitled to her own moral convictions and preferences, but the key aspect here is that social entrepreneurs intend to *act* on their moral convictions, and intervene in situations where their convictions have consequences for the lives of other people. In the national park example above, nature preservation and tourism development are considered to be more important than the rights of the current inhabitants. That might very well be a valid choice, but it will be valid only from a particular perspective (the one which centres on the arguments in favour of nature and tourism development); this means to 'devalue' other possible perspectives (e.g. that of the farmers' union, which might suggest a different kind of development for the area in question).

A similar entanglement with ethics can be seen with social innovation. Fontrodona (2013) claims that ethics itself is a practice focussed on improvement (of the self, of others and/or of situations), which means that ethics is intrinsically innovative. In the case of *social* innovation, this connection is possibly even more prominent, as this practice demands the explicit involvement of the needs, desires and values of the people who are part of the innovation process. This is not merely a definitional issue, as Fontrodona goes on to argue. Involving ethics in a business decision means to introduce a new dimension beyond the economic one – apart from, e.g. measurable profitability and shareholder value, much less easily measured factors become prominent, and often even dominant, such as the social and environmental effects of business decisions, the opportunities for durable social development facilitated by those decisions and the extent to which a company's employees and the relevant stakeholders accept and support the chosen course of action. Ethical factors are not always relevant in such decisions, but when they are, they are usually very important, as they intrinsically involve people as people, and not merely as economic entities. In a way, profit-based businesses have reasonably clear success criteria (i.e. the bottom line – creating monetary value), whereas the additional bottom lines (in particular, the second bottom line as mentioned above – serving a *social* good) that can be added in value-based businesses tend to be more subjective and contestable.

11.4.1.4 Ethical guidelines for social entrepreneurs and social innovators

How, then, can social entrepreneurs or social innovators move forward with their activities in an ethically appropriate manner? Durieux and Stebbins say that there are three ethical issues which often arise in social entrepreneurial projects, and being mindful of these pitfalls might be a good place for an entrepreneur to start: being honest with one's team, treating those team members fairly and avoiding exploitation of volunteers (2010).

In a more normative sense, Fabian and Fabricant (2014) suggest four principles that should define an ethical framework for innovation projects. They claim that, ideally, innovation projects should be humanistic: ('solving big problems through human ingenuity, imagination and entrepreneurialism that can come from anywhere'), non-hierarchical ('drawing ideas from many different sources and incubating small, agile teams to test and iterate on them with user feedback'), participatory ('designing *with* (not *for*) real people') and sustainable ('building skills even if most individual endeavours will ultimately fail in their societal goals').

The issue that makes these guidelines both interesting and complex is that they are still very much open to interpretation, depending on whatever practical context they would need to be implemented in. This means that the moral character of the social entrepreneur or social innovator, and her ability to align her own values and motivation with those of the people her actions affect, continue to be of utmost importance.

In the following case the complexity of social entrepreneurship and the potential moral ambiguity of its practices will be explored.

Case 11.4.2: Social entrepreneurship using voluntourism

Introduction

Volunteer tourism, or 'voluntourism' for short, is a popular way for (mostly young) people to learn about a different country and culture, and contribute something positive to their destination. An example of a voluntourism trip is to work at an orphanage in Africa for two months, or to help build a school there. Voluntourism can be part of a social entrepreneur's strategy to improve the living conditions in a disadvantaged area, by using voluntourists as workers to realise the project, by investing the money those voluntourists pay for their trip (which can involve substantial amounts) in the project, and by using the involvement of the voluntourists to improve cross-cultural interaction between developed and developing countries. However, despite the apparent optimistic aims of such projects, there is also potential for substantial criticism of the realised outcomes, as the following considerations might indicate.

Adverse outcomes of voluntourism

A voluntourist, looking back with some regret on her own experience, wrote:

> Participants pay for the opportunity to live and work in a developed country. In my case, I paid a couple thousand dollars to spend two weeks living in San Jose [sic], Costa Rica, while volunteering at an afterschool program for low-income students. The experience was personally formative, no doubt, but I now question the impact I actually had; and whether similar experiences being had by more and more people each year may actually be to the long-term detriment of impoverished communities. (Marsman, 2014)

Her doubt, and perhaps fear, that the impact of voluntourism activities might not always be positive is shared by others. In an article in *The Guardian*, Ian Birrell says the following:

> Wealthy tourists prevent local workers from getting much-needed jobs, especially when they pay to volunteer; hard-pressed institutions waste time looking after them and money upgrading facilities; and abused or abandoned children form emotional attachments to the visitors, who increase their trauma by disappearing back home. (2010)

Additionally, Raymond and Hall (2008) state that one of the goals of voluntourism projects can be to improve cross-cultural understanding, but that such projects need to be managed very carefully in order to avoid the reinforcement of cultural stereotypes. If that is not done – and more often than not the idea of cross-cultural understanding is treated as an automatic

(continued)

> ### Case 11.4.2: Social entrepreneurship using voluntourism (*continued*)
>
> outcome to be expected rather than a goal that needs to be managed – the latent and overt prejudices of voluntourists and the receiving community might reinforce rather than mitigate each other.
>
> ### Questions for discussion
>
> - When a voluntourist goes to work at (say) an orphanage in a developing country, based on which moral values might she make the decision to do so? What does she hope to achieve, and for whom?
> - Suppose that a voluntourist goes on her trip with genuine intentions to do good, but the description of the negative results as sketched in the description above is correct (see paragraph 11.4.2.2). Is she then to blame? In other words, can an action be considered 'good' if someone's intentions are good (even if the outcomes are bad), or if the outcomes are good (even if the intentions are bad)?
> - Even if a voluntourist's intentions are good, can she still be blamed for not doing proper research in advance about the *real* local effects of voluntourism practices? In other words, does ignorance in ethical matters exempt one from blame for moral failure? How would you judge her behaviour if she did do the research, but decided to go anyway?
> - Suppose the entrepreneur organising the voluntourism trips claims that she understands the negative effect of her activities on the labour market in the orphanage's area, but that 'at least the orphans are being taken care of'. Is her decision to continue with her activities a valid outcome of weighing these arguments pro and contra? What other arguments are possible to support the continuation of these activities, even in light of the counterarguments outlined in the example?
> - Can you design a modified scenario, based on the case above, in which the social entrepreneur tries to realise her ambitions (improving the local situation in the developing country, e.g. the fate or local orphans, by using voluntourists) in the form of a social innovation project? If so, how could one realise the four ethical guidelines as specified by Fabian and Fabricant (see paragraph 11.4.1.4)?

11.5 Concluding thoughts

Although often used interchangeably for describing the attitudes and approaches which drive (economic) activities within business contexts, the concepts 'business' and 'entrepreneurship' are fundamentally not synonyms. Whereas business roughly stands for economic activity, which proceeds from an existing idea or concept that is based on competition and aims at making profit, entrepreneurship proceeds from a new or unique idea or concept that is based on cooperation and aims at being of value to people or communities. This passion for creating value, be it social, aesthetic or even emotional, usually pushes entrepreneurs towards taking risks and leads them to create new markets for existing products or services or to invent new products and or services. Entrepreneurs are often described as inventors, innovators and pioneers; people who recognise and grab opportunities when they emerge; people who, in pursuing their passion, often bring change to the world – also in social contexts. Entrepreneurship, therefore, presupposes a specific mindset, which could also be present (and valued) in 'traditional, well-established organisations', since it allows for change, creativity, result-oriented action and innovation – traits which are of great benefit to doing business in the 'regular way'.

As far as the relationship between entrepreneurship and ethics is concerned: entrepreneurs also face several complex ethical dilemmas and problems, since creating new ventures is usually a dynamic endeavour which is embedded in contexts of high risk, and often not supported by generous financial means. Amongst other challenges, entrepreneurial activity has to deal with dilemmas regarding the division of financial gains, considering the well-being of employees, satisfaction of customers, ways of producing and distributing goods and services (innovation), and being accountable to society. Values like responsibility, honesty, fairness and doing no harm are arguably most important in dealing with those ethical dilemmas. Realising success should be balanced with fulfilment, happiness and human flourishing – of the entrepreneur him/herself, but also of other individuals and society at large.

Further reading

Bornstein, D. and Davis, S. (2010). *Social Entrepreneurship: What Everyone Needs to Know*. Oxford/New York: Oxford University Press.

Franz, H-W., Hochgerner, J. and Howald, J. (2012). *Challenge Social Innovation: Potentials for Business, Social Entrepreneurship, Welfare and Civil Society*. Berlin/Heidelberg: Springer-Verlag.

Hoholm, T., La Rocca, A. and Aanestad, M. (Eds.) (2018). *Controversies in Healthcare Innovation: Service, Technology and Organization*. London/New York: Palgrave Macmillan.

Minniti, M. (Ed.) (2007). *Entrepreneurship: The Engine of Growth. Vol. I. People*. Westport/London: Praeger.

Osburg, T. and Schmidpeter, R. (Eds.) (2013). *Social Innovation: Solutions for a Sustainable Future*. Berlin/Heidelberg: Springer-Verlag.

Owen, R., Bessant, J. and Heintz, M. (Eds.) (2013). *Responsible Innovation: Managing the Responsible Emergence of Science and Innovation in Society*. Chichester, UK: John Wiley &Sons.

Pate, L. and Wankel, C. (2014). *Emerging Research Directions in Social Entrepreneurship*. New York/London: Springer.

Ratten, V. (2017). *Entrepreneurship, Innovation and Smart Cities*. London/New York: Routledge.

References

Abu-Saifan, S. (2012). Social Entrepreneurship: Definition and Boundaries. *Technology Innovation Management Review*, 2(2): 22–27.

Berkhout, K. (2016, 17 March). Geef de dure pil sneller aan de patient. *NRC.nl*. Retrieved 15 March 2019 from http://www.nrc.nl/next/2016/03/17/geef-de-dure-pil-sneller-aan-de-patient-1600043.

Birrell, I. (2010, 14 November). Before You Pay to Volunteer Abroad, Think of the Harm You Might Do. *The Guardian*. Retrieved 14 December 2014 from http://www.theguardian.com/commentisfree/2010/nov/14/orphans-cambodia-aids-holidays-madonna.

Cox, K.R. (1933). The Local and the Global in the New Urban Politics: A Critical View. *Environment and Planning D: Society and Space*, 11(4): 433–448.

Faramceuten Gebruiken Ziekenhuis als Reclamespotje. (2016, 19 April). *De Volkskrant* 27. Retrieved 15 March 2019 from https://www.volkskrant.nl/economie/farmaceuten-gebruiken-ziekenhuis-als-reclamespotje~bf6744ce/.

Durieux, M.B. and Stebbins, R.A. (2010). *Social Entrepreneurship for Dummies*. Indianapolis, IN: Wiley Publishing, Inc.

Ehni, H.-J. (2014). Expensive Cancer Drugs and Just Healthcare. *Best Practice & Research Clinical Gastroenterology*, 28(2): 327–337.

Fabian, C. and Fabricant, R. (2014). The Ethics of Innovation. Retrieved 7 July 2017 from https://ssir.org/articles/entry/the_ethics_of_innovation.

FIFA. (2012). Fair play reigned for football's first Corinthians. Retrieved 25 April 2016 from http://www.fifa.com/classicfootball/history/news/newsid=1967575/index.html.

Fontrodona, J. (2013). The Relation between Ethics and Innovation. In Osburg, T. and R. Schmidpeter (Eds.), *Social Innovation – Solutions for a Sustainable Future*. Berlin/Heidelberg: Springer-Verlag.

Gibson, O. (2016, 27 February). Gianni Infantino and Fifa Must Turn Greed into Need for Game's Global Good. *The Guardian*. Retrieved 15 March 2019 from https://www.theguardian.com/football/blog/2016/feb/27/gianni-infantino-fifa-greed-need-president-football.

Glöckner, H. H. and Weijers, S.J.C.M. (2009). *Logistiek in de Zorg*. Groningen/Houten: Noordhoff Uitgevers.

Greene, A.J. (2003). Staged Cities: Mega-Events, Slum Clearance, and Global Capital. *Yale Human Rights & Development Journal*, 6(1): 161–188.

Haferburg, C. and Steinbrink, M. (2017). Mega-Events in Emerging Nations and the Festivalization of the Urban Backstage: The Cases of Brazil and South Africa. In Hannigan, J. and Richards, G. (Eds), *The SAGE Handbook of New Urban Studies* (pp. 267–290). London: Sage.

Hall, T. and Hubbard, P. (1998). *The Entrepreneurial City: Geographies of Politics, Regime, and Representation*. Chichester, UK: John Wiley & Sons.

IAAF at the Centre of New Doping Controversy after Major Blood Test Leak. (2015, 2 August). *RTE Sport*. Retrieved 14 March 2019 from https://www.rte.ie/sport/athletics/2015/0802/718818-doping.

Loewy, E. H. (1996). *Textbook of Healthcare Ethics*. New York/London: Plenum Press.

Marsman, V. (2014). Volunteering Gone Wrong: The Ugly Side of Voluntourism. *PanAm Post*. Retrieved 1 November 2017 from https://panampost.com/valerie-marsman/2014/05/07/volunteering-gone-wrong-the-ugly-side-of-voluntourism/.

McNamee, M. (2007). Sport, Ethics and Philosophy; Context, History, Prospects. *Sport, Ethics and Philosophy*, 1(1): 1–6.

Meagher, G. (2016, 14 January). IAAF Council 'Could Not Have Been Unaware' of Doping in Athletics – As it Happened. *The Guardian*. Retrieved 19 December 2016 from https://www.theguardian.com/sport/live/2016/jan/14/athletics-doping-scandal-wada-releases-part-two-of-report-live.

NOCs of Austria, Germany, Sweden and Switzerland (2014). Olympic Agenda 2020: The Bid Experience. Evaluation of the Winter Games Bids 2010–2018 and Recommendations for the IOC's Olympic Agenda 2020. Retrieved 25 April 2016 from https://www.dosb.de/fileadmin/Bilder_allgemein/Veranstaltungen/Olympische_Spiele/Dokumente/140612_OlympicAgenda_JointPaper.pdf.

Osburg, T. (2013). Social Innovation to Drive Corporate Sustainability. In Osburg, T. and Schmidpeter, R. (Eds.), *Social Innovation – Solutions for a Sustainable Future*. Berlin/Heidelberg: Springer-Verlag.

Parasuraman, A., Zeithaml, V.A. and Berry, L.L. (1985). A Conceptual Model of Service Quality and Implications for Future Research. *Journal of Marketing*, (49): 41–50.

Ponzini, D., Fotev, S. and Mavaracchio, F. (2016). Place-Making or Place-Faking? The Paradoxical Effects of Transnational Circulation of Architectural and Urban Development Projects. In Russo, A.P. and Richards, G. (Eds), *Reinventing the Local in Tourism: Travel Communities and Peer-Produced Place Experiences* (pp. 153–170). Bristol: Channel View.

PricewaterhouseCoopers. (2011). Changing the Game: Outlook for the Global Sports Market to 2015. PricewaterhouseCoopers. Retrieved 25 April 2016 from http://www.pwc.com/sportsoutlook.

Ramaswamy, C. (2015). Hosting the Olympics: the Competition No One Wants to Win. *The Guardian*, Retrieved 6 June 2016 from https://www.theguardian.com/sport/shortcuts/2015/nov/30/hosting-olympics-hamburg-drop-out-2024-games.

Raymond, E.M. and Hall, C.M. (2008). The Development of Cross-Cultural (Mis)Understanding through Volunteer Tourism. *Journal of Sustainable Tourism*, 16(5): 530–543.

Richards, G. (2013). Events and the Means of Attention. *Journal of Tourism Research & Hospitality*, 2(2). Retrieved 7 July 2016 from http://www.scitechnol.com/2324-8807/2324-8807-2-118.pdf.

Richards, G and Palmer, R. (2010). *Eventful Cities: Cultural Management and Urban Revitalization*. London: Routledge.

Richards, G. and Wilson, J. (2006). Developing Creativity in Tourist Experiences: A Solution to the Serial Reproduction of Culture? *Tourism Management*, 27: 1209–1223.

Rijksoverheid. (2013). *Kabinet: Overheidsparticipatie bij Doe-democratie. Rijksoverheid*. Retrieved 12 October 2016 from http://www.rijksoverheid.nl/nieuws/2013/07/09/kabinet-overheidsparticipatie-bij-doe-democratie.html.

Sharma, J. (2016). A Neoliberal Takeover of Social Entrepreneurship? Retrieved 7 July 2017 from https://ssir.org/articles/entry/a_neoliberal_takeover_of_social_entrepreneurship.

Sport Business. (2016). Rio 2016: Study Lifts the Lid on the Cost of Hosting the Olympic Games. In *Sport Business*. Retrieved 19 December 2016 from http://www.sportbusiness.com/sportbusiness-international/rio-2016-study-lifts-lid-cost-hosting-olympic-games.

Stebbins, R.A. (2010). Social Entrepreneurship as Work and Leisure. *LSA Newsletter* (85): 30–33.

Trends in de zorg. (n.d.). In *Atlas van Zorg & Hulp*. Retrieved 15 March 2019 from http://www.zorghulpatlas.nl/zorgwereld/trends-in-de-zorg/. [This site contains information about developments in the care sector for clients, caregivers and care entrepreneurs.]

Veen, C. van. (2015). Kankerpatienten krijgen dure medicijnen niet altijd. *NRC.nl Nieuws*. Retrieved 14 March 2015 from http://www.nrc.nl/nieuws/2015/06/16/kankerpatienten-krijgen-dure-medicijnen-niet-altijd. [Article about cancer patients who do not always receive the expensive drugs they need.]

Volksgezondheidenzorg. (n.d.). Retrieved 15 March 2019 from https://www.volksgezondheidenzorg.info/. [This site gives facts and figures on healthcare in the Netherlands.]Warshaw, A. (2016, 5 June). FIFA Chief Gianni Infantino under Pressure Once Again as His Presidency Reign Moves into its 100th Day. *Mail Online*. Retrieved 4 June 2016 from http://www.dailymail.co.uk/sport/sportsnews/article-3625665/Fifa-chief-Gianni-Infantino-pressure-presidency-reign-moves-100th-day.html.

Werken mit dbc's. (n.d.). In *Nederlandse Zorgautoriteit*. Accessed 15 March 2019 from https://werkenmetdbcs.nza.nl/. [This site contains information about working with DBCs in different sectors (diagnostic treatment combinations).]

Zorguitgaven stijgen langzamer. (2016, 19 May). In *CBS*. Accessed 15 March 2019 from https://www.cbs.nl/nl-nl/nieuws/2016/20/zorguitgaven-stijgen-langzamer.

Chapter 12

Information technology and business

Hayleigh Bosher, Marnix van Gisbergen, Adriaan van Liempt and Pieter de Rooij

12.1 Introduction to information technology and business

Hayleigh Bosher

Technology itself is neutral, in the sense that it can be developed and used for positive or negative purposes. New technologies can provide exciting opportunities for consumers, creators and business. In the last decade, many types of digital technologies have been developed, particularly in relation to consumer-related technologies. For example, streaming technologies have facilitated the easy consumption of music and film.

New technologies enable everyone to express their creativity and have inspired new ways of creating, using, sharing and exploiting creative works. Technology has enabled connectivity, mobility and crowdsourcing, has helped to develop healthcare, space exploration and sustainable energy, and has made social media possible, not to mention inventions such as high-speed Wi-Fi, smartphones, 3D printing, virtual reality, robotics, drones and Google Glass. However, technology can equally be used to illegally download and share copyright-protected works, such as through illicit file-sharing websites. Unfortunately, technology can also be used to invade a person's privacy and violates freedom of expression.

It is clear that the development of technology is quickly progressing and more and more human services are being replaced with machines and applications (apps). Furthermore, human interaction with new technology has become far-reaching, with that technology almost in fact, becoming an extension of the self (Shaw, 2015: 246). This can be on a small scale, such as using a phone's memory to store information that might otherwise have been retained in the mind. Alternatively, on a larger scale, it could be argued that it technology can afford an extension of the personality through social media, online games and virtual realities (Shaw, 2015: 246). As culture becomes further submerged into the virtual world, 'the Internet, transforms digital technology from being a tool of second life into an increasingly central part of real life' (Keen, 2012: 23).

Cultural behaviours are changing, consumer expectations are developing and as a result businesses must adapt in order to stay relevant. When businesses respond, adapt and utilise developing technologies they need to consider the ethical and legal implications that arise.

12.1.1 Copyright and human rights: A necessary balance

In the digital age, copyright has become more relevant to individuals in society. This is because, previously, copyright cases tended to take place between companies. However, due to the development of technology and, as a result, behaviour, copyright is now more often enforced against the individual user. Technology, such as software and social media platforms, has also encouraged and enabled users to become creators.

As such, the paradox of copyright regulation and human rights such as freedom of expression and privacy are prevailing. Any business operating in the digital environment needs to balance such legal and ethical considerations. It is extremely important to understand who the owner of a particular copyright work is – and this may not be straightforward. The copyright owner is usually the creator; therefore if users are co-creating with businesses this brings into question the ownership of the work. For example, this may apply in cases whereby gamers develop a game which was originally created by a company, but involves the possibility to contribute to the development of the game. However, this issue can easily be solved in the terms and conditions of purchase, where the company can specify who owns the copyright.

Equally, it is important that the copyright owner's rights are balanced with those of the users or the public interest. Copyright is limited by time and scope in order to accommodate this. There are also a number of copyright exceptions, which are circumstances in which a work can be used without the permission of the copyright owner; for example, for the purpose of creating a parody or reporting news.

Nevertheless, there are other factors to consider, such as the human rights of privacy and freedom of expression. These fundamental rights and freedoms are 'the foundation of justice and peace in the world and are best maintained on the one hand by an effective political democracy and on the other by a common understanding and observance of the Human Rights upon which they depend' (The European Convention on Human Rights, 2010: 5). A right to respect for private life is a condition of human well-being, part of the good life which ethical behaviour seeks to promote or preserve (Horner, 2014: 180).

Cases such as His Royal Highness (HRH) Prince of Wales vs Associated Newspapers 2006 demonstrate that breach of privacy and copyright infringement can be argued in the same circumstances. In this example, a newspaper printed extracts from the journal of HRH Prince of Wales without his permission. Charles was primarily concerned about his breach of privacy. However, he was able to use copyright infringement to restrict the use of the diary.

Freedom of speech is the right to articulate one's opinions and ideas without fear of government retaliation, censorship or sanction. This is also crucial to society, for example for education, to enable individuals to develop, to help communities and to ensure everyone has access to justice. However, according to the Freedom

House Report only 13 per cent of the world's population enjoys a free press (where coverage of political news is robust, the safety of journalists is guaranteed, state intrusion in media affairs is minimal and the press is not subject to onerous legal or economic pressures). Moreover, global press freedom declined to its lowest point in 12 years in 2015 (Freedom House, n.d.).

In the landmark case of Ashdown vs Telegraph Group, the UK court held that the limitation of copyright already affords sufficient protection to the principle of freedom of expression in most circumstances. In Germany, the courts have invoked the constitutional guarantee of freedom of expression as a limitation on copyright. In Austria, the Supreme Court has in at least two cases refused to allow freedom of expression to be used as a defence in copyright infringement cases. In the Netherlands, courts have acknowledged that, in principle, copyright may conflict with the guaranteed right to freedom of expression.

Many argue that the expansion of rights afforded to copyright holders has increased the tension between copyright and fundamental rights, as they have not been matched with an expansion of human rights (Helfer, 2008; Patterson, 1987). Nevertheless, these values are upheld by the courts, and should also be considered in the ethical decision-making of any digital business.

Therefore, regulators must take these rights into consideration. Equally, when copyright owners are enforcing their copyright they must not breach others' right to privacy or freedom of speech. To learn more about the different stakeholder perspectives on balancing copyright with freedom of speech and privacy, see Copyright User (n.d.).

12.1.2 Digital copyright infringement: The need for business to adapt

The Copyrightuser.org resource provides an interesting video on copyright and creativity, which highlights that the main challenge for copyright law is to adjust to the rapid changes in technology while fulfilling its purpose of encouraging learning and the spread of knowledge in a balanced way. It is incredibly easy to illegally access copyright materials online. 'Digital assistants in our pockets (...) provide at any time and any place a gateway to all people and information in the global village' (van Santen, Khoe and Vermeer, 2010: 111–112).

In recent years, a tension has grown between the entertainment industries and the younger demographic, facilitated by the development of the Internet, in particular online technologies that facilitate the copying and sharing of copyright works (Strangelove, 1994: 7). Bahanovich and Collopy have stated that the younger population do not have moral or ethical concerns about the practice of online copyright infringement (2012). As a result, digital copyright infringement is recognised as a social norm (Bowrey, 2005; Schultz, 2006; Lessig, 2008).

The entertainment industry has claimed some progress through technological solutions such as blocking (British Recorded Music Industry, 2013) and adaptive market strategy (Levine, 2012). However, the proportion of illegal as opposed to legal activity continues to increase (Belleflamme and Peitz, 2012: 491). This is only likely to intensify as technology becomes more advanced – Gordon Moore's forecast is that the increase rate of technological power will double every two years and lower in price accordingly, has been upheld for forty years (Mollick, 2006).

As such, copyright holders cannot rely on ethical, legal or technological motivations alone to stop young people from illegally accessing their copyright material. Instead, it has been argued that the most appropriate response is to adapt to the times and update the business models. For example, this would involve making copyright material easily accessible for the user, as has been demonstrated with the payment of monthly music subscriptions – examples being Spotify and Apple Music.

12.1.3 Ethical and legal issues in big data and marketing

In running any digital business in the current technological environment, it is likely that the company will be collecting information about their customers. This might take the form of storing personal information about the customer, or finding out about their interests through their social media or search history. This helps the company to tailor its marketing to its target audience, providing targeted communications that are more consistent with its consumers' needs and wants. It also supports companies in their decision-making, such as on which products to sell or which TV show to commission.

However, the collection of information about customers inevitably brings up legal and ethical issues. As explained above, privacy is a vital part of a healthy society and as such people are very concerned about their privacy and the way in which their information is collected, stored, used and distributed.

In the European Union data protection is regulated by the Data Protection Directive 95/46/EC, ePrivacy Directive 2002/58/EC, and has been updated by Directive 2009/136/EC and the General Data Protection Regulation EU-2016/679, which was implemented in May 2018. It is also important to be aware of the local laws and relevant codes of practices when dealing with data collection.

There are two different types of personal data that can be collected about a person. These are called personal data and sensitive personal data. Personal data is information which relates to a person who can be identified from that data alone or together with other information which is in the possession of the data controller, for example a name, e-mail address or geographical address. Sensitive personal data is more detailed information such as racial or ethnic origin, political opinions, religious beliefs, memberships, health or sexual life. Collecting this type of information evidently requires more care.

The development of social media in particular has left users vulnerable to the use of their data. Social media platforms encourage the mass sharing of personal information (Castell, 2011). As a result, the behaviours of users have changed and the sharing of personal information has become a social norm (Ball, Ramim and Levy, 2015). One of the main issues around these circumstances is that users are often not aware that they are providing data for the company. The terms and conditions of the website usually specify this, but it is well known that users do not tend to read these and even if they do, these documents are long and their wording is complex.

One way in which companies could address this would be to simplify the customer agreements and make them more transparent and visual to the user. For example, Hull, Lipford and Latulipe have argued that Facebook need to do a better job of making their data collection and privacy information more transparent to users (2011: 301). Another way to address this is the development of more transparent data collection through the use of cookies. A cookie is a data file placed on a computer that identifies that individual computer. A cookie can recognise a returning user as a 'remember me' option visitor. It can track trends on a website, for example, the number of returning visitors, or track trends across websites, for example, through pay-per-click marketing cookies which can attribute revenue back to the original source.

Cookies were always there, but users were not always informed of their existence. However, one might have noticed that a drop-down box now appears on the computer screen when entering certain websites. The box informs the user that the website he/she is on is using cookies. This is because the law has recently changed. As a result, a website must now inform the user that a cookie is there, explain what the cookie is doing and obtain the user's consent to store the cookie in their device (for more details see: Cookie Law, n.d.).

12.1.4 In conclusion

It has been stated above that new technologies enable people to express their creativity. They have inspired new ways of creating, using, sharing and exploiting creative works. Technology has enabled positive developments such as connectivity, mobility, crowd sourcing, sustainable energy, social media, and the like but, it can equally be used to illegally download and share copyright-protected works, such as through illegal file-sharing websites, which is a negative development. On the other hand, technology can also be used to invade one's privacy and violate freedom of expression. It is also clear that consumer behaviours adapt to rapid technological development. Therefore, businesses also need to adapt in order to stay relevant. It is important that they look for a balance between copyright and the privacy of customers, and consider, for example, the legal and ethical issues related to big data and marketing. Copyright, freedom of expression and privacy are major constituents in this regard.

In the following, three discussions with aligned cases reflecting moral issues and ethical dilemmas are presented. These stories demonstrate that there are many juxtaposed perspectives involved, and making a decision therefore requires a skilful balancing act. The first case, introduced by van Gisbergen and Bosher, reflects on intellectual property (IP) and privacy in the entertainment industry. The authors show that copyright is a regulatory tool for remunerating creators which provides restrictions on the use of works such as books, films, music and pictures. This is demonstrated by reflection on the moral and legal implications of football fans filming in stadiums without the consent of the organisers of the game or owners of the stadium. The second case, presented by van Liempt, revolves around the theme of downloading films and the ethical customer. He shows that the uploading and downloading of copyright-protected material on the Internet, without permission or a licence, is considered illegal under European law, but that many studies demonstrate that this behaviour does not resonate, particularly with younger people, as an ethical wrong. In order to address this, digital businesses and copyright holders must adapt to meet the consumer's needs. De Rooij introduces the third case in this chapter, which deals with the issue of big data and marketing. This case ponders upon the question of whether a good cause legitimises the use of big data, and if so, to what extent. The answer seems to align with the statement that while the use of data can be extremely valuable to marketers, the collection and use of such data must also be balanced with people's privacy rights.

12.2 Intellectual property (IP) and privacy in the entertainment industry

Marnix van Gisbergen and Hayleigh Bosher

12.2.1 Introduction to IP and privacy

The construct 'intellectual property' (IP) is contested. It is defined as the monopoly that has been assigned to a creation of the intellect by law and is usually expressed through protection measures such as trademarks, patents, designs and copyright. Whereas patents protect inventions, trademarks protect logos, brand names and slogans. In addition, design rights protect, for example, the design itself or the aesthetic appearance of a product. But IP could also apply to artwork, literature and inventions such as symbols. Critics, in referring to the confusing and vague connection between 'property' and its association with 'rights' would rather define IP as 'intellectual monopoly' or 'intellectual rights'. The latter is seen as a broader concept that also embraces moral rights, for example (see Intellectual Property, n.d.). Against the background of major inventions in the field of knowledge, information and technology a redefinition of 'intellectual property' has become more urgent. This is because society has come to increasingly depend on its ability to use and even exploit knowledge and information. The use of information naturally implies some kind a responsibility, which in turn, implies a moral positioning regarding the impacts, more specifically potential harm, that could be caused to parties. One can therefore state that there has been a shift in the relationship between the public and private spheres, which has an effect on the subject matter of IP as well (Lenk et al., 2007: 2–3). It has become more complex. Yet fundamentally the meaning of the construct still refers to any invention or creation of tangible and intangible nature that is used to raise revenue. For the purpose of this discussion, and related case, IP will be conceived of as those rights parties have with regard to their intellectual creations, specifically in the entertainment domain, and the rights (of use) others have.

12.2.1.1 The media content exchange ethical dilemma

In general there are five forms of exchange in which consumers give something in return for media content. First, the most traditional form, is paying for the media content. A simple exchange: the makers create content and the consumer pays money to receive it. The second form introduced was the exchange of media content for a small 'piece of your life'. This is the advertising model: in exchange for media content the consumer agrees to spend time viewing persuasive media messages such as advertisements. Although not investigated, the average consumer probably gives away a few years of his life in exchange for 'free' media content.

This is a very popular strategy in traditional media such as print magazines. For an overview of paid and advertising revenue models see Ostwalder and Pigneur (2010). The third strategy concerns 'co-creation'. This means the user actually produces (part of the) media content and in return receives aligned media content or gets access to unrelated media content (think of fan-based websites). A fourth, currently very popular exchange strategy, concerns data: the user explicitly or implicitly (automatic) gives away personal data and in return receives access to media and media content. This is a very popular exchange form when it concerns social media (such as Facebook) and media accessed via smartphones. The fifth and final form deals with data as well: the 'selling' of network data: data of the user's friends, family and others (think of popular 'member-get-member' actions, or opening up online user profiles to gain access to and make use of online media). Interestingly, more often companies provide consumers with a choice regarding the kind of exchange agreement they prefer (think of streaming services such as Spotify and Netflix) (Belleflamme, 2016).

Within this model there are many ethical dilemmas from a company perspective. However, often it is the consumer who acts 'unethically'. They break all five agreements made with the companies: (a) they do not pay and instead illegally get access to media content (downloading games and music for instance); (b) they break the agreement by not watching or listening to the commercial content, and simply walk away, for instance, during TV commercial breaks, or even create and use online tools that automatically avoid commercial messages such as banners (Krammer, 2008); (c) they create low-quality content or grab content created by others (Agichtein et al., 2008); and (d) they provide fake data (e.g., wrong e-mail addresses and/or incorrect dates of birth) and 'sell' non-existent friends and peers (Chahal, 2015).

There are good arguments for consumers to act in a 'seemingly unethical' manner, such as unclear exchange rules, protection of privacy, unclear 'contract' agreements, non-informed consent and freedom-of-expression concerns. However, these actions just seem like simply unethical behaviour (Bilton, 2015). And how should a company deal with that behaviour? Of course, companies try to deal with this by applying IP and copyright rules, for instance, to owned, earned and paid media categories respectively (van Gisbergen et al., 2014). But is copyright, for instance, a solution to secure the media deal made with consumers, or a dead end only leading to the use of more innovative strategies to break the media content exchange agreement?

12.2.1.2 Copyright

Copyright is a type of IP right that protects artistic and literary works. The purpose of copyright is to encourage creativity and the spread of knowledge. It does this in two main ways.

Firstly, it does so by granting the rights holder the exclusive right to copy or communicate the work to the public. The copyright owner can then sell or license the work for a fee in order to be remunerated for his or her efforts, which allows him or her to continue to create. Usually, this is done through an organisation such as a publisher or a record label, who are encouraged to disseminate the work on the same basis. Copyright is a highly lucrative asset and as such many companies, particularly in the entertainment and creative industry, profit significantly from licensing the use of or selling their copyright works.

Secondly, copyright encourages the creation and spread of knowledge by balancing these exclusive rights that are granted to the copyright owners with the need for the public to access and use copyright works. It does this by limiting the powers granted to the rights holder, for example through copyright exceptions, which are circumstances in which the work can be used without permission, such as for news reporting or creating a parody.

Thus, copyright acts as a balancing mechanism between the interests of the rights holders and the general public. However, as copyright enables rights holders to regulate the use of their work by stopping other people from copying it without permission, it can sometimes interfere with a persons' fundamental rights. For instance stopping someone from taking a photograph or video could conflict with their freedom of expression, and regulating their photographs or videos could conflict with their privacy rights.

12.2.1.3 Freedom of expression

The European Convention on Human Rights (ECHR) states that everyone has the right to freedom of expression, meaning that everyone has the right to hold an opinion and to receive and express information and ideas (2010: 11).

As copyright can restrict the use of copyright-protected works, it could inhibit a person's freedom of expression, if that expression involves the use of copyright-protected material. Therefore, while copyright works are protected for the benefit of the owner, the public must still be able to make use of the material in certain circumstances.

12.2.1.4 Privacy

The ECHR states that everyone has the right to respect for his or her private and family life, home and communications (2010: 10). This means that there must be a balance between the economic interests of society and people's rights to privacy.

Therefore, while copyright enables creators and owners to benefit from their creations – which has an economic benefit for society as a whole – it must also be balanced and ensure that when copyright owners are enforcing their copyright they are not breaching others' right to privacy.

The case study below contemplates the tensions between copyright, freedom of expression and privacy in the context of the entertainment industry, as has been explicated above. In particular, these issues are considered within the media content exchange framework and a real user case concerning the context of photographs and videos taken inside a football stadium. It considers the interaction between copyright ownership of the football stadium and the freedom of expression and privacy rights of the spectators, based on media content exchange agreements between different stakeholders and consumers.

Case 12.2.2: Photographs and videos taken inside a football stadium

Introduction: Filming and taking photos inside football stadiums

One example of a circumstance which incorporates all of the above-mentioned issues relates to the ownership and regulation of photographs and videos taken inside a football stadium.

There is no copyright in an event, for example a football match, per se. The Court of Justice of the European Union stated, in the joined cases C-403/08 and C-429/08 (Lindholm and Kaburakis, 2013) that the Premier League 'cannot claim copyright in the Premier League matches themselves, as they cannot be classified as works'.

However, the organisers of the event are able to make a substantial amount of money from selling the broadcasting rights of the event. The broadcast is a work that can be protected by copyright. Therefore, the owners of the event space can use contractual agreements to regulate the taking of photos and videos inside the stadium. As such, the terms and conditions of the ticket purchase can prohibit the taking of photographs or videos inside the stadium grounds.

In 2014 the Premier League announced that it was going to 'clamp down on fans posting unofficial videos of goals online' ('Premier League Warns about Posting Goal Videos Online', 2014). Fans posting photographs and videos from the stadium presents a problem for the owners as it interferes with their digital or broadcasting agreements. For example, the Premier League is currently under a £20 million agreement with News International, which allows the latter the exclusive right to present clips of key moments that occur during the football match (Sweney, 2013). The Premier League is also under broadcasting agreements with Sky and BT, which allow these organisations to broadcast the football matches in return for £3 billion over three years.

Therefore, if fans are recording clips and taking photographs of the football matches and uploading them to the Internet, where other consumers can access them for free, for example on social media platforms, the value of the rights sold to News International, Sky and BT by the Premier League are undermined.

The difficulty for the Premier League, of course, is enforcement. It cannot realistically stop fans from taking photos or videos on their phones and uploading them to the Internet. It can make takedown requests on the website on which the photos or videos appear, but this can be time-consuming and expensive.

Potential solutions and assessing ownership of IP

A potential solution to this problem was created by FanSauce (FanSauce, n.d.). They created a mobile software that allows the owners of a stadium to have instant access to photos and videos taken by the fans. The software is utilised in a mobile app; when the spectator presses the capture button on their phone, the image is then automatically and instantly shared with the owner of the event. Therefore, the FanSauce app offers a way for stadium owners to utilise the photos and videos taken at their event without facing the unrealistic challenge of preventing photos and videos being taken. Hereby stadium owners use this technology to both regulate photos and videos taken at the football matches and use them for their own purposes.

However, it is possible, and likely, that in the terms and conditions of their app, the stadium could obtain the copyright in the photos or videos taken. This would secure the copyright that was previously absent for the Premier League and better enable it to restrict the fans' use of the material. Furthermore, the stadium owner would then be able to make use of the fans' photos in any way they wish, without the need to seek permission or licence from the photographer.

A fan might argue that he or she is entitled to take photos or videos at a football match because of freedom of expression. However, the Premier League argues that the sharing of photographs and videos is a breach of its copyright (Williams, 2014). Hendersen et al. argue that, as there is no copyright in the sports event, the Premier League cannot claim copyright infringement in photographs or videos taken in the stadium (2014). Nevertheless, the football stadium owners use contractual agreements, usually in the terms and conditions of the ticket purchase, to regulate the use of their property in the football stadium.

A fan might argue that using his photograph without permission might be copyright infringement or invasion of privacy. However, the football stadium might argue that the photograph was taken on its private property, under the terms and conditions of the ticket purchase and therefore it is entitled to do so in order to protect the value of its IP.

Questions for discussion

- Do you think that restricting the taking of photos and recording of videos at an event on private property – such as a football stadium – through copyright or contractual means is a threat to freedom of expression? Why or why not?
- Which moral and ethical arguments could be conveyed in *favour* of the protection and regulation of IP?
- Can you think of moral objections *against* laws for the protection of IP?
- Do you think that a different media exchange strategy could help to solve the ethical dilemma explicated in the case, and if so, how?
- Consider the notion that IP rests upon an *idea* that someone has come up with, and that an idea can never be copyrighted, only an expression of it. Why do you think this is true or not true?

12.3 Downloading films and the ethical customer
Adriaan van Liempt

12.3.1 Introduction to downloading films and the ethical customer

12.3.1.1 To download a car, or not to download a car – online piracy, a matter of convenience or lack of ethics?

The first part of the title of this text is *borrowed* and *mashed up* from two different sources of what can be considered as IP. The first source is the often-used quote from William Shakespeare's play *Hamlet* ('To be, or not to be', n.d.), the second is an infamous quote from one of the anti-piracy videos ('Piracy is a Crime', 2006) displayed to the millions of people that either bought, rented, or downloaded a DVD in the early 2000s. The latter message was comparable to the dramatic 'Home taping is killing music' slogan of the 1980s, which has also been parodied plentifully ('Home taping is killing music', n.d.). The practice of borrowing and reinterpreting products of creativity and culture is a creative process in which it is not always clear who actually 'owns' the creative offspring, nor whether it is 'creative enough' in its own right, and which can lead to claims by the original IP holders. In this text, however, the focus will be limited to a less grey area called online piracy, which is simply illegal. It will be argued that those involved in copyright infringement may do so because the industry fails to deliver a distribution model that meets the desires and expectations of consumers in the digital era, and not because their ethics and morals are questionable.

12.3.1.2 Downloading and sharing

The practice of downloading, or the act of sharing (where the user uploads what he/she downloads simultaneously), illegal digital content is at the core of what seems to be a fight between consumers and producers and owners of IP. Downloading and sharing are commonly referred to as digital piracy, and their practice varies widely from country to country. For the scope of this text I primarily focus on music and films, and my frame of reference is mostly countries with modern capitalist economies and advanced digital infrastructures. For a more global comparison of software piracy see BSA (2012).

In the Netherlands people also download music, films, series, books software and even scientific articles (Rosenwald, 2016), and they do so en masse. In order to substantiate the Dutch passion for downloading, data was retrieved from the LISS panel (CentERdata, 2014a, 2014b) and analysed in order to determine the basic characteristics of people that are downloading in the Netherlands. Although in the survey downloading was not limited to illegal downloading, the results do not deviate strongly from international studies (Cox and Collins, 2014; Jimenez et al., 2015). Dutch downloaders are usually young. Roughly 68 per cent of people aged 15–24 download digital content, and this goes down to 47 per cent for people aged 25–34. Secondly, downloaders are often male. Approximately 42 per cent of the male population downloads, while 25 percent of the female population does so.

As such, the Dutch do not deviate markedly from other countries, except perhaps in that they download on a larger scale in comparison to other EU countries (Ernesto, 2016). One explanation for this phenomenon may be the fact that downloading of illegal content was made illegal in the Netherlands in April 2014, relatively late compared to other EU countries (Seegers, 2014). Before that time, only the uploading of illegal content was considered unlawful. It should be noted that, in the meantime, people in the Netherlands were taxed more heavily for items that could store data via private copying regulations (Thuiskopie, 2016). Also, it is reasonable to think that 'not explicitly stating' that downloading is illegal is not quite the same as assuming the Dutch government had no problems with the practice of copyright infringement. It is, e.g., feasible to assume that changing the law sooner was just not possible.

Still, it is interesting that Dutch legislation deviated for so long from that of other European countries in this respect, as it supports the notion that downloading illegal content might be different from stealing a car, which is illegal everywhere, and that there are different ways of dealing with the same problem (private copying regulations versus making the activity illegal). Actions can be made illegal through defining them as such via laws. The notion of the relativity of the illegality of downloading may seem like a different discussion, but it is relevant in the context of the consumer who is legally bound by the laws made by legislators. What was legal one day, was made illegal the next.

The matter that will be addressed next deals with the following question: why does the consumer download illegally, and what part do ethical concerns play in that choice?

12.3.1.3 Why do people download illegal digital content?

In Jimenez et al. (2015), which used a sample of 50,000 Spanish 'pirates' (people that infringe copyrights), respondents were asked for their reasons for downloading. The results were divided into five main categories, as follows: (1) economic reasons (downloading is cheaper); (2) practical reasons (downloading is easier); (3) impunity (downloading does not have legal repercussions); (4) Internet users' rights (downloading is okay because I pay for content indirectly through my TV subscription); and (5) civil disobedience (downloading as a form of protest). These five categories fit neatly with the so-called attitudinal factors mentioned in the 'Acquisition-Mode Framework for Music Piracy' developed by Coyle et al. (2009: 1031–1032). This model considers three basic constructs, which include attitudinal factors, demographics and the actual purchasing or piracy behaviours. In the model, consumer attitudes are assumed to be based on four types of considerations: ethical, legal, economic and consumer behaviour.

12.3.1.3.1 ETHICAL CONSIDERATIONS

Essentially Coyle et al. (2009) assume, based on (Reidenbach et al., 1991), that what consumers' ideas of what is appropriate and what is normatively prescribed will influence their actions. Coyle et al. (2009) refer to the studies of Bhattacharjee et al. (2003) and Wang (2005) which showed that, indeed, individuals of a more ethical disposition did download less pirated music than others. At the same time, however, Coyle et al. (2009) argue that several studies (Fetto, 2000; Freestone and Mitchell, 2004) have shown that consumers tend to feel that downloading illegal content is less wrong than other types of questionable behaviour possible on the Internet. However, Coyle et al. (2009) do not refer to the studies that, according to Krawczyk et al. (2015), suggest that age has an effect when it comes to the ethical considerations of consumers (Al-Rafee and Cronan, 2006; Ford and Richardson, 1994). This is odd, as Coyle et al. (2009) are working on a model that also includes demographic characteristics such as age. The authors do, however, argue that legal and ethical considerations must be assessed in relation to each other.

12.3.1.3.2 LEGAL CONSIDERATIONS

Coyle et al. (2009) refer to a number of studies that convey different reasons why downloaders may not concern themselves too much with legal issues. They mention: group pressure (Albers-Miller, 1999); teens' and young adults' ignorance of copyright law (Atkinson, 2004); the notion that consumers do not directly interact with other humans when downloading, but rather with machines or unknown persons (Gundlach and Murphy, 1993); and the belief that they will not get caught (Fetto, 2000).

12.3.1.3.3 ECONOMIC CONSIDERATIONS

Coyle et al. (2009) link economic considerations strongly to ethical considerations in the sense that they argue, using Blalock and Wilken (1979), that a person's actions are strongly influenced by that individual's perception of the consequences of their actions. These perceived consequences, which can range from negative to positive, include manufacturer loss (the effect of digital piracy on the industry as a whole), musician loss (the effects on individual musicians) and consumer loss (the extent to which people feel they are being ripped off by the music industry).

12.3.1.3.4 CONSUMER BEHAVIOUR CONSIDERATIONS

Coyle et al. (2009) basically use consumer behaviour considerations as a leftover category, which includes factor such as the following: piracy as a form of evaluation/sampling (Raymond, 2001); demographic characteristics (age, gender and income); past piracy (if you have downloaded in the past, you are also likely to do so in the future) (Taylor, 2004); and music consumption (if you own a lot of music, you are also more likely to download music) (Aron et al., 2004).

12.3.1.4 Are those explanations plausible?

What is problematic in Coyle et al.'s study and some of the studies they reference is that causality is not always questioned and that, in fact, a causal relation might also work the other way around, such as in the case of the study by Aron et al. (2004). Aron et al. state that people that own a lot of music are also the ones that download a lot. It is entirely possible that because people download a lot, they get introduced to new music that they wish to own.

The model that Coyle et al. (2009) developed is able to explain 75 per cent of the variance in piracy intentions within their sample of undergraduate students. Two variables with the strongest effects were past piracy and legal/ethical considerations. The 'past piracy' variable can be perceived as trivial, since it is similar to explaining the intentions a person has to drive to work, when he or she has already driven to work in the past. However, the ethical/legal considerations are noteworthy to consider, as they are a strong predictor that does not rely on past behaviour and demographic effects; this indicates that ethical/legal considerations do indeed matter.

12.3.1.5 What happens in a world where ethical and legal considerations matter and people download because of those considerations?

The answer is simple; it adapts, it changes strategies. Property rights and their protection and enforcement are fundamentally important to the development of societies (Acemoglu and Robinson, 2012; North, 1982). However, things apparently change when there is no physical property involved, when the property itself is not altered and when the property can be infinitely reproduced. We have observed the changes in an industry rigorously fighting downloading and sharing behaviour via the law, a tactic which, so far, has had little effect on eradicating piracy entirely. We have also seen and are seeing an industry that is changing because new parties are entering the market and providing content in a manner that seems to suit the consumer very well. Netflix reported having 65 million subscribers in its quarterly report for the first half of 2015 (Netflix, 2015). This was a significant rise compared to 2014 when they had reported 50 million subscribers. In the Netherlands over 1 in 10 households has a Netflix subscription (Reijerman, 2015). Business models like the one Netflix has introduced provide content in a manner that gives the consumers what they want. Although academic research still has to confirm whether content distributors like Netflix do indeed reduce the downloading behaviour of consumers, Netflix meets a lot of the desires and wishes of those consumers that essentially empowered themselves through copyright infringements because they could, and were ethically 'okay' with that decision. Original content providers have a huge problem when people are downloading their content illegally on a large scale; they should rethink their strategy of criminalising consumers and replace it with smarter business models that work in their favour.

There will most likely always be a group of young, technically apt individuals that will look for ways to obtain materials for free, but the larger share of people, seeking a hassle-free option, will overwhelmingly adopt legal alternatives over downloading. They will, however, only do so if these alternatives give them the ease and access they want. In that sense, Netflix's early 2016 move disallowing use of VPN services by its subscribers in order to access Netflix's international content all over the world, is a step in the wrong direction (VPN is a network technology that creates a new (secure) network connection between the user and the web service) (Greenberg, 2016). This action once again limits the consumers' sense being able to access the content they want in a convenient fashion and may have a negative impact on their ability and willingness to indulge in the act of copyright infringement (Greenberg, 2016; Seitz, 2016).

In the case below, an illegal service is presented that perfectly matches consumers' wishes regarding access to all possible content through one easy service.

Case 12.3.2: Killing Popcorn Time

Introduction: Sharing with Popcorn Time

Androidplanet.nl reported on August 29, 2014 that supposedly 1.3 million devices in the Netherlands had installed the illegal streaming service Popcorn Time, and that this number was growing with 15,000 installations per day (Verlaan, 2014). The same website claims, that in the Netherlands, approximately 100,000 persons actively use the software on a daily basis. Other sources also indicate that both Dutch and Flemish people, particularly males aged 15–24, are prone to downloading illegal content. Forty-six per cent of Flemish people have downloaded illegal content at some time during their lives (Vanhaelewyn et al., 2014).

Basically, the software works like the famous BitTorrent file-sharing software with the big difference that you can start watching the films almost immediately, rather than having to download the full content first. Just like legal streaming services such as iTunes, Netflix, Hulu, Bandcamp, Spotify etc., content is provided to a device that can play the content. The big exception is that it is free and the choice of what is offered is virtually limitless. Where content-streaming providers such as Netflix often change what they offer, Popcorn Time is solely dependent on what users are sharing. From the perspective of the user, Popcorn Time is an amazing library of content that is accessible with the click of a button. Any imaginable content, video or music, is accessible through one convenient portal. Had providers been able to 'provide' this service themselves, they would have created a cultural Valhalla for users. But, in fact, they were not amused.

Do clampdowns work?

The private Dutch anti-piracy organisation BREIN has been going after websites that support Popcorn Time, and was successful in taking down six such websites that were hosted in the Netherlands, in early 2015 (Stichting BREIN, 2015). The organisation admits that taking down the six websites is not a 'watertight' move, as the same content is provided on websites outside the Netherlands as well, but that it is 'water resistant'. Ideally BREIN wants to shut down all illegal services, but claims that Internet Service Providers (ISPs) are resisting such pressures.

There are several ethical dilemmas at stake here at the same time, because what does 'resisting pressures' actually imply? Would cooperation mean that ISPs are responsible for the actions of their users? Are they responsible for actively monitoring users' activities on the Internet? Are they responsible for potentially violating the privacy rights of their users by handing over details that could potentially help BREIN pursue their users? Because all of the above would have negative effects for the ISPs themselves.

Also, one can wonder to what extent shutting down illegal services would solve the problem. There is a vast consumer base that has shown itself to be willing to pay for content when it is offered conveniently. BREIN is simply trying to make it more difficult for consumers to find the music and movies they want to see, but they will look for illegal alternatives as BREIN is not working towards providing legal alternatives that can compete with the illegal alternatives.

The work of Jimenez et al. (2015) has demonstrated that 'pirates' download illegally for different reasons. An important one of those reasons is convenience, and one wonders whether BREINS' actions are indeed the best way to address a serious ethical issue whereby a significant portion of our society, granted, mainly young males, are positioned as criminals.

Questions for discussion

- What do you deem the most important reasons for downloading, for example, music, without paying for it? How do you evaluate that ethically?
- Which business model would you propose to find a solution for downloading music and other products from the Internet that would satisfy both content providers and customers?
- Do you think that it was right for BREIN to take down Popcorn Time? Could you give moral arguments to back up your answer?
- Are providers, to your mind, responsible for the actions of their users? Underpin your answer with ethical arguments.
- Does content and nature of use determine whether unpaid downloading is ethically justified or not (e.g. scientific articles, pornography, software, films, music, etc.)?

12.4 Big data and marketing

Pieter de Rooij

12.4.1 Introduction to big data and marketing: It takes two to tango

Knowledge of customer behaviour is more important than ever before. Marketers use customer knowledge to increase the effectiveness of marketing communication by individualising messages. Therefore, gathering, analysing and applying customer information has become an important task for marketing departments. In contemporary society, every consumer leaves a great variety of digital personal data behind. This 'big data' is a key opportunity for organisations to individualise marketing communication. At the same time, several ethical issues arise.

12.4.1.1 Changes in the marketing environment

The marketing environment in which organisations operate has changed considerably the last few decades. A few of these trends are discussed here. Firstly, customisation has replaced mass marketing. Consumers no longer demand general products, but are more likely to seek out personalised ones (e.g. your own name on your favourite sports shoes). The quality of a product is in many cases no longer an issue because high quality standards are often met. Nowadays, the symbolic value of products is more important because the products we consume symbolise who we are. Customised products increase the possibility of differentiating ourselves from others. Secondly, it is often stated that the use of traditional segmentation variables (such as demographics or social class) have become less effective in targeting customers. These variables are too general and lack a clear relationship with specific behaviour. Because marketers want to influence consumption behaviour, behavioural segmentation is gaining increasing support. Many consumption patterns in leisure and tourism seem to consist of routine behaviour. Therefore, previous behaviour is regarded a good indicator of future behaviour. Moreover, consumers leave many digital behavioural traces, which are sources of information. Thirdly, the accountability of the actions of a marketing department is more important than ever. Marketers need to reach their customers in an effective way. Therefore, marketing communication channels 'follow' their customers. This implies a shift from marketing spending in print media (such as newspaper and magazines) to online media (such as websites, Facebook, Google, mobile phone apps). In conclusion, marketers increasingly use knowledge about previous customer behaviour in order to effectively personalise their communication efforts and sell their products. Marketers want to get in contact with their customers and get to know them better. This implies a growing need for increased customer insights.

12.4.1.2 Customer insights

There are several sources marketers can use to build customer insights. They can, for example, conduct quantitative and qualitative studies amongst consumers. Mostly, this information is of a general nature, which means that details cannot be connected to individuals. As discussed before, these individual details are important because they provide marketers with the opportunity to communicate on a personalised level with (potential) customers. Therefore, marketers also make use of another source: the analysis of customer databases. Organisations store their customers' personal details (such as name, address, e-mail, phone number) and purchase history (products or services acquired) in their databases. Marketers use this information in order to get to know their customers and to personalise their messages and start an interaction. The information stored in these databases may be referred to as 'small data'. Customers provide their details to organisations and give them permission to use this information for future communication. Because customers have bought products from the organisation before (or showed interest in the organisation before), there is already a kind of relationship with these organisations. Therefore, sometimes customers provide additional personal details (such as product preferences, consumption details) and allow these organisations to contact them again. The marketers, in analysing this data, create either customer pyramids, which distinguish between small, middle and top clients, or chart the categories of products bought, customer preferences and communication channels used. This allows organisations to effectively approach customers in order to encourage them to rebuy, or to make them loyal.

Apart from these details, customers deliberately provide personal information to organisations. Yet sometimes, the same customers probably unintentionally provide other details as well. In our hyperconnected society customers leave many traces, such as social network insights (e.g. Facebook), web search history (e.g. Google) and location history (by using their phones), known as big data. Since this big, unstructured data has a commercial value, organisations are increasingly interested in using it.

The question arises: 'What counts as "big data"' and which ethical challenges does it bring up? These issues will be discussed next.

12.4.1.3 What is big data?

There is no single definition of big data. Various stakeholders, such as academics, professionals and the media, express different views on this topic. Ward and Barker (2013) define big data as 'the storage and analysis of large and or complex data set using a series of techniques'. Boyd and Crawford (2012: 663) define big data as a cultural, technological, and scholarly phenomenon that rests on the interplay of technology (maximising computation power and algorithmic accuracy), analysis (of large data sets to identify patterns) and mythology (the belief that these large data sets offer a higher form of intelligence). Professional industry and academia often characterise big data as consisting of 3 V's: volume, variety and velocity (Ward and Barker, 2013; McAfee and Brynjolfsson, 2012).

Firstly, there is a high volume of big data. This is the reason why it is referred to as 'big' data. Back in 2011, 5 billion gigabytes were already produced every two days. It was later estimated that in 2015 a total of 5 billion gigabytes would be produced every 10 seconds (Zwitter, 2014). And in May 2018, an estimated '2.5 quintillion bytes of data' were produced every day (Marr, 2018)

Secondly, a high level of variety refers to the effect of 'datafication' in our hyperconnected society: various sources can be combined in order to create a digital image reflecting an individual's reality (Zwitter, 2014). Individuals leave digital historical traces behind such as call and location history, social network insights (friendships and preferences), web search history, online buying behaviour, the use of apps on mobile phones and facial recognition (Crisan et al., 2014; Richards and King, 2014). This data represents a cluster of figures, narratives, images, audio messages, videos and so on. Our lives are mirrored in a varied, digital reality which is recorded and analysed by large corporations (Zwitter, 2014).

Thirdly, high velocity is related to the availability of real-time or nearly real-time data and the challenge is how to use this data quickly. If organisations are able to use big data in time, they might be able to influence the customer in decision-making processes (Nunan and Di Domenico, 2013). Old data is supposed to have less influence because customer needs might have changed since it was collected.

In addition, Crisan et al. (2014) relate a fourth characteristic of big data: personal character. Big data represent a combination of individual data on various topics. This personalised data can be combined to create a clear customer profile on behaviour, preferences and relationships. Given their improved information and communications technology (ICT) knowledge and the combination of high-volume, high-variety and high-velocity data, organisations are able – with an increasing accuracy – to monitor and manipulate consumers' behaviour. Big data can be very useful for general purposes in society. Google, for instance, was able to track the swine flu epidemic in 2009 faster than official health institutions could (Crisan et al., 2014). Big data are also applied to prevent terrorist attacks. But, as stated earlier, big data represent a commercial value for the private sector as well. Some organisations have transformed into data-generating machines, selling personalised data to marketing departments. Specialised data brokers gather, analyse and sell personalised data to companies requiring personal profiling to make optimal use of their advertising budget. This, in turn leads to actual or potential ethical dilemmas for the companies.

12.4.1.4 Big data and ethical issues

The rise of big data brought with it the following ethical issues and challenges. The first issue is related to knowledge and power. Consumers have a lack of knowledge about the data which is collected (Zwitter, 2014). Many individuals are not aware that personal details are stored and analysed. They neither read the regulations, nor do they understand them. Instead, they passively agree to the long set of terms, just before starting to use a service. This implies that they do not actively or consciously grant the company full permission to store their individual details. In cases where individuals are indeed aware of this storage, they actually might want these details *not* to be stored. Take for example WhatsApp. Due to the success and widespread use of apps like this, consumers consciously choose to use these apps. If they do not, they cannot communicate with their friends. However, in fact, they would have preferred to have an opportunity to use the app without all personal details being stored. Another example is the use of cookies on many websites. These cookies allow companies to track consumer's online behaviour. Google is able to combine customer details from various sources (Gmail, the Google search engine, mobile phones running on Android, Google Shopping) enabling them to create personalised advertisements (Peeperkorn, 2015). These examples point to the power some organisations have, and the lack of individual power, free will and consent on the part of the consumer.

The second issue relates to individual privacy, which is threatened by the use of big data (Nunan and Di Domenico, 2013). Some researchers argue that commercial use of big data undermines individuality on a personal level because organisations such as Facebook are able to guess the consumer's personality type and are therefore capable of manipulating behaviour (Schroeder and Cowls, 2014). Moreover, this becomes more serious when data is somewhat sensitive, such as data on health or political issues. Big data has along memory, which means that our digital footprint is increasing every day. How do organisations use this information? Do they have ethical standards in analysing information? Do they have strong security measures, preventing unauthorised access? There have been many examples of hacked computers and electronic identity theft, ranging from Edward Snowden leaking information from the National Security Agency (NSA) to the hacked dating website

Ashley Madison. This forms the background of the current discussion in Europe of 'the right to be forgotten' (Schroeder and Cowls, 2014).

Differences in legislation between countries bring us to a third issue. Europe and the United States have different rules about dealing with privacy (Crisan et al., 2014). European countries have tight governmental regulations, while in the United States self-regulation by the industry applies. In Europe, governments have introduced a high standard in data protection, setting up criteria for data collection and the use of data. For example, in the Netherlands organisations are legally obliged to inform consumers beforehand about commercial use of cookies (e.g. for profiling purposes).[1] Other kinds of cookies, such as functional cookies (used to facilitate log-in and ordering processes) and analytical cookies (used to improve website quality) are allowed to be used without informing consumers in advance. In practice, many organisations inform consumers about the cookies policy beforehand and provide them with the option to reject certain cookies on websites. Another example is the legal battle that was waged between five privacy committees from European countries and Facebook. In 2015, Facebook changed its conditions of use, thereby enabling the application of individual details to the creation of personalised advertisements (Vervaeke, 2015). Even consumers without a Facebook account may be tracked and traced after writing a positive review or comment about a company on its website. Given the international character of consumption and the differences in legislation between countries, legal issues are very complicated. This makes the privacy issue a particularly fraught one.

12.4.1.5 Integrating value for marketers and individual interests

It has become clear that ICT possibilities enable marketers to create deep customer knowledge. Sometimes it seems that they have all the power in their relationship with their customers. Two interesting questions arise here. Firstly, do all customers want to have a relationship with these companies? It has been suggested that many brands may be seen as 'uninvited crashers' on social media (Fournier and Avery, 2011: 193). The idea is that many consumers will most likely not be interested in getting personalised information from a company. They may view this as an inappropriate marketing action. A second question is about the extent to which customers would want to be in control of this relationship. Does the customer want to be proactive and take action himself/herself, or is he or she dependent on the company for its purchasing suggestions? LinkedIn, for example, may suggest contacts to whom a member could send an invitation, but does the person always have a factual or fruitful professional relationship with these contacts? How does LinkedIn know that a private exchange between two members has taken place the day before? Indeed, it seems that Big Brother is watching.

In reflecting on the interests that are in play within this discussion, we can distinguish between two types: the interest of the marketer and the interest of the customer. It seems that there is an imbalance between these two. The interests of the marketer take priority above those of the customer. This is because many organisations are looking for the next sale. They are more 'transaction focussed' than 'relationship focussed'. They approach consumers as 'living wallets' instead of human beings. They put emphasis on 'value from the customer', instead of 'value to the customer', although the customer is supposed to be central in marketing.

Therefore, marketers should realise that it is important to offer real value to customers, something which is determined by customers themselves. Marketers should also realise that it is important to establish long-term relationships with their customers. Building trust is crucial in building relationships (Morgan and Hunt, 1994). Therefore, organisations should not only innovate products and services from a customer perspective. They should also apply a customer-friendly communication policy. They should show respect to consumers' interests and be aware of their needs and potential conflicts. For example, it is important that organisations are transparent in their privacy policies (Richards and King, 2014). Simplification of the long list of agreement rules and a clear explanation of how companies use cookies would help with this. When it comes to building a good relationship with the customer, it takes two to tango.

The ways in which the insights discussed above blend together will be demonstrated in the fictitious case below.

Case 12.4.2: Using customer data at Carnegie Hall

Introduction: Increasing Carnegie Hall's number of consumers

Carnegie Hall is a large performing arts organisation in New York (Carnegie Hall, n.d.). Its mission is to make great music accessible to as many people as possible. Carnegie Hall presents music performances ranging from orchestral works, jazz, and recitals by singers, pianists and violinists. On an annual basis they present 170 music performances and organise several education and community programmes, with a total reach of 400,000 consumers. The marketing department consists of three teams: the publishing and creative services team, the marketing and visitor services team and the e-strategy team. A total of 29 marketing professionals are employed by the marketing department.

   Neill, the director of the marketing department, calls the members of the marketing and visitor's service teams together for a meeting. Apart from the regular running issues, one item features very prominently on the agenda: 'Increasing Carnegie Hall's number of customers'. After opening the meeting Neill introduces the main point of discussion and points out that, in the past, Carnegie Hall collected, analysed and used various small data (such as name, address, phone number, purchase behaviour, membership of friends and music interests) for communication purposes. Carnegie Hall also collects big data, but until that moment they have had no strategy with regard to analysing and using this data for marketing purposes. Given the difficult times and the need to innovate and move forward with regard to the educational programmes, the time has come for Carnegie Hall to consider a change in policy – especially with regard to the exploitation of big data. The target ambition is to increase the number of consumers over the next five years from 400,000 to 500,000. Neill writes a project plan, which is subsequently presented.

Exploiting big data for a good cause

Neill's plan consists of two phases. He proposes that Samantha, who was appointed as online marketer two months ago, should take responsibility for the first phase. She has been commissioned to make the website content fluid in collaboration with an external company. Previous website visits and purchase behaviour should be analysed within a 'marketing automation machine'. This automated analysis results in a fully personalised website for each customer. The result of Samantha's work would also enable Carnegie Hall to include paid advertisements from external companies (such as banks and insurance companies) on their website. Neill expects that this strategy will improve the effectiveness of marketing communication and at the same time increase revenue. In turn, this revenue could be used to improve the educational programme, which provides opportunities for young people on low incomes to learn to play a music instrument.

The responsibility for the second phase of the project was entrusted to Colin, who concentrates in particular on international marketing. He has worked at Carnegie Hall for six years now and this proposed policy is quite new to him. Neill's vision is that Carnegie Hall should attract more European visitors. Colin must work towards creating advertisements on Facebook for individuals who have shown any interest in attending New York. This will make it possible to communicate directly with potential European visitors after they sign up for the monthly newsletter. This newsletter could be individualised based on their interests, which they could make known after signing up to the newsletter, and also on their website behaviour.

Neill asks Samantha and Colin to study the project plan and in particular to reflect on the ethical implications of those two phases. They are expected to have it ready for presentation at the next meeting of the team in two weeks' time.

Questions for discussion

- Place yourself in Samantha's and Colin's shoes. How would you evaluate the ethical implications of your assignment?
- Is there, to your mind, a reasonable and ethical balance between Carnegie Hall's interests and those of potential customers?
- How do you morally judge Carnegie Hall's new business plan? If you do not approve, what would you advise Neill to alter in his plan? Refer to those principles you regard as fundamental for ethical marketing.
- Does working for a good cause – in this case creating opportunities for poor people to realise their creative dreams – legitimise jeopardising other people's right to privacy? Give arguments for your answer.
- Under which circumstances would it be morally justified for a government to allow the gathering and analysis of all the available personal and private data of individuals?

12.5 Concluding thoughts

Technology, in a generic sense, refers to the intelligent organisation and manipulation of materials, such that they can be used and applied in a better and more innovative manner. This definition also applies to IT, which has influenced the lives of people, organisations and even communities quite dramatically in recent years. It involves the use of computers in saving, studying, organising, transferring and manipulating data or information. With the growth of the Internet the capture and storage of (personal) information has increased, with the result that organisations and businesses are more and more dependent on information systems. This technology is mainly used in a business setting and usually excludes personal and entertainment technologies. Business uses IT to improve on and innovate with their services and products, and increase their profit margins. But, as it is often the case with the good things in life: there could be a negative side to it. It is also possible for IT to be used by third parties like criminals and hackers who commit fraud, corrupt data and steal personal information such as passwords from people and companies. So safety and protection are major themes as well.

But, apart from third-party risks and threats, companies themselves – as they work to increase their profits and protect their interests – are also in danger of using data in a dubious and even illegal way. This is especially the case when dealing with issues like IP (ownership), piracy and privacy rights within the context of, for instance, sales and marketing, and communications with (potential) customers. All in all, businesses should not only reflect retrospectively on their (moral) use of IT, but due to the nature and pace of current technological innovation, also prospectively on the potential (moral) impacts of IT on business and society, and the implications thereof for law- and policymaking.

Note

1 A cookie is a small text document which can be placed on an individual's computer during his or her use of a website. The server of an organisation can track behaviour and recognise the consumer's browser in case of a repeat visit.

Further reading

Freeman, L.A. and Peace, A.G. (2005). *Information Ethics: Privacy and Intellectual Property*. London/Melbourne: Information Science Publishing.
Gordon, A.D., Kittross, J.M., Merrill, J.C., Babcock, W. and Dorscher, M. (Eds.). (2011). *Controversies in Media Ethics*. Abingdon, UK/New York: Routledge.
Hick, D.H. and Schmücker, R. (Eds.) (2016). *The Aesthetics and Ethics of Copying*. London/Oxford: Bloomsbury.
Reynolds, G.W. (2010). *Ethics in Information Technology* (3rd ed.). Boston, MA: Cengage Learning.
Schultz, R.A. (2006). *Contemporary Issues in Ethics and Information Technology*. Hershey/London: IRM Press.
Tavani, H. T. (2013). *Ethics and Technology: Controversies, Questions and Strategies for Ethical Computing* (4th ed.). Hoboken, NJ: John Wiley & Sons.

References

Acemoglu, D., and Robinson, J. A. (2012). *Why Nations Fail: The Origins of Power, Prosperity and Poverty.* London: Profile Books.

Agichtein, E., Castillo, C., Donato, D., Gionis, A., and Mishne, G. (2008). Finding High-Quality Content in Social Media. In *Proceedings of the 2008 International Conference on Web Search and Data Mining,* Palo Alto: ACM: 183–194.

Albers-Miller, N. D. (1999). Consumer Misbehavior: Why People Buy Illicit Goods. *Journal of Consumer Marketing,* 16(3), 273–287.

Al-Rafee, S. and Cronan, T. P. (2006). Digital Piracy: Factors that Influence Attitude toward Behavior. *Journal of Business Ethics,* 63(3): 237–259.

Aron, M. L., Dato-on, M. C. and Rhee, K. (2004). Money for Nothing and Hits for Free: The Ethics of Downloading Music from Peer-to-Peer Web Sites. *Journal of Marketing Theory and Practice,* 12(1), 48–60.

Atkinson, C. (2004). Grammys Take Hard-Line Against Online Music Piracy. *Advert Age,* 75(6): 3.

Bahanovich, D. and Collopy, D. (2012). *Music Experience and Behaviour in Young People: Winter 2012–2013* [2011 National Survey]. Vienna: International Association of Music Business Research.

Ball, A. L., Ramim, M. M. and Levy, Y. (2015). Examining Users' Personal Information Sharing. *Online Journal of Applied Knowledge Management,* 3(1): 180–207.

Belleflamme, P. (2016). The Economics of Digital Goods: A Progress Report. *Review of Economic Research on Copyright Issues,* 13(2): 1–24. Retrieved 6 August 2017 from https://papers.ssrn.com/sol3/papers.cfm?abstract_id=2903416.

Belleflamme, P. and Peitz, M. (2012). Digital Piracy: Theory. In Peitz, M. and Waldvogel, J. (Eds.), *The Oxford Handbook of the Digital Economy* (pp. 489–530). New York: Oxford University Press.

Bhattacharjee, S., Gopal, R. D. and Sanders, G. L. (2003). Digital Music and Online Sharing: Software Piracy 2.0? *Communications of the ACM,* 46(7): 107–111.

Bilton, R. (2015). What Would Kant Do? Ad Blocking Is a Problem, But It's Ethical. *Digiday.* Retrieved 7 May 2017 from http://digiday.com/publishers/kant-on-ad-blocking/.

Blalock, H., & Wilken, P. (1979). *Intergroup Processes: A Micro-Macro Approach*: New York: Free Press.

Bowrey, K. (2005). *Law and Internet Cultures.* Melbourne: Cambridge University Press.

British Recorded Music Industry (2013). *Digital Music Nation Report.* London: BRMI.

Boyd, D. and Crawford, K. (2012). Critical Questions for Big Data. *Information, Communication & Society,* 15(5): 662–679.

BSA. (2012). *Shadow Market – 2011 BSA Global Software Piracy Study.* Retrieved 20 August, 2015 from http://globalstudy.bsa.org/2011/downloads/study_pdf/2011_BSA_Piracy_Study-Standard.pdf.

Carnegie Hall. (n.d.). www.carnegiehall.org. Retrieved 15 March 2019.

Castell, M. (2011). *The Rise of the Network Society: The Information Age: Economy, Society, and Culture.* Hoboken, NJ: Wiley-Blackwell.

CentERdata. (2014a). *Background Variables,* Retrieved 20 January 2017 from http://www.lissdata.nl/dataarchive/study_units/view/322.

CentERdata. (2014b). *Social Integration and Leisure.* Retrieved 20 January 2017 from http://www.lissdata.nl/dataarchive/study_units/view/563

Chahal, M. (2015). Consumers are 'dirtying' databases with false details. *Marketing Week* (July). Retrieved 4 September, 2017, from https://www.marketingweek.com/2015/07/08/consumers-are-dirtying-databases-with-false-details/.

Cookie Law (n.d.). www.cookielaw.org.

Copyright User (n.d.) www.copyrightuser.org/educate/a-level-media-studies/prompt-4/.
Cox, J. and Collins, A. (2014). Sailing in the Same Ship? Differences in Factors Motivating Piracy of Music and Movie Content. *Journal of Behavioral and Experimental Economics,* 50, 70–76.
Coyle, J. R., Gould, S. J., Gupta, P. and Gupta, R. (2009). 'To Buy or to Pirate': The Matrix of Music Consumers' Acquisition-Mode Decision-Making. *Journal of Business Research,* 62(10): 1031–1037.
Crisan, C., Zbuchea, A., and Moraru, S. (2014). Big Data – The Beauty or the Beast? In Bratianu, C., Zbuchea, A., Pinzaru, F. and Vatamanescu, E-M. (Eds.). *Strategica: Management, Finance, and Ethics* (pp. 829–849). Bucharest: Tritonic Publishing House.
Ernesto. (2016). Movie Industry Demands €1.2 Billion Piracy Damages from Dutch Govt. *Torrent Freak.* Retrieved 7 May 2017 from https://torrentfreak.com/movie-industry-demands-e1-2-billion-piracy-damages-from-dutch-govt-160205/
FanSauce. (n.d.). Retrieved 10 April 2017 from http://www.fansauce.com/pages/index.html.
Fetto, J. (2000). Penny for Your Thoughts. *American Demographics.* Retrieved 6 February 2017 from http://adage.com/article/american-demographics/penny-thoughts/43252/.
Ford, R. C. and Richardson, W. D. (1994). Ethical Decision Making: A Review of the Empirical Literature. *Journal of Business Ethics,* 13(3): 205–221.
Freedom House. (n.d.). Retrieved 7 May 2017 from https://freedomhouse.org/report/freedom-press/freedom-press-2016.
Fournier, S., and Avery, J. (2011). The Uninvited Brand. *Business Horizons,* 54(3): 193–207.
Freestone, O. and Mitchell, V. (2004). Generation Y Attitudes towards E-Ethics and Internet-Related Misbehaviours. *Journal of Business Ethics,* 54(2): 121–128.
Gisbergen, M.S. van, Hoogervorst, D., Kreek, S. and Witteman, R. van (2014). Media Planning: Create a Brand POEM. *Admap,* 49(559): 17–19.
Greenberg, J. (2016). For Netflix, Discontent over Blocked VPNs Is Boiling. *Wired.* Retrieved 20 April 2017 from http://www.wired.com/2016/03/netflix-discontent-blocked-vpns-boiling/.
Gundlach, G.T. and Murphy, P.E. (1993). Ethical and Legal Foundations of Relational Marketing Exchanges. *Journal of Marketing,* 57(4): 35.
Hendersen, A., Munn, J. and Blood, D. (2014). Digital and Social Media Rights: Can the Fans Be Forced to Take Down Online Goal Videos and Should They Be? *Law in Sport.* Retrieved 26 March 2016 from https://www.lawinsport.com/blog/snr-denton-blog/item/digital-and-social-media-rights-can-the-fans-be-forced-to-take-down-online-goal-videos-and-should-they
Helfer, L. R. (2008). The New Innovation Frontier? Intellectual Property and the European Court of Human Rights. *Harvard International Law Journal,* 49(1): 1–52.
Home Taping is Killing Music. (n.d.) Retrieved 6 April 2016 from https://en.wikipedia.org/wiki/Home_Taping_Is_Killing_Music.
Horner, D. (2014). *Understanding Media Ethics.* London: Sage.
Hull, G., Lipford, H. R. and Latulipe, C. (2011). Contextual Gaps: Privacy Issues on Facebook. *Ethics and Information Technology,* 13(4): 289–302.
Intellectual Property. (n.d.) Retrieved 7 May 2017 from https://en.wikipedia.org/wiki/Intellectual_property.
Jimenez, H., Martin, B. and Palao, I. (2015). *Piracy Observatory and Digital Contents Consumption Habits 2014.* In La Coalicion. Retrieved 20 March 2017 from http://lacoalicion.es/wp-content/uploads/executive-summary-2014.pdf.
Keen, A. (2012). *Digital Vertigo: How Today's Online Social Revolution is Dividing, Diminishing and Disorientating Us.* London: Constable and Robinson.
Krammer, V. (2008). An Effective Defence against Intrusive Web Advertising. In *Privacy, Security and Trust.* Proceedings of the IEEE's Sixth Annual Conference: 3–14.

Krawczyk, M., Tyrowicz, J., Kukla-Gryz, A. and Hardy, W. (2015). 'Piracy is Not Theft!': Is It Just Students Who Think So? *Journal of Behavioral and Experimental Economics*, 54: 32–39.

Lenk, C., Hoppe, N. and Andorno, R. (2007). *Ethics and Law of Intellectual Property: Current Problems in Politics, Science and Technology*. Hampshire/Burlington, VT: Ashgate.

Lessig, L. (2008). *Remix: Making Art and Commerce Thrive in the Hybrid Economy*. New York: Penguin Press.

Levine, R. (2012). *Free Ride: How the Internet Is Destroying the Culture Business and How It Can Fight Back*. London: Vintage.

Lindholm, J. and Kaburakis, A. (2013). Cases C-403/08 and C-429/08: FA Premier League Ltd and Others v QC Leisure and Others; and Karen Murphy v Media Protection Services Ltd, 4 Oct 2011. In Anderson, J. (Eds.), *Leading Cases in Sports Law*. The Hague: Asser Press.

Marr, B. (2018, 18th May). How Much Data Do We Create Every Day? The Mind-Blowing Stats Everyone Should Read. *Forbes*. Retrieved 14 March 2019 from https://www.forbes.com/sites/bernardmarr/2018/05/21/how-much-data-do-we-create-every-day-the-mind-blowing-stats-everyone-should-read/#340b2e5a60ba.

McAfee, A., and Brynjolfsson, E. (2012). Big Data: The Management Revolution. *Harvard Business Review* (1): 61–68.

Mollick, E. (2006). Establishing Moore's Law. *IEEE Annals of the History of Computing*, 28(3): 62–75.

Morgan, R., and Hunt, S. (1994). The Commitment-Trust Theory of Relationship Marketing. *Journal of Marketing*, 58(3): 20–38.

Netflix. (2015). Netflix 2nd Quarter 2015 Figures. Retrieved 7 May 2017 from https://ir.netflix.com/results.cfm.

North, D.C. (1982). *Structure and Change in Economic History*. London/New York: W.W. Norton & Company.

Nunan, D., and Di Domenico, M. (2013). Market Research and the Ethics of Big Data. *International Journal of Market Research*, 55(4): 1–13.

Ostwalder, A. and Pigneur, Y. (2010). *Business Model Generation*. Hoboken, NJ: John Wiley & Sons.

Patterson, L. R. (1987). Free Speech, Copyright and Fair Use. *VanderBilt Law Review*, 40(1): 1–66.

Peeperkorn, M. (2015). Brussel: Google Misbruikt Marktpositie. *De Volkskrant*, 16 April: 8–9.

Piracy Is a Crime. (2006). *YouTube*. Retrieved 10 April 2017 from https://youtu.be/fS6ncGEyszc.

Premier League Warns about Posting Goal Videos Online (2014). *BBC Newsbeat Online*. Retrieved 20 March 2017 from http://www.bbc.co.uk/newsbeat/article/28796590/premier-league-warns-about-posting-goal-videos-online.

Raymond, J. (2001). Profit in Sharing. *American Demographics, 38*(9).

Reidenbach, R. E., Robin, D. P. and Dawson, L. (1991). An Application and Extension of a Multidimensional Ethics Scale to Selected Marketing Practices and Marketing Groups. *Journal of the Academy of Marketing Science*, 19(2): 83–92.

Reijerman, D. (2015). Een op de Tien Nederlanders Heeft Netflix-abonnement. *Tweakers*. Retrieved 10 March, 2017 from http://tweakers.net/nieuws/102503/een-op-de-tien-nederlanders-heeft-netflix-abonnement.html.

Richards, N. and King, J. (2014). Big Data Ethics. *Wake Forest Law Review*, 49(2): 393–432.

Rosenwald, M. S. (2016, 30 March). This Student Put 50 Million Stolen Research Articles Online: And They're Free. *Washington Post*. Retrieved 10 April 2017 from https://www.washingtonpost.com/local/this-student-put-50-million-stolen-research-articles-online-and-theyre-free/2016/03/30/7714ffb4-eaf7-11e5-b0fd-073d5930a7b7_story.html.

Santen, R. van, Khoe, D. and Vermeer, B. (2010). *2030 Technology that Will Change the World*. Oxford: Oxford University Press.

Schroeder, R. and Cowls, J. (2014). Big Data, Ethics and the Social Implications of Knowledge Production. Data Ethics. Proceedings of KDD Data Ethics Workshop, 24 August 2014, New York. *GitHub*. Retrieved 20 August 2015 from https://dataethics.github.io/proceedings/BigDataEthicsandtheSocialImplicationsofKnowledgeProduction.pdf.

Schultz, M. F. (2006). Copynorms: Copyright and Social Norms. In Yu, K.P. (Ed.), *Intellectual Property and Information Wealth: Issues and Practices in the Digital Age, Vol. 1: Copyright and Related Rights* (pp. 202–236). Westport, CT: Praeger Publishers.

Seegers, J. (2014). Kabinet Verbiedt Downloaden uit Illegale Bron. *NRC*. Retrieved 10 April 2017 from http://www.nrc.nl/nieuws/2014/04/10/illegaal-downloaden-per-direct-verboden-in-nederland/.

Seitz, L. (2016). Netflix Vs. VPN. *Secure Thoughts*. Retrieved 10 March 2017 from https://securethoughts.com/netflix-vs-vpn/.

Shaw, J. A. (2015). From Homo Economicus to Homo Roboticus: An Exploration of the Transformative Impact of the Technological Imaginary. *International Journal of Law in Context*, 11(3): 245–264.

Stichting BREIN Richt Pijlen op Popcorn Time. (2015). *NOS*. Retrieved 8 February 2017 from http://nos.nl/op3/artikel/2020973-stichting-brein-richt-pijlen-op-popcorn-time.html.

Strangelove, S. (1994). The Internet as Catalyst for a Paradigm Shift. *Computer-Mediated Communication Magazine*, 1(8): 7.

Sweney, M. (2013, 23 January). Premier League Agrees Highlights Deal with News International. *The Guardian*. Retrieved 20 May 2017 from https://www.theguardian.com/media/2013/jan/23/premier-league-highlights-news-international.

Taylor, S. L. (2004). Music Piracy—Differences in the Ethical Perceptions of Business Majors and Music Business Majors. *Journal of Education for Business*, 79(5): 306–310.

The European Convention of Human Rights (ECHR) (2010). Strasbourg: Council of Europe. Retrieved 7 May 2017 from http://www.echr.coe.int/Documents/Convention_ENG.pdf.

Thuiskopie. (2016). About Thuiskopie. Retrieved 7 May 2017 from http://www.thuiskopie.nl/nl/about-thuiskopie.

To Be, or Not to Be. (n.d.) In *Wikipedia*. Retrieved 10 April 2017 from http://en.wikipedia.org/wiki/To_be,_or_not_to_be.

Vanhaelewyn, B., Pauwels, G., Maes, M. and De Marez, L. (2014). *Measuring Digital Media Trends in Flanders, Aug-Sept 2014*. Digimeter. Retrieved 7 May 2017 from http://www.iminds.be/~/media/files/digimeter/digimeter-2014.ashx?la=nl.

Verlaan, D. (2014). Popcorn Time Groeit Sterk: 100.000 Actieve Nederlandse Gebruikers. *Android Planet*. Retrieved 7 May 2017 from http://www.androidplanet.nl/apps/popcorn-time-gebruikers/.

Vervaeke, L. (2015, 22 June). Facebook Bespioneert Niet-gebruiker. *De Volkskrant*, 15.

Wang, C.-C. (2005). Factors that Influence the Piracy of DVD/VCD Motion Pictures. *Journal of American Academy of Business*, 6(1): 231–237.

Ward, J. and Barker, A. (2013). *Undefined By Data: A Survey of Big Data Definitions*. Arxiv.org. Retrieved 9 July 2015 from http://arxiv.org/pdf/1309.5821.

Williams, M. (2014). Premier League Warns About Posting Goal Videos Online. *BBC Newsbeat Online*. Retrieved 26 March 2017 from http://www.bbc.co.uk/newsbeat/article/28796590/premier-league-warns-about-posting-goal-videos-online.

Zwitter, A. (2014). Big Data Ethics. *Big Data & Society*, 1(2): 1–6.

INDEX

accountability 115, 133, 144, 149, 153, 158, 232, 274
account manager 164
Acquisition-Mode Framework for Music Piracy *see* piracy
Aesthetics 64
AirBnB 187, 188
Alagappan, P. 170
Albrecht, S. 136
altruism: reciprocal 185
Aquinas, T. 23
argumentation 65
Aristotle 23, 27, 29, 34, 87
Arthur Andersen 133

Bauman, Z. 24
behaviour: ethical behaviour 5, 6, 7, 8, 15, 21, 36, 38, 39, 57, 59, 81, 90, 92, 101, 103, 105, 109, 113, 170, 259; human behaviour 22, 23, 27, 28, 67; moral behaviour 2, 40, 63, 64, 65, 66, 68, 73, 83, 93; organisational behaviour 49, 54, 80, 114, 123, 124, 144; person-and task-oriented behaviour 130; professional behaviour 9, 40, 103, 104, 105, 106, 118; responsible behaviour 1, 110, 145
benefit corporations 42
big data 11, 36, 261, 273, 275–6; and ethics 262, 276–7; and marketing 261, 273
biophilia 187
bisignis 28
BREIN 272–3
bribery 39, 53, 107, 111, 136, 206, 227, 236, 245, 246

British Hospitality Association (BHA) 104
Brundtland report 115
business: as an academic discipline 36; aims and purpose of 28, 31, 32, 34; characteristics of 31; and culture 114; and ethics 48, 51, 57; as a form of applied ethics 36 (*see also* business ethics); history of 29; negotium 28; responsible business 8, 13, 14, 35, 40, 42, 59, 80, 83, 93, 111, 127, 139, 144; and society 32, 34, 36, 43, 186, 250, 280
business ethics: definition, scope and domain of 21, 38–40; history of 34; (new) approaches to business ethics 40–2
business models: ethical business models 182; new business models 42, 181, 183, 250; sustainable business models 40, 183–4; traditional business models 9, 183
business responsibility: four types of 150

Cadbury report 134
capitalism: Chinese capitalism 53; a higher form of 179
carbon footprint 9, 13, 183, 194, 197; CO_2 emissions 195, 196, 198, 200
Carmacal 196
CARMATOP 196
Carnegie Hall 278
categorical imperative 23, 67, 74, 87
China 48, 50, 53, 168
Christianity 67
Church fathers 23
Cicero 35

Index

cities: entrepreneurial cities 235, 243; green cities 191; liveability of 191, 192, 193
citizens: corporate citizens 151, 184; global citizens 1, 5, 15
Ciulla, J. 181–2, 185
Civil Society Organisation (CSO) 152
climate change 1, 9, 32, 35, 179, 183, 194–5, 197–8, 217
Coca-Cola 208
co-creation 125, 126, 250, 264
Code Liberation Foundation 212
code of conduct 39, 51, 85, 152, 156, 160, 170
Code of Hammurabi 34
collective creativity 131, 132, 250
collectivism 52, 58
common good 5, 88, 194
community: international community 9, 57, 207; local community 165, 186, 187, 188
compliance 35, 36, 89, 117, 118, 137, 152, 154, 155, 156, 157, 159, 208, 209, 225
Confucianism 24, 53
consequentialism 25, 41, 93
consumer behaviour 262, 269, 270
control mechanisms 8, 127, 135, 138, 152
cookies: analytical cookies 277; functional cookies 277
copyright 259; copyright infringement 260–1
corporate citizenship 151, 184
corporate moral agency 41
corporate social responsibility (CSR) 9, 14, 102, 149, 150–3, 154, 156, 162, 165–6, 170, 173, 181, 185, 235; CSR 2.0 180
corruption 39, 52, 55, 107–8, 110, 135–6, 159, 194, 198, 227, 236, 245, 246
COSO model 135
creative industries see industry
Cressey, D. 135
culture: and business 49, 51–2; Chinese culture 53; and complexity 52–4, 55; cultural collectivism 52; cultural industries (see industry); cultural pluralism 56; cultural practices 53, 124; cultural relativism 56; cultural revolution 53; cultural values 53–6, 59, 124; and the individual 54–5; as a metaphor 51; as a variable 51

data 82, 138, 227, 261–2; fake data 264; personal data 261, 264, 273
data protection directive 261
decision-making 2, 8, 14, 37; constituents of 78; core of 82; and ethics 82; formal and informal approaches 84; frameworks of 78, 82, 84; inclusive decision-making 123; and the law 83–4; and organisational culture 89, 93
decision-making models 78, 83, 93; cognitive behavioural model 89; cognitive moral development model 90
deontology 25, 41, 90, 91, 93
Dewey, J. 15
dilemma: nature of 78–9
Dionesian Roman law 35
Disney 223–6
doping 236, 244, 246
Doux commerce hypothesis 181

economy: circular economy 169; global economy 103, 122, 207; and growth 136, 183, 190; history of 29–31
education 1–3, 5–6, 205, 207, 233
egoism 24, 4, 90
Egypt 35, 67
Einstein, A. 15, 101
Electronic Arts 139
Electronic Industry Code of Conduct (EICC) 170
emotional intelligence 129
emotions 65–9
employee: competences 115; crunch 143; professional role of 5, 125; reward 103
employer responsibilities 8, 127
Enron 108, 133, 149
entrepreneurs: leisure entrepreneurs 160, 233; professional entrepreneurs

286

160, 162; social entrepreneurs 172, 234–5, 248–9
entrepreneurship 237–40; and cities 243; and ethics 255; responsible entrepreneurship 234–5
Epicure 23
epistemology 23, 49, 79, 124
Ernst & Young 136
ethicality 5, 12, 86; bounded 75
ethicmentality 5
ethics: as an activity 125; applied 26, 26, 88; Arabic 24; behavioural 6, 75, 81; and business (see business ethics); of care 25, 72; Chinese 24; code of 92, 99, 101, 115; contextual 124; descriptive 24; Eastern 24; ethical approaches 24–5; ethical awareness 2, 6, 14, 115; ethical behaviour 36, 38, 57, 92, 99, 101; ethical compliance officer 117–18; ethical conduct 89, 102, 112, 158, 247; ethical consumerism 114; ethical culture 109, 115; ethical customer 262, 268; ethical decision-making 2–6; ethical dilemma 3–6, 8, 11–14; 127, 154, 166, 180, 196–7, 217, 239, 263; ethical four component model 83; ethical naturalism 68, 71, 72; ethical obligations 28, 36, 88, 115; ethical principles 26, 56, 70, 77, 80–3, 94, 160, 193; ethical process 89; ethical risk 84; ethical scandals 133; ethical screening 8, 83–4; ethical situational variables 81, 92; ethical sourcing 154, 165; ethical standards 86, 100; ethical statements/judgments 2; ethical triage 84, 93; and factual statements 64; Greek ethics 23; individual ethics 28; and the law 26, 34, 36; managerial ethics 114–15; medieval ethics 23; meta-ethics 24, 36; normative ethics 24; personal ethics 58, 115; practical 24, 26, 36, 40; prescriptive 122, 124; professional 100–3; purpose of 2, 27; relational ethics 123, 127; teaching ethics 2, 5–6; theoretical ethics 24, 26; virtue ethics 25, 28, 41, 81

ethnocentrism 56
eudaemonia 27–8; *see also* flourishing; happiness; self-fulfilment; well-being
eudaemonism 25
European convention on human rights (ECHR) 265
events 80, 101, 127, 189; sports 235, 244–5

fairness 15, 25, 37–8, 68, 82, 106, 236
Falkenberg, L. 6
FanSauce 266–7
FIFA World Cup 236, 244–8
film: download of 268–71; in football stadiums 266
flourishing 25, 27, 42, 255; *see also* eudaemonia
fraud 10, 35, 39, 107–10, 127, 133, 135–6, 227, 246
Fraud Triangle (FT) 135–6
freedom of expression 217, 258–61
Freeman, E. 32, 149
Friedman, M. 32, 102, 105, 206, 209

Gamasutra 211
games: Assassin's Creed 210; Call of Duty 210; Cancer 142; Candy Crush 210; Depression Quest 142; Dragon Age 211; Fable 211; Far Cry 3 211; 50 Cent Bulletproof 210; Gamespot 142; gender in 210; Gone Home 142; Grand Theft Auto V 142, 210; Hatred 142; Hurt me Plenty 211; indie 139–42; Mass Effect 211; Minecraft 210; minorities in 210, 215; New York Dawn 212–15; The Path 211; sexuality in 211; That Dragon 142
GDP-growth 136
Germany 160, 209, 22, 225
Gilligan, C. 8, 69, 71–2
Global Code of Ethics for Tourism 216
Global e-Sustainability Initiative (GeSI), 170
globalisation 39, 49, 50, 51, 55; and culture 49
Global Reporting Initiative (GRI) 153
glocalisation 51
Golden Rule 66, 67

Goldman Sachs 109
Goleman, D. 129
good life 7, 23, 26, 27–8, 33, 37–8, 42, 83, 259
governance: good corporate 8, 39, 127, 133–5
Greece 67
greed 109–10, 225
greenhouse gas 165, 194, 195; see also carbon footprint
Greenpeace 166
guanxi 53

happiness 25, 27–8, 255; see also eudaimonia
Hare, R. M. 67
healthcare: complexity of 237; and ethical dilemmas 239; functional quality of service in 237, 242; managing costs of 237–8; technical quality of service in 237, 242
hedonism 25, 27
Heertje, A. 33
Heinz Dilemma 70
Hippocratic Oath 100
Hobbes, T. 23
Hofstede, G. 48, 52, 58
home medical equipment 116
hospital 84
hospitality 103; industry (see industry); remuneration in 104; sustainable hospitality 186; 2.0 186
hotel: Hilton 162; Holiday Inn 162
human dignity 41, 42, 209, 210, 223
humanism 67
humanistic management network 42
human resource 8, 103, 140
human rights 25, 35, 43, 51, 84, 166, 205–9; and copyright 259–60; Declaration of 57, 209, 216, 223; economic human rights 206; and the law 208
Hume, D. 23

ID&T 152
India 24, 56, 99, 106
industry: aviation 195; catering 163–4; creative 4, 125, 126, 130–3, 211, 265; cultural 4; electronics 170; entertainment 11, 260, 262, 263, 265; games 139–43; healthcare 237, 240; hospitality 8, 80, 103–5, 106, 134, 136, 162, 186–7; leisure 80, 160, 161; media 142; pharmaceutical 239, 242; service 4, 7, 80, 194, 223, 237, 242; tourism 80, 110, 136, 192, 194, 219
information: credible and incredible 109
innovation: and ethics 250–2; social 235, 236, 248, 250, 252
integrity 7, 9, 15, 38–40, 80, 92, 103, 112–13, 118, 129, 14, 135, 144, 155, 157–8; managerial integrity 155, 156; in sports 244, 248
intellectual property (IP) 262, 263
Intercontinental Hotel Group (IHG) 152
International Association of Athletics Federations (IAAF) 244, 246
International Chamber of Commerce (ICC) 206
International Covenant on Economic, Social and Cultural Rights 216
internationalisation 36, 39
International Labour Organisation (ILO) 206
International Olympic Committee (IOC) 243
Internet Service Providers (ISPs) 272
Islam 24, 67
ISO 26000 42, 57

justice 25, 35, 42, 72, 88, 91, 109, 165, 182, 205, 212, 259

Kant, I. 23, 67, 81, 87
Kaplan Financial Limited 41
Knoepffler, N. 23, 26
knowledge: episteme 5; techne 5
Kohlberg, L. 69–73
Koran 35
Kramer, M. 179, 180, 18, 185

labour 9, 35, 80, 104, 105, 114, 140, 154, 157, 159, 160–2, 166, 206, 217, 220; slave labour 180

law: copyright law 260, 270; European law 11, 262; mortgage law 164; universal law 67, 74
leader: personal identity 129; professional identity 129
leadership (theory): contingency theory 128; dynamic leadership 8, 127; effective leadership 127–32; emergent leadership 130; ethical leadership 181–2, 185, 186; hierarchical leadership 123; participative leadership 128; situational theory 128; six leadership styles 129; systemic leadership 130; trait theory 127; transformational leadership 128
legal system 37, 51
leisure 3, 4, 9, 28, 161, 216, 234, 274; otium 28; serious leisure 250
Levinas, E. 24
Lewin, K. 128
library 132
locus of control 81
logistics 3, 14, 80, 100, 166; reverse logistics 167, 169; sustainable logistics 169
loyalty 39, 58, 87, 103, 108, 110–12, 118, 151
Lynn, W. 22, 26, 36

McDonaldization 50
Machiavelli, N. 109
majority opinion 65, 66, 69
management 99–100, 105, 108
manager: roles of 117
Mandela, N. 15
Mann, M. 5
market: direct selling market 116; free market 35, 183, 185, 232, 234; marketing 139, 158, 217, 224, 243, 246, 261, 273, 274, 277, 279; marketing cookies 262; marketisation 109
media content exchange 263–4
metaphysics 23
Middle Ages 30, 35
Millennium Development Goals (MDGs) 57

Mill, J. S. 87
misogyny 141, 142
moral: assessment 89, 194; awareness 6, 26, 34, 75, 81, 92, 194, 200; behaviour 2, 40, 63, 64, 68, 73, 93, 112; debate 89; decision 6, 25, 64, 72, 73–7; development 2, 6, 19, 6, 73, 90, 116; dialogue 89; disengagement 75; failure 78, 79, 93, 254; growth 63; intent 6, 83, 92; judgments 24, 63, 64–6, 73, 80, 82, 89, 92, 103; obligation 32, 36, 58; philosophy 21–2; positioning 63, 73, 263; psychology 63, 64; reasoning 64–75; reasoning styles 72; sensitivity 3, 6, 15, 34; value(s) 10, 21, 33, 39, 43, 55, 77, 80, 87, 92, 128, 215, 234, 236, 254
morality 22–3, 24, 27, 35, 37, 43, 49, 63, 68, 85, 99, 109, 222; common sense 66, 101, 124

National Olympic Committee (NOC) 243, 245
National Security Agency (NSA) 276
negotium see business
neo-liberalism 109, 181, 185
Netflix 264, 271, 272
neuroscience 68
New Testament 35
normativity 69

Ockham, W. 23
oeconomicus 29
Old Testament 34
Olympic Games 236, 243, 244–8
ontology 49, 79
Organisation for Economic Cooperation and Development (OECD): OECD better life initiative 42; OECD guidelines for multinational enterprises 42
organisations: as a closed system 122, 123; demand driven organisations 236; as an entity 123; as machine 122; as a (network of) conversation(s) 123; non-governmental (NGO) 156, 158, 166; as an open complex system 123; supply driven organisations 237

Index

original equipment manufacturers (OEMs) 170
otium 28; *see also* leisure

Palestine 208, 209, 217–20
performance: financial performance 77, 116, 180–2, 184; social performance 180
personal intuition 65–6, 92
PetroFina 206
phronesis 5, 25; *see also* wisdom
Piaget, J. 69, 71–2
piracy: Acquisition-Mode Framework for Music Piracy 269; and consumer behaviour 269; digital piracy 268, 270; online piracy 268
Plato 23
politics 57, 74, 102, 221, 243
Popcorn Time 272
Porter, M. 179, 180, 18, 185
poverty: eradication of 9, 12, 183, 198, 200, 226, 249
Premier League 266–7
Priddat, B. P. 30, 31, 33
Principles of Corporate Governance 134
privacy 239, 258, 260, 261, 263–4, 265–7, 273, 276, 277, 280
problem-based learning 6
productivity: capital productivity 9, 112, 161–3; labour productivity 9, 154, 161
products: life cycle of 166–7, 171; safety of 35, 108, 114, 117, 157; sub-standard products 14
profession 100
profit: for-profit 29, 232, 235, 249; maximisation 206, 208; non-profit 29, 108, 249
Protestantism 51
psychiatry 68
psychology 6, 40, 49, 63, 66, 68, 100

Rachels, J. 22
racism 142, 215
Rand, A. 27
rational: deliberation 64, 66, 68; justification 65, 68
Rawls, J. 87; *see also* veil of ignorance

Raw Materials Initiative 169
research: ethnographic 49, 55
Resource Efficiency Roadmap 169
respect 15, 24, 40, 55, 57, 68, 84, 89, 118, 126, 141, 144, 201, 206, 208, 209, 216, 226, 259, 265, 278
responsibility 5, 7, 9, 32, 34, 38–43, 44, 65, 72, 82, 89, 102, 112, 115, 118, 126, 129, 144, 156, 188, 193, 206, 208, 217, 225, 231, 232, 234, 239, 246, 255, 263, 279; pyramid of social responsibility 156; reactive responsibility 103, 114
Rest, J. 6, 81, 83; *see also* ethics, ethical four component model
return on investment (ROI) 31, 162, 236, 250
rhetoric: classical stages of 89
rights: cultural rights 208; and duties 14, 81, 89, 222, 223, 225, 226; to be forgotten 277; minority rights 110; women's rights 110; to work 205, 222
risk assessment 135, 155
Rossouw, D. 38

Sarbanes-Oxley Act 134
Sarkeesian, A. 210
Save the Children 166
Scholasticism 23
Scotus, D. 23
self-destruction hypothesis 181
self-fulfilment 28; *see also* eudaimonia
service industries *see* industry
Seventh Environment Action Plan 169
shareholder 33, 102, 105, 110, 134, 143, 165, 180, 182, 184; shareholder value 32, 252
Shell 208
Singer, P. 22
social: constructionism 123, 124, 126; welfare 115
Social Enterprise Initiatives (SEIs) 42
Socrates 23
sports: and ethics 244–5
stakeholders: engagement 150; management 150, 180; matrix 150; multi-stakeholder 32, 33

Index

Statement on Auditing Standards no. 99 (SAS99) 135
Stoicism 23
suppliers 32, 38, 44, 50, 80, 103, 114, 116–17, 144, 149, 154, 156, 158–9, 169, 184, 187, 208; and code of conduct 170
supply chain: closed-loop supply chain 169; ethical supply chain 157; supply chain integrity 9, 154, 155–6, 159; supply chain management 6, 155; sustainable supply chain 157, 158
sustainability: and business 179; climactic 183, 198–9; social sustainability 166, 193; sustainable environment 115
sustainable development: dimensions of 184
Sustainable Development Goals (SDGs) 42, 57

teaching methods 2, 6
technology: and business 258; design for recycling technology (DFR) 170; digital technology 258; games technology 210; homecare technology 239; information technology (IT) 36, 50, 156, 276; technological revolution 122
teleology 23, 25, 41
theme parks 161, 224
theory: of complexity 129; of mind 68
thinking: aboutness 125; withness 125
TOIL-payment 143, 144
tourism: Bill of Rights 216; city 189, 191; destinations 12, 200; ethical tourism 217; religious 219; rural 190; slum 190; sustainable 183, 189, 190, 191–3
trade 28, 115, 167, 172, 194, 198, 207, history of 29, 30
trade union 39, 110, 208
transnational corporations (TNCs), 207–9
transparency 9, 35, 40, 57, 115, 144, 149, 153, 154, 155, 171, 238, 240
transport: air 195–7
triple-p baseline/bottomline 149

trust 32, 38, 57, 77, 82, 89, 91, 99, 101, 115, 116, 124, 133, 135, 145, 150, 156, 158, 181, 193, 278

Ubuntu 52, 53, 55
UNESCO 4
United Nations Global Compact (UNGC) 42, 134
United Nations Human Rights Norms for Corporations 209
United Nations Sustainable Development Goals (SDGs) see Sustainable Development Goals (SDGs)
United Nations World Commission on Environment and Development (UN-WCED) 115
United Nations World Tourism Organisation (UNWTO) 194, 198, 216
universalism: biological 67
utilitarianism 25, 41, 90

values: cultural 53, 54, 55, 56, 59, 81, 114, 124; economic 3, 33, 179, 180, 182, 185, 231, 235; environmental 149, 217, 234; moral 10, 21, 33, 39, 43, 45, 77, 80, 87, 92, 128, 215, 234, 236, 254; personal 6, 91, 93; professional 2, 5, 14, 43, 81, 86, 118; shared 116, 179–80, 182, 185; social 3, 10, 113, 142, 151, 152, 180, 185, 234, 235, 236, 249
veil of ignorance 87
video games: race and gender in 214; stereotypes in 212, 213, 214
virtue ethics 25, 28, 41, 81, 91
virtues 5, 7, 27, 33, 34, 37, 38–41, 43, 44, 69, 88, 180, 185
voluntourism 236, 248, 253, 254; adverse outcomes of 253
Vuuren, L. van. 38

wages: fair 35, 115; minimum 10, 22, 104, 209, 221, 225
waste: electronic (e-waste) 9, 12, 154, 165, 167–9, 172, 173; recycling of 169

Index

Waste and Resources Action Plan (WRAP) 169
Weber, M. 51, 151
well-being: of cities 189; economic 216; employee 184, 235, 255; for future generations 9, 21, 32, 44, 154; human 9, 27, 183, 194, 259; social well-being 149, 194, 216
whistle blowing 48, 103, 107–10
wisdom: practical 5, 6, 25; see also phronesis

work: safe working conditions 35, 117, 208, 266; working poor 209, 220–3, 224, 225
World Anti-Doping Agency (WADA) 246
World Commission on Environmental Development (WCED) 156
World Health Organisation 114
world 2.0 130
World Wildlife Fund (WWF) 166

Yukl, G. A. 128